Logic and Language Models
for Computer Science

Logic and Language Models for Computer Science

HENRY HAMBURGER
George Mason University

DANA RICHARDS
George Mason University

PRENTICE HALL
Upper Saddle River, New Jersey 07458

Library of Congress Cataloging-in-Publication Data

CIP data on file.

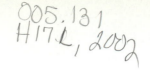

Vice President and Editorial Director, ECS: *Marcia Horton*
Senior Acquisitions Editor: *Petra J. Recter*
Vice President and Director of Production and Manufacturing, ESM: *David W. Riccardi*
Executive Managing Editor: *Vince O'Brien*
Managing Editor: *David A. George*
Production Editor: *Lakshmi Balasubramanian*
Composition: *PreTEX, Inc.*
Director of Creative Services: *Paul Belfanti*
Creative Director: *Carole Anson*
Art Director: *Jayne Conte*
Art Editor: *Greg Dulles*
Cover Designer: *Bruce Kenselaar*
Manufacturing Manager: *Trudy Pisciotti*
Manufacturing Buyer: *Lisa McDowell*
Marketing Manager: *Jennie Burger*

© 2002 by Prentice Hall
Prentice-Hall, Inc.
Upper Saddle River, NJ 07458

Printed in the United States of America

10 9 8 7 6 5 4 3 2 1

ISBN 0-13-065487-6

Pearson Education Ltd., *London*
Pearson Education Australia Pty. Ltd., *Sydney*
Pearson Education Singapore, Pte. Ltd.
Pearson Education North Asia Ltd., *Hong Kong*
Pearson Education Canada, Inc., *Toronto*
Pearson Educaciòn de Mexico, S.A. de C.V.
Pearson Education—Japan, *Tokyo*
Pearson Education Malaysia, Pte. Ltd.
Pearson Education, *Upper Saddle River, New Jersey*

To Judith, with love. —H.H.

To Nelda, for her patience and support. —D.R.

Contents

Preface

So you are a computer science (CS) major and you are sitting down to see what this book is about. It has been assigned, the course is required, you have no choice. Still you chose your institution, your major. Maybe your instructor made a good choice. Let's hope so.

Okay, you are not a computer science major, perhaps not even a student, but you have picked up this book. Maybe the title intrigued you. Will you be able to read it, to learn from it? We think so. We will try to interest you too.

Or you are teaching a course that might use this book, maybe in discrete math, maybe including logics or formal language or both. If you want your CS students to see the applicability of mathematical reasoning to their own field or your math students to see the usefulness of their field outside itself, it is your students whom we have in mind.

If you are a CS major, you have already noticed that this course is different from the others you have taken so far. It is not an introduction to computing, programming, problem solving, or data structures. No, this book is about something called *models*—models of language and knowledge. It is also about formal methods.

You know something about models if you have built or seen a model airplane. In Kitty Hawk, North Carolina, you can see the wind tunnel that the Wright brothers built to test the lift capabilities of various wing shapes. A model can help us simplify and think more clearly about a complex problem (powered flight) by selecting a part (the wing) and focusing on some aspect of it (its aerodynamics). The other, temporarily ignored parts and aspects must ultimately be addressed, of course, if the original problem is to be solved.

The models in this book are simplifications too, but not of material objects like airplanes. For computer scientists, the objects of study lie mainly in the world of symbols. In this book, it is computer software, and especially the programming languages in which that software is written, from which we draw our models and to which we apply them.

A model, then, is a collection of precisely stated interacting ideas that focus on a particular aspect or part of our subject matter. A good model can simplify a topic to its essence, stripping away the details so that we can understand the topic better and reason precisely about it. The model keeps only those parts and processes that are of interest.

We reason both formally and informally. Informal methods draw on analogies to your knowledge of other things in the world in general and your common sense, typically expressed in a human language like English and perhaps a diagram. Formal methods use abstract symbols—like the famous "x" of high school algebra—and clearly stated rules about how to manipulate them. A formal method based on a simple but precise model of a situation can enable us to *prove* that we have got things right at least as reflected in the model.

If this concern with precision and proof makes you think this is a theory book, you are partly right. If you think that means it is not of practical value, we ask you to think again. It is often said that experience is the best teacher. However, learning from experience means transferring ideas across situations by seeing the essential similarities in nonidentical situations. This abstracted essence, by which we learn from history or from our mistakes, is an informal model. Formalizing the model and reasoning carefully about it—that is, theory—is the scientist's and engineer's path to knowledge and action in the real world.

So what do we theorize about? We have chosen to focus on language, the crucial link between hardware and software. Programming languages permit software to be written and language processors—compilers, interpreters and assemblers—permit hardware to run that software. Sometimes a model proves to be so interesting and widely applicable that it becomes an object of study in its own right. That is the case with the logic and language models in this book.

Two key aspects of language are structure and meaning. We study models of each. The structure of language has to do with the arrangement of symbols into permitted sequences—called *sentences* in human language and *statements* in programming languages. This topic is usually called formal models of language. It underlies key aspects of compilers, the study of what computers can do efficiently and the processing of human language for translation and easy interaction between people and computers.

Symbol arrangements are of interest not only in their own right, but also because they express ideas about meaning and computation. Expressing meaning can be done in various ways, including logic. Of the many logics, the simplest is propositional logic. It finds application in the tiny hardware components called *logic gates*, in the conditions for branching and loops in high-level programming languages and in mathematical rules of proof that can be applied via software throughout engineering and science. Predicate logic builds on propositional logic to permit knowledge representation in database systems, artificial intelligence, and work on program correctness in software engineering.

Computer science students may notice that several phrases in the prior paragraphs are the names of upper division courses in computer science. To further emphasize the practical value of the two major topics of this book, we introduce an important programming language based on each. Lex, based on formal language, is a tool for building a *lexical scanner*—a key component of a compiler. Prolog, a programming language whose core is based on predicate logic, supports rapid prototyping of intelligent systems.

Formalisms for language and logic have ancient roots: India for language and Greece for logic. Each field has enjoyed renewed attention in more recent times, starting in the nineteenth century for logic and early in the twentieth century for language. These latter thrusts are more formal yet still independent of computing. The venerable histories of logic and linguistics suggest the inherent fascination that each has held for human minds. Building on that motivation, this book stresses the relationship of each to computer science. The two fields are also related to each other in various ways that emerge in this text. Watch for these important links among logic, formal language, and computing.

- Complementarity: Logic and formal language share the job of modeling, with logic providing models of meaning and formal language paying attention to form.

- Recursion: In logic, formal language and elsewhere, recursive definitions provide a finite means to specify expressions of unlimited size.

- Proofs: Logic supports proofs of results throughout formal language, mathematics, and computer science, notably in the area of program verification.

- Correspondences: Language categories defined by grammar types are in direct correspondence to the recognition capabilities of types of automata (models of computing).

- Compiling: Design strategies for some (pushdown) automata reflect language processing techniques for compilers. Concepts of formal languages and automata directly support compiler tools.

- Computation: Another class of automata (Turing machines) provides an apparently correct characterization of the limits of computing.

- Programming: Logic-based languages such as Prolog support the declarative style of programming. Prolog in turn is used to implement some automata and database concepts.

H. HAMBURGER
D. RICHARDS

Chapter 1

Mathematical Preliminaries

This text is concerned with formal models that are important to the field of computer science. Because the models are formal, we make substantial use of mathematical ideas. In many ways, the topics in this book—logic, languages, and automata—are a natural extension of a Discrete Mathematics course, which is generally required for computer science (CS) majors. This text steers clear of excessive mathematical notation, focusing instead on fundamental ideas and their application. However, it is impossible to appreciate the power that comes from the rigorous methods and models in this book without some background in discrete mathematics. This chapter is a brief overview of the needed mathematical background and may be useful for self-evaluation, review, and reference.

1.1 Operators and Their Algebraic Properties

Operators are crucial to all of mathematics, starting with the first one we learn in childhood—the addition operator of ordinary arithmetic. The things that an operator operates *on* are called its *operands*.

Each operand of an operator must come from some *domain*. For present purposes, we assume that both operands of addition are from the domain of real numbers, which includes things like -273, π, .406, and $\sqrt{5}$. The real numbers are *closed* under addition, because the result of adding two of them is also a real number; roughly speaking, "closed" means staying within a domain.

In the case of addition, the order of the operands does not affect the result. For example, $2 + 3$ and $3 + 2$ are both 5. More generally, $x + y = y + x$ for any x and y. Since that is the case, the operator is *commutative*. Multiplication is also commutative, but subtraction and division are not. Being commutative, or the

1

property of commutativity, is one of several properties of operators that is of interest to us.

Another key property of addition is *associativity*. Like commutativity, it can be expressed by an equality. To say that addition is associative—which it is—is the same as saying that $(x + y) + z = x + (y + z)$ for any x, y, and z. The *identity* element for addition is 0 (zero) since, whenever it is one of the operands, the result is the other operand: $x + 0 = x$ for any x. Every real number x has an *inverse*, $-x$, such that the two of them add up to the identity: $x + (-x) = 0$.

Multiplication of reals is commutative and associative. It has an identity element, 1, and for each element except 0 there is an inverse. The multiplication operator is often left invisible, as in xy, the product of x and y. Here the operator has been expressed by simply writing the operands next to each other.

A property of the interaction of addition and multiplication is *distributivity*, the fact that multiplication distributes over addition. This fact is written $x(y + z) = xy + xz$, for all x, y, and z. Addition does not distribute over multiplication, however, since it is *not* true in general that $x + yz = (x + y)(x + z)$.

Equality, less than ("<"), and greater than (">") are known as *relational* operators. The pairwise combinations of them are also relational operators: inequality ("$\neq$"), less than or equal ("$\leq$"), and greater than or equal ("$\geq$"). An important property of all these operators except "$\neq$" is *transitivity*. For example, to say that less than is transitive means that if $x < y$ and $y < z$ are both true, then $x < z$ must also be true.

Operators apply not only to numbers, but to other categories as well. An excellent example occurs in the next section, where sets and their operators are introduced. We find that not only are the two key operators, union and intersection, both commutative and associative, but also each distributes over the other. In later chapters, we see that discussions of operators and their algebraic properties are highly significant for the principal topics of this book—logic and formal languages.

1.2   Sets

A *set* is a collection of distinct *elements*. The elements are typically thought of as objects such as integers, people, books, or classrooms, and they are written within braces like this: {*Friday, Saturday, Sunday*}. When working with sets, it can be important to specify the *universe*, $\mathcal{U}$, of elements (e.g., the set of days of the week) from which the elements of particular sets are drawn. Note that the universe is a set: the set of all elements of a given type. Sometimes the universe is only tacitly specified, when the reader can easily figure out what it is. The elements are said to be *in* the set and may also be called its *members*.

Sets can be presented in two forms. The *extensional* form enumerates the elements of the set, whereas the *intensional* form specifies the properties of the elements. For example:

$$S = \{11, 12, 13, 14\}$$

$$S = \{x \mid x \text{ is an integer, and } 10 < x < 15\}$$

are extensional and intensional forms of the same set. The second of these is read "those x *such that* x is an integer greater than 10 and less than 15." Note that the universe, the set of integers, is tacit in the first example and only informally specified in the second. The *empty set* is a set with no element and is denoted $\emptyset$.

Because the elements of a set are distinct, you should write sets with no repetition. For example, suppose a student database includes countries of origin and shows the participants in a seminar as being from China, France, China, Egypt, and France. Then the set of countries represented in this class is $\{China, France, Egypt\}$. Further, there is no concept of ordering within a set; there is no "first" element, and so on. For example, the sets $\{4, 2, 3\}$ and $\{2, 3, 4\}$ are the same set; it does not matter which form is used.

If ordering is important, then one speaks of a *sequence* of elements. In the extensional form of a sequence, the elements appear in order, within parentheses, not braces. For example, the sequence $(4, 2, 3)$ is different from $(2, 3, 4)$. Further, sequences need not have distinct elements, so the sequence $(2, 3, 3, 4)$ is different from $(2, 3, 4)$. Sequences are often implemented as one-dimensional arrays or as linked lists. A sequence of length 2 is called an *ordered pair*. A sequence of length 3, 4, or 5 is called a *triple*, *quadruple*, or *quintuple* respectively; in the general case of length n, the word is *n-tuple*.

Set operators let us talk succinctly about sets. We begin with notions of membership and comparison. The notation $x \in S$ means that x is an element of the set S, whereas $x \notin S$ means that x is *not* in S. With $S = \{11, 12, 13, 14\}$ as in the prior example, $12 \in S$ and $16 \notin S$. We say that S_1 is a subset of S_2, written $S_1 \subseteq S_2$, if each element of S_1 is also an element of S_2. For example, $\{12, 14\} \subseteq \{11, 12, 13, 14\}$. Since (of course) a set contains all of its own elements, it is correct to write $S \subseteq S$. Now consider subset T, which is *not* equal to S because it is missing one or more elements of S. Although it is correct to write $T \subseteq S$, we may choose to write $T \subset S$, which states that T is a *proper subset* of S. For contrast, one may refer to any set as an *improper subset* of itself.

Two sets are equal, $S_1 = S_2$, if (and only if) they contain exactly the same elements. It is important to observe that $S_1 = S_2$ exactly when $S_1 \subseteq S_2$ and $S_2 \subseteq S_1$. To show that $S_1 = S_2$ one needs to argue that both $S_1 \subseteq S_2$ and $S_2 \subseteq S_1$.

The empty set is a subset of any set. Thus, for any set S, it is correct to write $\emptyset \subseteq S$.

The *cardinality* of a set S is the number of elements in S and is denoted $|S|$. For example, $|\{11, 12, 13, 14\}| = 4$. When the cardinality is an integer, the set is *finite*; otherwise it is *infinite*. Notice that an infinite set, such as the set of integers divisible by 3, must be written intensionally, not extensionally, because it would take forever to write down all its elements. The empty set has cardinality 0, $|\emptyset| = 0$.

The *power set* of S is the set of all subsets of S, and it is typically written 2^S. For example, if $S = \{1, 2, 3\}$, then $2^S = \{\emptyset, \{1\}, \{2\}, \{3\}, \{1, 2\}, \{1, 3\}, \{2, 3\}, \{1, 2, 3\}\}$ is the power set of S. Notice that the power set in this example has exactly $8 = 2^3$ elements. This is no accident; for any set S, the cardinality of its power set, $|2^S|$, is equal to $2^{|S|}$. In fact, it is this exponential (power) relationship that motivates the name of the power set and the notation for it.

Earlier we saw the operators for membership and comparison. Now consider binary operations that take two sets and produce a single set as their result. The most common of these are union, intersection, and subtraction (set difference). The *union* of S_1 and S_2, denoted $S_1 \cup S_2$, is the set of elements in either S_1 or S_2 or both. The *intersection* of S_1 and S_2, denoted $S_1 \cap S_2$, is the set of elements that are in S_1 as well as being in S_2. The *set difference* of S_2 from S_1, written $S_1 \setminus S_2$, is the set of elements that are in S_1 but not in S_2. The *complement* of a set S, denoted $\overline{S}$, contains exactly those elements of the current universe $\mathcal{U}$ that are *not* in S. We can write $\overline{S} = \mathcal{U} \setminus S$, which may help stress the important point that the complement depends crucially on what the universe is understood to be. Let us look at a few examples using the universe of one-digit integers, $\mathcal{U} = \{0, 1, 2, 3, 4, 5, 6, 7, 8, 9\}$.

$$\{1, 2, 3, 4\} \cup \{3, 4, 5, 6\} = \{1, 2, 3, 4, 5, 6\}$$

$$\{1, 2, 3, 4\} \cap \{3, 4, 5, 6\} = \{3, 4\}$$

$$\{1, 2, 3, 4\} \setminus \{3, 4, 5, 6\} = \{1, 2\}$$

$$\overline{\{0, 2, 4, 6, 8\}} = \{1, 3, 5, 7, 9\}$$

The *cross-product* of S_1 and S_2, denoted $S_1 \times S_2$, is the set of ordered pairs of elements in which the first is in S_1 and the second is in S_2. Formally,

$$S_1 \times S_2 = \{(x, y) \mid x \in S_1 \text{ and } y \in S_2\}.$$

For example, $\{a, b\} \times \{c, d, e\} = \{(a, c), (a, d), (a, e), (b, c), (b, d), (b, e)\}$. Just as the elements of $S_1 \times S_2$ are ordered pairs, so the elements of $S_1 \times S_2 \times S_3$ are triples, and so on.

1.3 Strings

It is commonplace in discussions of computer programming to say that "HELLO" is a "string" or a "string of 5 characters." In the terminology of the preceding section, this would be a *sequence* of characters, of length 5, denoted (H,E,L,L,O). Since such sequences are used so extensively in computer science, we adopt a more concise and natural approach.

A *string* is a finite sequence of elements. The elements are typically called *symbols*, and the set of all symbols under consideration in any example or situation is denoted Σ. The set of symbols may also be called an *alphabet* especially when each symbol is a single letter, but even in other cases. Just as the empty set is a set with no elements, it is convenient to define the *empty string* to be a string with no characters. We call it Λ. Thus, if the alphabet is $\Sigma = \{a, b, c\}$, the following are examples of "strings over the alphabet Σ":

$$\Lambda, \quad ab, \quad bbc, \quad abacab$$

The principal operation on strings is concatenation. The *concatenation* of strings x and y, simply denoted xy, is a string consisting of the characters of x followed by the characters of y. For example, if $x = ab$ and $y = bca$, then $xy = abbca$. Either x or y could be the empty string; if $x = ab$ and $y = \Lambda$, then $xy = ab$. In general, concatenation is not a commutative operation, so we cannot expect $xy = yx$. However, concatenation is an associative operation, so when we extend such concatenations to three or more strings we can write the expression without parentheses: $(xy)z = x(yz) = xyz$. A *prefix* consists of consecutive letters at the beginning of a string, so ab is a prefix of $abcbb$ and x is always a prefix of xy.

The *length* of the string x, the number of characters in it, is denoted $|x|$ (the same notation used for the cardinality of a set). For example, $|ab| = 2$ and $|abacab| = 6$. The empty string has zero length—that is, $|\Lambda| = 0$. Recall that by definition a string is finite, so $|x|$ is always an integer. Finally, note that $|xy| = |x| + |y|$.

Sets of strings are studied extensively in this text. We use the term *language* to refer to a set of strings. For example, $L = \{ab, bbc, abacab\}$ is a language of three strings, $|L| = 3$. It is important to remember that, although a language may contain an infinite number of strings, each string in the language is finite. We will postpone any formal discussion of strings and languages until Part II, where they receive extensive treatment.

1.4   Relations and Functions

A *binary relation* is a set of ordered pairs. More formally, a relation R from the set S_1 to the set S_2 is a subset of the cross-product of those sets, $R \subseteq S_1 \times S_2$. For example, if E is a set of employees and P is a set of projects, we can specify a relation R from E to P that indicates which employees are assigned to which projects. In this case, each element of R has to be an ordered pair (x, y) with $x \in E$ and $y \in P$. More specifically, if $E = \{e_1, e_2, e_3\}$ is the set of employees and $P = \{p_1, p_2, p_3, p_4\}$ is the set of projects, we might have $R = \{(e_1, p_2), (e_1, p_3), (e_3, p_2)\}$, indicating that employee e_1 is assigned to both p_2 and p_3 while e_3 is assigned only to p_2 and e_2 is unassigned.

It is possible to have a relation from a set to itself. In this case, we say that we have a relation *on* that one set. More formally, a relation R on the set S is a subset of the cross-product of S with itself, $R \subseteq S \times S$. Take, for example, in the domain of English royalty, the set S = {George VI, Elizabeth II, Prince Charles} and the relation P that relates a child to the parent. Then $P = \{$(Prince Charles, Elizabeth II), (Elizabeth II, George VI)$\}$.

Some relations are explicitly constrained to have just one ordered pair for each possible first element; such a relation is a *function*. In the earlier example, if each employee had been assigned to just one project, then the relation from employees to jobs would be a function. In that case, we would want to use the familiar function notation, $R(x) = y$, rather than the relation notation, $(x, y) \in R$. (One might also be inclined to call the function f.) Since a function can be regarded as a *mapping* from one set to another, this relationship can be described with the notation

$$R : E \rightarrow P,$$

which indicates that R is a function that maps elements of E to (unique) elements of P. E is called the *domain* of R and P is the *codomain* of R.

Such a function is a *one-to-one correspondence* between E and P if every element of E is mapped to an element of P and every element of P has exactly one element of E mapped to it. It follows that if there is a one-to-one correspondence between E and P, then $|E| = |P|$. In fact, we formally say two sets have the same cardinality if and only if such a mapping exists. If the function R fails to map some elements of E, we call it a partial function. In contrast, a total function provides mappings for all elements of E.

Analogous to binary relations, there are also ternary (3-ary) and n-ary relations. A ternary relation is a set of triples, and an n-ary one is a set of n-tuples. More formally, a relation R on the sets S_1, S_2, and S_3 is a subset of their cross-product, $R \subseteq S_1 \times S_2 \times S_3$, and similarly for n-ary relations.

The previous statement—that a function maps one set to another, $R : E \to P$,—is more permissive than it may seem. That is because the set E (or P for that matter) may be a cross-product set. For example, consider a chart, G, of gross national product (GNP) with countries and years as the rows and columns. With C as the set of countries and $\mathcal{N}$ as the set of integers (for years and dollars), we can write:

$$G : C \times \mathcal{N} \to \mathcal{N}$$

where G is a function that maps countries and years into dollars. For an example that relates back to Section 1.3, let $\mathcal{S}$ be 2^S, the set of subsets of S. Then we can write $\cap : \mathcal{S} \times \mathcal{S} \to \mathcal{S}$; that is, intersection takes a pair of sets and produces a set.

1.5   Growth Rates of Functions

A numeric function, $f(n)$, maps numbers to numbers, either integers or reals. Sometimes we wish to discuss the growth rate of a numeric function in rough terms. For example, for the functions $3n^2 + 12n$ and $10n^2$, it may be useful to emphasize that they are both quadratic functions, rather than to point out their differences. The "big-O" notation was devised to characterize the growth of functions while ignoring the constant coefficients and the lower order terms (such as $12n$ above) that have negligible impact on the growth rate for large n.

In particular, we say a numeric function "$f(n)$ is $O(g(n))$" if

$$\frac{f(n)}{g(n)} \leq c(n), \quad \text{and} \quad \lim_{n \to \infty} c(n) = c$$

for some constant c. For example, $3n^2+12n$ is $O(n^2)$. There are other ways to bound the growth of functions. These are typically discussed more fully in an algorithms course, when proving bounds on the execution times of algorithms. We use this notation sparingly, so we do not go into further details.

1.6   Graphs and Trees

Graphs are an important mathematical concept to model relationships within a set. Formally, a *graph* G is a pair of sets, $G = (V, E)$, where V is a set of elements called *vertices* and E, the set of *edges*, is a relation from V to V, so that $E \subseteq V \times V$. If $(x, y) \in E$, we say there is an edge from vertex x to vertex y; pictorially such an edge is drawn as an arrow from a point labeled x to another point labeled y.

As defined in the preceding paragraph, a graph is sometimes specifically called a *directed graph*, or just a *digraph*, to distinguish it from the related concept of an undirected graph. An *undirected graph* is a graph in which an edge does not imply any directionality. In other words, if $(x, y) \in E$, we do *not* say that there is an edge from x to y; instead we simply say x and y are connected by the edge. Such an undirected edge is depicted as a line (with no arrowhead). If (x, y) is in E, then there is no need to include (y, x) in the specification of E since that conveys no additional information.

A directed *path* of length k from vertex x to vertex y is a sequence of vertices

$$x = x_0, x_1, x_2, \ldots, x_k = y$$

such that $(x_{i-1}, x_i) \in E$ for each $1 \leq i \leq k$. An undirected path is defined analogously, but there is no implied concept of following the arrows as one traverses such a path. A *cycle* is a path for which $x = y$. A graph is *acyclic* if it contains no cycles. An undirected graph is *connected* if there is a path from each vertex to every other vertex; a directed graph is *strongly connected* if there is a directed path from each vertex to every other vertex.

An undirected graph is a *tree* if it is connected and acyclic. A directed acyclic graph is often called a *dag* in view of its initials. A dag is a *rooted tree* if it has a distinguished vertex, called the *root*, and a unique path from the root to every other vertex. Rooted trees, in contrast to real trees that grow in the ground, are usually drawn with the root at the top and all the edges pointing downward. If this is done consistently, we can omit the arrowheads in the drawings. Each edge points from a *parent* vertex to a *child* vertex. A vertex with no outward arrows (i.e., no children) is called a *leaf*. Sometimes the order of the children of a parent vertex is significant so that it is natural to speak of the "leftmost child," also called the "first child," and so on. When the children in a rooted tree have such an ordering, then we have an *ordered tree*. Among the many facts known about trees, perhaps the most crucial is that the number of edges is one less than the number of vertices, $|E| = |V| - 1$. Ordered trees (with labels on their vertices) play a key role in specifying and analyzing the structure of programming languages in Part II.

1.7   Computing with Mathematical Objects

Sets, strings, and other mathematical objects are introduced in this chapter for conceptual purposes, but it is often important to implement them in the computer as data structures. That means deciding how to store the objects and designing algorithms to determine the results of applying the operators. If you have already taken some programming courses, the ideas presented here are familiar, but worth reviewing in the present context.

How difficult it is to implement a class of objects depends on the particular programming language. Many modern high-level languages provide, for example, a string class along with a concatenation operator. In that case, you can use those capabilities to go about your work without worrying about the hidden details. It is rarer that a graph class is provided within a language, although you may be able to find one implemented in a library for your programming language. Here we touch on a few important issues by discussing the implementation of sets. We assume that both the reader and the programming language can handle the concepts of arrays and (linked) lists.

Sets can be stored by putting the elements into a list. Doing this imposes an ordering on them in the computer. However, as noted in Section 1.2, sets are not ordered, so we should regard the actual order within a list as arbitrary. Our lists do not have repetitions since sets have distinct elements. We assume that the language lets us build a list, node by node, by operations that allocate a new node, link it into a list, and assign it a value.

An algorithm to find the intersection of two sets, X and Y, can traverse X and for each element either copy it to the result or not depending on whether it is also in Y as determined by traversing Y. Since this involves traversing Y repeatedly, it may not be the most efficient way to do things. The set difference can be done similarly by taking just those elements of X that are *not* in Y. The algorithm for union is left as an exercise.

Alternatively, sets can be expressed as arrays of 1s and 0s, with array size equal to the number of elements in the current universe. Array positions correspond to some convenient ordering for the elements of that universe. The array for any particular set has 1s at the positions for its elements and 0s elsewhere. With a universe of the five vowels, for example, and assuming alphabetical ordering, the diagram below shows an array of size 5 representing the set $\{a, i, o\}$. Union and intersection can be computed with a single traversal of each array, but now the number of positions to be traversed is the size of the universe, not of the sets.

1	0	1	1	0

For sets over a large universe, if space is an issue, each 1 or 0 can be stored as a single bit. Thus, each set over a 320-element universe requires only ten 32-bit words of memory. If you know something about computing hardware, you may have noticed an additional advantage of this method with respect to efficiency. It allows set operations to be put into correspondence with fast, parallel bitwise logical operations in hardware.

Exercises

1.1 Express each of the following in formal set notation.

    (a) The commutativity and associativity of union.

    (b) The commutativity and associativity of intersection.

    (c) The distributivity of intersection over union.

    (d) The distributivity of union over intersection.

1.2 Give an expression for the cardinality of $S_1 \times S_2$.

1.3 What is the identity element for

    (a) the union operator?

    (b) for the intersection operator?

1.4 For each of the following, answer the question and explain.

    (a) Is the subset relation transitive?

    (b) Is every set closed under cross-product?

1.5 What is the cardinality of the language $\{x \mid x$ is a string over $\{a, b, c\}$ and $|x| \leq 2\}$?

1.6 Express $f(n) = 6n^3 - n \log n + 10n$ using big-O notation.

1.7 Describe an algorithm for computing the union of two sets:

    (a) for the list implementation.

    (b) for the array implementation.

Part I

Logic for Computer Science

Introduction to Part I:
Logic for Computer Science

Logic has many uses for computer scientists. Perhaps the best known is the role of *propositional* logic in the design and analysis of the digital circuits from which computers are built. A richer form of logic known as *predicate* logic underlies work in a much broader range of computer science topics, including artificial intelligence, databases, and software engineering. There are even programming languages based on predicate logic.

But logic is not only a source of applications. It is also an aid to careful thought about precisely defined subject matter such as that of mathematics and computer science. We see how so-called *rules of inference* can be used to establish confidence in the truth of each assertion in a sequence of assertions, culminating in proofs of important results. In fact, we not only prove things, but also discuss proofs as problem-solving activities and stress the relationship between inference rules and everyday commonsense reasoning.

Computer science has long been concerned with the manipulation of data. Increasingly these days, it also deals with the manipulation of *knowledge*. This shift, which underlies important applications like expert systems and intelligent databases, has been made possible by finding ways to write down what we know about real-world subject matter in a form that is sufficiently precise so that a computer can do useful things with it.

Because logic is a way to express knowledge, various forms of it have played important roles in these endeavors. Here we introduce propositional logic and predicate logic (also called predicate calculus), which are formal systems for expressing knowledge and reasoning about it to get new results. Both of these approaches to knowledge representation and reasoning ignore some aspects of knowledge. This simplification helps both the beginner and the field as a whole by permitting clarity

14

and rigorous proofs about how the reasoning works. There are important representation and reasoning systems (not treated here) that build on predicate logic, extending it to deal with time, uncertainty, approximation, and other important aspects of knowledge.

Propositional logic is presented in Chapter 2. It then serves, in Chapter 3, as the basis of a discussion of proof techniques that are widely used in both mathematics and computer science. Building on this foundation, we move on to predicate calculus and additional proof methods that it supports, in Chapters 4 and 5, respectively. This material in turn is the basis for two different parts of computer science. Verification, the topic of Chapter 6, is concerned with proving programs correct as opposed to just testing them on some inputs. Finally, Chapter 7 shows that predicate logic can even form the basis of programming itself, by presenting the rudiments of Prolog, a logic programming language.

Chapter 2

Propositional Logic

Logic is a useful framework for models of knowledge. Logical models simplify the world to focus on key ideas. The focus in propositional logic is on statements that are simply *true* or *false* and on the ways in which such statements can be combined and manipulated. Requiring statements to be true or false means that we never say something is likely or unlikely: There is never a 70% chance of rain in propositional logic. Nor do we ever say that a statement is close to the truth or far from it; statements are never vague or approximate. These restrictions allow us to focus on essential ideas about precise reasoning and, in Chapter 3, to uncover a remarkable array of useful ways to prove important results.

2.1 Propositions

Propositional logic is about true and false statements, which we call **propositions**. Often propositions appear in the notation of arithmetic, set theory, or some other formalism, but they may also be expressed as ordinary sentences in English or some other human language. Here are a few examples:

$$5 > 3$$
$$\text{FISH} \subset \text{MAMMALS}$$
It is raining.

The first of these is clearly true. The second is clearly false. The third is a bit problematic, but if we imagine that it is spoken to you as you are reading this, then it is reasonable to say that either it is true or it is false. Besides allowing ourselves this explanation about the time and place of the rain, we also conveniently ignore borderline misty conditions. To deal with these additional factors would require a more complex system of representation. When we come to predicate logic, we go into greater detail, so that in the case of "5 > 3", we look inside the proposition, at the 5, the 3, and the operator. For propositional logic, we care only whether the whole statement is true or false.

Because its focus is on true and false sentences, the formal study of propositional logic begins with the set {TRUE, FALSE}, called the set of **logical constants**. Some people refer to them as the Boolean constants in honor of George Boole, the founder of modern symbolic logic. Calling them constants contrasts them with logical variables, soon to be introduced here. Yet another term for them is the *truth values*, which emphasizes their similarity to numerical values in arithmetic. Just as we combine numerical values, like 2 and 3, using arithmetic operators, like plus, to get a resulting value, so here we combine the truth values TRUE and FALSE, using logical operators, to get resulting values.

A **logical variable** (or Boolean variable) is one that can take on only the value TRUE or FALSE. For example, with the variable p understood to represent the idea that 5 exceeds 3, we can write $p = $ TRUE. A proposition can be just a logical constant or a logical variable or it may be a more complex expression built out of logical variables and logical constants (either or both of them) along with operators corresponding roughly to "and", "or", and "not". In particular, if we let p be the proposition that it is raining and let q be the proposition that 5 > 3, then (not surprisingly) the expression "p and q" stands for the proposition that both are true: that it is raining and 5 > 3. Similar comments apply to "p or q" and to "not p". We also use the operator $\wedge$ for "and", $\vee$ for "or", and $\neg$ for "not", giving us three ways to express the propositions.

It is raining and 5 is greater than 3.	p and q	$p \wedge q$
It is raining or 5 is greater than 3.	p or q	$p \vee q$
It is not raining.	not p	$\neg p$

Although the English words "and," "or," and "not" are suggestive here, using English words can lead to ambiguity. Specifically, the word "or" is often used in English to mean "one or the other *but not both*," for example, when offering a choice between two alternatives. In logic, contrastingly, we most often use the *inclusive* interpretation: "one or the other *or both*." It is therefore actually less confusing in the long run to introduce special symbols. As shown earlier, we write these expressions as $p \wedge q$, $p \vee q$, and $\neg p$, respectively. The operators $\wedge$, $\vee$, and $\neg$ are called **logical operators** (or connectives). The $\vee$ symbol is read as "or", but it is *always* understood to have the inclusive meaning (allowing the possibility of both). If we need to talk about exclusive "or", we use a different symbol.

The expression $p \wedge q$ is regarded as a proposition, as well as being an expression involving other propositions; by analogy, $1 + 2$ is a number, 3, although it is also an expression involving numbers. The following definition is one way to specify all the propositions discussed.

Definition 2.1 Propositions

- Each of the two logical constants, TRUE and FALSE, is a proposition.

- Logical variables, such as p, q, r, ..., are propositions.

- If α and β are propositions, then so are $(\alpha \wedge \beta)$, $(\alpha \vee \beta)$, and $(\neg \alpha)$.

- Nothing else is a proposition.

The third line of this definition can be used repeatedly to build up complex propositions. Each of the symbols α and β can stand not only for a logical constant (TRUE or FALSE) or a logical variable, but also for another proposition already formed in accord with this same third line of the definition. For example, with $\alpha = p$ and $\beta = (q \wedge r)$, the form $(\alpha \vee \beta)$ becomes the complex proposition $(p \vee (q \wedge r))$. It is also important to realize that this third line of the definition is **recursive**, in that it defines propositions in terms of (smaller) propositions. Recursion plays an important role in both mathematics and computer science.

Parentheses play an important role in the definitions. Without their parentheses, the expressions $(p \vee (q \wedge r))$ and $((p \vee q) \wedge r)$ would look the same since each would be left with just $p \vee q \wedge r$. But $(p \vee (q \wedge r))$ can have a different value than $((p \vee q) \wedge r)$, just as $(2 + 3) \times 4 \neq 2 + (3 \times 4)$. So we do need the possibility of parentheses. However, the definition goes beyond what is necessary in this regard. First, it unnecessarily requires parentheses around the outside of all expressions except simple ones that consist of a single constant or variable. Second, it does not take advantage of precedence. Just as $2 + 3 \times 4$ is understood to mean that the $\times$ is to be applied before the $+$, so too is the unparenthesized expression $p \vee q \wedge r$ understood to mean that the $\wedge$ is to be applied before the $\vee$. Despite these drawbacks, however, the definition we have chosen is indeed correct and has the advantage of simplicity.

2.2 States, Operators, and Truth Tables

We often refer to the value of a proposition as its **state**, so a proposition can be in one of two states: TRUE or FALSE. More generally, when we are dealing with a collection of propositions, we can speak of the state of the collection. That combined state is then the ordered list of the states of each proposition in the collection. For example, two propositions, p and q, can be in one of the four states listed next. Three propositions can be in one of eight states and k propositions in one of 2^k states. States are sometimes called *assignments of truth values.*

<table>
<tr><td rowspan="4">The 4 states for p and q have these pairs of values for p, q, respectively:</td><td>1. TRUE, TRUE</td></tr>
<tr><td>2. TRUE, FALSE</td></tr>
<tr><td>3. FALSE, TRUE</td></tr>
<tr><td>4. FALSE, FALSE</td></tr>
</table>

The operator $\wedge$ is read "and" and is often called the **conjunction** operator. It has two operands (propositions that it operates on) and is defined by giving its value in each of the four states of those two operands. Specifically,

$$p \wedge q = \text{TRUE} \qquad \text{when both } p = \text{TRUE and } q = \text{TRUE, and}$$
$$p \wedge q = \text{FALSE} \qquad \text{in the other three states.}$$

The operator $\vee$ is read "or" and is often called the **disjunction** operator. It too is defined by giving its value in each of the four states of its two operands. Notice how this definition is inclusive in the manner mentioned before.

$$p \vee q = \text{FALSE} \qquad \text{when both } p = \text{FALSE and } q = \text{FALSE, and}$$
$$p \vee q = \text{TRUE} \qquad \text{in the other three states.}$$

Finally, we define $\neg$, the **negation** operator:

$$\neg p = \text{TRUE} \qquad \text{when } p = \text{FALSE, and}$$
$$\neg p = \text{FALSE} \qquad \text{when } p = \text{TRUE.}$$

These definitions are presented graphically in the following truth tables, in which each cell (or box) corresponds to a state of the two variables p and q. After that comes Definition 2.2, which combines the information in the truth tables with the information provided in Definition 2.1 about constructing all the possible propositions. It is sometimes said that Definition 2.1 provides the **syntax** or structure of the propositions and Definition 2.2 combines this with the **semantics** or meaning of the propositions.

Truth Tables

p \ q	T	F
T	T	F
F	F	F

$p \wedge q$

p \ q	T	F
T	T	T
F	T	F

$p \vee q$

p	
T	F
F	T

$\neg p$

Definition 2.2 Evaluating Propositions

- TRUE and FALSE are propositions. The value of each is itself.

- Variables like p, q, r, . . . are propositions with value either TRUE or FALSE.

- If α and β are propositions, then

   (a) $(\neg \alpha)$ is FALSE if α is TRUE and vice-versa.

   (b) $(\alpha \wedge \beta)$ is TRUE if both α and β are TRUE, and otherwise is FALSE.

   (c) $(\alpha \vee \beta)$ is FALSE if both α and β are FALSE, and otherwise is TRUE.

- Nothing else is a proposition.

It is of some interest to show how propositional logic can be discussed in the formal framework of sets and functions introduced in Chapter 1. To begin, note that the logical constants constitute a two-element set, which we call $\mathcal{B}$, so that $\mathcal{B} = \{\text{TRUE}, \text{FALSE}\}$. Next, the conjunction and disjunction operators can also be regarded as *functions* of two variables. A function symbol is typically written ahead of its arguments—for example, $f(x, y)$—so by analogy you would write $\wedge (p, q)$. This is like writing $+(x, y)$ for the sum of x and y. However, it is much more common to use $\wedge$ and $\vee$ as infix operators, writing them between their arguments (or operands), as we have done except in this discussion.

Putting the ideas of sets and functions together, we can regard the conjunction operator, $\wedge$, as a function from pairs of $\mathcal{B}$-elements to a single $\mathcal{B}$-element. We write this idea as $\wedge : \mathcal{B} \times \mathcal{B} \to \mathcal{B}$, where the symbol "$\times$" denotes the cross-product of sets—in this case, all pairs of $\mathcal{B}$-elements. The elements of $\mathcal{B} \times \mathcal{B}$ are the four states of (p, q) mentioned at the beginning of this section. The disjunction operator, $\vee$, involves the same sets, so $\vee : \mathcal{B} \times \mathcal{B} \to \mathcal{B}$. For the operator $\neg$, which simply has $\mathcal{B}$ as its domain, one writes $\neg : \mathcal{B} \to \mathcal{B}$.

2.3   Proofs of Equivalence with Truth Tables

Look back at the truth tables for the three propositional operators. Notice that we have a one-dimensional table for the unary (one-operand) operator, $\neg$, and a two-dimensional table for each of the binary (two-operand) operators, $\wedge$ and $\vee$, since each variable gets its own dimension. Expressions with more variables would require more dimensions, so this approach to making diagrams on two-dimensional book pages is of limited usefulness.

An alternative tabular form for truth tables is illustrated next. Looking at the rows of this new kind of table and recalling the idea of states (beginning of Section 2.2), notice that each possible state has its own row. There are two variables, so there are 4 ($= 2{\times}2$) states and the table has four rows of truth values. The states are expressed in the first two columns taken together. For brevity, we put T and F in place of TRUE and FALSE.

p	q	$p \wedge q$	$\neg\,(p \wedge q)$	$\neg\,p$	$\neg\,q$	$\neg\,p \vee \neg\,q$
T	T	T	F	F	F	F
T	F	F	T	F	T	T
F	T	F	T	T	F	T
F	F	F	T	T	T	T

Confirm for yourself that the third column contains exactly the same information as the truth table for $p \wedge q$. Similarly, each of the columns contains the truth values of a different expression. Therefore, we can think of this table as a whole collection of the earlier kind of truth tables.

Moreover, this table is not just an arbitrary collection of information. Notice that the fourth and seventh columns have identical truth values, and therefore the expressions heading those two columns are the same in all possible states and there is no logical difference between them, although they look different. Two propositional expressions that have the same value for each and every state like this are said to be **equivalent**. The other columns (the third, fifth, and sixth) gradually lead up to these results, starting from the four possible states of p and q in the first two columns. Taken as a whole, the table demonstrates the equivalence. Using the standard symbol "$\equiv$" for "is equivalent to," the equivalence of the two expressions is written like this:

$$\neg\,(p \wedge q) \equiv \neg\,p \vee \neg\,q.$$

The truth table is a systematic and visually clear way to present our exhaustive consideration of all four cases of the possible state combinations for p and q. The table is thus a summary of a proof by **exhaustive case analysis**. The important concept of case analysis (not always exhaustive) arises again in Chapter 3, where it serves as the basis of an inference rule and is used in a proof.

Why use three bars ("$\equiv$") for equivalence instead of just the two in an ordinary equals sign ("$=$")? The difference between an equation and an equivalence is that an equivalence is always true (in all states). An equation does not make such a claim. For example, $3x^2 = 12$ is not a claim that $3x^2$ must be 12, no matter what value x has. Although an equation may hold for all values of its variables, more often the variables must have particular values (called *solutions*). Some equations have no solution at all, and others, like this one, may have multiple solutions (here, 2 and -2).

We have seen one example of equivalence and how to prove it in a case with just two variables. Now consider a more complex truth table proof—for the equivalence of the following two propositions:

$$p \wedge (q \vee r)$$

$$(p \wedge q) \vee (p \wedge r)$$

In these expressions, there are three variables, so eight ($= 2 \times 2 \times 2$) states are needed for all possible combinations of values. Consequently, the required table, given next, has eight rows of truth values. Thinking of T and F as the binary digits, the eight rows contain—in the first three columns—the binary representation of the integers from 7 through 0—that is, 111, 110, ..., 000.

p	q	r	$q \vee r$	$p \wedge (q \vee r)$	$p \wedge q$	$p \wedge r$	$(p \wedge q) \vee (p \wedge r)$
T	T	T	T	T	T	T	T
T	T	F	T	T	T	F	T
T	F	T	T	T	F	T	T
T	F	F	F	F	F	F	F
F	T	T	T	F	F	F	F
F	T	F	T	F	F	F	F
F	F	T	T	F	F	F	F
F	F	F	F	F	F	F	F

The truth values for the eight states of the first expression, $p \wedge (q \vee r)$, appear in the fifth column of the truth table shown, and those of the other expression appear in the last column. Comparing the values in these two columns, we see that they correspond exactly, each having three Ts followed by five Fs. Since the two expressions have the same truth value for each of the (eight) possible states of their logical variables, we have another equivalence:

$$p \wedge (q \vee r) \equiv (p \wedge q) \vee (p \wedge r).$$

There is another important kind of result, besides equivalences, that truth tables can prove. A **tautology** is a proposition that is equivalent to TRUE. In other words, it has the value TRUE regardless of the state of its variables, so in the truth table there will be a column for that proposition that is all TRUEs. Find that column in each of the following truth tables. The first involves a single variable and proves that $p \vee \neg p$ is a tautology. A tautology involving two variables is $(p \wedge q) \vee \neg p \vee \neg q$, as is proved in the second truth table.

p	$\neg p$	$p \vee \neg p$
T	F	T
F	T	T

p	q	$\neg p$	$\neg q$	$p \wedge q$	$(p \wedge q) \vee \neg p$	$(p \wedge q) \vee \neg p \vee \neg q$
T	T	F	F	T	T	T
T	F	F	T	F	F	T
F	T	T	F	F	T	T
F	F	T	T	F	T	T

It is good to be aware of some other terms used to describe expressions in logic. An expression is said to be **valid** if it is a tautology—that is, if its column in a truth table is all TRUEs. One whose truth table has *some* TRUEs (one or more) is said to be **satisfiable**. An expression whose column is all FALSEs is **unsatisfiable**.

2.4   Laws of Propositional Logic

This section lists some short, useful equivalences often called **laws of propositional logic**. You already know the one shown next, since it was proved in the preceding section. Below it, for comparison, is the familiar distributive law for numbers.

$$p \wedge (q \vee r) \equiv (p \wedge q) \vee (p \wedge r)$$

$$x \times (y + z) \equiv (x \times y) + (x \times z)$$

In arithmetic, multiplication distributes over addition. The logical equivalence here is similar to the arithmetic one and by analogy is also called a *distributive law*. It says that conjunction ($\wedge$) distributes over disjunction ($\vee$). Propositional logic, unlike arithmetic, has not just one, but *two* distributive laws: Each operator ($\wedge$ and $\vee$) distributes over the other. Just as we can use the distributive law of arithmetic to transform one (arithmetic) expression into another, so too we can use this propositional equivalence to transform one (propositional) expression into another. Just as in arithmetic, manipulating expressions is an important technique to generate new but equivalent expressions.

The lists in Figures 2.1 and 2.2 give some of the most important equivalences for manipulating logical expressions. Each equivalence can easily be established by comparing columns of appropriate truth tables. We now have a new way to prove things besides truth tables: substitution, that is, the replacement of an expression by another one that has been shown to be equivalent to it.

Additional propositional equivalences are given in the next section. Taken together, the set of equivalences for propositional logic is richer and more symmetric than the set of analogous rules for arithmetic. An example of the richness is that there is nothing in arithmetic like DeMorgan's laws. An example of the symmetry can be found in the two distributivity laws. Another symmetry emerges below when we prove a new subsumption law that looks just like the first one, except that the roles of the operators are interchanged.

The equivalences in the two figures for this section, as well as Figure 2.3, are correct as they stand, but they can also be understood more broadly. Not only do they apply to the propositions p, q, and r, but they can also be applied to arbitrary propositional expressions. Symbols like the α and β used in Definitions 2.1 and 2.2 would in fact be more appropriate since they do refer to whole expressions. For example, the second DeMorgan law in Figure 2.2, $\neg(p \vee q) \equiv \neg p \wedge \neg q$, is really

$$\neg(\alpha \vee \beta) \equiv \neg \alpha \wedge \neg \beta.$$

For example, suppose we substitute into this new version of the law the expression $\neg p$ for α and q for β. The result is

$$\neg(\neg p \vee q) \equiv \neg \neg p \wedge \neg q \equiv p \wedge \neg q.$$

As another example, we begin by rewriting the first distributive law as $\alpha \vee (\beta \wedge \gamma) \equiv (\alpha \vee \beta) \wedge (\alpha \vee \gamma)$ and then apply it using p for both α and β, and q for γ, thereby getting the initial step of the following proof of a second subsumption law, $p \vee (p \wedge q) \equiv p$. Be sure you can supply the reasons for the additional steps.

$$p \vee (p \wedge q) \equiv (p \vee p) \wedge (p \vee q) \equiv p \wedge (p \vee q) \equiv p$$

Law of negation:
$$\neg\,\neg\,p \equiv p$$

Combining a variable with itself:

$$p \vee \neg\,p \equiv \text{TRUE} \qquad \text{Excluded middle}$$
$$p \wedge \neg\,p \equiv \text{FALSE} \qquad \text{Contradiction}$$
$$p \vee p \equiv p \qquad\qquad\quad \text{Idempotence of } \vee$$
$$p \wedge p \equiv p \qquad\qquad\quad \text{Idempotence of } \wedge$$

Properties of constants:

$$p \vee \text{TRUE} \equiv \text{TRUE}$$
$$p \vee \text{FALSE} \equiv p$$
$$p \wedge \text{TRUE} \equiv p$$
$$p \wedge \text{FALSE} \equiv \text{FALSE}$$

Figure 2.1: Equivalences with One Variable

Commutativity:

$$p \wedge q \equiv q \wedge p$$
$$p \vee q \equiv q \vee p$$

Associativity:

$$p \vee (q \vee r) \equiv (p \vee q) \vee r$$
$$p \wedge (q \wedge r) \equiv (p \wedge q) \wedge r$$

Distributivity:

$$p \vee (q \wedge r) \equiv (p \vee q) \wedge (p \vee r)$$
$$p \wedge (q \vee r) \equiv (p \wedge q) \vee (p \wedge r)$$

DeMorgan's laws:

$$\neg\,(p \wedge q) \equiv \neg\,p \vee \neg\,q$$
$$\neg\,(p \vee q) \equiv \neg\,p \wedge \neg\,q$$

Subsumption:

$$p \wedge (p \vee q) \equiv p$$

Figure 2.2: Equivalences with Multiple Variables

2.5 Two Important Operators

A third approach to proving things—besides truth tables and replacing things by their equivalents—is to make use of *rules of inference*. This technique, which is the topic of Section 3.2, involves an especially important operator that we now introduce. We give it a strange name, $\triangle$, so we can talk about it without prejudging what the expression $p \triangle q$ might mean. The new operator has the following truth table:

p \ q	T	F
T	T	F
F	T	T

$$p \triangle q$$

What does this truth table tell us? First, notice that it has three Ts. Therefore, to assert $p \triangle q$ is a weak claim, in that it only narrows down the possible states from four to three. By contrast, asserting $p \wedge q$ is a strong claim that narrows the possible states to just one, thereby telling us what p must be (TRUE) and also what q must be (TRUE).

Suppose you were somehow assured that proposition $p \triangle q$ was TRUE. Then, consulting the truth table, you would see that you were in one of the three states other than the upper right corner. That is, you could conclude the state $p = $ TRUE and $q = $ FALSE was not the current state. Now suppose you also learned that $p = $ TRUE. What can the truth of p tell you in the presence of the truth of $p \triangle q$? Whenever $p = $ TRUE, we are in the top half of the truth table, but whenever $p \triangle q = $ TRUE, we are not in the upper right. That leaves the upper left, where both p and q are true. So we conclude that both p and q are true.

To summarize, $p \triangle q = $ TRUE lets us use the information that $p = $ TRUE to establish that, in addition, $q = $ TRUE. In other words, it tells us that (the truth of) p leads to (the truth of) q. So henceforth we pronounce $\triangle$ as "leads to" or "implies" and write it as $\rightarrow$. This arrow shows the direction of our reasoning. The operator it represents, called either **implication** or the **conditional** operator, plays a crucial role in proving assertions by rules of inference (see Chapter 3).

We also read the expression $p \rightarrow q$ as "if p then q". This English-language phrasing can be just as confusing as "or" (inclusive vs. exclusive) unless we are careful to remember that, as with the other operators, the definition is the truth table, not the English phrase. Although in English "if p then q" does not seem to mean much when p is false, we have seen that it is useful to have this operator, which is defined to give TRUE in both of the states where p is FALSE. The important point is that the truth of both p and $(p \rightarrow q)$, together, ensures the truth of q, and that we can prove it with the truth table.

Another important operator has the truth table shown next. Once again, we use a strange name at first, this time $\Diamond$, to avoid any preconceptions. As you can see from the truth table, the expression $p \Diamond q$ is true in those (two) states for which p and q have the same truth value: either both TRUE or both FALSE.

q

p	T	F
T	T	F
F	F	T

$$p \Diamond q$$

The same kind of reasoning used for the conditional works here too. Suppose we know that $p \Diamond q$ is true (putting us in either the upper left or lower right of the truth table) and we then learn that p is true (putting us in the top row). The only possible state is therefore the upper left, where both p and q are true. So from the truth of *both* p and $p \Diamond q$, we can conclude that $q = $ TRUE too.

So far, this reasoning is just like that for the conditional. Now notice what happens if we assume the truth of q (instead of p as before) along with the truth of $p \Diamond q$. The truth of q requires our state to lie in the left column. This along with the truth of $p \Diamond q$ (upper left or lower right) again puts us in the upper left, where $p = $ TRUE. In summary, when $p \Diamond q = $ TRUE, we can reason either from p to q or from q to p. Because each leads to the other, we use a two-way arrow for this operator, writing $p \leftrightarrow q$. The $\leftrightarrow$ operator is sometimes called the **biconditional**, in view of the fact that it is equivalent to two conditionals; that is, $p \leftrightarrow q \equiv (p \rightarrow q) \wedge (q \rightarrow p)$. This equivalence is stated later.

We read $p \leftrightarrow q$ as "p if and only if q", or more succinctly, "p iff q". It may also help to say it less succinctly as "p if q, and also p only if q". We can rephrase the "p if q" part as "if q, p" or "if q then p", which is the same as $q \rightarrow p$. As for the "p only if q" part, it indicates that when q is false, so is p; that is, $\neg q \rightarrow \neg p$. This in turn gives $p \rightarrow q$ by the contrapositive law. That law appears in Figure 2.3, preceded by two other new laws, one for each of our new operators, the conditional and the biconditional. Each of the three new laws can be proved by a truth table proof with four rows (see the exercises).

For computational purposes, it simplifies various algorithms to convert logical expressions to a *normal* (or standard) *form*. The first of the normal forms we

Conditional law:
$$p \rightarrow q \equiv \neg p \vee q$$

Biconditional law:
$$p \leftrightarrow q \equiv (p \rightarrow q) \wedge (q \rightarrow p)$$

Contrapositive law:
$$p \rightarrow q \equiv \neg q \rightarrow \neg p$$

Figure 2.3: Equivalences with the Conditional

introduce here is used in artificial intelligence, the second in hardware design. We begin by using two of the laws just introduced to get rid of the biconditional operator in $p \leftrightarrow q$ and obtain an expression in which the only operators are $\wedge$, $\vee$, and $\neg$. Be sure you can justify each step by stating the equivalences used.

$$
\begin{aligned}
p \leftrightarrow q &\equiv (p \rightarrow q) \wedge (q \rightarrow p) \\
&\equiv (\neg p \vee q) \wedge (\neg q \vee p)
\end{aligned}
$$

Notice that the last expression is a conjunction of disjunctions in which the negation operator ($\neg$) applies only to simple variables (p, q). Such an expression is said to be in **conjunctive normal form** (CNF). As a further exercise, we continue our manipulations to get an equivalent expression that is a disjunction of conjunctions of variables or negated variables—that is, an expression in **disjunctive normal form** (DNF). Continuing from before,

$$
\begin{aligned}
&\equiv (\neg p \wedge \neg q) \vee (\neg p \wedge p) \vee (q \wedge \neg q) \vee (q \wedge p) \\
&\equiv (\neg p \wedge \neg q) \vee \text{FALSE} \vee \text{FALSE} \vee (q \wedge p) \\
&\equiv (\neg p \wedge \neg q) \vee (q \wedge p)
\end{aligned}
$$

Notice the use here of various equivalences, including one of the distributive laws. Also useful for converting logical expressions into the normal forms are DeMorgan's laws, which help in getting the $\neg$ symbol to apply only to variables.

The conditional law, $p \rightarrow q \equiv \neg p \vee q$, allows us to replace an expression containing the conditional operator ($\rightarrow$) by one not containing it. However, we did not introduce this operator simply to get rid of it by using some other equivalent expression. Rather, as noted at the beginning of this section, that operator is useful for stating and using rules of inference. These rules give us a new and more powerful way to prove things, as Chapter 3 shows.

Exercises

2.1 Consider the effect of parentheses.

(a) Give a set of truth values for p, q, and r for which the values of $(p \vee q) \wedge r$ and $p \vee (q \wedge r)$ are different.

(b) What does the answer to (a) indicate about parentheses in these expressions?

(c) There are two set of values for p, q, and r that could answer (a); give the other one.

2.2 Section 2.2 introduces square 2×2 truth tables for the individual logical operators $\wedge$ and $\vee$. Each table has four cells.

(a) Suppose we have an empty table of this type and size and wish to fill one of its four cells with the logical constant TRUE and the other three cells with FALSE. There are four possible ways to do this depending on the location of TRUE. Each of the resulting four truth tables corresponds to a simple expression of logic. (Because of equivalences, it may also correspond to other expressions, some of which are not so simple.) Copy the following answer chart and fill each empty cell with an appropriate expression, using whatever you need from the nine symbols p, q, $\wedge$, $\vee$, $\neg$, $\leftrightarrow$, $\rightarrow$,) and (. Use as few occurrences of the operators as you can. Use parentheses only where necessary.

Location of TRUE	Simple Logic Expression
upper left	$p \wedge q$
upper right	
lower left	
lower right	

(b) Do the same thing as in part (a), except that this time each truth table is to have one occurrence of FALSE and three of TRUE. This time the left column of your answer chart should be labeled "Location of FALSE."

(c) At the end of Section 2.2, it is noted that the binary propositional operators, $\wedge$ and $\vee$, can be regarded as functions, $f : \mathcal{B} \times \mathcal{B} \rightarrow \mathcal{B}$. Four such functions are specified in part (a) and four others are specified in part (b). Using one or more complete and clear sentences, Explain why there exist 16 such functions in all.

2.3 Use two-row truth tables like the one in the text for $p \vee \neg p$ to show that each of the expressions given here is a tautology. That is, show that each of them has the value TRUE for both possible states of p. Explain for each, in one or more complete and clear sentences, why it *should* always be true.

(a) $p \vee \text{TRUE}$

(b) $\neg (p \wedge \neg p)$

(c) $p \rightarrow p$

2.4 Section 2.3 shows how to use truth tables to prove equivalences. In particular, this distributive law is proved there: $p \wedge (q \vee r) \equiv (p \wedge q) \vee (p \wedge r)$. Examine that proof. Using the same technique, prove the equivalences given here. Confirm from Figure 2.2 that these are, respectively, one of DeMorgan's laws and the other distributive law. For the first proof you need two identical columns in a four-row truth table. The second requires an eight-row table.

(a) $\neg (p \vee q) \equiv \neg p \wedge \neg q$

(b) $p \vee (q \wedge r) \equiv (p \vee q) \wedge (p \vee r)$

2.5 Use truth tables to prove the conditional, biconditional, and contrapositive laws repeated here. Note that the 2×2 truth tables introduced for $\triangle$ and $\diamond$ are actually the ones for $\rightarrow$ and $\leftrightarrow$.

(a) $p \rightarrow q \equiv \neg p \vee q$

(b) $p \leftrightarrow q \equiv (p \rightarrow q) \wedge (q \rightarrow p)$

(c) $p \rightarrow q \equiv \neg q \rightarrow \neg p$

2.6 Use truth tables to show that each of the expressions given here is a tautology, by showing that each of them has the value TRUE for all four possible states of p and q. Explain for each, in one or more complete and clear sentences, why it makes sense and *should* always be true.

(a) $p \rightarrow (p \vee q)$

(b) $q \rightarrow (p \rightarrow q)$

(c) $((p \rightarrow q) \wedge p) \rightarrow q$

(d) $((p \rightarrow q) \wedge \neg q) \rightarrow \neg p$

2.7 Using truth tables as in Exercise 2.6, prove that each of the following conditional expressions is a tautology. This time there are three propositional variables, so there are eight possible states. Once again, explain why each makes sense.

    (a) $((p \rightarrow q) \wedge (q \rightarrow r)) \rightarrow (p \rightarrow r)$

    (b) $((p \vee q) \wedge (p \rightarrow r) \wedge (q \rightarrow r)) \rightarrow r$

2.8 The operator "$\oplus$" expresses the idea of exclusive "or," that is, a choice between alternatives. Thus $p \oplus q$ is TRUE when exactly *one* of p, q is TRUE but it is FALSE when both or neither is TRUE.

    (a) Give the shortest possible equivalence for $p \oplus q$.

    (b) Give an expression equivalent to $p \oplus q$ containing only $\wedge$, $\vee$, and $\neg$ as its operators.

2.9 Prove that $p \vee (\neg p \wedge q) \equiv (p \vee q)$ is a tautology in each of the following ways:

    (a) By a truth table.

    (b) By substitution, starting with distributivity.

2.10 Prove each of the conditional expressions in Exercise 2.7 by substitution. Start by getting rid of all the conditional operators by using the conditional law. Then use DeMorgan's law repeatedly to get all the negation signs operating on the individual symbols p, q, and r getting rid of double negations wherever they crop up. You may also make use of the formula proved in Exercise 2.9.

2.11 Prove distributivity *from the right* of $\wedge$ over $\vee$, algebraically. That is, use a sequence of equivalences to show that

$$(p \vee q) \wedge r \equiv (p \wedge r) \vee (q \wedge r)$$

2.12 Converting a propositional expression from CNF (conjunctive normal form) to DNF (disjunctive normal form) is analogous to multiplying out an arithmetic expression originally in factored form: $(a + b) \times (c + d) = a \times c + \ldots$. Convert the following expression to DNF by algebraic methods—that is, by a sequence of equivalences.

$$(p \vee q) \wedge (r \vee s)$$

Fully justify each step. Hint: Rewrite a distributive law in terms of α, β, and γ, and then use $(p \vee q)$ as α.

2.13 Prove algebraically the distributivity of $\vee$ over 3-conjunct conjunctions like $(q \wedge r \wedge s)$.

2.14 Prove algebraically that if $\vee$ distributes over $(n-1)$-conjunct conjunctions like

$$(q_1 \wedge q_2 \wedge \ldots \wedge q_{n-1})$$

then it also distributes over n-conjunct conjunctions.

Chapter 3

Proving Things: Why and How

In this chapter, we present the notion of a proof by rules of inference. The proofs are formal since not only are they expressed in terms of symbols, but in addition each step is justified in terms of explicit rules for manipulating the symbols. The rules-of-inference approach to proving things turns out to apply much more broadly than the methods of Chapter 2. Truth tables—although essential as the foundation of other methods—are limited to a role within logic. By contrast, the approach introduced in this chapter, enriched with predicates (Chapter 5), applies throughout mathematics and, as we see in Chapter 6, to computer science.

3.1   Reasons for Wanting to Prove Things

As a practical matter, it is useful to have beliefs that correctly match up with what is true in the world. Some of our beliefs are based on direct observation, some come from believing what people that we trust write or tell us, and still others come indirectly by reasoning. Of course, in the case of reasoning, it has to be sound reasoning if it is to yield correct results. Proofs are really just particularly careful reasoning in a sequence of justified steps. Rules of inference concern what kinds of steps are justifiable.

Proving things has several benefits to people in general, to technical specialists and specifically to computer scientists. For starters, of course, a correct proof shows you that the particular thing proved is true, given that it starts from true assumptions. It also shows you why it is true, helping you to understand the subject matter more deeply. More generally, proofs give good practice in careful thinking.

Turning to computing, you know that computer programs need to be correct in general for all possible data. It is not enough for them just to work on a few arbitrary test sets of data. There are many disaster stories in the real world that turn on software error. There are several approaches to software reliability, one of which is to actually prove that a program is correct. This is discussed in Chapter 6.

The proving process can be automated. In fact, logic programming languages, like Prolog, actually work by proving things, as discussed in Chapter 7. In other programming languages (whether logic-based or not), it is possible to write a theorem prover. Another application area for automated reasoning is expert systems. These systems apply humanlike reasoning to aspects of medicine, science, engineering, law, business, and education. They reason with logic where appropriate, but can also reason about uncertain things with degrees of uncertainty.

In commonsense reasoning and in ordinary discussion, frequent informal use is made of many strategies given here, such as counterexamples and case analysis. Thus, formal proofs do not differ from ordinary reasoning so much in what is an acceptable step in an argument, but rather in using symbols for precision and in proving quite subtle results by long chains of reasoning, involving many different strategies within a single proof.

3.2   Rules of Inference

A **proof** is a sequence of assertions meant to convince the reader of the truth of some particular statement. The proved statement is called a **theorem**. Usually a theorem is not obvious at the outset, but the proof is intended to inspire confidence that it is actually true. A theorem should also hold some interest possibly because it is useful in applications or it may be of indirect use because it helps prove other important results.

The actual presentation of the proof greatly depends on the (assumed) sophistication of the reader and the rigor of the given statement. Here we begin with a rather formal view of proofs, rather than rough sketches of proofs, for two reasons. First, it is hard to make sense of a rough sketch of something you have never seen; to recognize the structure of a sketch of a formal proof, we need to know the components of a formal proof. Second, formal proofs arise in several computer application areas, such as "inference engines" and "mechanical theorem provers."

Proofs succeed in convincing people by (i) starting from agreed truths and (ii) continuing by agreed methods. Some of these truths and methods may seem so simple that it is hardly worth stating them, but that is just what we want. The starting point of a proof consists of assertions chosen from among a collection of **axioms**. These simple statements are widely accepted as being clearly true. The methods for moving onward from the axioms are called **inference rules**.

In addition, we sometimes introduce an assertion tentatively, as an **assumption**, despite not knowing whether it is true, just to explore its consequences. A formal proof is a sequence of assertions, ending with the statement that is being proved, in which each assertion is either an axiom or an assumption or else follows by an inference rule from one or more particular assertions earlier in the sequence. It is crucial to keep track of which assertions depend on which assumptions and to achieve the final result in such a way that it does not depend on any of the assumptions.

Even in a formal proof, an axiom may be considered so common and well accepted that it is not mentioned. In arithmetic, for example, we typically do not bother to state explicitly that "4 is the successor of 3" or "0 is the smallest element of $\mathcal{N}$" (where $\mathcal{N}$ is the set of non-negative integers). Furthermore, even when something is mentioned, a lot of "background knowledge" underlying it may be left tacit. For example, we would not hesitate to state without proof that a positive number above 1 is smaller than its square, although that is, strictly speaking, the consequence of other axioms and not an axiom itself. Further, our background knowledge includes inference rules about specific domains (or subject matter). For example, continuing in the domain of non-negative integers, if $a < b$ and $b < c$, we can infer that $a < c$. This inference rule, known as the transitivity of less than, is so common that it is often left unstated without confusing anyone.

To avoid possible confusion about unstated background knowledge, we begin with proofs about material that is explicitly stated in this text. This means using propositional logic for everything: the axioms and theorems are propositions and the rules of inference are also based on propositional logic. In later chapters, we include predicate logic for these roles. Ultimately, we apply logic-based inference to prove properties of numbers and computer programs about which we do assume some background knowledge.

Substitution is a method that you have used in algebra and that is also valid with equivalent propositions. Suppose that within an expression that we have already proved there appears one side of some equivalence. Then we can substitute the other side of that equivalence in our original true (already proved) expression to get a new true expression. A proof that proceeds entirely in this way is sometimes called an *algebraic proof* (even when we are not talking about elementary algebra) since it has the style of algebraic manipulation. In contrast, a proof that proceeds entirely by rules of inference without substitution is sometimes called a *rules of inference proof*. It is also permissible to mix the two, and in fact we include substitution below in our display of rules of inference.

A straightforward and exceedingly useful rule of inference is the one called **modus ponens** (or the rule of detachment). It states that if we know (the truth of) both $(p \rightarrow q)$ and p, then we can infer (the truth of) q. This inference rule follows directly from our earlier discussion of the conditional operator. It is written this way:

Modus ponens:
$$p \rightarrow q$$
$$p$$
$$\overline{}$$
$$q$$

Another rule of inference, called **modus tollens**, states that if we know both $(p \rightarrow q)$ and $\neg q$, then we can infer $\neg p$. Notice that here we are concluding the truth of a negation, $\neg p$. This conclusion is justified by an argument in which we consider the possibility that the conclusion is false and show that doing so leads to a contradiction. Thus, suppose that $\neg p =$ FALSE. Then p would be TRUE. Further, by modus ponens with p and $p \rightarrow q$, we would know that $q =$ TRUE, contradicting the originally given information, $\neg q$. We say the supposition that $\neg p =$ FALSE is **absurd**: it is absurd to believe something that leads to a contradiction. Having determined that $\neg p$ must not be FALSE, we have arrived at (the truth of) $\neg p$.

Modus tollens:
$$p \rightarrow q$$
$$\neg q$$
$$\overline{}$$
$$\neg p$$

These rule names are Latin phrases. *Modus* means way or in this context a method. *Ponens* and *tollens* mean putting and taking away. Imagine that you have $p \rightarrow q$ in a container of truths. If you *put p* in, then q is in too. If you *take out q* (assert that it is false), then p comes out too.

Several important inference rules, including modus ponens and modus tollens, appear in a standard format in Figure 3.1. Expressing this format more formally enables us to see in general terms how these rules are established. First, note that each rule has a horizontal bar with an assertion below it and some number of assertions above it. The material above the bar, known as the **premises** (or antecedents), must be sufficient to justify the **conclusion** (or consequent) written below the bar. Symbolically, we use β to refer to whatever propositional expression appears below the bar. Above the bar we use α for a single expression, α_1 and α_2 if there are two expressions, α_3 for a third, and so on as needed. For example, in modus ponens, α_1 is $p \rightarrow q$.

To justify an inference rule consisting of a propositional expression α above the bar and a propositional expression β below it, we claim that one need only prove the

Modus ponens:

$$p \rightarrow q$$
$$p$$
$$\overline{}$$
$$q$$

Modus tollens:

$$p \rightarrow q$$
$$\neg q$$
$$\overline{}$$
$$\neg p$$

$\leftrightarrow$ introduction:

$$p \rightarrow q$$
$$q \rightarrow p$$
$$\overline{}$$
$$p \leftrightarrow q$$

Contrapositive:

$$p \rightarrow q$$
$$\overline{}$$
$$\neg q \rightarrow \neg p$$

Case analysis:

$$p \vee q$$
$$p \rightarrow r$$
$$q \rightarrow r$$
$$\overline{}$$
$$r$$

Vacuous proof:

$$\neg p$$
$$\overline{}$$
$$p \rightarrow q$$

$\wedge$ introduction:

$$p$$
$$q$$
$$\overline{}$$
$$p \wedge q$$

$\wedge$ elimination:

$$p \wedge q$$
$$\overline{}$$
$$p$$

$\vee$ introduction:

$$p$$
$$\overline{}$$
$$p \vee q$$

Contradiction:

$$p$$
$$\neg p$$
$$\overline{}$$
$$\text{FALSE}$$

Substitution:
(when $\alpha \equiv \beta$)

$$\alpha$$
$$\overline{}$$
$$\beta$$

Tautology:
(when $\alpha \equiv \text{TRUE}$)

$$\overline{}$$
$$\alpha$$

Figure 3.1: Rules of Inference

conditional $\alpha \rightarrow \beta$. To see that this makes sense, recall that the truth table for $\rightarrow$ has FALSE in its upper right corner. It follows that if α is TRUE when β is FALSE, we do not *have* $\alpha \rightarrow \beta$ in the first place. So if we do have $\alpha \rightarrow \beta$, then having α TRUE means β cannot be FALSE.

Similarly, $\alpha_1 \wedge \alpha_2 \rightarrow \beta$ justifies the inference rule with α_1 and α_2 above the bar and β below. For example, from the prior discussion, the modus ponens rule has the form $\alpha_1 \wedge \alpha_2 \rightarrow \beta$ with $p \rightarrow q$ in the role of α_1, with p for α_2 and q as β. In general, there can be any number n of items above the bar provided that we can prove the corresponding conditional statement $\alpha_1 \wedge \alpha_2 \wedge \ldots \wedge \alpha_n \rightarrow \beta$.

Patterns for inference rules
with 1 or 2 premises:

$$\frac{\alpha}{\beta} \qquad \frac{\begin{array}{c}\alpha_1 \\ \alpha_2\end{array}}{\beta}$$

This line of reasoning has brought us to a result of crucial importance: *Each potential rule of inference is equivalent to an expression of propositional logic and can therefore be evaluated in terms of truth tables.* In particular, all the entries in Figure 3.1 that we *claim* are rules of inference (by calling them that in the caption of the figure) can actually be *proved*, by truth tables, to be valid rules. In fact, having learned the material of Chapter 2, you can actually do this yourself. The next two examples clarify how this is done.

Example 3.1 Verify the inference rule, Contradiction.

Consulting Figure 3.1, we see that this rule has $\alpha_1 = p$ and $\alpha_2 = \neg p$ as its premises and $\beta =$ FALSE as its conclusion. Thus, to establish this rule of inference, we need to prove that $p \wedge \neg p \rightarrow$ FALSE. The truth table proof of this expression, appearing next, shows that it is a tautology (i.e., that it is always TRUE, as you can see from the last column).

p	$\neg p$	$p \wedge \neg p$	FALSE	$(p \wedge \neg p) \rightarrow$ FALSE
T	F	F	F	T
F	T	F	F	T

Example 3.2 Verify the inference rule, $\vee$ introduction.

According to Figure 3.1, this rule has only one premise, $\alpha = p$. The conclusion is $\beta = p \vee q$. The rule of inference is established next by proving with a truth table that $p \rightarrow (p \vee q)$.

p	q	$p \vee q$	$p \to (p \vee q)$
T	T	T	T
T	F	T	T
F	T	T	T
F	F	F	T

Somewhat more complicated is the proof for the rule modus tollens. Take a look at Proof 1 of Theorem 3.2 in Section 3.5, which provides the layout of the required truth table. The expression in the theorem appears as the heading of the last column in the truth table. You should now be able to put that expression into the form of a rule of inference, getting the modus tollens rule. Also see Exercise 3.1.

3.3 Proof by Rules

Now let us prove something with rules of inference. While we are at it, we prove a result that can be recast as a rule of inference. Thus, the result is able to contribute to future proofs. This is just like the enlightened software practice of building reusable subroutines and accumulating a library of such routines.

Before starting on a particular proof, we ask what one should look like; that is, how would we recognize—and confirm—a proof if we saw one? Thus, suppose we have a list of assertions that someone claims is a proof. For now, we take the case in which no assumptions are involved. To check the claim that these assertions constitute a proof, we must check each one of them. Checking an assertion means (i) finding an inference rule whose conclusion (below its bar) matches the assertion being considered, and (ii) finding earlier assertions in the would-be proof that match what is above the bar of that rule. Matching may involve substitution so long as the same substitution is in use consistently throughout the checking of each assertion.

The idea of our first proof, Example 3.3, is the following: Whenever we know that one or the other (possibly both) of a pair of propositions is true but we also know—perhaps by some separate line of reasoning—that a particular one of them is false, then the other must be true. In everyday language, this line of reasoning is a commonsense matter of eliminating an alternative.

Example 3.3 Prove formally, by rules of inference, that taking $(p \vee q) \wedge \neg p$ as true permits a proof that q must be true. Note that line 5 relies on the fact that $q \to q$ is a tautology; this is true since FALSE $\to$ FALSE is true as is TRUE $\to$ TRUE.

1.	$(p \lor q) \land \neg p$	given
2.	$p \lor q$	$\land$ elimination, with line 1
3.	$\neg p$	$\land$ elimination, with line 1
4.	$p \to q$	vacuous proof, with line 3
5.	$q \to q$	tautology
6.	q	case analysis, with lines 2, 4 and 5

In light of the first and last lines of Example 3.3, we have demonstrated the validity of the following new inference rule:

Alternative elimination: $(p \lor q)$
                                        $\neg p$

$$\rule{3cm}{0.4pt}$$

                                            q

Our next example of a proof by rules of inference concerns propositions that contradict each other. We know that p has a single value, so it is impossible to have both p and $\neg p$. To show another reason for not wanting to allow these two propositions to hold at the same time, suppose they did. We now show that it would be possible to prove any proposition whatsoever, such as the arbitrary unrelated proposition, q. It would follow that *everything* is true—surely a bizarre and undesirable outcome.

> **Example 3.4** Use rules of inference to show that taking $p \land \neg p$ as true allows proof of an arbitrary unrelated proposition q.

1.	$p \land \neg p$	given
2.	$\neg p$	$\land$ elimination, with line 1
3.	$p \to q$	vacuous proof, with line 2
4.	p	$\land$ elimination, with line 1
5.	q	modus ponens, with lines 3 and 4

3.4   Assumptions

Assumptions play an important role in proofs. In fact, at least one of them appears in almost every proof from this point on. As noted earlier, an assumption is unlike an axiom in that it is only introduced tentatively. We do not claim to know that the assumption is true, and it is essential to indicate that lack of commitment.

There are two parts to the notation for an assumption. First, we put the assumed statement in brackets (e.g., [p]). Second, we indent the statement *and everything else proved from it*, so that we do not confuse what is really known and what is only based on our tentative assumption. We sometimes say that the indented expressions are only true "relative to the assumption." This use of indentation is analogous to the use of indentation for prettyprinting of a structured program in, say, Pascal or C++. The indentation makes explicit the scope of the assumption. As we will see, we can have nested assumptions. When that occurs, we use nested indentation, just as in structured programming style.

One inference rule that uses an assumption is reduction to an absurdity, as shown next. It states what we can conclude after assuming that p is true and, relative to that assumption, finding that FALSE would be a valid line later in our proof. In that context, it is absurd to allow the possibility that p could be true. Therefore, the assumption that p is true must have been incorrect, so we infer that p is false. Therefore, $\neg p$ is TRUE. Notice that the conclusion $\neg p$ is *not* indented, since we really do believe $\neg p$ after having found that p leads to FALSE. The contradiction rule looks like this:

$$\text{Reduction to absurdity:} \qquad \begin{array}{c} [p] \\ \text{FALSE} \\ \hline \neg p \end{array}$$

You can find several expressions with the conditional operator ($\rightarrow$) among the inference rules introduced in Figure 3.1. Notice, however, that it occurs mostly above the bar, which means we need to have already arrived at a conditional expression in order to use the rule. The question thus naturally arises, how can we manage to obtain expressions containing the conditional?

The inference rule shown next (which, like the preceding one, also uses an assumption) allows us to *introduce* an expression containing an instance of $\rightarrow$. Therefore, this " $\rightarrow$ introduction" inference rule (also called *conditional introduction*) is arguably the most important of all the inference rules. It states that if we assume p to be true and relative to that assumption we can prove that q would have to be true, then we can infer that $p \rightarrow q$ really is a true statement. The rule does *not* merely state that $p \rightarrow q$ is true only relative to the assumption that p is true. Rather, the rule permits us to assert $p \rightarrow q$ as a true statement irrespective of the assumption that p is true. Later parts of the proof are not conditioned on that assumption.

$$\rightarrow \text{introduction:} \qquad \begin{array}{c} [p] \\ q \\ \hline p \rightarrow q \end{array}$$

As an intuitive example of the idea of → introduction, suppose there is a triangle behind your back. Let p be the proposition that its angles are 30°, 60°, and 90°, and let q be the proposition that one of its sides is twice as long as another one. Since the triangle is behind your back, you cannot see its angles so you do not know whether p is true and you cannot see its sides so you do not know whether q is true. However, if you were to assume p, you would be able to prove q, so you do know that $p \to q$.

Now that we have the → introduction rule, let us use it. The following theorem reformulates the proof in Example 3.3. Instead of saying that the expression $(p \lor q) \land \neg p$ is *given*, as in that example, we now make it an *assumption*, in line 1. Lines 2 through 6 are the same as in Example 3.3. The last line is identical to the original statement of the theorem—an essential aspect of a successful proof.

Theorem 3.1 $((p \lor q) \land \neg p) \to q$

Proof:

1.	$[(p \lor q) \land \neg p]$	assumption
2.	$p \lor q$	∧ elimination, from line 1
3.	$\neg p$	∧ elimination, from line 1
4.	$p \to q$	vacuous proof, based on line 3
5.	$q \to q$	tautology
6.	q	case analysis, with lines 2, 4 and 5
7.	$((p \lor q) \land \neg p) \to q$	→ introduction, with lines 1 and 6

Notice that the result in Theorem 3.1, $((p \lor q) \land \neg p) \to q$, has the form $(\alpha_1 \land \alpha_2) \to \beta$, with

$$\alpha_1 = p \lor q$$
$$\alpha_2 = \neg p$$
$$\beta = q.$$

Therefore, Theorem 3.1 justifies the "Alternative Elimination" rule in a more formal way than Example 3.3 did.

Assumptions can be nested. That is, within the context of an assumption, we can make an additional assumption so that both are in force. Watch for this technique as we now prove the transitivity of the conditional operator. In symbolic form, the claim is that $((p \to q) \land (q \to r)) \to (p \to r)$. Since the top level operator is a " → " (the one that connects major parenthesized subexpressions), our strategy is to use → introduction. The first thing to do is to write down the theorem as the *last* line of proof, preceded by the material needed to justify it, as shown in the following sketch of a plan for the proof.

$$[(p \to q) \land (q \to r)] \qquad \text{Assumption}$$
$$\vdots$$
$$p \to r \qquad \text{[to be shown]}$$
$$((p \to q) \land (q \to r)) \to (p \to r) \qquad \to \text{introduction}$$

In the right-hand column are justifications. For $p \to r$, the justification is "[to be shown]". We want to prove it, but do not yet know how we will do so. This is just a plan, not the finished proof. Next, planning to prove $p \to r$ is handled similarly: We again use $\to$ introduction to plan for a (sub)proof. This leads to the following more detailed proof outline. You should try to complete it using $\land$ elimination and modus ponens as needed.

$$[(p \to q) \land (q \to r)] \qquad \text{Assumption}$$
$$\vdots$$
$$[p] \qquad \text{Assumption}$$
$$\vdots$$
$$r \qquad \text{[to be shown]}$$
$$p \to r \qquad \to \text{introduction}$$
$$((p \to q) \land (q \to r)) \to (p \to r) \qquad \to \text{introduction}$$

The prior proof—once it has been completed—establishes a theorem in the form $\alpha_1 \land \alpha_2 \to \beta$. It therefore justifies a new rule of inference, called the transitivity of $\to$ (below), that we can use in future proofs. At first we justified rules of inference only by truth tables. Then, in the proof of alternative elimination and again here with this proof of the transitivity of $\to$, we take the important methodological step of using existing inference rules to establish new ones that can be reused in further proofs.

$$\text{Transitivity of } \to : \qquad p \to q$$
$$q \to r$$
$$\underline{}$$
$$p \to r$$

3.5 Proof Examples

To illustrate and compare the three kinds of proofs that have been introduced, we now prove a single result three times, once by each of the three proof methods. The proofs concern the concept—a familiar one by now—of modus tollens (i.e., that $p \rightarrow q$ together with $\neg q$ provides justification for concluding $\neg p$). However, instead of writing this idea as a rule of inference, we write it—see the statement of Theorem 3.2—as the propositional expression that serves to *justify* the modus tollens rule of inference. Since we are able to prove modus tollens as a theorem, we do not really need to include it as an axiom.

Dramatizing the differences among three proof styles in this way may make you wonder when to use each one. Truth tables are useful in getting the whole field started since they justify equivalences and rules of inference. The latter two styles are often used together. It is also fair game to ask whether there are yet other proof methods. Indeed there are others. Another approach, which we do not discuss further, is the method of semantic tableaus, which focuses on whether an expression is satisfiable (see Section 2.3). It is used to prove that the negation of some expression of interest *must* be FALSE—that is, it is *unsatisfiable*. The method has the effect of putting an expression into disjunctive normal form (see Section 2.5). Then one looks at each of the (disjoined) conjunctions to see whether it includes a pair of mutually contradictory conjuncts, such as p and $\neg p$. If—and only if—every one of the conjunctions does include such a pair, the expression is unsatisfiable.

Theorem 3.2 $((p \rightarrow q) \wedge \neg q) \rightarrow \neg p$

Proof 1: Here is a start of a proof of Theorem 3.2 using a **truth table**. Completing it is left as an exercise. You want to get all TRUEs in the final column, which means that the expression at the top of that column—which is the theorem—is TRUE no matter what the state is. Thus, you show that it is a tautolgy. Look at the other headings in the table. Could you have supplied the correct column headings yourself given only the statement of the theorem? Students often wonder, "How can I think up a proof or a problem solution?" How does an author, instructor, or professional practitioner know what step comes next?

p	q	$p \rightarrow q$	$\neg q$	$(p \rightarrow q) \wedge \neg q$	$\neg p$	$((p \rightarrow q) \wedge \neg q) \rightarrow \neg p$
T	T					
T	F					
F	T					
F	F					

To answer this question, it is frequently useful to think *recursively*—that is, to make a recursive plan. This entails working backward rather than forward—asking not about the next step, but about earlier results. In a truth table, that means working from *right to left* instead of forward. Here, in order to get values for the formula to be proved, $((p \rightarrow q) \wedge \neg q) \rightarrow \neg p$, one first seeks values for its major parts, before and after the top-level conditional operator—that is, for $((p \rightarrow q) \wedge \neg q)$ and $\neg p$. The first of these needs to be broken down further until we get down to expressions like $p \rightarrow q$ and $\neg q$ for which the truth tables are known.

Once this planning stage is complete so that all the expressions in the top row have been determined, it is time to work forward, filling in the table from left to right with TRUEs and FALSEs as appropriate. (Do it!) Notice that this entire process is the sort of thing that occurs when a recursive function in called. If you write a recursive function to evaluate propositional formulas, put a trace on it, and then input some values for p and q, you will see this process work through, starting with the backward breakdown of the formula and continuing with the forward determination of a resulting truth value for the particular input values of p and q. Recursion is a powerful aid to both thought and computation. It is a way to "divide and conquer" many problems.

Proof 2: This proof of Theorem 3.2 proceeds entirely by **substitution**. (As noted earlier, one may call such a proof algebraic.) As in the preceding discussion (in Proof 1) of how to come up with the column headings in the truth table, we again begin with the expression in the theorem statement and work backward. In this case, our procedure is to show that the given expression is equivalent to smaller and smaller ones down to TRUE. (The exercises ask you to state the equivalence that justifies each step and also to give a shorter proof.)

$$
\begin{aligned}
((p \rightarrow q) \wedge \neg q) \rightarrow \neg p \ &\equiv\ \neg ((\neg p \vee q) \wedge \neg q) \vee \neg p \\
&\equiv\ \neg ((\neg p \wedge \neg q) \vee (q \wedge \neg q)) \vee \neg p \\
&\equiv\ \neg ((\neg p \wedge \neg q) \vee \text{FALSE})) \vee \neg p \\
&\equiv\ \neg (\neg p \wedge \neg q) \vee \neg p \\
&\equiv\ (p \vee q) \vee \neg p \\
&\equiv\ (p \vee \neg p) \vee q \\
&\equiv\ \text{TRUE} \vee q \\
&\equiv\ \text{TRUE}
\end{aligned}
$$

Proof 3: Finally we come to a **rules-of-inference proof**. Recall that the theorem we are trying to prove is an expression that captures the idea of modus tollens, so it hardly seems interesting or even fair to do it by using the rule modus tollens. Here, we use only rules other than modus tollens. As in Proof 1, we finish by arriving at the desired result, but it is the *first* thing we write down when planning the proof.

Notice that the last line is not indented since its truth does not depend on any
assumption. One of the exercises asks you to justify each line of this proof.

$$[(p \rightarrow q) \wedge \neg q]$$
$$p \rightarrow q$$
$$\neg q$$
$$[p]$$
$$q$$
$$\text{FALSE}$$
$$\neg p$$
$$((p \rightarrow q) \wedge \neg q) \rightarrow \neg p$$

A longer example of an inference proof is the one for Theorem 3.3 given next.
Note that this theorem is directly analogous to the conditional law, $p \rightarrow q \equiv \neg p \vee q$,
so it hardly needs to be proved. Still, the following rules-of-inference proof—
composed without the conditional law—is a good opportunity to see a number of
useful proof techniques at work. The proof structure is visible in the indentation
of its several nested assumptions. Although this proof looks complex, the following
discussion shows how most of it arises in a natural and straightforward manner.

Theorem 3.3 $(p \rightarrow q) \leftrightarrow (\neg p \vee q)$ is true for all values of p and q.

Proof:

	Justification or comment
$[\neg p \vee q]$	Assumption
$[\neg p]$	Additional assumption
$p \rightarrow q$	
$\neg p \rightarrow (p \rightarrow q)$	End of first case
$[q]$	
$[p]$	
q	
$p \rightarrow q$	
$q \rightarrow (p \rightarrow q)$	End of second case
$p \rightarrow q$	
$(\neg p \vee q) \rightarrow (p \rightarrow q)$	End of first major subproof
$[p \rightarrow q]$	Assumption
$p \vee \neg p$	Excluded middle (tautology)
$[p]$	
q	
$\neg p \vee q$	
$p \rightarrow (\neg p \vee q)$	End of first case

$$[\neg p]$$
$$\neg p \vee q$$
$$\neg p \rightarrow (\neg p \vee q) \qquad \text{End of second case}$$
$$\neg p \vee q$$
$$(p \rightarrow q) \rightarrow (\neg p \vee q) \qquad \text{End of second major subproof}$$
$$(p \rightarrow q) \leftrightarrow (\neg p \vee q) \qquad \leftrightarrow \text{ introduction}$$

How did someone dream up this proof? First look at what we have to prove (the statement of the theorem). The main operator is a biconditional, $\leftrightarrow$. Any proof of a $\leftrightarrow$ must use the $\leftrightarrow$ introduction rule, and so the proof necessarily divides into two subproofs each using the $\rightarrow$ introduction rule. The first half of the proof begins by assuming the right side of the biconditional, $\neg p \vee q$, from which we have to prove the left side, and the second half does the opposite. Once we make the assumption $\neg p \vee q$, it seems like a good idea to use the case analysis rule, first assuming $\neg p$, then assuming q, and trying to prove the left side in each case.

In the second half of the proof, it is less clear what to do. For this part, we set up a case analysis by invoking the law of the excluded middle. Note that a *tautology* can be introduced into a proof at any time. Our decision to use this technique depends somewhat on experience with proofs, but really it is good common sense: When you cannot determine whether something is true or false, check out both possibilities.

The foregoing examples give the flavor of how formal proofs proceed. The statement of Theorem 3.2 is of the form "if p then q," whereas Theorem 3.3 has the form "p if and only if q." These are two common types of theorems. Next we give a few hints about how to approach these kinds of theorems.

3.6 Types of Theorems and Proof Strategies

The issue of how to think of a proof has already been raised, especially in the discussions of the example proofs in the preceding section. It is also important to remember that once a theorem has been proved, it can be used as part of the proof of something else. In effect, the already proved theorem is used just like an axiom or a rule of inference. Here are some additional pointers.

The type of theorem to be proved may suggest the style of proof. Many theorems, for example, take the form of conditional expressions. In that event, we want to prove the conditional so that it can then be used—with modus ponens, transitivity of $\rightarrow$, and so on—to prove other results. We first give some ways to obtain conditionals and biconditionals and then some strategies involving disjunction.

Proving a conditional, $p \to q$

- **Direct proof:** The proof can begin by assuming that p is true and show that q would then be a consequence. In other words, use the $\to$ introduction rule. This method is used in Proof 3 of Theorem 3.2 and in each of the two major subproofs for Theorem 3.3.

- **Indirect proof:** Alternatively, assume $q =$ FALSE and show that $p =$ FALSE would be a consequence. This lets us conclude (by $\to$ introduction) that $\neg q \to \neg p$, which is the contrapositive of $p \to q$, hence equivalent to it. Making this substitution completes the proof.

- **Proof by contradiction:** Assume that $p \to q$—the thing we want to prove—is false, and show that this assumption leads to a contradiction (i.e., a FALSE line in our proof). Notice that the truth table definition of $p \to q$ tells us that for it to be false we must have both $p =$ TRUE and $q =$ FALSE.

Proving a biconditional, $p \leftrightarrow q$

- **Two-way proof:** Use the biconditional law so that there are two main subproofs, one to prove $p \to q$ and one to prove $q \to p$. This is the top-level strategy for the proof of Theorem 3.3.

- **Set equality:** A theorem that the sets A and B are equal can be rewritten $x \in A \leftrightarrow x \in B$. Since it therefore requires proof of a biconditional, its proof can be viewed as a special case of two-way proof.

Proofs with disjunction, $p \lor q$

- **Case analysis I:** If the truth of the disjunction $p \lor q$ has been *given or already proved* and the desired final result is r, prove that r holds in either case. That is, prove both $p \to r$ and $q \to r$. This method is used within each half of the proof of Theorem 3.3.

- **Case analysis II:** To prove a disjunction, say $r \lor s$, in a context where another one, $p \lor q$, is already established, prove that $p \to r$ and $q \to s$.

- **Excluded middle:** For either of the prior two kinds of case analysis, it may be helpful to introduce—for some judiciously chosen proposition u—the disjunction $u \lor \neg u$. Being a tautology, this expression can be introduced at any time. Then u can play the role of p in either of those strategies, and $\neg u$ would play the role of q.

- **Eliminating an alternative:** If $p \vee q$ has been given or already proved, try to eliminate p. Then $q =$ TRUE, as we proved earlier. Since q is a stronger statement than $p \vee q$, it may be more useful in continuing the proof.

Proofs are often presented informally, and this can be a good thing. Still a sound informal proof retains the underlying structure of a formal proof and relies on inference rules even if they are not always mentioned explicitly. Ultimately, we are interested in real proofs—that is, proofs that are not just for showing how to prove things, but whose purpose is to make a convincing argument about something. Unfortunately, real proofs are usually so cluttered with background knowledge (or clouded by its absence) that it can be a struggle to find the underlying formal outline of the logical proof. That is why it can be helpful to spend some time thinking about the proving process, as we have done here.

Exercises

3.1 Complete Proof 1 of Theorem 3.2 by copying the table there and filling it in. State what pattern in the completed table establishes the theorem.

3.2 Prove by truth tables that

$$(p \rightarrow q) \wedge \neg (p \leftrightarrow q) \rightarrow \neg (q \rightarrow p).$$

Explain why this tautology makes sense.

3.3 Prove the case analysis rule of inference by truth tables. In other words, prove by truth tables that $((p \vee q) \wedge (p \rightarrow r) \wedge (q \rightarrow r)) \rightarrow r$. You need eight $(= 2 \times 2 \times 2)$ rows. You also need eight columns: three for p, q, and r, three more for the three conjuncts; one for their conjunction; and one for the whole formula. This last column should have all TRUEs, thereby establishing the tautology. Explain, in whole sentences, why the fourth, fifth, and sixth columns have two FALSEs each.

3.4 For each of the eight steps (lines) in Proof 2 of Theorem 3.2, name the equivalence that justifies that step. If a particular step requires the use of two equivalences or requires using one twice, say so.

3.5 Give a much shorter equivalence proof of Theorem 3.2 by making use of one of DeMorgan's laws right after using the conditional law.

3.6 Prove the tautology in Exercise 3.2 by substitution. Hint: Do *not* use the conditional law; use the biconditional law, one of DeMorgan's laws, distributivity, contradiction, and a property of constants.

3.7 Here is a proof that the conditional operator is transitive. It has an algebraic style: We keep substituting equivalent expressions. The proof shows that the initial expression is a tautology, since it is equivalent to TRUE; that is, it is true for any values of p, q, and r. Sometimes two or more rules are used for a step. State the equivalence(s) used at each step.

(a) $((p \to q) \wedge (q \to r)) \to (p \to r)$

$$
\begin{array}{lll}
\equiv & \neg((\neg p \vee q) \wedge (\neg q \vee r)) \vee (\neg p \vee r) & \text{i} \underline{\hspace{2cm}}\\
\equiv & (\neg(\neg p \vee q) \vee \neg(\neg q \vee r)) \vee (\neg p \vee r) & \text{ii} \underline{\hspace{2cm}}\\
\equiv & ((\neg \neg p \wedge \neg q) \vee (\neg \neg q \wedge \neg r)) \vee (\neg p \vee r) & \text{iii} \underline{\hspace{2cm}}\\
\equiv & (p \wedge \neg q) \vee (q \wedge \neg r) \vee \neg p \vee r & \text{iv} \underline{\hspace{2cm}}\\
\equiv & ((p \wedge \neg q) \vee \neg p) \vee ((q \wedge \neg r) \vee r) & \text{v} \underline{\hspace{2cm}}\\
\equiv & (\text{TRUE} \wedge (\neg q \vee \neg p)) \vee ((q \vee r) \wedge \text{TRUE}) & \text{vi} \underline{\hspace{2cm}}\\
\equiv & \neg q \vee q \vee \neg p \vee r & \text{vii} \underline{\hspace{2cm}}\\
\equiv & \text{TRUE} \vee \neg p \vee r & \text{viii} \underline{\hspace{2cm}}\\
\equiv & \text{TRUE} & \text{ix} \underline{\hspace{2cm}}\\
\end{array}
$$

(b) Write down the *new rule of inference* that is now justified by the proof in part (a).

3.8 Prove each of these equivalences by substitution, *one* step at a time. State which equivalence in Section 2.4 or 2.5 justifies each step.

(a) $((p \vee q) \wedge (\neg p \wedge \neg q)) \equiv \text{FALSE}$

(b) $p \vee q \vee r \vee s \equiv (\neg p \wedge \neg q \wedge \neg r) \to s$

3.9 Complete the proof in Section 3.4 that the conditional operator is transitive.

3.10 Consider the formula $q \to (p \to q)$. Roughly speaking, it says that if something is true, anything implies it. This turns out to be true. Construct a *plan* for a proof in the manner of the proof-planning in Section 3.4. To begin, write down the desired final result as the last line. Then determine which "$\to$" separates the principal parts of the expression and write those in earlier lines, using indentation and bracketing appropriately. Then proceed similarly with the other "$\to$". That will give you five lines of proof, which turns out to be all you need. Add the justifications for each line and you are done.

3.11 Using rules of inference with no substitutions, prove that

$$(p \land (p \to q) \land (q \to r)) \to r.$$

Use the rules-of-inference format. Name the rule of inference that is used at each step. Hint: The top-level operator in the formula here is a conditional (the $\to$ symbol). Begin by writing everything to the left of that symbol (within the large parentheses) on the first line of the proof, in brackets and indented, as an assumption. Leave some space and put the entire formula that you are to prove as the last line, not in brackets and not indented. Try to get an indented r on the next-to-last line. Of course, the lines before it must justify putting it there.

3.12 Annotate Proof 3 of Theorem 3.2 by stating, for each line, the rule of inference that justifies it, along with the previous lines on which it depends. No previous line or justification is needed for an assumption.

3.13 Use rules of inference with one substitution to prove the result in Exercise 3.2. Annotate the proof by numbering each line and for each line indicating the rule of inference that justifies it, along with the previous lines upon which it depends. No justification is needed for assumptions.

3.14 The *contrapositive* equivalence, $p \to q \equiv \neg q \to \neg p$, was introduced in Chapter 2. It is useful in a rules-of-inference proof for recasting what is to be proved. In particular, we can prove "if p then q" by assuming $\neg q$ and then proving $\neg p$. Formally prove

$$(\neg q \to \neg p) \to (p \to q)$$

using rules of inference with no substitutions.

3.15 This exercise extends the idea of case analysis to situations with *three* cases. Give a proof in the rules-of-inference format for

$$((p \lor q \lor r) \land (p \to s) \land (q \to s) \land (r \to s)) \to s.$$

Avoid substitution except for using the associative law to replace $p \lor q \lor r$. Annotate your proof by numbering each line and for each line indicating the rule of inference that justifies it, along with the previous lines upon which it depends. No justification is needed for an assumption.

3.16 In several of the foregoing exercises, you are asked to establish a tautology of the form $\alpha_1 \wedge \alpha_2 \wedge \ldots \wedge \alpha_n \to \beta$. Find four of them—with $n = 1, 2, 3,$ and 4—and rewrite them as rules of inference. Provide each with a brief descriptive name.

Chapter 4

Predicate Logic

Our study of propositions has led to some important results and provided a relatively simple environment in which to examine three styles of proof. Unfortunately, when it comes to representing knowledge, the simplicity of propositions is a significant weakness. Recall that propositions reflect only whether a sentence is true or false, without looking at the complex conceptual structure within the sentence—at the things, properties, actions, and relationships it talks about.

Predicates do look at those kinds of things, and in that way they are a big step up with respect to this issue of representing knowledge. Even with predicates, we retain the use of the logical constants, TRUE and FALSE, as the only possible values of logical expressions, so that like propositions they ignore all forms of vagueness and uncertainty. Still the representational power of predicate logic—sometimes called predicate calculus—is so great that, with some adjustments, it forms the basis of the so-called *logic programming languages*, notably Prolog, which is the topic of Chapter 7.

4.1   Predicates and Functions

In contrast to propositional logic's atomistic, true-or-false view of propositions, predicate logic breaks them apart to take a more detailed look. You may recall from Chapter 2 that our first example of a proposition was 5 > 3. Looking now inside that proposition, we focus on the operator, ">". This operator—which turns out to be our first predicate—can be regarded as a function of two numerical arguments. To make the connection to functions clearer, let us give this operator (">") a name that looks more like the name of a function and also write its name first like this: GREATERTHAN(5,3). Thus, GREATERTHAN is a function defined on pairs

of numbers, let us say pairs of reals. Letting $\mathcal{R}$ be the reals and using the terminology of Chapter 1, the domain of GREATERTHAN is $\mathcal{R} \times \mathcal{R}$. The codomain of
this function—that is, the set to which things are mapped—is $\mathcal{B}$, the set of logical
constants, {TRUE, FALSE}. To summarize, GREATERTHAN : $\mathcal{R} \times \mathcal{R} \to \mathcal{B}$. We are
now ready to define predicates and relate them to propositions.

> **Definition 4.1 Predicates:** A predicate is a function whose codomain
> is $\mathcal{B}$, the set of logical constants.

Thus, GREATERTHAN is a predicate. It also follows from the definition that a
predicate *with specific arguments* is a member of $\mathcal{B}$ and so is a proposition. For
example, GREATERTHAN(5,3) is a proposition—one whose value happens to be
TRUE. Although the codomain of every predicate is $\mathcal{B}$, the *domain* is much more
flexible. We used pairs of reals as the domain in this introductory example, but
later examples use predicates with domains of people, symbols, and other numerical
sets. Indeed the domain of a predicate can be any set whatsoever.

Predicate logic and variations of it are knowledge representation languages. Like
English, Japanese, C++, Prolog, and other languages, the language of predicate
logic gives us the means to express things, but it is largely up to us what to express and how to express it. As an example of this freedom, consider a new predicate GREATERTHANTHREE, which takes one argument and yields TRUE for values
greater than 3. Then the same values of x that give GREATERTHAN$(x, 3) = $ TRUE
also give GREATERTHANTHREE$(x) = $ TRUE. Despite this freedom, of course, certain sensible and conventional ways of doing things should be heeded. Thus, for
example, no one has succeeded in getting a special operator symbol for the idea
of GREATERTHANTHREE into widespread use, whereas the far more useful concept
expressed by GREATERTHAN does have a conventional symbol, (">").

In reasoning about predicates, it is important to understand their relationship
to propositions. It is reasonable to think of a predicate as a kind of shorthand for
a family of propositions, one for each element in the domain. For example, suppose
that p represents the predicate we have been calling GREATERTHANTHREE. Then
$p(-2)$ is a proposition whose value is FALSE and $p(7)$ is a proposition with the
value TRUE. Carrying over our understanding of the $\wedge$ operator to expressions
that include predicates, we have propositions like $p(-2) \wedge p(7)$. This proposition
happens to be false since $p(-2) \wedge p(7) = $ FALSE $\wedge$ TRUE $ = $ FALSE.

> **Example 4.1** Let q be the predicate that means its argument is less
> than 7. Using q along with the predicate p earlier, what does $r(x) =$
> $p(x) \wedge q(x)$ mean?

Here r is a predicate that is true in case both p and q are true. In other words, r is the property of being between 3 and 7. We can also write

$$r(x) = p(x) \land q(x) = (x > 3) \land (x < 7).$$

So, for instance, $r(6.8) = p(6.8) \land q(6.8) = \text{TRUE} \land \text{TRUE} = \text{TRUE}$, but $r(-16.5) = \text{FALSE}$. Although r is more complicated than p and q, it is like them in that each takes only a single argument. Thus, r takes one real to a logical constant, and we can write $r : \mathcal{R} \to \mathcal{B}$.

Non-numerical arguments are also of great interest. For example, let $\mathcal{P}$ be the set of persons. Then we can define MOTHER to be a predicate such that for two members, x and y, of the set $\mathcal{P}$, MOTHER(x, y) is true if and only if x is the mother of y. To take a well-known senator, for example, MOTHER(Hillary, Chelsea) $= \text{TRUE}$. In this case, MOTHER: $\mathcal{P} \times \mathcal{P} \to \mathcal{B}$.

It is often just assumed that there is some obvious domain or universe (reals, persons, etc.) with elements that can serve as possible values for a variable. Sometimes when speaking in general terms, with no particular universe in mind, we may just call the universe $\mathcal{U}$.

4.2 Predicates, English, and Sets

Human languages express the idea of predicates in many ways. For example, in the preceding section, we borrowed the word "mother" from English for our logic predicate MOTHER, as in MOTHER(x, y), meaning that x is the mother of y. Human language is not always precise and unambiguous, and even a simple word like "mother" can be used differently, say in a metaphor like "necessity is the mother of invention." Still we assume that such examples are clear enough. Let us look at some more examples of how predicates are expressed in English. Of course, every other human language expresses ideas similar to those discussed.

Nouns like "aunt," "brother," and the words for other family relations translate readily to two-argument predicates, just like "mother." Adjectives of nationality, like "Chinese" and "Egyptian," can be used as one-argument predicates, as in CHINESE(Deng). Notice, however, that there is nothing about the idea or the definitions of predicate logic to stop us from writing this idea as a two-argument predicate like NATIONALITY(Deng, Chinese) or CITIZENSHIP(Deng, China), and indeed that may well be more convenient from a computational viewpoint. It is up to us how to use the framework that logic provides. Names too are a matter of choice, just as they are in computer programs. Thus, although we meant Deng here as former Chinese leader Deng Xiao-Ping, the constant Deng can stand for someone (or something) else so long as we are consistent about it.

Adjectives for color can be expressed with one argument, as in BROWN(Desk-1). Yet here again, as in the case of nationality, it is often useful to use the general idea—in this case, color—as the predicate. Doing so again leads to two arguments: COLOR(Desk-1, Brown). Other adjectives, like those for size, express a property that really applies not to a single thing, but to that thing in relation to its class. For example, a big ant is nowhere near as big as a small elephant. So a big ant is big with respect to ants only, and not with respect to animals or things in general. To capture this idea in predicate logic, we may wish to write BIG(Ant-3, Ant), meaning that Ant-3 is big for an ant. Taking the more general notion of size as the predicate would lead to having three arguments: SIZE(Ant-3, Ant, Big).

> **Example 4.2** Use the three-argument predicate SIZE to express the fact
> that Jumbo the baby elephant, although small for an elephant, is a
> big mammal.

$$\text{SIZE(Jumbo, Elephant, Small)} \;\wedge\; \text{SIZE(Jumbo, Mammal, Big)}$$

Verbs are another source of predicates. The verb "borders" corresponds to a predicate meaning that two countries border each other: BORDERS(India, Pakistan). This predicate is symmetric since its two arguments can always be interchanged without altering the value of the proposition. Another geographical example is one stating that a river runs through a country. This predicate corresponds to the meaning of a verb combined with a preposition: RUNSTHROUGH(Amazon, Brazil). Here we have a many-many mapping since a river may run through more than one country and a country may have more than one river. Unlike RUNSTHROUGH, the predicate MOTHER is one-many since each person has exactly one (biological) mother. Consequently, we can define a directly related function as in Example 4.3.

> **Example 4.3** Let m be a function for which $m(x) = y$ means that y is
> the one and only mother of x. Then with MOTHER as defined earlier,
> what is the meaning and truth value of MOTHER($m(x)$, x)?
>
> This expression, which must be true for every x, says that "the
> mother of x is the mother of x," where the first occurrence of "mother"
> in this sentence is a translation of the one-argument function m and
> the second comes from the two-argument predicate MOTHER.

Each one-argument predicate has an interesting and important relationship to a particular set—namely, the set of values that makes the predicate true. This set is called the **truth set** of the predicate. The truth set of p is written $\mathcal{T}(p)$. As a formal definition of $\mathcal{T}$, we write $\mathcal{T}(p) = \{x \mid p(x) = \text{TRUE}\}$. This definition is read "$\mathcal{T}(p)$ is the set of those x for which $p(x)$ is true." Notice that x is just an arbitrary variable in this definition, and we could just as well have used y or some other variable throughout. It is p, the predicate, that is related to the set $\mathcal{T}(p)$, its truth set.

> **Example 4.4** Suppose that VOWEL is a predicate that takes letters as its legal inputs. Also assume that its value is TRUE for vowels and FALSE for other letters. Use this predicate in true and false propositions. Use its truth set in true and false propositions.
>
> VOWEL('e') = TRUE. VOWEL('g') = FALSE. The truth set of VOWEL is $\mathcal{T}(\text{VOWEL}) = \{\text{'a', 'e', 'i', 'o', 'u'}\}$. It follows that 'e' $\in \mathcal{T}(\text{VOWEL})$ but that 'g' $\notin \mathcal{T}(\text{VOWEL})$. If $\mathcal{L}$ is the set of all 26 letters, we can also write $\mathcal{T}(\text{VOWEL}) \subseteq \mathcal{L}$.

Predicates with two (or more) arguments also have truth sets, but the members of these sets are ordered pairs. For example, $\mathcal{T}(\text{RUNSTHROUGH})$ contains the ordered pairs (Amazon, Brazil) and (Volga, Russia). Similarly, $(5,3) \in \mathcal{T}(\text{GREATERTHAN})$; also note that $\mathcal{T}(\text{GREATERTHAN}) \subseteq \mathcal{R} \times \mathcal{R}$. Finally, if SEPARATES is a three-argument predicate, meaning that its first argument is a river forming part of the border between the two countries that are its other two arguments, then the ordered triple (RioGrande, Mexico, USA) is a member of $\mathcal{T}(\text{SEPARATES})$.

4.3 Quantifiers

So far we have used predicates to make assertions about only one thing at a time. **Quantifiers** give us a compact, precise, formal way to make assertions about a whole set at once. The situation is somewhat analogous to loops in programming languages, which let us carry out the same operation on a whole set of entities. In fact, it turns out that one of the quantifiers (the universal quantifier, to be introduced shortly) is just what we need to help describe the consequences of a loop in proofs of program correctness (see Chapter 6). The examples in the rest of this chapter make frequent reference to the following sets:

$$\mathcal{P}: \quad \text{the set of living people}$$
$$\mathcal{Q}: \quad \text{the set of all people, living or not}$$
$$\mathcal{I}: \quad \text{the integers}$$

$\mathcal{N}$:   the nonnegative integers (including zero)

$\mathcal{R}$:   the real numbers

$\mathcal{U}$:   an arbitrary set

The **universal** quantifier means "every" or "for all" and has the symbol $\forall$. It says that every element of some set has a certain property, so to use it we need to specify the set and property we have in mind. Properties are expressed by one-argument predicates, so $\forall x \in \mathcal{U} : p(x)$ can be read, "For all members x of the set $\mathcal{U}$, $p(x)$ is true" or, more simply, "Every member of $\mathcal{U}$ satisfies p." The set ($\mathcal{U}$ here) is called the **domain** or **universe** of the quantification.

Example 4.5 Express the statement "Every integer has a square that is greater than or equal to 0" using $\forall$.

Here are two ways, each specifying a set and a property. The set in each case is $\mathcal{I}$, representing the integers. The property appears as a predicate p in the first case and is spelled out in familiar mathematical notation in the second.

$$\forall x \in \mathcal{I} : p(x), \text{ where } p(x) \leftrightarrow x \text{ has a non-negative square}$$

$$\forall x \in \mathcal{I} : (x^2 \geq 0)$$

Each of the universally quantified expressions in Example 4.5 means that $0^2 \geq 0$ *and* $1^2 \geq 0$ *and* $(-1)^2 \geq 0$ and so on. Notice the use of *and* in the preceding sentence, which indicates a close relationship between conjunctions and the universal quantifier. More generally, for a universe, $\mathcal{U} = \{x_1, x_2, ...\}$, we can write

$$(\forall x \in \mathcal{U} : p(x)) \equiv p(x_1) \wedge p(x_2) \wedge \cdots$$

The **existential quantifier** means "for some" or "there exists ... such that" and has the symbol $\exists$. It too requires us to specify a set and a property.

Example 4.6 Express the following statement using $\exists$: "There exists an integer between 3 and 7."

$$\exists x \in \mathcal{I} : ((x > 3) \wedge (x < 7))$$

This existentially quantified expression means that either 0 is between 3 and 7 *or* 1 is between them *or* -1 is between them, *or* ....

This use of "or" is, as usual, intended to be understood in the inclusive sense. That is, like the $\lor$ operator, $\exists$ is inclusive: It is satisfied when one or more arguments satisfy the predicate. The preceding statement is thus true because the predicate is true when $x = 4$ or 5 or 6.

A general and more formal statement of the relationship between $\exists$ and $\lor$ is

$$(\exists x \in \mathcal{U} : p(x)) \equiv p(x_1) \lor p(x_2) \lor \cdots$$

For a universe of just two elements, $\mathcal{U} = \{x_1, x_2\}$, we can rewrite the first of DeMorgan's laws from Chapter 2 as

$$\neg\,(p(x_1) \land p(x_2)) \equiv \neg\,p(x_1) \lor \neg\,p(x_2)$$

Moving to a potentially larger yet still finite universe, $\mathcal{U} = \{x_1, x_2, ..., x_n\}$, permits us to state the following generalizations of DeMorgan's laws, which are identical to the preceding equivalence when $n = 2$. They can be proved using the earlier general equivalences for the quantifiers in terms of $\land$ and $\lor$ by repeated application of the original DeMorgan's laws.

$$\neg\,(\forall x \in \mathcal{U} : p(x)) \equiv \exists x \in \mathcal{U} : \neg\,p(x)$$

and

$$\neg\,(\exists x \in \mathcal{U} : p(x)) \equiv \forall x \in \mathcal{U} : \neg\,p(x).$$

Notice that in each of these two equivalences parentheses have been used to restrict the scope of the universal quantifier so that it applies only to the left side. Now look specifically at the first equivalence. Its left side denies that every x (in the finite universe $\mathcal{U}$) satisfies p. Its right side says the same thing from a different perspective: There is an x that fails to satisfy p. It is like the difference between saying "It is false that all dogs are brown" versus "There is (at least) one dog that is not brown." You should create a similar example with the second of the prior equivalences. (We have supported the previous equivalences only with informal comments. Formal proof of this generalization to arbitrary n also requires mathematical induction, introduced in Section 5.4.)

Informally the DeMorgan generalizations say that negation can move through quantification while changing it from universal to existential or vice versa. In trying to understand how negation interacts with the scope of quantifiers, it may help to think about the meanings of analogous sentences in English.

Example 4.7 Express each of the following English sentences as a quantified expression, using symbols of predicate logic, $\mathcal{P}$ for the set of people and the one-argument predicate, IsCarOwner.

It is *not* the case that *some*one has a car. $\neg\, \exists x \in \mathcal{P} : \text{IsCarOwner}(x)$

*Some*one does *not* have a car. $\exists x \in \mathcal{P} : \neg\, \text{IsCarOwner}(x)$

No one is without a car. $\neg\, \exists x \in \mathcal{P} : \neg\, \text{IsCarOwner}(x)$

Frequently, a form like "$x \in \mathcal{I}$" in a quantification is shortened to just "x". This is reasonable provided that the universe within which x can range is clear from the context. However, it is often clearer to give the universe explicitly. For example, it is true that

$$\exists x \in \mathcal{R} : 3 < x < 4$$

since there are reals (like π and 3.45) that lie between 3 and 4, but replacing $\mathcal{R}$ by $\mathcal{I}$ would make this expression false. You can see that the $\mathcal{R}$ here really is more important than the x since x could just as well be replaced throughout by y or any other variable, but $\mathcal{R}$ could not be replaced by $\mathcal{I}$. It is about $\mathcal{R}$ that we are asserting something; x is just being used to help say it. In this sense, it is like a parameter of a programming function or a dummy variable in a summation or an integral. In such cases, we say that the variable is **bound** by the quantification and that it is a **bound variable**. A variable that is not bound is a **free variable**.

Example 4.8 Is the formula $\exists y \in \mathcal{N} : (y = x^2)$ about x or about y?

Note that y is bound but x is free, so, according to the prior comments, the proposition says nothing about y. However, it does say something about the free variable x: that some non-negative integer is the square of x.

Empty sets can be a source of confusion. For perspective, let us look at set size in general. To discuss quantification, we have introduced sets that are infinite (e.g., the integers), large (e.g., all people), or of unspecified but finite size, $\{x_1, x_2, \ldots x_n\}$. The last-mentioned one may appear to have at least *some* members, but there is no guarantee of that since, in general, it is possible for n to be zero, unless that possibility is explicitly ruled out. Other set specifications too may permit a set to be either empty or not. Thus, it is important to be aware of how quantification works with the empty set, which is as shown in the following formulas. Note that these hold *no matter what p is.*

$$(\forall x \in \emptyset : p(x)) \equiv \text{TRUE}$$

$$(\exists x \in \emptyset : p(x)) \equiv \text{FALSE}$$

For example, consider the set of unicorns, which is empty because the unicorn is a mythical animal that does not exist. It is FALSE that "there is a unicorn that has a horn" (although they all did, in myth). This is reasonable in that there is no unicorn to serve in the role of horn-bearer. Next, it is TRUE that "every unicorn can leap tall buildings in a single bound." Let us go to a tall building and see if any unicorns fail the test. None do (none can since none exist), so there is no fact contrary to the universal quantification.

4.4 Multiple Quantifiers

Just as one quantifier can be applied to a predicate with one variable, so two (or more) quantifiers can be applied to a predicate with two (or more) variables. We begin with examples that use only universal quantifiers and then go on to examples with both kinds of quantifiers. All of the examples express useful ideas.

Example 4.9 What do the following quantified expressions mean?

$$\forall x : \forall y : (\text{PARENT}(x, y) \wedge \text{FEMALE}(x) \leftrightarrow \text{MOTHER}(x, y))$$

$$\forall x : \forall y : \forall z : (\text{MOTHER}(y, x) \wedge \text{FATHER}(z, x) \leftrightarrow \text{OFFSPRING}(x, y, z))$$

Both of these propositions are definitions. The first one uses two universal quantifiers to define a mother as a female parent. The second one uses three universal quantifiers to define a predicate that expresses the three-way relationship among a person and his or her (biological) parents.

Example 4.10 Write a quantified expression that expresses the property of symmetry for the predicate BORDERS introduced earlier.

$$\forall x : \forall y : (\text{BORDERS}(x, y) \leftrightarrow \text{BORDERS}(y, x))$$

Example 4.11 Use both kinds of quantifiers in a single expression stating that every integer has a square that is also an integer and is non-negative. Compare this with Example 4.5, where the square is not claimed to be an integer.

$$\forall x \in \mathcal{I} : \exists y \in \mathcal{N} : y = x^2$$

Although the existential quantifier claims that there is *at least* one appropriate value of y, in fact we know that there is exactly one. Exercise 4.5 introduces a special quantifier meaning "there is exactly one," which would be useful for Example 4.11 and also for stating that everyone has exactly one mother. Here we just use the ordinary existential quantifier.

> **Example 4.12** Write a two-quantifier formula stating that every living person has at least one mother among the set of all people, living or not.
>
> $$\forall x \in \mathcal{P} : \exists y \in \mathcal{Q} : \text{MOTHER}(y, x)$$

Notice that without the "$\forall x \in \mathcal{I}$:" at its beginning, the proposition in Example 4.11 becomes the same as Example 4.8, with a free variable, x. Thus, by including the quantification, we have bound the variable. Whereas Example 4.11 says that numbers *have* perfect squares, Example 4.13 lets us say that if a number meets certain conditions it *is* a perfect square. In fact, Example 4.13 defines the notion of a perfect square. Notice that, like the definitions in Example 4.9, this one begins with a universal quantifier and contains a biconditional operator.

> **Example 4.13** Define the predicate ISPERFECTSQUARE, which is true of integers like 0, 1, 4, 9, 16, and so on, which are perfect squares.
>
> $$\forall x \in \mathcal{I} : \text{ISPERFECTSQUARE}(x) \leftrightarrow (\exists y \in \mathcal{I} : x = y^2).$$

The *order of quantification* is very important. In Examples 4.11 through 4.13, the existence of some y is claimed with respect to an already introduced x, and so the choice of y may depend on which value of x is under consideration as we move through all the members of x's set. In such a case, one says that y is within the **scope** of x. The scope of a quantifier extends to the end of its formula unless otherwise indicated by parentheses. In Example 4.13, take 9 and then 49 as values of x. One of them (9) is a perfect square because of the y-value -3 or 3, and the other (49) is also a perfect square, but on the basis of a different y-value, either -7 or 7.

Reversing the order of quantification in a true expression often yields a false one as the next example shows.

> **Example 4.14** Reverse the quantifier order in the expressions in Examples 4.11 and 4.12 and in each case state whether the result is true or false.

The results appear next. The first expression is false because it states that there is a (special) number that serves as the square of every integer. (It allows that there may be additional special numbers with this property, but requires at least one.) The second expression is false because it claims that there is one particular person who is the mother of everyone.

$$\underline{\text{this is false:}} \quad \exists y \in \mathcal{N} : \forall x \in \mathcal{I} : (y = x^2)$$

$$\underline{\text{this is false:}} \quad \exists y \in \mathcal{Q} : \forall x \in \mathcal{P} : \text{MOTHER}(y, x)$$

Of course, there are times when we really *do* want the existential operator to come first as the next two examples show.

Example 4.15 State in a quantified expression that there is a (special) member of $\mathcal{N}$ that is less than all the others. (In fact, that special member of $\mathcal{N}$ is zero.)

$$\exists y \in \mathcal{N} : \forall x \in \mathcal{N} : (y \leq x)$$

Example 4.16 In a network of computers, $\mathcal{C}$, we define the predicate DIRECT to give TRUE if its two arguments are either the same or directly connected. Write a quantified expression that means there is one computer (say, the server) directly connected to all the others; there may also be other connections.

$$\exists y \in \mathcal{C} : \forall x \in \mathcal{C} : \text{DIRECT}(x, y)$$

When both quantifiers (or all of them) are of the same kind, the order of quantification does not matter. For universals, the expression $\forall x : \forall y : p(x, y)$ means that the predicate p holds for all (x, y) pairs and that is also what $\forall y : \forall x : p(x, y)$ means. As examples, look back at the definitions of MOTHER and OFFSPRING at the start of this section. With existentials, the expression $\exists x : \exists y : p(x, y)$ means that the predicate p holds for at least one (x, y) pair and this is also what $\exists y : \exists x : p(x, y)$ means.

Definition 4.2 Formulas of Predicate Logic

- If *pred* is an n-argument predicate and each of $a_1, a_2, \ldots, a_n$ is either an element of the domain or a variable over the elements, then $pred(a_1, a_2, \ldots, a_n)$ is a formula.

- If α is a formula and β is a formula, then $(\neg\alpha)$, $(\alpha \vee \beta)$, and $(\alpha \wedge \beta)$ are formulas.

- If α is a formula and x is a variable over the elements of the domain, then $(\exists x : \alpha)$ and $(\forall x : \alpha)$ are formulas.

- Nothing else is a formula.

The first part of this definition establishes the **atomic formulas**. The second and third recursively build all formulas. As with propositions (Definition 2.1), we keep the definition simple by allowing an excess of parentheses. Avoiding them here would require not only specifying the precedence among the propositional operators, but also a statement about what is covered by a quantification. In fact, it is understood that in the absence of parentheses *a quantifier covers everything to its right*—that is, to the end of the entire (largest) formula containing it. Another simplifying decision about the definition is that it does not bother to distinguish between free and bound variables; it allows both. Finally, all quantification is assumed to be over the same tacit universe.

Domains, variables, and quantifiers are what distinguish predicate logic from propositional logic. The elements of the domain may be numbers, people, or whatever else we find useful. Because the variables here (x, y,...), range over *elements of a domain*, they are much more flexible than the variables (p, q, ...) in the definition of propositions, which range only over *truth values*.

After defining the propositions in Chapter 2, we gave an additional definition that included their truth values. That is harder to do here, but still possible if the universe is finite and the truth values are known (specified) for all atomic formulas without variables. In that case, the truth value of any formula that has only bound variables can be determined in the steps listed next. A formula with no free variables has a truth value and so is a proposition.

- Eliminate quantifiers and variables, making use of the equivalences in Section 4.3 to express them in terms conjunctions and disjunctions.

- Replace each atomic formula by its truth value.

- Evaluate the result, which is a proposition, in accord with Definition 2.2.

4.5 Logic for Data Structures

Two important data structures for computer science are the string and the graph. This section shows how to express some essential ideas of these data structures in terms of predicate logic. Both strings and graphs can be implemented as arrays, which in turn are crucial to so many computing applications that they were built into the first high-level language, Fortran. Arrays may have one, two, or more dimensions, and may have numbers, characters, or other forms of data as their elements. Strings are typically implemented as one-dimensional arrays of characters, and graphs often use a two-dimensional array of edges.

The **sequence** (or ordered set) is an abstract notion that corresponds directly to a one-dimensional array. A sequence is like a set in being a collection of elements, but it differs in two ways from an ordinary set. First, the ordering of elements is significant. For example, the sequence (a, b) is not the same sequence as (b, a), whereas $\{a, b\}$ and $\{b, a\}$ are just two ways of writing the same (ordinary, unordered) set. Second, a sequence may have repeated elements, and each occurrence counts when determining the **length** of the sequence.

> **Example 4.17** Let A be the sequence $(b, o, o, k, k, e, e, p, e, r)$. The length
> of A is 10, including 3 occurrences of e. The set of elements appear-
> ing in the sequence is $\{b, e, k, o, p, r\}$, which has a cardinality (size)
> of 6.

When the elements of a sequence are letters, characters, or symbols, the sequence may be called a **string**. As Example 4.17 suggests, each word of English is a string or sequence of letters (with an occasional hyphen or apostrophe). Many programming languages implement strings as one-dimensional arrays of characters. In the study of formal language (Part II), strings are defined as sequences of symbols.

General notation for a finite sequence is $A = (a_1, a_2, \ldots, a_n)$. In the next few examples, A and B are each sequences of n letters, with $A = (a_1, a_2, \ldots, a_n)$ and $B = (b_1, b_2, \ldots, b_n)$. We use $\mathcal{I}_n$ for the set of the first n positive integers, $\{1, 2, \ldots, n\}$. All quantification in these examples is with respect to $\mathcal{I}_n$. These examples involve formal descriptions of constraints on A and B, using quantifiers, set notation, and the predicates "$=$", "$\neq$", and "$\prec$" as needed, where $x \prec y$ means "x precedes y alphabetically."

> **Example 4.18** State formally that some letter appears in the same po-
> sition in the two sequences A and B specified earlier.
>
> $$\exists i \in \mathcal{I}_n : a_i = b_i$$

> **Example 4.19** State formally that within every pair of elements of A
> each of the two elements equals the other. Then state that every
> element of A is equal to its first element. Notice that these are
> equivalent; if either is true, then both are true.

$$\forall i \in \mathcal{I}_n : \forall j \in \mathcal{I}_n : a_i = a_j$$

$$\forall i \in \mathcal{I}_n : a_i = a_1$$

Example 4.20 Express the following quantified expression in English.

$$\forall i \in \mathcal{I}_{n-1} : a_i \prec a_{i+1}$$

This says that A is sorted in strictly alphabetical order. Notice the use of $\mathcal{I}_{n-1}$ rather than $\mathcal{I}_n$. We want to avoid comparing the last element to the one after it, since *nothing* comes after it. The situation is analogous to avoiding references beyond the bounds of an array.

The idea of a graph, introduced in Chapter 1, is simple yet remarkably useful, and whole books are devoted to graph algorithms. Here we confine attention to the **undirected graph** and its relationship to predicate logic. An undirected graph $G = (V, E)$ consists of two things: (i) a set V of vertices and (ii) a set E of edges that are (unordered) pairs of elements of V. It helps to visualize a vertex as a point and regard an edge as a line segment connecting two points. Vertices and edges can be, respectively, computers and cables, airports and roundtrip flights, people and friendships, nations and bilateral treaties, or whatever else we find it useful to apply them to. Each edge represents a *direct* connection.

To make the connection with predicate logic, let $\text{EDGE}(x, y)$ mean that x and y are connected by an edge—that is, $\{x, y\} \in E$. Since we are talking about undirected graphs, whenever $\{x, y\} \in E$, it is also true that $\{y, x\} \in E$. Therefore, EDGE is a symmetric predicate.

Example 4.21 Suppose that $V = \{a, b, c, d\}$ and the edges correspond to $\text{EDGE}(a, b)$, $\text{EDGE}(b, c)$, and $\text{EDGE}(a, d)$. State whether the following quantified expression is TRUE or FALSE.

$$\forall x \in V : \exists y \in V : \text{EDGE}(x, y)$$

This is true for the given graph since for each vertex there is a vertex connected to it, but notice that we need to appeal to the symmetry of EDGE. Thus, for the case of d, since we have $\text{EDGE}(a, d)$, we also have $\text{EDGE}(d, a)$.

Example 4.22 For the graph in Example 4.21, evaluate the following quantified expression:

$$\exists x \in V : \forall y \in V : x = y \lor \text{EDGE}(x, y)$$

This is false. It claims that one particular vertex is directly connected to each of the others and this is not so.

Exercises

4.1 Express in predicate logic the meaning of each of the following sentences of English. Use negation, whatever quantifiers you need, and the one-argument predicate ISCAROWNER, which is true for anyone who owns at least one car. Also, state which of your answers are equivalent to each other.

(a) It is not the case that everyone has a car.

(b) No one has a car.

(c) Someone does not have a car.

(d) Someone has a car.

(e) It is false that everyone is without a car.

4.2 Consider the definitions in Examples 4.9 and 4.13.

(a) Definitions often make use of the biconditional operator. Why?

(b) Definitions often make use of the universal quantifier. Why?

4.3 The following formulas define what it means for two things to be the same or different from each other.

$$\forall x : \text{IDENTICAL}(x, x)$$

$$\forall x : \forall y : \neg \text{IDENTICAL}(x, y) \leftrightarrow \text{DIFFERENT}(x, y)$$

(a) Use PARENT and DIFFERENT along with quantifiers as needed (but no other predicates) to define PARENTINCOMMON(x, y), meaning that x and y have one of the following (biological) relationships: sister, brother, half-sister, or half-brother. You share two parents with a sister, but only one with a half-sister. You are not your own sister.

(b) Now define SISTER(x, y) to mean that x is either the sister or half-sister of y. Assume that there are one-argument predicates MALE and FEMALE with the obvious meanings. Use PARENTINCOMMON from (a).

(c) Define FIRSTCOUSIN(x, y) to mean that x is the first cousin of y. Note that first cousins must have a grandparent in common, but they must be different people with different parents.

4.4 The existential quantifier says that there is at least one of something, but sometimes we have more accurate information than that. Sometimes there must be exactly one of something, as noted in the discussion of Example 4.11. Express the fact that there is exactly one integer between 4 and 6 by using an existential quantifier to state that there is at least one such integer and also that if there were two such integers (say x and y), they would have to be equal to each other.

4.5 The quantifier $\exists!$ is sometimes used to assert that exactly one of something exists. That is, $\exists!x \in \mathcal{I} : p(x)$ means that there is exactly one integer with property p. Use this quantifier to state that

(a) Every living person has exactly one mother, living or not.

(b) Every integer has exactly one square.

4.6 The Pythagoreans of ancient Greece studied what they called triangular numbers as well as the squares. These are 1, 3, 6, 10, ..., which are equal to 1, 1+2, 1+2+3, 1+2+3+4, and so on. Define a predicate TRIANGULAR that is true of these numbers and no others. Your definition may allow zero to be triangular.

4.7 *Evaluate* each of the following propositions and explain your reasoning for arriving at your result. $\mathcal{N}$ is the set of non-negative integers, $\{0, 1, 2, \ldots\}$. $\mathcal{I}^+$ is the set of positive integers, $\{1, 2, \ldots\}$. $\mathcal{I}$ is the set of all integers, including the negatives. To evaluate an expression means to find the constant to which it is equal or equivalent. For a proposition, that means determining that it is equivalent to TRUE or to FALSE. Justify your answers.

(a) $\forall i \in \mathcal{N} : \forall j \in \mathcal{N} : i^2 + j^2 \geq 0$

(b) $\exists i \in \mathcal{I}^+ : \exists j \in \mathcal{I}^+ : (5 < i^2 + j^2 < 10) \wedge (i \neq j)$

(c) $\forall i \in \mathcal{I} : \exists j \in \mathcal{I} : (i + 2j = 0) \vee (2i + j = 0)$

(d) $\exists j \in \mathcal{I} : \forall i \in \mathcal{I} : ij = -i$

4.8 Consider the graph (V, E) with vertices, V, and edges, E. Let EDGE(x, y) mean that x and y are connected by an edge, although it is more common to write $(x, y) \in E$.

(a) Express the fact that EDGE is symmetric.

(b) Write a formula stating that for every pair, (x, y), of vertices in V there is a path of length 2 connecting x to y.

(c) Let PATH(x, y) mean that there is a sequence of 0, 1, 2, or more edges connecting x and y. Using quantifiers and EDGE, give a *recursive* definition of PATH.

4.9 Using the terminology of Exercise 4.8, with $V = \{a, b, c, d\}$, state whether each of the formulas (i)-(iv) is TRUE or FALSE when

(a) EDGE(a, b), EDGE(b, c) and EDGE(b, d) are TRUE, but these are the only edges.

(b) EDGE(a, b), EDGE(b, c) and EDGE(c, d) are TRUE, but these are the only edges.

(i) $\forall x \in V : \forall y \neq x \in V : \text{EDGE}(x, y)$

(ii) $\forall x \in V : \forall y \in V : \text{PATH}(x, y)$

(iii) $\forall x \in V : \exists y \in V : \text{EDGE}(x, y)$

(iv) $\exists x \in V : \forall y \neq x \in V : \text{EDGE}(x, y)$

4.10 As in the sequence examples of Section 4.5, let A and B each be sequences of letters, with $A = (a_1, a_2, \ldots, a_n)$ and $B = (b_1, b_2, \ldots, b_n)$. Describe each of the following situations formally, using quantifiers with respect to $\mathcal{I}_n = \{1, 2, \ldots, n\}$, set notation, and the predicates "$=$", "$\neq$", and "$\prec$" (precedes alphabetically) as needed.

(a) There is no occurrence of "c" in A.

(b) Some letter appears twice in A.

(c) No letter appears twice in A.

(d) A and B are the same list.

(e) The set of letters appearing in A is a subset of the set of letters appearing in B.

(f) The set of letters appearing in A is the same as the set of letters appearing in B.

(g) Each element of A is no later in the alphabet than the corresponding element of B.

4.11 Using the notation of Exercise 4.10, give a formal specification of conditions that are both necessary and sufficient to make A occur earlier in an ordinary dictionary than B. In such a case, we say that A *lexicographically* precedes B. You may assume that both sequences have the same length, n, and are padded on the right by blanks, which alphabetically precede all the letters. Also note that $\mathcal{I}_1 = \{1\}$ and $\mathcal{I}_0 = \emptyset$.

4.12 Two solutions are provided to the question posed in Example 4.19. Show that one of them corresponds to an algorithm with a single loop and in that way is preferable to the other, which in effect specifies a less efficient algorithm with nested looping.

4.13 With $\mathcal{U} = \{a, b, c\}$, rewrite the following formula from Section 4.3 without using any quantifiers. Use the $\wedge$ and $\vee$ operators. It may help to look at the equivalences in Section 4.3.

$$\neg\,(\forall x \in \mathcal{U} : p(x)) \equiv \exists x \in \mathcal{U} : \neg\, p(x)$$

Chapter 5

Proving with Predicates

Predicates and quantification—added to the earlier apparatus of propositional logic—provide a much broader foundation for proving important results both within logic and applied to outside areas like mathematics and computer science. With a view to achieving these results, the first two sections develop new inference rules and strategies for using them. The capability of logical inference to apply beyond logic itself then makes its first appearance with proofs in mathematics in the last two sections, preparing the way for an application to computer science in the next chapter.

5.1   Inference Rules with Predicates

As we begin to prove things about subject matter expressed with predicates, it is important to remember that propositions are still part of the picture because, as noted, a formula in predicate logic *is* a proposition. Therefore, our propositional rules of inference are often still useful. Moreover, many inference rules for propositions have analogous versions for predicates. For these reasons, proofs by rules of inference with predicates may have a reassuringly familiar look. Here is the predicate version of $\rightarrow$ introduction. We use the same name as before, but it is clear in any particular context which kind of $\rightarrow$ introduction is meant.

$\rightarrow$ Introduction:

$$[p(x)]$$
$$q(x)$$
$$\overline{}$$
$$p(x) \rightarrow q(x)$$

To realize that the preceding rule is not really new, remember that $p(x)$ is a proposition: that x satisfies the predicate p. Of course, some inference rules with predicates go beyond just restating propositional rules. For example, the next rule is a generalization of an inference rule for propositions. It is often called **instan-tiation**, but here it is called ∀ elimination to emphasize that it generalizes the propositional rule, ∧ elimination. In fact, in a universe of just two elements, this rule is identical to ∧ elimination. It states that if the predicate p is true for all possible arguments, it must be true for any particular one.

$$\forall \text{ Elimination:} \qquad\qquad \frac{\forall x \in \mathcal{U} : p(x)}{p(a)}$$

The next rule, ∀ introduction, follows from the observation that the only thing assumed about x is that it belongs to some set, $\mathcal{U}$. Thus x is a completely arbitrary element of $\mathcal{U}$. The second line says that this (weak) assumption has led to the truth of $q(x)$. Thus, the predicate q must hold for every member of $\mathcal{U}$, as concluded below the line.

$$\forall \text{ Introduction:} \qquad\qquad \frac{\begin{array}{c}[x \in \mathcal{U}]\\ q(x)\end{array}}{\forall x \in \mathcal{U} : q(x)}$$

Another way to look at this rule of ∀ introduction is to express membership in $\mathcal{U}$ as a predicate, INU. In this way, we make this inference rule analogous to → introduction, with the predicate p replaced by the new predicate, INU. Now the assumption of $p(x)$ is replaced by the assumption of $\text{INU}(x)$. Correspondingly, the conclusion becomes $\text{INU}(x) \to q(x)$, which is just another way to say $\forall x \in \mathcal{U} : q(x)$, as written in the concluding line of ∀ introduction.

Turning now to the existential quantifier, consider how to make use of the knowledge that *some* member of $\mathcal{U}$ satisfies p. In this event, we proceed to name that thing "a". The name "a" must *not* be the name of some particular member of $\mathcal{U}$, and furthermore it must *not* have been previously mentioned in the proof because we do *not* know—unlike the case with ∀ elimination—that any specific thing satisfies p. Other than that, the thing a stands for is an arbitrary member of $\mathcal{U}$.

$$\exists \text{ Elimination:} \qquad\qquad \frac{\exists x \in \mathcal{U} : p(x)}{a \in \mathcal{U} \wedge p(a)}$$

Conversely, if at least one member of $\mathcal{U}$ satisfies the predicate p that justifies the introduction of the existential quantifier,

$\exists$ Introduction: $\qquad a \in \mathcal{U} \wedge p(a)$

$$\overline{\exists x \in \mathcal{U} : p(x)}$$

5.2 Proof Strategies with Predicates

The foregoing rules of inference, like the ones for propositions, allow us to prove many important results. Here are a few proof strategies for theorems with predicates and quantifiers.

1. Theorems of the form "$\exists x \in \mathcal{U} : p(x)$"

   Theorems like this can be proved using $\exists$ introduction simply by *exhibiting* a specific x and showing that it is the case that $p(x)$ is true. (It is a common mistake to use this proof technique when a universal quantification is to be proved; in that case, a "proof by example" is inadequate and is not a proof.) Sometimes, rather than explicitly showing such an x, we can give a technique for finding such an x (and argue the technique cannot fail); this is called an *algorithmic proof.*

2. Theorems of the form "$\forall x \in \mathcal{U} : p(x)$"

   This kind of theorem clearly requires $\forall$ introduction. As noted, however, the theorem really says that $(x \in \mathcal{U}) \rightarrow p(x)$ is a true proposition. So the proof, using the $\rightarrow$ introduction rule, assumes $x \in \mathcal{U}$ and shows $p(x)$ is a consequence. It is crucial that when using this technique you assume x is an *arbitrary* element of $\mathcal{U}$; making any further assumption about x invalidates the proof.

3. Theorems of the form "$\neg\, \forall x \in \mathcal{U} : p(x)$"

   Here we are to prove that p does not hold throughout $\mathcal{U}$. By DeMorgan's law, this is equivalent to "there exists an $x \in \mathcal{U}$ such that $\neg p(x)$". Using strategy 1, we can prove this by exhibiting an x such that $\neg p(x)$ is true. This is a *proof by counterexample.*

4. Theorems of the form "$\forall x \in \mathcal{N} : p(x)$"

   This is an extremely common type of theorem; we want to show that p holds for all x such that $x \geq 0$. One technique used to prove such a theorem is *mathematical induction.* This powerful and widely used tool fits neatly into a logical framework, as Section 5.4 explains.

5.3   Applying Logic to Mathematics

Logic has been playing a double role in many of our examples. Its rules of inference have been our principal source of reasoning techniques, and it has also served as the domain of application. We have applied logic to logic. However, the power and significance of logic are clearer when its proof methods are put to use outside of logic. The most important applications of logic lie within mathematics and computer science because, like logic itself, they are expressed in general terms and so are broadly applicable. Chapter 6 applies logic to computer science, specifically to the challenge of proving the correctness of programs. This section and the next one pave the way, by applying logic to arithmetic, or more precisely to number theory. In this domain, the claims are easy to understand but not trivial to prove, so it is a good place to start.

For any new application domain, it is necessary to develop new predicates and sometimes even new inference rules specific to that domain. Sometimes the special predicates and inference rules for a particular topic are given explicitly, but usually they are tacit or couched as definitions. Part of the difficulty of understanding and writing proofs is to recognize these components of our background knowledge. For example, next are four items of background knowledge for sets and numbers. The task of casting them into the inference rule format of Chapter 3 is left as an exercise.

- Subset rule:

    $A \subseteq B$ follows from the assertion $\forall x \in A : (x \in B)$.

- Set equality rule:

    $A = B$ follows from $A \subseteq B$ and $B \subseteq A$.

- Transitivity of $<$:

    This inference rule states that $a < c$ follows from the combination of $a < b$ and $b < c$. We saw in Chapter 3 that the conditional operator, $\rightarrow$, is also transitive. Several other operators and relations, including equality, equivalence, and subset, are transitive as well.

- Pigeon-hole principle:

    If $n + 1$ occurrences are assigned to n categories, there must be one category with at least two occurrences (e.g., given eight people, at least two were born on the same day of the week).

Some inference rules follow directly from definitions. For example, earlier we defined the predicate ISPERFECTSQUARE, which is true for each of the perfect squares. Therefore, if in a proof we have a line asserting that ISPERFECTSQUARE(a) is true then we can infer that there exists an integer b such that $a = b^2$. The proof in Example 5.1 uses this rule, although very informally. The proof in Example 5.2, which is more formal, defines the predicate ODD, converts it to a rule of inference and uses that in a proof that the product of odd numbers is odd.

Example 5.1 Prove that every perfect square is either a multiple of 3 or one greater than a multiple of 3.

This proof is informal, but we point out its use of some formal rules of inference, specifically case analysis and ∨ introduction. The basic idea of the proof is that when examining numbers in the context of multiples of 3, each integer falls into one of three categories depending on its value modulo 3. That is, for every n, one of the following holds:

For some m, $n = 3m$, or
For some m, $n = 3m + 1$ or
For some m, $n = 3m + 2$.

The disjunctive form of this statement (its use of "or") suggests a proof by *case analysis*, with three cases (see Exercise 3.15). To complete the proof, we show that each case leads to the result. A perfect square is the square of an integer n, so continuing each of the cases, the square, n^2, is one of these:

$$n^2 = (3m)^2 = 3(3m^2) \text{ or}$$
$$n^2 = (3m + 1)^2 = 3(3m^2 + 2m) + 1 \text{ or}$$
$$n^2 = (3m + 2)^2 = 3(3m^2 + 4m + 1) + 1.$$

In the first case, the square is a multiple of 3 and in the other two cases it is one greater than a multiple of 3. Now look at the problem statement. It can be written in the form $p(n^2) \lor q(n^2)$, where p is the property of being a multiple of 3 and q is the property of being 1 more than a multiple of 3. In one of the three cases we have proved $p(n^2)$, and in the other two cases we have proved $q(n^2)$. In each case, one then uses ∨ *introduction*, a step so straightforward it often goes unmentioned.

Example 5.2 Prove that if the integers a and b are odd then ab is odd.

In other words, the product of two odd numbers is odd. This proof is more formal than that of Example 5.1, but they are alike in putting to use the idea of domain-specific inference rules. The first step is to give a formal *definition* of "a is odd":

$$\forall x \in \mathcal{N} : \text{ODD}(x) \leftrightarrow \exists w \in \mathcal{N} : (x = 2w + 1).$$

The proof uses this definition as an inference rule in two ways, replacing its left-hand side by its right-hand side and vice versa. Nearly all theorem statements have their logical structure hidden by the use of ordinary (English) language. Our earlier phrasing, "the product of odd numbers is odd," is an example of such informality. To clarify what is really being said, it is helpful, at this point, to state explicitly the logical structure of what is to be proved:

$$\forall a \in \mathcal{N} : \forall b \in \mathcal{N} : ((\text{ODD}(a) \wedge \text{ODD}(b)) \to \text{ODD}(ab)).$$

The main idea is that, taking x and y to be arbitrary integers, $2x+1$ and $2y + 1$ are arbitrary odd numbers, and their product can be manipulated by algebraic equivalences into $2(2xy + x + y) + 1$, which must be odd. Here is a (more nearly) formal proof.

$[a \in \mathcal{N} \wedge b \in \mathcal{N}]$
$\quad [\text{ODD}(a) \wedge \text{ODD}(b)]$
$\quad \text{ODD}(a)$
$\quad \exists w \in \mathcal{N} : (a = 2w + 1)$ definition of ODD
$\quad a = 2x + 1$ $\exists$ elimination
$\quad \text{ODD}(b)$
$\quad \exists w \in \mathcal{N} : (b = 2w + 1)$ definition of ODD
$\quad b = 2y + 1$ $\exists$ elimination
$\quad ab = 2(2xy + x + y) + 1$
$\quad ab = 2z + 1$
$\quad \exists w \in \mathcal{N} : (ab = 2w + 1)$ $\exists$ introduction
$\quad \text{ODD}(ab)$ definition of ODD
$\quad (\text{ODD}(a) \wedge \text{ODD}(b)) \to \text{ODD}(ab)$
$\forall a \in \mathcal{N} : \forall b \in \mathcal{N} : ((\text{ODD}(a) \wedge \text{ODD}(b)) \to \text{ODD}(ab))$ $\forall$ introduction, twice

The foregoing proof begins with the assumption that we have an arbitrary a and b from the domain, which is how we typically prove any universally quantified logical expression. Our earlier definition of ODD is used in both directions, as promised, forward in the fourth and seventh lines and then backward in the third-to-last line.

The rule of $\exists$ elimination is used twice in this proof, each time to let us choose a name for something we know exists. Also used here is $\exists$ introduction, which lets us say that if something is true of a particular number, then it is true of some number.

Finally note that we have used the initial assumption, that a and b are integers, in two subtle ways: We used ODD(a), which is only defined for integers and we perform algebraic manipulations (to get the ninth line), from our background knowledge, that are allowed for integers.

5.4   Mathematical Induction

Computer scientists need to know things about infinite sets. For example, consider a `while` loop and a set of propositions $P(0)$, $P(1)$, $P(2)$, ... Suppose that each $P(i)$ (for $i = 0, 1, 2, \ldots$) states something that is supposed to be true after i iterations of the loop and that we want to prove all of these propositions. Of course, we hope that the loop will not go on forever, but we probably do not want to impose an arbitrary limit on the number of iterations for two reasons. Suppose we did limit a loop to, say, 10,000 iterations. One trouble with this is the possibility of running into a data set that causes the loop to need 10,001 or 20,000 iterations or more. Second, proving 10,000 propositions one by one would take too long. In contrast, many proofs for infinite sets are not very difficult. This section introduces a technique called **mathematical induction** that is used to prove things about infinite sets.

Proofs about the behavior of loops—that they do what they are supposed to—are introduced in Chapter 6. Here we use easier examples about integers, so we can focus our attention on the methods of proof. You have already seen one proof of an infinite set of propositions. This was the proof that the product of any two odd numbers is odd. The proof was done rather formally, concluding by using the rule of inference known as $\forall$ introduction. We assumed the oddness of the two numbers but nothing else about them, so the result held for any pair of odd numbers. Each odd number is an *arbitrary representative* of an infinite set (here the odd numbers).

Mathematical induction (MI) builds on the method of using arbitrary representatives and $\forall$ introduction. MI is for proving things about infinite sets of propositions. MI is a powerful method, allowing us to prove things that would at best be difficult to prove using only arbitrary representatives. The key idea of MI is that when trying to prove proposition $P(n)$—where n is an arbitrary representative of the positive integers—we can act as if the truth of $P(n-1)$ has already been established. The assumption of $P(n-1)$ is called the **inductive hypothesis**.

This extra help can be crucial, as we will see, but is it justified? To see that it is, let us be a little more precise. First, it is important to realize that a proof by MI has two parts—proof of a base case and proof of the so-called inductive step. Typically, the **base case** (or basis) is $P(0)$. Typically, the **inductive step** is to prove that $P(n-1) \to P(n)$. If this step is carried out with no assumptions about n except that $n \geq 1$, then it is true for any $n \geq 1$, so the base case together with all the results that come from the inductive step are:

$$P(0)$$
$$P(0) \quad \to \quad P(1)$$
$$P(1) \quad \to \quad P(2)$$
$$P(2) \quad \to \quad P(3)$$
$$\vdots$$
$$P(n-1) \quad \to \quad P(n)$$
$$\vdots$$

From the first two lines, modus ponens lets us infer $P(1)$. From $P(1)$ and the third line, modus ponens lets us infer $P(2)$. Then we can infer $P(3)$ and so on through $P(n)$. Thus, repeated use of the inductive step with modus ponens justifies all these arrows for any positive integer n.

$$P(0) \ \text{(from Base)} \to P(1) \to P(2) \to P(3) \to \cdots \to P(n)$$

Having introduced the general idea of mathematical induction, we now show how it can be used. You will notice that nothing we have said tells you *what* to prove. MI is only a method of proof. One starts with a guess or conviction that a certain result is both true and useful. If the result involves an infinite set, there is often a chance that MI will help with the proof. It is also worth noting that MI is one of several concepts that expresses in a finite way something about sets of unlimited size. Other such concepts are loops in programs, recursive functions in programs, recursive definitions, universal quantification ($\forall$), summations (Σ), and products (Π).

Example 5.3 Show that, for any non-negative integer n, the sum of the first n integers is $n(n+1)/2$. That is, prove all propositions

$P(n), n \geq 0$ where $P(n)$ is the following equality:

$$\sum_{i=1}^{n} i = \frac{n(n+1)}{2}$$

Proof: We show, by MI, that the preceding formula is true for all n. The base case, $P(0)$, is the proposition that the sum of no (zero) numbers is $0(0+1)/2$ or 0, which is clearly true. To establish $P(n)$, we proceed as follows:

$$\sum_{i=1}^{n} i = n + \sum_{i=1}^{n-1} i$$

$$= n + \frac{(n-1)((n-1)+1)}{2} = \frac{n(2+(n-1))}{2} = \frac{n(n+1)}{2}$$

Note that we appealed to the inductive hypothesis, $P(n-1)$, when we went to the second line.

One way to gain some confidence that this summation formula is correct is to check it for a couple of specific example cases. Thus, note that for $n = 4$, the left side is $1 + 2 + 3 + 4$ whereas the right side becomes $(4 \times 5)/2$, and the value of each of these expressions is 10. The following diagram lets you confirm this result visually. There are 10 little squares laid out so as to indicate the sum $1 + 2 + 3 + 4$. You can see that this is exactly half of the 4 by 5 rectangle and that a similar diagram can also be drawn for values of n other than 4.

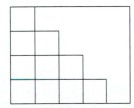

Mathematical induction can be expressed as a *rule of inference*. Above the bar are, as usual, the things that must be proved before using the rule. In the rule shown next, we need to prove the first and second lines, and we can then conclude that the last line is proved. Since this is for MI, we must prove the base case, which is the first line, as well as the inductive step, the second line. The final line is the result that is being proved by MI.

BC = Base Case
IH = Inductive Hypothesis
IC = Inductive Conclusion

Step	Rule or Comment

$\vdots$ Steps in proving BC

$P(0)$ BC proved

$\quad [n \geq 1]$ Assumption

$\qquad [P(n-1)]$ Assumption: IH

$\qquad \vdots$ Steps in proving IC

$\qquad P(n)$ IC proved

$\quad P(n-1) \to P(n)$ $\to$ introduction

$\forall n \geq 1 : P(n-1) \to P(n)$ $\forall$ introduction

$\forall n \geq 0 : P(n)$ Mathematical induction

Figure 5.1: Framework for Mathematical Induction proofs

Mathematical Induction:

$$P(0)$$
$$\forall\, n \geq 1 : P(n-1) \to P(n)$$

$$\overline{}$$

$$\forall\, n \geq 0 : P(n)$$

Notice that the second line, the inductive step, is expressed in terms of $\forall$ (universal quantification) and $\to$ (conditional). We need to get results in a form that includes these symbols to make use of this rule of inference, so we should expect to use $\forall$ introduction and $\to$ introduction along the way. For $\forall$ introduction, recall that proving something true of all positive integers can be achieved by proving that it is true of n, where we make no assumptions about n except that it is a positive integer. For $\to$ introduction, we assume the left-hand side and, using that assumption, proceed to prove the right-hand side. Notice that in the context of MI, assuming the left-hand side is called using the inductive hypothesis. Taken together, these strategic observations give the general framework in Figure 5.1 for proofs by mathematical induction. The framework can be seen to guide the proof in Example 5.4.

Example 5.4 Give a *formal proof* of the formula in Example 5.2 that the sum of the first n integers is $n(n+1)/2$.

Step	Rule or Comment

1. $\sum_{i=1}^{0} i = \frac{0(0+1)}{2} = 0$ — Proof of BC
2. $[n \geq 1]$ — Assumption
3. $\sum_{i=1}^{n-1} i = \frac{(n-1)n}{2}$ — Assumption: IH
4. $\sum_{i=1}^{n} i = n + \sum_{i=1}^{n-1} i = \ldots = \frac{n(n+1)}{2}$ — Algebra rules
5. $\sum_{i=1}^{n} i = \frac{n(n+1)}{2}$ — IC
6. $\sum_{i=1}^{n-1} i = \frac{(n-1)n}{2} \rightarrow \sum_{i=1}^{n} i = \frac{n(n+1)}{2}$ — $\rightarrow$ introduction
7. $\forall n \geq 1 : \sum_{i=1}^{n-1} i = \frac{(n-1)n}{2} \rightarrow \sum_{i=1}^{n} i = \frac{n(n+1)}{2}$ — $\forall$ introduction
8. $\forall n \geq 0 : \sum_{i=1}^{n} i = \frac{n(n+1)}{2}$ — Mathematical induction

Although it is instructive to put one MI proof into our standard proof format, we must admit that by doing so we have made the proof of a relatively simple result look much more complex and forbidding than is usual. The essence of this longer proof lies in lines 1 and 4, which made up the entirety of the earlier informal proof in Example 5.3. In effect, the unstated background knowledge for that informal proof was the MI framework in Figure 5.1.

Besides its useful and interesting relationship to loops in programming and to quantification in logic, MI suits our continuing concern with proof strategy. Already it has served as an example of how unstated background knowledge can be uncovered and brought into a formal proof as a strategy for proving infinitely many propositions at once. Here are a few more specific strategies for MI:

- If the predicate $Q(n)$ is true for all integers $\geq k$ but false for $k-1$, let $P(0) = Q(k)$ be the base case and more generally let $P(n) = Q(n+k)$.

- The preceding item is an idea that can be used for many variants of the method. For example, if the predicate Q is only true for odd integers, let $P(n) = Q(2n+1)$. For powers of 2, let $P(n) = Q(2^n)$.

- Use $P(n) \rightarrow P(n+1)$ as the inductive step (instead of $P(n-1) \rightarrow P(n)$). Sometimes this eases the algebraic manipulations. Possible values of n must now include zero, along with, as before, the positive integers.

- When $P(n-1)$ is not enough to prove $P(n)$, use **strong mathematical induction**, a proof method in which the proof of $P(n)$ is allowed to make use of all (or any subset of) the preceding propositions, from $P(0)$ through $P(n-1)$. This makes sense since all of these earlier propositions have already been proved by the time $P(n)$ needs to be considered. Ordinary MI, as originally introduced, is sometimes called **weak mathematical induction**.

- When $P(n)$ is an equation, say $L(n) = R(n)$, and when you can show that $L(n) = L(n-1) + \alpha = \cdots = R(n-1) + \beta = R(n)$, then also try to show that the expressions α and β are equal. Together with the induction hypothesis, that $L(n-1) = R(n-1)$, this completes the proof. This approach guided Example 5.2.

- Occasionally the proof $P(n-1) \to P(n)$ is by *contradiction* (rather than a *direct proof*); this is called a *proof by smallest counterexample*.

Now let us try one of these strategies, in particular the first one, which allows a starting point other than $P(0)$. In Example 5.5, the proposition for $n = 4$ is false, but it is true for all integers ≥ 5. We do not bother to define both P and Q as in the prior strategy description, but simply take $P(5)$ as the base case. This makes it reasonable—in fact appropriate—to allow the use of $n \geq 6$ in the proof of the inductive step.

The much simpler and more common style of MI proofs used in Example 5.3 is evident again in Example 5.5, which proves that exponentials outgrow squares. To be more precise, it is a proof that, for sufficiently large integers, $2^n > n^2$. In other words, exponentiating a sufficiently large number to base 2 yields a larger result than squaring the same number. Notice that the claim is not true for $n = 2$, 3, and 4; for example, since $2^4 = 4^2$, the strict inequality is not satisfied. Therefore, we start with $P(5)$ as the base case.

Example 5.5 Prove that $\forall n \geq 5 : 2^n > n^2$.

Base Case: $\qquad\qquad\qquad 2^5 = 32 > 25 = 5^2$

Inductive Hypothesis: $2^{n-1} > (n-1)^2$

Inductive Step: $\qquad\quad 2^n = 2 \times 2^{n-1} > 2(n-1)^2$ [by inductive hypothesis]
$$= 2(n^2 - 2n + 1) = n^2 + n^2 - 4n + 2$$
$$= n^2 + n(n-4) + 2 \quad \text{[with } n \geq 5\text{]}$$
$$> n^2$$

5.5 Limits of Logic

How many rules of inference are there? How many do we need? How many should we use? So far, we have not asked such questions, but have been content to look at individual rules and evaluate them in isolation. Evaluating a rule has meant showing with a truth table that an expression corresponding to it must be true in all states (is a tautology). Such a rule is said to be **sound**. Clearly we want only sound rules. It may also appear that we are evaluating a rule positively when we make favorable comments about how reasonable it seems. For example, we observed that rules like case analysis and the elimination of an alternative seem to make good common sense. Reasonableness is nice, but for formal proofs soundness is essential.

Now recall that some sound rules, like case analysis and modus ponens, were collected together into a kind of starter set or initial set of inference rules in a figure (Figure 3.1), whereas other equally sound rules, like transitivity of the conditional and the elimination of an alternative, we saw fit to prove not by truth tables but from other inference rules (whether from the initial set or previously proved or both). How should one decide which rules to start with and which to prove using other rules? It is possible to build more and more complex sound inference rules without limit (something we do not prove here), so there are infinitely many of them, and we cannot put them all into the initial set. However, we certainly do want to start with a big enough or diverse enough collection to be able to prove everything that is true.

A *system* of logic is informally defined as a set of axioms and a set of rules of inference. A system that makes it possible to have a proof for everything that really is true is said to be **complete**; in particular, a system is complete if every expression is provably true or provably false. A system is **consistent** if it is impossible to prove any expression to be both true and false. So what we seek is a system with sound rules that is complete and consistent.

It turns out that for propositional logic it is indeed possible to come up with a finite collection of rules that is complete and consistent, although to show this is beyond the scope of this book. (This is intuitive since "everything that is true" in propositional logic is that which can be proved with a truth table.) Yet logic is not always so clean and intuitive.

It turns out that if we look at systems of logic based on predicate logic, our intuition is betrayed. This was first discovered by Gödel in the 1930s. He considered a minimal system for proving statements about number theory (such as the statements in Section 5.3). He was able to show that if the system was consistent, then it must be incomplete! After Gödel, people have replicated this paradoxical situation with many other systems. It is known that if a system is sufficiently complex, in a very technical sense, it cannot be both consistent and complete—there is always a true but unprovable expression.

Exercises

5.1 Prove that for any n its successor times its predecessor is 1 less than its square. In other words, prove that $\forall n \in \mathcal{N} : P(n)$, where $P(n)$ is $(n + 1)(n - 1) = n^2 - 1$. You do *not* need mathematical induction for this. Use $\forall$ introduction and arithmetic manipulations involving distributivity and associativity. You may regard other rules of algebra as common knowledge that do not need to be explicitly provided as justifications. Lay out your proof like the rules-of-inference proofs in Chapter 3, justifying each step by stating its rule of inference.

5.2 Prove by mathematical induction that the sum of the first n positive odd integers is n^2.

5.3 Prove by mathematical induction that

$$\left(\sum_{i=1}^{n} i \right)^2 = \sum_{i=1}^{n} i^3.$$

You may make use of the fact that $\sum_{i=1}^{n} i = \frac{n(n+1)}{2}$.

5.4 Prove by mathematical induction that for any integer $n \geq 10$, $2^n > n^3$.

5.5 Prove algebraically that $\lor$ distributes over n-conjunct conjunctions like

$$(q_1 \land q_2 \land \ldots \land q_n)$$

given, as in Chapter 2, that this is true for $n = 2$.

5.6 Recast the following inference rules into the formal line-by-line notation introduced in Chapter 3.

    (a) Subset rule.

    (b) Set equality rule.

    (c) Transitivity of the conditional operator.

    (d) Pigeon-hole principle. Hint: Let f be a function from set A to set B; that is, $f : A \to B$. Remember that $|A|$ is the number of elements in A.

Chapter 6

Program Verification

Often we write computer programs that we believe to be correct. Still it would be desirable, especially for important programs, to *know* that they are correct, by proving it. But how would you prove a program correct? This question defines the challenge of **program verification**—a subfield of software engineering. This chapter lays out a predicate logic approach to verification, incorporating special new rules of inference to express our background knowledge of computer programming. The material can thus sharpen your predicate logic skills while demonstrating their relevance.

6.1 The Idea of Verification

When a program compiles successfully, the compiler has, in effect, certified that the program is *syntactically* correct. However, this only means that it consists of permitted symbols in recognized categories that have been strung together in ways that the programming language allows. As an example, for English "Fast trees see" is syntactically correct in that an adjective, "fast," precedes and combines with a noun, "trees," to make a plural subject for the verb "see." However, this is a weak notion of correctness, having nothing to do with whether the sentence means anything. Since trees have neither speed nor sight, the words do not combine in a meaningful way. The sentence is syntactically acceptable, but since it has no meaning we say that it is *semantically* unacceptable.

Semantics is the formal study of meaning. The idea is to introduce notation for the semantics of each kind of programming statement and have these combine to give the semantics of whole programs. Here we take the semantics of a programming statement to be its effect on the values of variables and on the properties of those values, such as being an odd integer, a positive real, or less than another number. We use new inference rules to describe these effects. These rules are language dependent, in that some of the rules for C++ have to be different from those for Perl. However, the rules introduced here are for central concepts, shared by many programming languages.

Our intent is to prove, for a given program, that it not only runs, but actually accomplishes its goal. We begin by specifying that goal—what the program is supposed to compute—in the form of a logical assertion. We also describe in logic the initial state of the program. The process of program verification then consists of repeatedly applying our new inference rules (for the statement types in our programming language) to successive statements in the program until, finally, the inference rule for the last statement allows us to infer the logical assertion that was originally given as the program's goal. In other words, we are trying to prove a theorem of the form "executing the code S when p is known to be true will result in q being true".

This process has actually been automated and used to verify the correctness of relatively small programs, but we are far from achieving that for large real-life programs. The last section of this chapter is a consideration of some of the difficulties in program verification. Now let us see what all this really looks like.

6.2   Definitions

Typically the *proof* that a program is correct is divided into two subproofs. First, one shows the program's **partial correctness**: If the program **terminates**, then indeed it computes what it should. Second, one shows that, in fact, the program terminates. This chapter treats only the first part, proofs of partial correctness, since proofs of termination can be subtle and problematic.

To keep our discussion largely language independent, we constrain our attention to just a few types of statements common to most procedural languages. In particular, in addition to some elementary statements, such as assignment statements, we use the three standard mechanisms for generating structured code out of elementary statements: sequencing of statements ("S_1 ; S_2" for S_1 followed by S_2), conditional statements ("if B then S_1 else S_2"), and iteration statements ("while B do S"). It is worth noting that these last three kinds of statements are the core of structured programming and are also the easiest to prove assertions about. This supports the notion that programmers who use structured programming write code that is most readily shown correct, however informal that proof might be.

We choose to write programming statements not in any real programming language, but in a pseudolanguage that captures key ideas yet keeps us from appearing to rely on the peculiarities of any particular real language. This approach lets us promote clarity of the formulas by stripping away practically all punctuation. It also lets us avoid C's and C++'s use of the equals sign for assignment statements, so that the mathematical equals signs in the proofs are unambiguous. Some may recognize the pseudocode as being Pascal-like. It is worth noting that such a style is still sometimes used in presenting algorithms, even though the Pascal language has slipped from the educational landscape. For example, users of C++ will find it easy enough to read "`while B do S`", for example, as "`while (B) S`". Unlike both languages, we use new-line breaks and indentation where possible to indicate program structure.

We *specify* what a program is supposed to compute by giving two propositions. First, we give the **initial assertion**, which indicates the initial state of the computation. This is a conjunction of propositions about the initial values of the variables used by the program. Second, we give the **final assertion**, which specifies the final state of the computation. This too is a conjunction of propositions—in this case, about the final values of the variables and/or the output of the program. Notice that the specification says nothing about the method used to compute the desired final state; any number of correct programs based on different methods could all be correct.

The notation typically used in program verification is called the **Hoare triple**: $p\,\{S\}\,q$. This notation indicates that if the proposition p is true for the initial state of the code S and, further, S terminates, then q is true for the final state. One could put this into the standard format for inference rules by writing

p is true immediately before S is executed.

S is executed.

_____

q is true when S concludes.

Notice that S need not be just a single statement; in fact, it can be an entire program. We call p the **precondition** and q the **postcondition**. When S is the entire program, then the precondition is the initial assertion and the postcondition is the final assertion.

6.3   Inference Rules

The simplest inference rules are for the elementary statements like the assignment statement. We use "$\Leftarrow$" as the assignment operator, rather than the "$=$" of C and

C++ or the ":=" of Pascal, to emphasize that our reasoning is language independent. With this notation, the general form of an assignment statement is v ⇐ e, where v is a variable and e is an expression like 3 or x+1 or 2*sin(theta). This kind of statement has the following semantics (meaning): Evaluate e and assign the resulting value to v. Here is the rule of inference for assignment statements:

Assignment: $p(e) \{v \Leftarrow e\}\, p(v)$

The idea here is that if the value of e satisfies some predicate p before the statement is executed, then the value of v will satisfy that same predicate afterward (assuming execution terminates). Of course, all variables other than v will retain their values—an observation that may seem too obvious to mention, but that nonetheless is needed.

Example 6.1 Letting p be the predicate ODD, which is true when its argument is odd, permits the following Hoare triples:

$$\text{ODD}(3)\{y \Leftarrow 3\}\text{ODD}(y)$$

$$\text{ODD}(y)\{x \Leftarrow y + 2\}\text{ODD}(x)$$

$$\text{ODD}(x)\{x \Leftarrow x + 1\}\text{EVEN}(x)$$

In the first triple, the precondition, ODD(3), is true from arithmetic and does not really need to be written. Arithmetic steps are often omitted from correctness proofs. Thus, the second triple uses the fact that the sum of 2 and an odd number is odd without bothering to prove or even take note of that fact. In the third triple, it is important to distinguish two different meanings of x. Obviously, x cannot be both odd and even at the same time. The value of x is odd in the precondition, before execution, and it is even in the postcondition, after execution.

To distinguish the values of the variable x at different times, let x_0 be the value of x before execution of the statement and let x_1 be the value afterward. This move allows us to use ordinary mathematical notation; that is, $x_1 = x_0 + 1$, so if x_0 is odd then x_1 must be even. This notation may *look* more complicated, but it clarifies what is really going on, so we use it again shortly.

Inference rules for input and output statements would be similar to the one for assignment. Thus, for a read statement, one might use $p(b_1)$ {read(v)} $p(v)$, where b_1 is the next value in the input buffer. We do not say anything more about input or output.

The rule of inference for the sequencing of statements is:

Sequence:
$$\begin{array}{c} p\,\{S_1\}\,q \\ q\,\{S_2\}\,r \\ \hline p\,\{S_1; S_2\}\,r \end{array}$$

This inference rule is applicable when we have analyzed two successive statements, S_1 and S_2, and have established that q, the *pre*condition of the second, is also the *post*condition of the first. Thus, S_1 establishes what S_2 requires. In such a case, it is correct to conclude that we know the precondition and postcondition for the two-statement sequence as a whole. Note that a sequence is a kind of statement sometimes called a *compound statement*. Therefore, repeated use of this rule on longer and longer compound statements allows us to handle programs of any size.

Example 6.2 Suppose it is known that x must be 1 on entry to the code

   y ⇐ 3; z ⇐ x + y.

Substitute appropriate parts of this code into the sequence rule for the values of S_1, S_2, p, q, and r. You need to use your knowledge of elementary arithmetic and programming to get the postconditions.

$$\begin{array}{lll} (x=1) & \{\; \text{y} \Leftarrow 3 \;\} & (x=1) \wedge (y=3) \\ (x=1) \wedge (y=3) & \{\; \text{z} \Leftarrow \text{x + y} \;\} & (z=4) \\ \hline (x=1) & \{\; \text{y} \Leftarrow 3;\; \text{z} \Leftarrow \text{x + y} \;\} \quad (z=4) & \end{array}$$

Example 6.3 For the compound statement {x ⇐ x + 1; y ⇐ y + 1}, show that if the equality $x = y$ holds on entry to the code it also holds on exit.

$$\begin{array}{lll} (x=y) & \{\; \text{x} \Leftarrow \text{x + 1} \;\} & (x=y+1) \\ (x=y+1) & \{\; \text{y} \Leftarrow \text{y + 1} \;\} & (x=y) \\ \hline (x=y) & \{\; \text{x} \Leftarrow \text{x + 1};\; \text{y} \Leftarrow \text{y + 1} \;\} \quad (x=y) & \end{array}$$

Example 6.3 involves the useful notion of incrementing variables (by 1). Notice that for the two-statement sequence (below the bar), the precondition is the same as the postcondition. Although each of the variables x and y has undergone a change in value, we are able to prove that the relationship of equality between them is maintained by the statement sequence as a whole. Such a relationship is called an **invariant condition** for that chunk of code. This idea is important in the later discussion of loops.

A potential source of confusion in the foregoing example is that we keep using x and y in the pre- and postconditions, but the actual values change as the code proceeds. Therefore, let us use subscripts as we did earlier to distinguish among the different values of the variable x at different times and similarly for y.

x_0 is the value of x at the outset.
x_1 is the value of x between the two statements.
x_2 is the value of x at the end.

Example 6.4 We use the subscript notation to show that $x = y$ is an invariant with respect to the two-statement sequence in Example 6.3. For $x = y$ to be an invariant means that *if* it is true at the outset it will be true at the end. In the subscript notation, that means proving that if $x_0 = y_0$ then $x_2 = y_2$.

From the assignment rule applied to the first statement, we have $x_1 = x_0 + 1$ and since, as noted, other variables are unaffected, $y_1 = y_0$. Similarly, $y_2 = y_1 + 1$ and $x_2 = x_1$. Using all these relationships, we can establish the required result—that $x_2 = y_2$ as follows:

$$x_2 = x_1 = x_0 + 1 = y_0 + 1 = y_1 + 1 = y_2.$$

Here we have yet another opportunity, in this new realm of programming code, to do the kind of thing we have stressed in earlier chapters: show what is really going on behind the scenes by converting an informal discussion into a formal proof. In this case, we restate the key points in the informally stated material of Examples 6.3 and 6.4, incorporating them into a formal proof that clarifies the structure of the argument. Notice that the fourth line of the formal proof is precisely the continued equality at the conclusion of Example 6.4.

Justification

$$[x_0 = y_0] \qquad \text{Assumption}$$

$$x_1 = x_0 + 1 \wedge y_1 = y_0 \qquad \text{Assignment (statement \#1)}$$

$$y_2 = y_1 + 1 \wedge x_2 = x_1 \qquad \text{Assignment (statement \#2)}$$

$$x_2 = x_1 = x_0 + 1 = y_0 + 1 \qquad \text{Repeats; Substitution}$$

$$= y_1 + 1 = y_2 \qquad \text{(continuation)}$$

$$x_2 = y_2 \qquad \text{Substitution (Transitivity of =)}$$

$$(x_0 = y_0) \to (x_2 = y_2) \qquad \to \text{Introduction}$$

$$x = y \text{ is the invariant} \qquad \text{Definition of Invariance}$$

The next rules of inference are for the conditional statements, involving `if, then` and possibly `else`.

If-Then:

$$(p \wedge B) \, \{S\} \, q$$
$$(p \wedge \neg B) \to q$$

$$\overline{}$$

$$p \, \{\text{if } B \text{ then } S\} \, q$$

If-Then-Else:

$$(p \wedge B) \, \{S_1\} \, q$$
$$(p \wedge \neg B) \, \{S_2\} \, q$$

$$\overline{}$$

$$p \, \{\text{if } B \text{ then } S_1 \text{ else } S_2\} \, q$$

Focusing only on the if–then rule, notice that the first line is a Hoare triple, whereas the second line is an ordinary expression in propositional logic. Also notice that the proposition p appears at the start of each, conjoined with B in one case and with $\neg B$ in the other. Together, therefore, they justify the concluding Hoare triple, in the bottom line, since when p is true, q either becomes true by execution of S when B is true or remains true when B is false by modus ponens using the second line. The if–then–else rule has a similar explanation, left as an exercise.

Example 6.5 For the statement $\{\text{if } \texttt{y < x} \text{ then } \texttt{y} \Leftarrow \texttt{x}\}$, show that from a precondition of $x = 7$ we can ensure a postcondition of $y \geq 7$.

In this if–then statement the condition B is $y < x$ and statement S is the assignment, $\texttt{y} \Leftarrow \texttt{x}$. Notice that $\neg B$, which in this example is $\neg (y < x)$, can be rewritten as $y \geq x$, since y's relation to x must be one of $\{>, =, <\}$. Also p is $x = 7$ and q is $y \geq 7$. Putting all this into the if–then inference rule gives the tableau shown next. Our

goal is the result below the bar; to prove it, we must establish the
two lines above the bar. Each is easy. The first line is true because
x is initially 7 and is copied to y, making y equal to 7, so certainly
$y \geq 7$ (by $\vee$ Introduction, strictly speaking). The second line is all
arithmetic: $y \geq x = 7$, so again $y \geq 7$. By the way, the 7 here could
just as well have been replaced by whatever value x might have at
the outset. Since x is not reassigned in the code, we actually have
the more general conclusion $y \geq x$ after the if–then statement is
executed.

$$(x = 7 \wedge y < x) \qquad \{\, \texttt{y} \Leftarrow \texttt{x} \,\} \qquad\qquad\qquad (y \geq 7)$$
$$(x = 7 \wedge y \geq x) \qquad\qquad \rightarrow \qquad\qquad\qquad\quad (y \geq 7)$$

$$\overline{(x = 7) \qquad\qquad \{\, \texttt{if y < x then y} \Leftarrow \texttt{x} \,\} \qquad (y \geq 7)}$$

Example 6.6 Implement the absolute value function and verify the code.

The code is below the bar. We use the precondition $p = \text{TRUE}$ to
indicate that we need no prior assumptions to draw our conclusion.

$$(\text{TRUE} \ \wedge x < 0) \quad \{\, \texttt{abs} \Leftarrow \texttt{-x} \,\} \qquad\qquad\qquad\quad (abs = |x|)$$
$$(\text{TRUE} \ \wedge x \geq 0) \quad \{\, \texttt{abs} \Leftarrow \texttt{x} \,\} \qquad\qquad\qquad\quad (abs = |x|)$$

$$\overline{(\text{TRUE}) \qquad\qquad \{\, \texttt{if x<0 then abs} \Leftarrow \texttt{-x else abs} \Leftarrow \texttt{x} \,\} \quad (abs = |x|)}$$

6.4   Loop Invariants

The inference rule for the while iteration statement is shown next. The condition
p in the rule is called the **loop invariant**. It is an invariant condition for the loop
body S because when S is allowed to execute—that is, when B is true—p is both a
precondition and postcondition for S.

While: $(p \wedge B) \, \{S\} \, p$

$$\overline{p \, \{\texttt{while } B \texttt{ do } S\} \, (p \wedge \neg B)}$$

A loop invariant is used in the correctness proof of a program in a way that
is strongly analogous to a proof by mathematical induction. To see this, imagine
that we are trying to prove the following theorem: "The assertion p is true after n
iterations of the code S, where $n \geq 0$." An induction proof has a basis, for $n = 0$,

which is trivially true here since it is given that p is true initially. The inductive step of an induction proof would try to show that if p is true after n iterations, then it is also true after $n + 1$ iterations. That is essentially what it means for p to be an invariant condition for S. However, the analogy with induction is limited. An induction proof would show that the theorem is true for all n. However, p is an invariant condition for S only as long as B remains true. Another difference is that the very fact that the loop stops tells us something. In particular, notice the occurrence of $\neg B$ in the postcondition of the While rule. We know that $\neg B$ holds at this point since what terminates the loop is a violation of B.

Example 6.7 Consider the following puzzle. You begin with a bag of M white and N black balls, say 17 white and 10 black balls. Then you repeatedly randomly draw two balls from the bag. If the two balls are of opposite color, you put the white one back. If they are the same color, you put a black ball back in the bag. (Assume you have a large enough supply of extra black balls to always be able to do this.) Note that at each iteration the number of balls in the bag decreases by 1, so eventually there will only be one ball left. The puzzle is: What is the color of that final ball?

It may seem that the answer depends on how the balls are selected at each step, but that is not so. For the particular example of 17 white and 10 black balls, the final ball must be white regardless of the sequence leading to it. This remarkable conclusion is based on consideration of a loop invariant. Let us begin by writing a program for the removal process specified in the puzzle. Note that we include in our pseudolanguage the increment ("++") and decrement ("--") operators from C/C++.

```
                        // m is the current number of white balls.
                        // n is the current number of black balls.
                        // random(2) returns 0 (black) or 1 (white),
                        // with probability 0.5 each.
    m  ⇐ M              // Initialize m to the white supply, M.
    n  ⇐ N              // Initialize n to the black supply, N.
    while (m+n > 1) do   // While at least 2 balls remain...
        a  ⇐ random(2)           // Select a color
        if a=1 then m-- else n--    // to remove.
        b  ⇐ random(2)           // Do it again.
        if b=1 then m-- else n--
        if a=b then n++ else m++    // Put one back.
```

The key step of establishing a loop invariant here involves a proof by *cases*; watch for this. The puzzle states that when the balls are of opposite color the white one is put back, so m, the number of white balls, is unchanged in that circumstance. Consider m in the other cases, and see if we can find an invariant. If both balls are black, one is returned, and so here too there is no change in m. Finally, consider m when two whites are picked. In this case, a black ball is put into the bag, so m has been lowered by 2. Taken together, these considerations show that in the only case where m changes, it changes by 2, so that its oddness (being odd or not) is unchanged at each iteration. Further, the oddness of the white balls at any time, $\text{ODD}(m)$, is the same as it was in the beginning, $\text{ODD}(M)$. We can therefore take the loop invariant p to be the proposition that $\text{ODD}(m) = \text{ODD}(M)$. Note that p must be true before the first iteration since m was initialized to be equal to M. Letting

S be the body of the while loop and
p be the loop invariant, $\text{ODD}(m) = \text{ODD}(M)$ and
B be the condition for staying in the loop, $m + n > 1$,

we have the requirements in place for applying the While inference rule:

$$(\text{ODD}(m) = \text{ODD}(M)) \wedge (m + n > 1)\ \{S\}\ (\text{ODD}(m) = \text{ODD}(M)).$$

Applying the rule gives

$$(\text{ODD}(m) = \text{ODD}(M))\ \{\texttt{while } (m + n > 1)\ \texttt{do } S\}$$

$$(m + n \leq 1) \wedge (\text{ODD}(m) = \text{ODD}(M)).$$

This solves the puzzle: The one ball left at the end is white—so that $m = 1$ and $\text{ODD}(m) = \text{TRUE}$—if and only if there was originally an odd number of white balls, so that $\text{ODD}(M) = \text{TRUE}$.

Strictly speaking, the preceding discussion leaves a minor mathematical loose end: $m+n \leq 1$ seems to allow $m+n = 0$. To sharpen the result, we really need a stronger loop invariant: $(\text{ODD}(m) = \text{ODD}(M)) \wedge (m + n > 0)$. The sum $m + n$ stays above zero because it is required to be at least 2 until exit from the loop and it decreases by exactly 1 in each iteration. It now follows that when the loop terminates, $m+n = 1$ (since $m + n$ is an integer above 0 but not above 1). A similar strengthening of the loop invariant is used in the next example as well.

Example 6.8 Find a loop invariant for the following program and use it to prove that the program computes $n!$.

```
i ⇐ 1;
f ⇐ 1;
while i < n do
        i ⇐ i+1
        f ⇐ f*i
```

How do we come up with a loop invariant? To answer this, we need to think about the *purpose* of the code. Here the purpose is to compute $n!$ in the variable f. Therefore, we take as part of the invariant that $f = i!$ at the start of each iteration. At the time of exit from the loop, we have $i = n$, making $f = n!$. In light of these considerations, we take the loop invariant p to be $(f = i!) \wedge (i \leq n)$. Note that for p to be true initially, we must know that $n \geq 1$. To show p is a loop invariant, we need to argue that:

$$(f = i!) \wedge (i \leq n) \wedge (i < n) \ \{\texttt{i} \Leftarrow \texttt{i} + 1; \ \texttt{f} \Leftarrow \texttt{f} * \texttt{i}\} \ (f = i!) \wedge (i \leq n).$$

Although this can easily be seen to be true, we could break the argument down into two steps and use the sequencing inference rule:

$$(f = i!) \wedge (i \leq n) \wedge (i < n) \ \{\texttt{i} \Leftarrow \texttt{i} + 1\} \ (f = (i - 1)!) \wedge (i \leq n).$$

$$(f = (i - 1)!) \wedge (i \leq n) \ \{\texttt{f} \Leftarrow \texttt{f} * \texttt{i}\} \ (f = i!) \wedge (i \leq n).$$

Once we have established p as a loop invariant, the inference rule gives:

$$(f = i!) \wedge (i \leq n) \ \{\texttt{while (i < n) do S}\} \ (f = i!) \wedge (i \leq n) \wedge (i \geq n),$$

so that when the loop terminates, $i = n$ and so $f = n!$.

Example 6.9 Look for the loop invariant in the following pseudocode, which is for reading characters from input until a nonblank is found.

```
read(c)
while c=' ' do
        read (c)
```

This loop does not seem to have a loop invariant. In fact, the loop invariant p is just TRUE, which is trivially proved. From the inference rule, we conclude

$$(\text{TRUE}) \, \{\texttt{while c = ' ' do read(c)}\} \, (\text{TRUE}) \wedge (c \neq \text{' '}),$$

so that really all we get is $c \neq$ ' '. Note that this is a good example of why these arguments are only for partial correctness. We do not claim to prove that the loop terminates, but only that if it terminates then $c \neq$ ' '.

6.5   The Debate About Formal Verification

For at least 30 years, the value of formal proofs of the correctness of programs has been appreciated. Much research has been done on designing languages and systems that facilitate such proofs, and on the underlying mathematical logic. There has also been much effort to teach programmers to incorporate these techniques as they build software. For example, a major algorithms text lists the explicit and frequent use of loop invariants as a significant improvement in its recent new edition. There is clear benefit to verifying the individual algorithms that are the building blocks of modern software.

Work on correctness proofs in major systems, however, has had only limited success. No large or even moderate-sized software projects have been formally proved to be correct. Additional reasons have been put forward for not using these techniques:

- They are too sophisticated for most programmers.

- They lead to straightforward algorithms, stifling creativity.

- They assume the specifications are correct when, in fact, the major source of real-life errors is in the specifications.

- They prove the underlying algorithm is correctly implemented, but the program runs on a complicated collection of hardware and software components, which may or may not be correct.

The hope is that the process can be automated since the inference rules can be applied mechanically. However the invention of the various preconditions, postconditions, and loop invariants seems to involve the programmer to some degree.

The good news is that knowledge of formal verification techniques helps *inform* the programmer even when only informal verification is being practiced. We already mentioned that structured programming principles derive from the desire to create code that is easily (either formally or informally) proved correct. Similarly, all good programmers document their subroutines with the preconditions and postconditions for that code (i.e., what is known about the parameters and about what the subroutine returns). In general, a good programmer always knows and documents at key points the state of the program—that is, the things that must be true about the values of important variables.

Finally, a note about partial correctness versus correctness. It usually is not difficult to argue that a program, or a section of code, will terminate. For example, the puzzle with balls certainly halts after $M + N - 1$ iterations. However, it is a deep result (from Turing Machine theory) that there cannot be a single technique that always allows us to decide if a program will terminate. (This is known as the "Halting Problem" and is discussed in Section 14.8.)

Exercises

6.1 The sequence rule could be used more widely and still be correct if it only required the postcondition of S_1 to *imply*, not to equal, the precondition of S_2. Express this revised rule formally.

6.2 Here is a simple piece of pseudocode that has the effect of replacing x by its absolute value. The precondition is provided; it states that all we know at the outset is that x is a real number. One could leave this out, but strictly speaking it is necessary, to guarantee that the less-than relation and the unary minus operator will be meaningful.

$$\text{REAL}(x) \quad \{\text{if } (\text{x} < 0) \text{ then x} \Leftarrow -\text{x}\} \quad [\text{ the postcondition }]$$

(a) Note that the variable x occurs three times in the pseudocode. Use x_{i-1} and x_i to distinguish between the values of x before (x_{i-1}) and after (x_i) the execution of this statement when it is the ith statement in a program. Copy the statement, replacing each occurrence of x as either x_{i-1} or x_i depending on which is appropriate.

(b) Continuing part (a), complete the Hoare triple by doing two things. First, copy down the given precondition. Second, drawing on your knowledge of what this piece of code accomplishes, write down an appropriate postcondition.

(c) Write down the rule of inference for the kind of statement used in this example.

(d) One way to show that the postcondition you gave as your answer to part (b) is justified by the rule of inference you gave in part (c) is to state what expressions in part (b) correspond to p and q in the pre- and postconditions, and to B and S in the IF statement, within the rule of inference. Referring to the if–then inference rule in Section 6.3, give the values of p, q, B, and S in this example.

6.3 Here is another piece of code, this one being a compound statement. Answer the same questions—(a), (b), (c), and (d)—as in Exercise 6.2 with the following differences. Use S_1 and S_2 as they are used in this chapter in the inference rule for compound statements. Use p, q, and r as pre- and postconditions as in the text. Use x_0 and y_0 in the precondition of the first statement, p; use x_1 and y_1 as well as x_2 and y_2 in a way that is appropriate, given the discussion of x_{i-1} and x_i in Exercise 6.2.

$$\{x \Leftarrow x + 1; y \Leftarrow y + 1\}$$

6.4 For this code, present a loop invariant and prove it.

```
i ⇐ 0;
s ⇐ 0;
while i < n do
    i ⇐ i+1
    s ⇐ s+i
```

6.5 Suppose that $s = i^2$ and you increase s by an amount i, increment i by 1 and again increase s by i.

(a) Show that the relation $s = i^2$ holds again at the end of the three operations described.

(b) Use this idea to write pseudocode for a program that computes squares of positive integers.

(c) Present a loop invariant for the loop in your answer to (b) and prove its invariance.

Chapter 7

Logic Programming

A good way to appreciate the precision and power of predicate calculus as a system for representing ideas is to watch it in action as the basis of a **logic programming language**, such as Prolog. This chapter focuses on the logic-like parts of Prolog, but also touches on some other capabilities, like data structures, arithmetic, and input/output, that are needed for practical programming.

Prolog lets you make assertions in predicate logic. These can be particular facts about individual objects or general statements about relationships among concepts. Then you can pose questions to the Prolog processor and it provides answers on the basis of what it can figure out or infer from what you have asserted. It does so by a **deductive inference** procedure consistent with what you have learned about predicate calculus. We touch lightly on how this process is carried out.

7.1   The Essence of Prolog and Its Relation to Logic

Three unusual and significant characteristics of Prolog are its relationship to logic, its **interactive** style, and its **declarative** nature. Although distinct, the three properties are related in a way that makes Prolog a powerful tool for rapid prototyping. That is, they can help a Prolog programmer get a working initial version of a program that represents complex concepts.

A Prolog interaction begins with a question—called a **query**—typed in by the user. This might be an end user, but here we envision a developer testing a piece of a new program. Then Prolog (strictly speaking, the Prolog interpreter) provides an answer to the query on the basis of some code that has been loaded for testing. This is a particularly convenient approach to informal testing.

Moreover, the code is simple in appearance because of its logical and declarative nature. Prolog is a declarative language in that you just state—or **assert**—what you know in a form equivalent to expressions of predicate logic. In the old imperative languages like Fortran and C, it is necessary to write many procedures to get things done. This is true even for languages like C++ that support some object-oriented techniques. In contrast, a Prolog program does not need to specify the procedure that puts its logical facts and rules to use. Instead, the Prolog processor supplies an **inferencer**—that is, a procedure for carrying out logical inferencing. (The programmer does exert some control over procedure by specifying rule ordering and by some advanced techniques.) The programmer, relieved of the need to write a procedure, can then focus better on the concepts in the subject matter of the application.

The assertions you can make in Prolog are of two varieties, **facts** and **rules**. Facts describe the properties of particular objects—which may be things, people, institutions, and so on—and the relationships between/among those objects. Rules apply more broadly and are used to infer new information. Let us look at an example with both facts and rules.

> **Example 7.1** Here are three facts about specific individuals and two
> rules about family relationships in general.
>
> ```
> parent(mary,john).
> female(mary).
> parent(ann,mary).
> mother(X,Y) :- parent(X,Y), female(X).
> grandparent(X,Y) :- parent(X,Z), parent(Z,Y).
> ```
>
> The first fact is intended to mean that someone named Mary is a
> parent of someone named John, and the second that Mary is female.
> These two facts together with the rule for `mother` will allow Prolog to
> tell us—when we ask it—that Mary is the mother of John. Of course,
> as in other programming languages, the use of English words to name
> the symbols has no significance to Prolog, although it may be helpful
> to human beings who read your program. Thus, the constant symbol
> `mary` can represent someone named Ma Ry or, for that matter, John.
> When typing Prolog facts and rules, be sure to avoid blanks between
> the predicate and the left parenthesis; blanks are okay elsewhere.

Each fact in Example 7.1 consists of a predicate with suitable arguments. This notation is like that of predicate logic except that there must be a period ("`.`") at the end. Prolog rules are also directly related to predicate logic, but the notation disguises that relationship quite a bit more than in the case of facts. First, variables like X, Y, and Z here are capital letters (or begin with a capital), whereas predicates like parent and constants like mary begin with lowercase letters. Prolog's operator symbols differ considerably from those in logic. The symbol ":-" means implication, but from right to left, opposite to the direction for predicate logic. You might think of it as a backward implication with a "←" symbol. Also, you can read ":-" as the English word "if." Each of the rules in Example 7.1 has two propositions to the right of the ":-" separated in each case by a comma. The comma can be read as "and" since it corresponds to "∧" in logic. Later we use a semicolon—read as "or"—to correspond to "∨".

Yet another way in which Prolog concepts resemble those of predicate logic but differ in notation is that each rule in Prolog is understood to begin with universal quantifiers on all of its variables. Putting all this together, and using the second rule in Example 7.1 as an example, we can reverse the implication and put in the quantifiers and ∧ sign to get the corresponding statement in predicate logic:

$$\forall X : \forall Y : \forall Z : \text{PARENT}(X, Z) \wedge \text{PARENT}(Z, Y) \rightarrow \text{GRANDPARENT}(X, Y)$$

A good way to read the Prolog version of this rule is as follows: To prove that X is the grandparent of Y, one proves that X is a parent of some Z and also that the same Z is a parent of Y. This is allowed for any values of X and Y given as input and for any Z that makes both parts of the statement true.

Having examined assertions—both facts and rules—it is time to turn to the question–answer part of Prolog. The assertions in Example 7.1 enable the Prolog inferencer to answer a variety of questions. For example, just the fact parent(mary, john) by itself lets us get answers not only to "Is Mary a parent of John?", but also to "Who is a parent of John?", "Who is Mary a parent of?", "Who is a parent of whom?", "Is Mary a parent?", and more. Using the rules of Example 7.1, Prolog can also give the correct answer to the likes of "Who is the mother of John" and "Is anyone a grandparent?" We will soon see what such questions look like in a form that Prolog can use.

7.2   Getting Started Using Prolog

Using Prolog is easy. As mentioned before, an important aspect of Prolog is that it is typically used interactively, with an interpreter rather than a compiler. This section is intended to give you a sense of what a Prolog session is like. In a typical Unix system, you can enter Prolog by typing "prolog", but before you start anything be

sure you know how to stop. In many implementations, you can stop by using the
input "`halt.`" — without quotes, but you do need to include the period and the
return (or enter).

Example 7.2 If the system prompt is "`=>`" and the Prolog prompt is
"`| ?- `" then the shortest possible session looks like this.

```
=> prolog
      [startup message from the software company]

| ?- halt.
=>
```

Before starting the Prolog interpreter, you should prepare a file containing some
facts and rules using your favorite editor. Then once you have started, you can get
those facts and rules into the session by means of the built-in predicate `consult`,
which takes a file name as its one argument. This predicate is understood as a
query about whether the file is loadable and also as a request to load it. So the
Prolog response is "**yes**" and the loading of the file takes place as a side-effect.
It is also possible to make assertions during a session using the special predicate
`assert`, but this is *not* recommended in general. If the file named `afile` contains
`parent(mary,john)`, the following have the same effect:

```
| ?- consult(afile).
| ?- assert(parent(mary,john)).
```

So let us say you have created a file called `family` containing the three facts and
two rules in Example 7.1. You have started a Prolog session and loaded the file.
Now you are ready—and able—to enter queries and receive answers based on the
facts and rules you have loaded.

Suppose you start with the query `parent(mary,john)`. Since this is identical to
one of the three facts you just loaded, it is not surprising that Prolog prints `yes` as its
response as shown in Example 7.3. In contrast, when you enter `parent(john,ann)`,
Prolog prints `no` because it is not among the facts you loaded, and your rules are
no help since they do not have the `parent` predicate on the left side. The same can
be said for the query `parent(bea,cal)`.

Example 7.3 What do queries about facts look like within a session?

```
| ?- consult(family).
yes
| ?- parent(mary,john).
yes
| ?- parent(john,ann).
no
| ?- parent(bea,cal).
no
```

As you look at the short Prolog session in Example 7.3, keep in mind that it is you, as the user, who has caused each new line to start by typing return (or enter). Some of these new lines come after your own query. (Remember that the period is part of your query.) Others come after Prolog's "yes" or "no" answer. All the material you type in must end with a period. Any time you hit return without remembering the period, just type a period and return again.

Example 7.4 Can Prolog give correct affirmative answers about a predicate for which there are no facts?

Yes. For the predicate **mother**, there is a rule but no facts. When Prolog is given the following query, it initially fails to find a directly relevant fact, but then proceeds to make use of the **mother** rule and gives the correct answer. Later we see just how Prolog manages to arrive at answers to this and even more difficult queries.

```
| ?- mother(mary,john).
yes
```

Example 7.5 What happens when a variable appears in a query?

The Prolog inferencer tries to prove that there are answers by finding suitable values for the variable. In simple examples, the Prolog variables correspond to the question words "who" and "what" in English. The following queries mean "Who is a mother of John?" and "Who is Mary a mother of?" (or "Whose mother is Mary?"). Note that we say "Who is *a* mother of John?", rather than "Who is *the* mother of John?", since the information given to Prolog does not rule out having more than one mother.

```
| ?- mother(X,john).
X = mary
yes
| ?- mother(mary,X).
X = john
yes
```

Example 7.6 Suppose you put variables in both positions?

Prolog again seeks suitable values for variables. With two variables, the corresponding English question is awkward but still understandable. For example, the query below asks "Who is a mother of whom?" or "Who is whose mother?" After receiving one answer, the user can request another by typing a semicolon (;) before $\boxed{\text{return}}$, as shown here. Typing additional semicolons yields additional answers if they exist. To get an example with multiple answers, we first assert the additional fact that Ann is female. If you keep typing semicolons until there are no more answers, Prolog ultimately prints "no," meaning "no more."

```
| ?- assert(female(ann)).
| ?- mother(X,Y).
X = mary, Y = john
yes;
X = ann, Y = mary
yes;
no
```

Example 7.7 Can I ask who is a grandparent without asking for a grandchild?

Yes, you can. Prolog has **anonymous** variables whose values are not reported. Anonymous variables have names that begin with the underscore character, "_", and need not have any additional characters. Thus, the query grandparent(P,_) asks if any object P is a grandparent of any object "_", but reports only the value of P. Since grandparent (like mother) is a predicate for which no facts have been asserted, Prolog invokes the grandparent rule to get started. Ultimately, it finds the correct answer, but prints a value only for

Prolog interaction	Paraphrase in English	Comments
`| ?- female(X).` `X = mary`	Who is female?	Value of named variable is given.
`| ?- female(_).` `yes`	Is anyone female?	Prolog is silent about "_".
`| ?- parent(X,john).` `X = mary`	Who is a parent of John?	
`| ?- parent(_,john).` `yes`	Is anyone a parent of John?	

Figure 7.1: Prolog queries and the corresponding questions in English.

the **named** variable, not the anonymous one. In English, this reads, "Who is a grandparent?"

```
| ?- grandparent (P,_).
P = ann
yes
```

We have now seen that the Prolog processor responds to queries in the form of predicates with three different kinds of arguments: constants like "mary", ordinary named variables like "X", and anonymous variables ("_"). A named variable in a query is printed out with its substitution value so that it has the effect of English words like "who" and "what". In contrast, there is no output provided for anonymous variables. Another difference between named and anonymous variables is that a named variable must take the same particular value throughout a clause, but each occurrence of "_" is treated as a different variable, so two occurrences of it do not necessarily have the same value, although they *may*, just as two different named variables *may* have the same value. Figure 7.1 shows Prolog at work on queries with one or another of the two kinds of variables. Then Figure 7.2 moves to some more challenging examples querying two variables at once. Included with each query is a paraphrase in English. You should check that "who" always corresponds to a named variable. The answers are based on the rules and facts of Example 7.1.

Prolog interaction	Paraphrase in English	Comments

`| ?- parent(_,X).`
`X = mary;`
`X = john`
	Who has a parent?	Semicolon to get another answer.

`| ?- parent(X,Y).`
`X = ann, Y = mary;`
`X = mary, Y = john;`
 	
`no`
	Who is a parent of whom?	Prolog gives x and y values.
		On request, Prolog gives
		    another answer
		Now there are no more answers.

`| ?- parent(X,X).` `no`	Who is his/her own parent?	

Figure 7.2: Two-variable queries in Prolog and English.

7.3   Database Operations in Prolog

You have seen several of the most important aspects of Prolog: its facts and rules, their declarative form and its similarity to logic, how to interact in a Prolog session using queries in several formats, and how these queries relate to varied and useful questions in ordinary English. To provide some practice with this knowledge while emphasizing its significance, we now put it to work in the world of databases.

Database management systems play a central role in the modern world, allowing individuals and organizations to store, manipulate, extract, and report information with a convenience and volume that would have astounded most people a generation ago. In this section, we introduce the three fundamental operations of the dominant database model and show how to express each of them in Prolog. The ease with which this can be done reflects a conceptual tie between logic and databases. Note, however, that Prolog is not a good language for the actual implementation of a full database system.

Although there are several ways to organize databases, we confine attention to relational databases, which are by far the most widely used. The main construct for representing data in this type of database is the **relation**. It may seem obvious that a relational database would use something called a *relation*, but it is perhaps a bit surprising that this word that is so familiar in a management context can be correctly understood here in terms of its mathematical definition.

Several concepts that were introduced in earlier sections have a role in the present discussion. Foremost among these is the notion of a relation, first mentioned back in Chapter 1. We assemble these ideas here with their definitions edited to emphasize the relationships among them. In particular, look for the similarities in the definitions of a *truth set*, *Prolog facts*, and a *database relation*.

- **Tuple**: a sequence, which may be a singleton, like (a), a pair, like (a, b), a triple, (a, b, c), and so on (see Section 1.2).

- **Cross-Product**: the set of all tuples whose successive elements come from the corresponding sets in that cross-product. This definition allows for a cross-product of a single set; its members would be singletons (see Section 1.2).

- **Predicate**: a function from a set, which may be a cross-product of sets, to the logical constants, $\mathcal{B} = \{\text{TRUE, FALSE}\}$ (see Section 4.1).

- **Truth Set** of a predicate: the set of elements or tuples for which the predicate is true (see Section 4.2).

- **Prolog Facts** for a predicate: assertions specifying tuples for which the predicate is true (see Section 7.1).

- **Relation**: a set of tuples that is a subset of the cross-product of sets. See Section 1.4.

- **Database Relation**: a relation (in the preceding mathematical sense) in which the tuples specify what is true.

- **Database Schema**: a specification of the structure of a database relation, giving a name for it, the sets that are components of its cross-product and the data type of each set. It plays the same role as the declaration for a record or structure in an ordinary high-level programming language.

Example 7.8 Let "EMPINFO" be a three-place predicate for employee information. Its first argument is an employee's five-digit identification number, the second is the year that employee joined the company, and the third is the company work unit to which he or she belongs. Thus, it might be the case that EMPINFO$(34567, 1998, unit23)$ is TRUE. Letting $Idnum$ be the set of all possible identification numbers, $Year$ the set of years, and $Unit$ the set of work units, we express this predicate's mapping as EMPINFO : $Idnum \times Year \times Unit \to \mathcal{B}$.

Corresponding to this EMPINFO predicate there is also a *relation* that consists of all the triples that—like (34567, 1998, *unit23*)—are in the truth set of the EMPINFO predicate. Suppose that a relation has four such triples. It is usual and convenient to present the corresponding database relation in the form of a table as shown here.

Idnum	Year	Unit
34567	1998	unit23
34612	2000	unit23
33927	1991	unit06
33825	1987	unit08

We are now in a position to get specific about Prolog. The initial steps, creating a file of facts and loading that file into a Prolog session, are done in the usual way. Each fact is a predicate with constants as arguments; e.g., `empinfo(34567, 1998, unit23)`. As a warmup exercise, we print out this database by creating a suitable Prolog query:

```
empinfo(X,Y,Z).
```

Three fundamental operations on relational databases are select, project, and join. The **select** operation chooses some of the rows on the basis of their contents in particular columns. Suppose we wish to select and print out the rows having *unit23* as the unit. Two Prolog queries for doing this are shown here:

```
empinfo(X,Y,unit23).
empinfo(X,Y,Z), Z = unit23.
```

The first query plugs the desired value directly into the appropriate argument position of `empinfo`. In the second query, we achieve the same result by using a variable in that position and then explicitly constraining it to be equal to—actually to unify with—the desired value.

As another example of the select operation, suppose we want all the rows with a year before 1995. The following query does this. Notice that to express a constraint other than having a specific value, we need a format like the second—not the first—of the two foregoing queries about *unit23*.

```
empinfo(X,Y,Z), Y < 1995.
```

It is also possible to write a rule that confines attention to these earlier years, yet retains information about all the columns of the database. The following rule for `early_empinfo` does exactly this. After the rule comes a query that uses it, followed by the response from Prolog.

```
early_empinfo(X,Y,Z) :- empinfo(X,Y,Z), Y < 1995.

| ?- early_empinfo(X,Y,unit23).
no
```

The **project** operation chooses columns. (To see why the choosing of columns is called *projection*, think of a point (x, y, z) in three-dimensional space being projected vertically to the point (x, y) in the two-dimensional plane.) Recall that the choice of rows was based on particular values in the table, but the choice of columns is based only on the labels at the top of the table. Next are Prolog rules for two projections. The rule for `year(Y)` selects only the second column, which contains the years in which current employees have been hired. The query "`year(Y).`" (or "`year(X).`" for that matter) then extracts those entries one at a time if the user keeps hitting the semicolon key. The second Prolog rule selects the last two columns, thereby restricting attention to year-and-unit combinations. These can be printed out using the query "`year_unit(Y,Z).`" and then using semicolons to continue.

```
year(Y) :- empinfo(_,Y,_).
year_unit(Y,Z) :- empinfo(_,Y,Z).
```

A relational database is a collection of relations, but up to now our database has contained just the one relation, EMPINFO. We now introduce a second relation and show how relations can be used together. The new relation, MANAGES, associates each work unit with its manager. (To avoid ambiguity, one should use managers' employee numbers rather than their last names, but the way we have done it here is easier to follow.)

Unit	Manager
unit06	Nguyen
unit23	Smith
unit17	Lee

We are now ready for the **join** operation. Actually, there are several related versions of joins, but we do not distinguish among them. Our one example concerns the so-called "natural join." Notice that our two relations have a field in common, the "*Unit*" field. Via this field, we can relate other fields in the two relations as shown in the next table. In effect, the new table merges the two relations on the *unit* field where possible—that is, wherever the two have the same value in that field. The new table has two rows for *unit23*, but none for *unit08* and *unit17*, one of which lacks a manager and the other, employees.

Idnum	Year	Unit	Manager
34567	1998	unit23	Smith
34612	2000	unit23	Smith
33927	1991	unit06	Nguyen

The following Prolog rule expresses the same ideas. As with "EMPINFO," we reuse the relation name "MANAGES" to name the Prolog predicate. More significant is how the requirement of identical values in the *unit* field is implemented by means of a shared variable (Y) in Prolog.

```
empinfo_aux(W,X,Y,Z) :- empinfo(W,X,Y), manages(Y,Z).
```

This concludes our brief demonstration of the similarity between predicate logic as implemented in Prolog and the relational algebra that plays a key role in many database management systems. The latter field is of course much more complex than what appears here. Built on top of relational algebra are query languages designed to let a user request needed information without having to understand even the logical organization of the data. Beneath the level we have been discussing, there are issues of storing the data in real physical devices and providing access to it for multiple users in overlapping time frames. These are topics for a more specialized and comprehensive treatment of the subject.

7.4   The General Form and a Limitation of Prolog

To explore just what we can do with Prolog, let us look at the general structure of rules. First, to broaden our range of examples, consider the rule for `ancestor` presented in the next example. This rule is more complicated than the rules for `mother` and `grandparent` in Example 7.1 in that it provides two ways, not just one, to prove that the predicate holds.

Example 7.9 The first part of this ancestor rule says that anyone who is your parent is one of your ancestors. The second says that your ancestors also include the parents of your ancestors. Each part of the rule ends with a period and is called a **clause**. So `ancestor` is a two-clause rule in contrast to the one-clause rules for `mother` and `grandparent`. The rule is accompanied by bits of explanation, each beginning with the Prolog comment symbol, "%".

```
ancestor(X,Y) :-   % First clause: X is an ancestor of Y if
    parent(X,Y).    %                X is a parent of Y.


ancestor(X,Y) :-   % Second clause:X is an ancestor of Y if
    parent(X,Z),    %                X is a parent of someone (Z)
    ancestor(Z,Y).  %                who is an ancestor of Y.
```

In general, a Prolog rule is a set of Prolog clauses, perhaps just one, sometimes two as in this case, and possibly more. Each clause has the form of a backward implication with exactly one proposition on the left side of the ":-" symbol. The right side, however, is more flexible: It may have any number of propositions (0, 1, 2, 3, ...). For example, each of the earlier rules—mother and grandparent—is a single clause with two propositions on the right side, whereas one of the ancestor clauses has just one proposition on the right. Later on, we see that one of the clauses for the different rule has *no* propositions on the right. Here is the general form of a Prolog clause:

$$P :- Q_1, Q_2, \ldots, Q_n.$$

The symbols P, Q_1, and so on are propositions, so each of them may actually stand for a predicate with one or more arguments, as in every example so far. For instance, to get the rule mother in Example 7.1, the proposition P here in the general pattern would be replaced by mother(X,Y)—that is, a predicate with two arguments— Q_1 and Q_2 would be, respectively, parent(X,Y) and female(X). To focus on what is true of all rules in general, it is convenient to use the general form, ignoring the more detailed level of specific predicates and arguments.

A clause in the general form may be read as "P is true if all of the Q_i are true." Note that when $n = 0$ the list of Q_i disappears, and for the case of $n = 1$ it becomes just Q_1. For $n = 2$, it is Q_1, Q_2, and so on. P is called the head of the clause and $Q_1, Q_2, \ldots, Q_n$ constitute the body. Now translating this form into the usual symbols of logic, with the implication symbol pointing to the right, we get the following propositional form, called a **Horn clause**.

$$[Q_1 \wedge Q_2 \wedge \cdots \wedge Q_n \rightarrow P]$$

By the way, it is possible for a Prolog program to include a clause with *nothing* on the left side like this: " :- $Q_1, Q_2, \ldots, Q_n$". This is not a rule, but is just used to get something done. As usual, the Prolog inferencer must prove the propositions on the right to establish what is on the left, although in this case there is nothing on the left to establish. In the following example, the propositions on the right are "nl", which simply starts a new line of output, and "write", which writes whatever single-quoted material is provided.

Example 7.10 Suppose file h contains two parent facts, parent(a,b) and parent(b,c), followed by ":- nl, write('parent data loaded from file h.').". What happens when this file is loaded?

In addition to the facts becoming available within your session, the "nl" starts a new line and the "write" causes the single-quoted material to appear on the screen.

```
=> prolog
     [startup message from the software company]

| ?- consult(h).
parent data loaded from file h.
yes
```

It is important to ask about the consequences of the restrictions in the Prolog general form $P :- Q_1, Q_2, \ldots, Q_n$. On the face of things, it looks like we are allowed conjunction operators but not disjunctions on the right side (remember that the commas are really $\wedge$ signs) and neither operator on the left. Note, however, that there is no limit on the number of clauses, so we can write things like this:

$$P \quad :- \quad Q_1.$$
$$P \quad :- \quad R_1, R_2.$$

The effect of these two clauses together (which are exactly the form of the rule ancestor) is that P can be proved by Q_1 *or* by the combination of R_1 and R_2. So we really do have the ability to express disjunction on the right, at least implicitly. In fact, Prolog lets us do so explicitly using a semicolon (";"), so the preceding clauses are equivalent to $P :- Q_1 ; R_1, R_2$. In correspondence with propositional logic, the semicolon (the $\vee$ operator) has lower precedence than the comma (the $\wedge$ operator).

Example 7.11 Here the ancestor rule from Example 7.9 is rewritten using a semicolon to mean "or". This version of the rule is equivalent to the earlier one so far as Prolog is concerned.

```
ancestor(X,Y) :- parent(X,Y) ; parent(X,Z), ancestor(Z,Y).
```

It is also possible to use multiple clauses to get the effect of conjunction on the left. Thus, the combination of $P :- R$ with $Q :- R$ would tell us that we can establish both P and Q by proving R. However, in this case, we must use two clauses as Prolog has no special notation for this situation. So now we have both conjunction and disjunction on the right, and we can get the effect of conjunction on the left by using multiple clauses.

When it comes to disjunction on the left, the restriction to Horn clause equivalents really is a restriction. You cannot have a rule for proving a disjunction in Prolog, and there are no disjunctive facts. An example of a disjunctive fact is that Bush is either from Texas or Connecticut. You simply cannot represent this idea in Prolog by directly translating from the appropriate disjunction in predicate logic, $\text{NATIVESTATE}(bush, texas) \lor \text{NATIVESTATE}(bush, connecticut)$. One way to get this idea into Prolog is to introduce a three-argument predicate and write the two facts `native-state(bush,texas,maybe)` and `native-state(bush,connecticut,maybe)`.

Prolog's restriction to Horn clauses makes it fall short of expressing everything representable in predicate logic. That is, there are no rules corresponding to $Q_1 \land Q_2 \land \cdots \land Q_n \rightarrow P_1 \lor P_2$ and no facts of the form $P_1 \lor P_2$. This was a deliberate choice for the sake of efficiency.

Finally, we rewrite the Horn clause shown earlier using the conditional law and then DeMorgan's law to get the forms shown next. The last form is a disjunction of propositions, of which all but one are negated. Since the various facts and rules of a program are all supposed to be true, they constitute one long conjunction of such disjunctions. Thus, a Prolog program is close to being in conjunctive normal form.

$$
\begin{aligned}
[Q_1 \land Q_2 \land \cdots \land Q_n \rightarrow P] &\equiv [\neg(Q_1 \land Q_2 \land \cdots \land Q_n) \lor P] \\
&\equiv [\neg Q_1 \lor \neg Q_2 \lor \cdots \lor \neg Q_n \lor P]
\end{aligned}
$$

7.5 How Prolog Works

To understand how the Prolog processor does logical inference, we first need to look at the **scope** of the variables in Prolog rules. We then step through some examples of how the inference proceeds. Concluding this section is an introduction to the special operator **cut**, for which processing is quite unusual.

To begin our look at the idea of scope, recall the rule `mother(X,Y) :- parent(X,Y), female(X)`. Clearly we want Prolog to require the X to mean the same person throughout one use of the rule. That is, we want it to find that Mary is the mother of John because *she* is female and is *his* parent, not because somebody else is a female parent of yet another person. Similarly, when `grandparent(X,Z) :-` `parent(X,Y), parent(Y,Z)` is used to show that Ann is the grandparent of John, it is necessary to prove things about Ann and John, and not about some arbitrary `X` and `Z`. Moreover, it is necessary to find a single individual, `Y`, satisfying both parent relationships on the right side: someone whose parent is Ann and who also is the parent of John. On the other hand, when proving a `grandparent` relationship, we certainly do *not* have to look at the variables in the rule for `mother`.

The foregoing considerations are part of the issue of the (lexical) **scope** of variable names. Since `grandparent` and `mother` are one-clause rules, it is hard to tell whether to say that scope extends to one clause or one rule. To make that determination, what we need is a two-clause rule, like the one for `ancestor`, repeated here.

```
ancestor(X,Y) :- parent(X,Y).
ancestor(X,Y) :- parent(X,Z), ancestor(Z,Y).
```

If you think of yourself as `Y` in this rule, what it says is that to prove someone is your ancestor, show that he or she is your parent (first clause) or is a parent of one of your ancestors (second clause). Although the two clauses work together, they do *not* need to share variables. In fact, we could change the variables in the first clause to `U` and `V`, making it `ancestor(U,V) :- parent(U,V)`, without changing the way it is processed by the Prolog inferencer. The clause would still mean "to prove that `ancestor` holds for two arguments, prove that `parent` holds for them." Therefore, we conclude that, in Prolog rules, the scope of variable names is one clause. (Note: Scope extends across semicolons, up to a period.)

With scope in mind, we look in some detail at how Prolog carries out its deductive inference on some queries. To match the facts and rules in a program against the questions that are asked, Prolog uses a matching technique called **unification**, which makes sensible use of variables from both the assertion and query sides. A variable from either side can be matched against a constant or variable from the other side, or even against a whole expression. The sequence of events in an inference is governed by a control strategy of depth-first search with backtracking, keeping track of proposed values for variables that arise from attempts at matching. The algorithm is not presented here, but we run through descriptions of how Prolog works on some simple examples.

> **Example 7.12** With the facts and rules of Example 7.1 loaded, what does the Prolog interpreter have to do to handle the query `mother(mary,john)`?

Upon finding that there are no `mother` facts loaded, the processor moves on to trying the `mother` rule. First, the inferencer makes a substitution list for the rule's variables, associating `X` with `mary` and `Y` with `john`. Since substitutions have scope over the entire clause, the right side leads to the subtasks of proving `parent(mary,john)` and `female(mary)`, each of which is then established simply by looking it up among the available facts. Finally, Prolog prints `yes` as its answer.

Example 7.13 Referring again to Example 7.1, how does the Prolog interpreter handle the query `grandparent(ann,john)`, meaning "Is Ann the grandparent of John?"?

This query has the same form as the one in Example 7.12: a predicate with two constants as its arguments. However, the interpreter's processing is a bit more complex here because the rule it uses, for `grandparent`, has *three* variables, one of which must be associated with an entity other than the two in the input.

As in Example 7.12, the variables on the left side of the rule are associated with the input arguments, here `X` with `ann` and `Y` with `john`. Because of scope, these substitutions are used on the right side, giving the subtasks `parent(ann,Z)` and `parent(Z, john)`. Now comes a more subtle use of scope. Since these subtasks came from the same clause, the inferencer must ensure that `Z` gets the same value for each of them. Working on `parent(ann,Z)`, the inferencer now seeks a `parent` fact with `ann` as first argument, which it can do since `parent(ann, mary)` fits this description. As a result, `Z` is now associated with `mary`. To obey scope, the inferencer now narrows the second subtask, requiring `Z` to be `mary` there too. The second subtask thereby becomes merely the confirmation that `parent(mary,john)` is a fact.

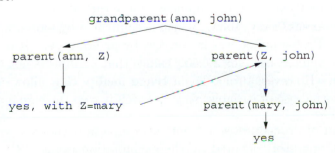

The next example shows how the Prolog processor handles the important idea of **recursion**. For this purpose, let us look back at the `ancestor` rule repeated here. The second clause of the `ancestor` rule is recursive because it expresses `ancestor` in terms of itself.

```
ancestor(X,Y) :-         % First clause: X is an ancestor of Y if
    parent(X,Y).         %                 X is a parent of Y.

ancestor(X,Y) :-         % Second clause:X is an ancestor of Y if
    parent(X,Z),         %                 X is a parent of someone (Z)
    ancestor(Z,Y).       %                 who is an ancestor of Y.
```

> **Example 7.14** Suppose we ask Prolog to prove `ancestor(ann,john)`, having loaded the facts `parent(ann,mary)` and `parent(mary,john)`. To use the first clause of the `ancestor` rule, the inferencer would need to prove `parent(ann,john)`, which is *not* a fact. It must therefore try the second clause. By substituting `ann` for `X` and `john` for `Y` in the second clause and then consulting the right side of that clause, the inference procedure comes up with the subtasks of proving `parent(ann,Z)` and `ancestor(Z,john)`.
>
> The inferencer succeeds at the first of these two subtasks by lookup, finding that `Z` can be `mary`, which alters the second subtask to `ancestor(mary,john)` and makes it the only remaining task. Notice that this is where recursion comes into play: We now have another `ancestor` task that is part of the original one. In this new use of the `ancestor` rule, we are asking about a different pair of arguments than before (`mary` and `john` rather than `ann` and `john`), so its variables must now get fresh values. Keeping the new values of these variables separate and distinct from the original ones is a crucial aspect of Prolog's inference algorithm.
>
> Using the first clause, the inferencer now reduces `ancestor(mary, john)` to `parent(mary,john)`, which is confirmed by look-up. When it finishes, Prolog announces its success by printing **yes**. It does not report the value it used for `Z` (`mary`) since that variable is not used in the query. (However, Prolog has a **trace** facility that allows you to see its internal use of variables as you watch it step through a proof.)

Our discussion of procedure would not be complete without a consideration of the so-called **cut** operator, denoted by the exclamation point: "!". The cut is a special operator for letting the programmer influence the procedure—in violation of Prolog's (mostly) declarative nature. Here is how it works. The inferencer regards a cut as logically true, so it continues to the next proposition on the right side of its clause. However, if a failure occurs later in this clause, after the cut, the inferencer does not go on to try the remaining clauses in the rule.

Here we use a cut for the indispensable purpose of ensuring that two things are different from each other using the Prolog code given next. This rule for the predicate `different` has two objectives: (i) to fail when given two identical arguments, but (ii) to succeed in all other cases.

```
different(X,X) :- !, fail.
different(_,_).
```

Example 7.15 How does Prolog achieve the twin objectives of the `different` predicate?

If you try `different(b,b)`, Prolog matches X to b on the left side, proceeds to the right, succeeds on the cut, continues to `fail` and then does not try the second clause because of the cut. The result is failure.

In contrast, if you try `different(c,d)`, Prolog matches the first X on the left side of the first clause to c and then it tries to match the second X on the left side to d. However, since X is already committed to c, this attempt fails. Processing then proceeds to the second clause, which succeeds with the first anonymous variable ("_") as c and the second one as d.

To see how the predicate `different` can be put to good use, consider the word "sibling," which means someone who shares at least one parent with you. If a pair of people have just one parent in common, they are "half-siblings". If they have two parents in common, they are "full siblings". The next example introduces a predicate that covers both of these concepts, both full siblings and half-siblings. It takes care to avoid letting you be your own sibling. Please note: When using `different`, be sure to put it at the *end* of a rule as in Example 7.16.

Example 7.16 Write a rule for the predicate `sibling` that is true for two people who are siblings of each other.

```
sibling(X,Y) :- parent(Z,X), parent(Z,Y), different(X,Y).
```

7.6   Structures

Like other languages, Prolog has built-in mechanisms for dealing simply with some important data structures. These include lists, which are the topic of the next section, and structured objects, or simply **structures**, taken up briefly here. Prolog structures resemble what are called *structures* or *records* in other programming languages. A Prolog structure consists of a name for a particular kind of structure, followed by parentheses that enclose one or more comma-separated elements. Each element may be a variable, a constant, or another (sub)structure.

> **Example 7.17** Suppose that `person` is a predicate that has a structure
> for each of its arguments like this: `person(names(john,smith),`
> `date(december,3,1970))`, which we take to mean that John Smith
> was born on December 3, 1970. Write Prolog queries that mean
> "What is the birth year of anyone named John with a birthday in
> December?" and "What are the first and last names of anyone born
> in 1970?"
>
> ```
> person(names(john,_), date(december,_,X)).
> X = 1970
> person(names(F,L), date(_,_,1970)).
> F = john, L = smith
> ```
>
> Notice the use of named variables in the positions about which our
> English language questions specifically ask, in contrast to the anony-
> mous variables ("_") for positions that our questions do not refer to.
> If facts had been loaded about several additional people, the user
> could keep getting answers by typing semicolon and $\boxed{\text{return}}$ after
> each answer until no more answers are forthcoming.

7.7   Lists and Recursion

Another data structure, and one of even greater flexibility than structured objects, is the **list**. Lists are important in a wide range of programming applications, especially in artificial intelligence (AI) programming, where they were first developed and extensively used as early as the 1950s, in a pioneering AI program for proving theorems in logic. The Lisp programming language, the only language besides Fortran in continuous use since the 1950s, was actually named for *list* processing. First we look at list representation in Prolog. Then come some simple Prolog programs for the basic list operations of membership, concatenation, adding new elements, and deleting existing ones.

For input and output, a Prolog list consists of its elements separated by commas and enclosed in brackets. The empty list appears as [ ] while [a,b,c] is a three-element list. Another way to write lists comes from the recursive definition of what a list is. A list is a data structure that is either empty or consists of two parts: a *head* and a *tail*. The head of a nonempty list is its first element and the tail is the rest. The tail in turn has to be a list (possibly the empty list). Therefore, Prolog lets us write a list in general with brackets and a vertical bar—that is, as [H|T], where H is the head and T is the tail.

You can see this list notation at work by typing [H|T] = [a,b,c] to the Prolog interpreter. The equals sign in Prolog is the unification (matching) operator. Using only its own built-in capabilities (with nothing loaded by you via consult), Prolog succeeds with this unification by matching the variable H to a and T to the list [b,c]. This also means that [a,b,c] = [a|[b,c]]. Try it! Another wrinkle in the list notation that can be useful at times is the variation that lets us put down the first few elements in the usual way, then a "|", and finally a symbol for whatever is left. Thus, [a,b,c,d,e] matches [a,b|X] with X as [c,d,e].

Now let us create some rules for lists, starting with the idea of whether some item is a member of a given list. The two-argument predicate member should have a rule that makes a query like member(c, [a,b,c,d]) yield a reply of "yes". A strategy for creating such a rule flows from the observation that for an item to be a member of a list it must be either (i) the first element or (ii) a member of the tail. Notice that part (ii) of this description is recursive: It defines member in terms of member. This is acceptable because the arguments get shorter and shorter until we reach a simple successful case or fail. We have already seen recursion at work in the ancestor rule.

Example 7.18 In this rule for member, the first clause succeeds when the item in question is found first in the list. The second clause is a recursive test of whether the item occurs later in the list.

```
member(H,[H|_]).
member(X,[_|T]) :- member(X,T).
```

Notice that the foregoing definition uses named variables like H in some places and the anonymous variable in other places. For example, in the first clause of member, the H appears in two places, thereby *linking* them—that is, requiring both to have the same value. The tail of the second argument does not need to be linked to anything, so it is appropriate to use the anonymous variable. You *can* use a named variable in that position; some Prolog processors issue a warning if you do ("singleton variable"), but the rule still works.

> **Example 7.19** Suppose you want a predicate that can tell you whether its argument is a list. The first clause here looks for the empty list. If that fails, the second one looks for any other list—that is, an arbitrary, nonempty list. The second clause succeeds on any list of length 1 by matching the first underscore to the list element and second underscore to the empty list. For lists of length 2 or more, the second underscore unifies with a list consisting of all elements of the input except the first.

```
list([ ]).
list([_|_]).
```

Whereas `member` and `list` give yes or no answers, the next few list-processing predicates—`append`, `push`, and `delete`—are often regarded as having two inputs in the first two argument positions and operating on them to produce a result that gets associated with a variable in the third argument position. Thus, each of them is a three-argument predicate and not, as you might have expected, a two-argument function. Once defined, however, these predicates can be used in other ways, as shown in Example 7.21 for `append`. We begin with a simpler example, implementing `push`.

> **Example 7.20** Pushing an item X into the beginning of a list L can be accomplished with the following rule for the predicate `push`. The third argument of `push` is a list consisting of X followed by all the elements of L.

```
push(X,L,[X|L]).
```

The `append` predicate is built into some versions of Prolog; when it is not, the recursive rule given here does the job.

> **Example 7.21** For concatenation of two lists to give a third one, we define the relation `append(L1, L2, L3)`, where L1, L2, and L3 are all lists, possibly empty, and L3 is the concatenation of the others. For example, we want the query `append([a,b], [c,d], Result)`.

to report success with the substitution `Result = [a,b,c,d]`. Interestingly, the rule given here can also be used in the other direction so that the query `append(First, [g,h], [d,e,f,g,h])` succeeds and reports `First = [d,e,f]`.

```
append([  ],L,L).
append([X|L1],L2,[X|L3]) :- append(L1,L2,L3).
```

The first clause of this rule indicates that the concatenation of an empty list "`[  ]`" with a list `L` is `L`. The second shows that the concatenation of `[X|L1]` with list `L2` is `[X|L3]`, where `L3` is the concatenation of `L1` and `L2`.

Next we look at deletion. As with **append**, there are three argument positions. The item to be removed appears as the first argument and the list comes second. The third argument is the list that results from removing the designated element. Thus, for the query `delete(a,[b,c,a,g,h],Result)`, Prolog's reply should be `Result = [b,c,g,h]`. This rule is yet another application of the important idea of recursion.

Example 7.22
```
delete(H,[H|T],T).
delete(X,[H|T],[H|U]) :- delete(X,T,U).
```

In Section 7.5 we looked at the actual operation of the Prolog processing mechanism in some detail. We now do the same in the context of list-processing, specifically for an example with **delete**.

Example 7.23 The easiest case is when the element to be deleted appears at the beginning of the list. Suppose the query is:

```
| ?- delete(a,[a,g,h],Result).
```

The Prolog interpreter tries to match the first clause of the rule with `H=a` and `T=[g,h]` and it succeeds, giving as the value of the user's variable `Result = [g,h]`. Now suppose the element to be removed is *not* at the beginning of the list.

```
| ?- delete(a,[b,a,g,h],Result).
```

The Prolog processor begins by trying to match this query to the first clause of the `delete` rule, `delete(H,[H|T],T)`. The matching in the first argument is `H=a`. For the second argument, matching requires `H` to be the first element of the user's list, `[b,a,g,h]`—that is, `H=b`. But `H` is already required to be `a`, so this attempt at matching fails. Prolog therefore moves on and proceeds to try the next `delete` clause,

$$\texttt{delete(X,[H|T],[H|U]) :- delete(X,T,U).}$$

Recall that the user's query is `delete(a,[b,a,g,h],Result)`. Prolog must first match the query to the head of the current clause. It succeeds with `X=a`, `H=b`, `T=[a,g,h]`, and `Result=[H|U]`. This works because, unlike the situation with the first clause, `X` is assigned to `a` and `H` is assigned to `b`, so there are no conflicts. We are off to a good start, but this clause only works if the Prolog processor can also manage to prove the right-hand side, `delete(X,T,U)`. That is, plugging in the matched values of `X` and `T`, we need `delete(a,[a,g,h],U)`.

Prolog takes on the challenge of proving this proposition as if it had come from a user. It consults the first clause of the `delete` rule, and, as in the earlier example, it succeeds immediately, with `U` matched to the tail of the second argument—that is, `U=[g,h]`. If you look back (really as Prolog's recursion unwinds back to the original use of the rule), you see that `Result=[H|U]` and that `H=b`. Thus, along with `U=[g,h]`, the Prolog interpreter concludes that `Result=[b,g,h]`, which is exactly what we want in this case.

If the element to be deleted appears even later in the list, the processing takes longer, but the idea is the same, with repeated recursive use of the second clause and one use of the first clause.

A powerful ingredient of programming in any language is the idea of identifying fundamental concepts and building on them. In list processing, concatenation is a fundamental concept. Having defined `append`, we can use it in rules for other predicates.

Example 7.24 Write a Prolog rule for the predicate `last(E,L)` for determining whether `E` is the last element in the list `L`.

```
last(E,L) :- append(_,[E],L).
```

The concept of reversal can apply to both strings and lists. Here we are interested in lists, but reversing a *string* is of some interest in the study of formal models of language. The next example is about a predicate called `reverse` with arguments that are lists. It checks whether each of these lists is in the reverse order of the other. The idea of a palindrome also applies to both strings and lists. A palindrome reads the same backward and forward. Examples of strings of letters that form palindromic English words are "pop", "deed", "radar", "redder" and "reviver".

Example 7.25 Write a recursive rule for the predicate `reverse` that determines whether two lists are reverses of each other. Use that predicate to write a rule for `palindrome` that determines whether a list is the reverse of *itself*.

```
reverse([ ],[ ]).
reverse([H|T],Result) :- reverse(T,R), append(R,[H],Result).

palindrome(X) :- reverse(X,X).
```

7.8 Built-In Predicates and Operators

The logical core of Prolog has been augmented by its designers to make it a real programming language. This has been done by including a substantial number of built-in predicates and operators that provide normal programming capabilities like the writing of output and that provide programming environment tools like tracing. You have already seen a few. This section briefly introduces a few more and then gathers them all into a couple of tables for convenient reference. Bear in mind, however, that the goal of this chapter is not a thorough treatment of Prolog, but rather to give a sense of how logic can be extended into a declarative approach to programming. For substantial projects, you should consult a Prolog text.

Several built-in predicates take a single argument and determine whether it has some particular type. In the section on lists, we wrote such a predicate ourselves, `list`. Prolog provides `integer` for integers, `float` for floating point numbers and `number` for either. The predicate `atom` succeeds for constant symbols like `a1` and `mary` as well as anything enclosed in a pair of single quotes like `'object-oriented design'` or `'New York'`. These are treated like strings in that they are appropriate arguments to `write`, which writes them to the output. The predicate `atomic` succeeds on all numbers and constant symbols. Example 7.26 shows some simple queries with these predicates. Later, in Example 7.28, we will use `atom` to avoid errors on the wrong kinds of input.

Example 7.26

```
| ?- integer(55).
yes
| ?- float(55).
no
| ?- float(55.0).
yes
| ?- atom(55).
no
| ?- atomic(55).
yes
| ?- atom(abc).
yes
| ?- atom(X).
no
| ?- atom('X').
yes
| ?- atom('Is this a string?').
yes
| ?- atomic(particle).
yes
```

The predicate **name** has two arguments. The first argument is a constant symbol. (These were described in the preceding paragraph.) The second is the corresponding list of ascii codes. As with other Prolog predicates, information can flow in either direction between the two arguments, as the simple queries in Example 7.27 show. This capability comes in handy for manipulations within a string (constant symbol) as in Example 7.28: **name** is used to break up the string at the outset and reassemble it later.

Example 7.27

```
| ?- name(abc,X).
X = [97,98,99]
| ?- name(Y,[97,98,32,99]).
Y = 'ab c'
| ?- name(a,[97]).
yes
```

Example 7.28 Implement a Prolog predicate called `upcase` that, when given a constant symbol as its first argument, converts each lowercase letter in it to the corresponding capital letter.

The ascii codes for the letters "a", "b", ... and "z" are 97, 98, ... and 122. First we create `upcasecode1` to take a single ascii code from lowercase to uppercase, if it happens to be lowercase. Notice the use of the cut (exclamation point). Without the cut, there would be two possible results for numbers from 97 to 122. Next, `upcasecodelist` handles all the codes in a list, using `upcasecode1` on the first and itself (recursively) on the rest. With these auxiliary rules in place, we take on the original task of creating `upcase`, using `name` twice, first to get at the codes and then to reassemble them after `upcasecodelist` has done the main work.

```
upcasecode1(X,Y) :- 96<X, X<123, !, Y is X-32.
upcasecode1(X,X).
upcasecodelist([ ],[ ]).
upcasecodelist([Xh|Xt], [Yh|Yt]) :- upcasecode1(Xh,Yh),
                         upcasecodelist(Xt,Yt).
upcase(X,Y) :- atom(X),
               name(X,Xcodes),
               upcasecodelist(Xcodes, Ycodes),
               name(Y,Ycodes).
```

Finally, we consider `setof` and `bagof`. To see the usefulness of these, suppose you have a Prolog-style database of `parent` facts and you want to know all the people that have our old friend `mary` as a parent. Although it is true that you can do this interactively with the query `parent(mary, X)`, using the semicolon as often as necessary, this approach does not let you do anything with the set of answers within a Prolog program. What we need is a way to collect those answers into a list. That is what `setof` and `bagof` let you do. The difference between them is that `setof` removes duplicates and sorts the list.

Example 7.29 Interactively show some individual's children in two different ways. First, using `parent`, show them one at a time as the multiple answers to a query. Then using `setof`, produce a list containing all of them.

```
| ?- parent(mary,X).
X = bea ;
X = cal ;
X = dot ;
no
| ?- setof(X, parent(mary,X), Y).
X = _9398,
Y = [bea,cal,dot] ;
no
```

Example 7.30 Write Prolog rules that take a string and produce a new
string containing one instance of each vowel of the original string
in alphabetical order. Also write Prolog rules to yield the vowel
substring of a string—that is, all the instances of vowels in the order
in which they appear in the original string.

We create Prolog rules `vowelset` and `vowelbag` using `setof` and
`bagof`, respectively. Each relies on the rule for `member`, repeated
here, and on a list of the codes for the five vowels. Try each of them
on inputs like `mississippi` and `pneumonia`.

```
member(H, [H|_]).
member(X, [_|T]) :- member(X,T).

vowelcode(X) :- member(X, [97,101,105,111,117]).
vowelset(X,Y) :- name(X,Xcodes),
        setof(U, (member(U,Xcodes), vowelcode(U)), Ycodes),
        name(Y,Ycodes).

vowelbag(X,Y) :- name(X,Xcodes),
        bagof(U, (member(U,Xcodes), vowelcode(U)), Ycodes),
        name(Y,Ycodes).
```

Here are the tables of built-in predicates and operators promised earlier. Following the name of each predicate is a slash and the number of arguments it requires. The operators are all binary, and each is used in infix position with one operand before and one after.

Predicate /arguments	What the predicate does
assert/1	is used to assert something during a Prolog session.
atom/1	is true if its one argument is an atom.
atom_char/2	is identical to name/2; see below.
bagof/3	is good for collecting possibly repeated answers.
consult/1	loads a file into a Prolog session. If the argument begins and ends with a single quote, it can be a path. Brackets are an abbreviation for consult.
fail/0	always fails
halt/0	terminates the Prolog session
integer/1	is true if its one argument is an integer.
name/2	succeeds of its two arguments are an atom and the corresponding list of ascii codes.
nl/0	writes a newline to the current output.
notrace/0	turns off tracing
read/1	reads the next Prolog expression in the current input.
see/1	redirects where Prolog looks for input when it reads.
setof/3	is good for collecting non-repeated answers. argument 1: a variable argument 2: an expression involving that variable argument 3: a list of values of the variable for which the expression succeeds.
tab/1	has one argument, which specifies how many blanks to output.
trace/0	turns on the tracing operation.
true/0	always succeeds.
write/1	has one argument that is written to the current output. If there are blanks, enclose everything in single quotes.
!/0	The "cut" succeeds whenever it is reached, but then it prohibits the use of any later clauses in its rule.

Operator	What it does
is	tries to compute the value of an arithmetic expression on its right and unifies the result with the operand on its left.
=	tries to unify (or match) its two operands. This can cause a variable to be associated with an appropriate value.
==	succeeds if it has two identical operands.
=:=	succeeds if it has two numerical operands that are equal.
> and <	greater than and less than.
>= and =<	greater-or-equal and less-or-equal; note the difference in where "=" goes.
=\=	the unequals operator uses a backslash.

Exercises

7.1 Suppose you have a database of people, with facts like those in Example 7.1. Besides parent(X,Y) and female(X), we now include a third predicate for facts, male(X), used to express things like the fact that John is male. Add rules for the following predicates. Where appropriate, make use of a predicate for which a rule has already been specified, either in this chapter or within your solution to this problem.

    (a) father(X,Y)

    (b) grandmother(X,Y)

    (c) child(X,Y) (opposite of parent(X,Y))

    (d) grandchild(X,Y)

    (e) descendant(X,Y)

7.2 Being careful to distinguish the conditional and biconditional operators,

    (a) Write the exact translation of the mother(X,Y) rule into logical notation.

    (b) Define "mother" in logical notation.

7.3 The logic version of the grandparent(X,Y) rule is repeated here.

$$\forall X : \forall Y : \forall Z : \text{PARENT}(X, Y) \wedge \text{PARENT}(Y, Z) \rightarrow \text{GRANDPARENT}(X, Z)$$

It is *not* correct to reverse the direction of the conditional operator. That is, replacing "→" by "←" gives a *false* statement. Explain why it is false and state how it must be changed.

7.4 Consider the following definition of GRANDPARENT

$$\forall X : \forall Z : [\text{GRANDPARENT}(X, Z) \leftrightarrow \exists Y : \text{PARENT}(X, Y) \land \text{PARENT}(Y, Z)]$$

Show that this definition implies the logic version of the `grandparent(X,Y)` rule, which is repeated in the preceding exercise.

7.5 Suppose that the family example (Example 7.1) is extended to include facts about people being married using the predicate `husband`. For example, `husband(bill,ann)` means that Bill is the husband of Ann.

   (a) Write a rule for `wife` in terms of `husband`.

   (b) Write a rule for `spouse` in terms of `husband` and `wife`. Do this both *with* a semi-colon and *without* one.

   (c) Write a rule for `spouse` using only `husband`.

7.6 Using the rules from this chapter and preceding problems as needed, write a rule for `aunt` that takes account of both kinds of aunt: sister of a parent and aunt via marriage to an uncle. Use a semicolon.

7.7 Write a Prolog rule for full siblings—that is, those who share two parents. You now need to use the `different` rule in two ways: as in the `sibling` rule, in Example 7.16, and also to require the two shared parents not to be the same person. (If you test your rule, which you should, be sure to load the `different` rule unless it happens to be built into your version of Prolog.)

7.8 Write a Prolog rule for first cousins using a criterion that says we are first cousins if you have a parent who is a full sibling of one of my parents, but we ourselves are not full or even half-siblings and of course first cousins must not be the same person. Use cut twice to exclude these possibilities. Note that the equals sign ("=") can be used to force unification of two variables. It simplifies matters to use the sibling rule and/or the rule for full siblings from in Exercise 7.7. (When testing your rule, be sure to load any other rules it depends on.)

7.9 Suppose we represent a world of stackable, cubical blocks of identical size by writing facts like `on(a,c)` to mean that block a is resting directly on block c, being in contact with it and supported by it. The predicate `higher` requires only that the first block be somewhere above the second within the same stack. While allowing physical contact, it does not require it, as `on` does. In the situation just described, suppose we add block `j` and have it sit directly on `a`. Then `higher(j,c)` holds, although not `on(j,c)`. Write a recursive rule that expresses `higher` using both itself and `on`.

7.10 Numerical predicates like "$<$" are expressed in Prolog in the familiar infix order used in mathematics, so we can write, for example, "$x < 4$" rather than something like `lessthan(x,4)`. Suppose that `age(John,33)` means that John is 33 years old.

   (a) Write a rule for `olderthan(X,Y)` that is true whenever person X is older than person Y.

   (b) Write a rule for `bigsib(X,Y)` that is true if person X is an older brother or an older sister of person Y.

7.11 Consider an employee database with facts of the form

$$\texttt{employee(730638,dee,hr,8,1998)}.$$

This particular Prolog example encodes the fact that the person with employee number 730638 is named Dee, works in the Human Resources division (expressed "`hr`" in this Prolog implementation) of the company, and was hired in August (the eighth month) of the year 1998. Write queries that extract the information specified below. Assume that the user will have to use repeated semicolons to get multiple answers.

   (a) the names (only) of the people who work in PP (Physical Plant)

   (b) the name and division of each person who joined the company in 1998 or after

   (c) the name of everyone hired in the 10 years ending June, 2000.

7.12 With `employee` facts as in Exercise 7.11, write rules that express the following concepts as Prolog rules related to the relational operators select and project.

(a) Confine attention to an employee's name and where in the organization he or she works.

(b) Confine attention to when people began work.

(c) Confine attention to (all information about) just those employees who are in the Payroll Office, which is expressed as `pay` in the Prolog facts.

(d) Confine attention to employees in Human Resources who joined the organization before 1997.

7.13 In part (a) of the preceding problem, use the built-in Prolog operator `setof` so that all the answers are returned at once and you are not obliged to keep on typing semicolons.

7.14 Along with the Prolog facts of the form `employee(730638,dee,hr,8,1998)`. introduced in Exercise 7.11, assume that we now also have facts about the month and year of an employee's date of birth that look like this: `dob(730638,3,1968)`.

(a) Write a Prolog rule for a new predicate—call it `all_info`—corresponding to a natural join of the `employee` and `dob` tables on the registration number. The result should have seven fields.

(b) Use the predicate `all_info` from part (a) in writing a rule for a predicate that accepts an employee's number and is true if that employee joined the organization during or after the month in which he or she turned 50.

7.15 With `employee` facts as in Exercise 7.11, write rules for the following predicates.

(a) `later(W,X,Y,Z)`, meaning that the month W of year X is later in time than the month Y of year Z. This does not depend on `employee` facts, so it may be useful not only in the next part but elsewhere as well.

(b) `senior_to(X,Y)`, meaning that the employee with number X has worked longer for this firm than the one with number Y. Use the predicate `later`.

(c) `senior_div_mate_of(X,Y)`, meaning that the employees with numbers X and Y are in the same division and X has worked longer for this firm than Y. Use the predicate `senior_to`.

7.16 Let `employs(a,b)` mean that person a owns a firm that employs person b. Note that it is possible to work in your own firm. Write 11 Prolog queries, each having an argument pattern that differs significantly from all of the others. For each of your 11 queries, write down a question in English that expresses the idea of that query.

One kind of significant difference between argument patterns is having a different kind of argument—constant versus named variable versus anonymous variable ("_")—in one of the argument positions. When two argument positions both have a constant (or both have a named variable) there is a significant difference between the case in which those two constants (or named variables), are the same and the case of them being different.

7.17 Implement and test Prolog rules for list predicates each having two arguments as follows:

(a) In the predicate `delete_first2`, the second argument can be found by deleting the first two elements of the first argument. Thus, Prolog should answer "yes" to `delete_first2([a,b,b,c,c],[b,c,c])`.

(b) In the predicate `delete_last2`, the second argument can be found by deleting the last two elements of the first argument. Thus, Prolog should answer "Result = [a,b,b]" to `delete_last2([a,b,b,c,c], Result)`.

(c) In the predicate `delete22`, the second argument can be found by deleting the first two and the last two elements of the first argument. Thus Prolog should answer "yes" to `delete22([a,b,c,d,e],[c])`.

7.18 Consider the Prolog rule `pal2(Z) :- append(X,Y,Z), reverse(X,Y).` for some, but not all, palindromes.

(a) For which palindromes does `pal2` fail?

(b) Why must `pal2` fail in these cases?

7.19 All of the recursive examples in the text involved direct recursion—that is, a predicate calling itself. In this exercise, you are asked develop two predicates that call each other, so that each calls itself not directly but indirectly via the other. Specifically, write predicates `evenlength` and `oddlength` that determine, respectively, whether the length of a list is even or odd, by calling each other on shorter and shorter lists—shorter by 1 each time. The resulting indirect recursion bottoms out when a call is ultimately made with the empty list, which should succeed for `evenlength` since zero is an even number, but not for `oddlength`. Hint: Use `evenlength([ ]).` as the base case.

7.20 Project:

Facts: Create a collection of Prolog facts using *only* the predicates `person` and `family`. They may concern any real or fictitious family, possibly your own. The arguments of `person` are a person's name, sex, and date of birth, [e.g., `person(mary,female,1988)`]. The arguments of `family` are a husband, a wife, and a list of offspring (children), [e.g., `family(bill,ann, [mary,lee])`]. For a couple with no offspring, the third argument is the empty list, `[ ]`. The purpose of these assignments is to extend the concept of a family by adding predicates with rules. The usual family relationships can be expressed in terms of parenthood, marriages and the sexes of individuals.

Some Predicates: Create a file with some facts about specific persons and families. Create another file with rules for the following six predicates: `sex`, `dob`, `husband`, `wife`, `mother` and `father`. Start a Unix script; start Prolog; load both files; enter one or two queries for each predicate; exit from Prolog; and exit from the script. You may edit your script *only* by adding your name at the beginning; adding empty lines for ease of reading; and entering clearly marked comments.

You may assume permanent marriages, so that one person is the sibling of another if they have (at least) one parent in common. Without this assumption, there would be half-sisters, ex-sons-in-laws, and so on. To begin, use the anonymous variable "_" (the underscore character) to create rules for `sex(X,Y)` as `person(X,Y,_)`, and similarly for a person's date of birth, `dob`. This technique also enables you to write rules for `husband` and for `wife`, working with the `family` predicate.

When it comes to `mother` (or `father`), you need to relate the second (or first) argument of `family` to the third, which is the list of offspring, and then have a second conjunct using the list-membership predicate, `member`. Unless member is a built-in predicate in your implementation of Prolog, you need the definition of member in Section7.6. (Notice that the approach here differs from that in Section 7.1 since here you are to define the relationships of mother and father before getting to the gender-neutral notion of parent.)

More Predicates: Continue by defining `parent` in terms of `mother` and `father`, either as a disjunction or using two clauses. For the offspring predicate, proceed in the other direction. That is, start with the gender-neutral predicate `offspring`, expressing it in terms of `parent` (of which it is the opposite), and then write rules for `son` and `daughter`, each in terms of `sex` and `offspring`.

You already have seen how to write the gender-neutral predicate `grandparent`. Do that and then use it to define `grandmother` and `grandfather`. Another gender-neutral term is *sibling*. Define the predicate `sibling` to express the idea that your sibling is someone who has the same mother (and/or father) as you, but is not you. To handle the requirement that two siblings must be different from each other, use the predicate `different`.

In addition to all the rules called for so far, also give rules for `ancestor`, `descendant`, and `uncle`. Note that there are two kinds of uncle: parent's brother and parent's sister's husband.

Product: The product that you hand in should include three things:

1. A printout of the file(s) that contains your Prolog facts and rules.

2. A script of a Prolog session, in which you enter Prolog, load your program, and then type in queries and receive answers.

3. Clearly written material including (i) comments in the program file, (ii) an introductory overview of what you accomplished, and (iii) discussion of how you selected your queries to provide an adequate test of your rules.

Part II

Language Models for Computer Science

Introduction to Part II: Language Models for Computer Science

Language models are tightly related to programming languages, which are central to practical computing. The study of language models addresses concepts and issues relevant to all programming languages. The field thereby seeks a better understanding of language in general, as opposed to a single language. In moving to this more general level, we follow our modeling strategy of focusing on a relatively small number of widely applicable concepts. The resulting language models clarify issues about compilers—the software that translates your programs into executable form. The study of language models can also help you learn and even design new languages.

Discussion is directed not only to programming languages, but also to human language, with examples from English. These examples are intended to be interesting and to aid understanding, but they also have computational significance. As computer interfaces make increasing use of human language, the subfield of artificial intelligence known as natural language processing has gained in importance, and this work too benefits from an understanding of language models.

In addition to modeling language, we also model computing machinery by introducing simple abstract machines called *automata*. We see some surprisingly close relationships between automata and language models. The study of automata also leads to the theory of computation. A category of automata known as Turing machines provides a simple but apparently correct way to model what it means to compute on any computer, no matter how complicated its construction. Then, given a model of what computation is, it becomes possible to talk about uncomputability. That is, one can actually prove that for some classes of computational problems there cannot be a general solution. From a practical standpoint, this work helps us formulate real problems in ways that are computable.

Chapter 8

Language and Models

The aim of this chapter is to motivate the study of language models and lay out fundamental conceptual themes. We set the stage by relating language models to actual programming languages as well as to human languages in ways that are precise yet broadly applicable. Attention is also directed to locating our field of study with respect to other parts of computer science. Complementing these big-picture concerns, the middle of the chapter introduces formal notation needed for speaking precisely about the issues of this chapter and provides a foundation for the chapters that follow. The final section lists and explicates the major recurring questions that have driven the development of the field.

8.1   Programming Languages and Computer Science

Programming languages are central to computing. They lie between software and hardware and connect the two of them. Software (a program) is written in a high-level language that people can understand. It is translated (compiled) into a machine language that some hardware understands. More precisely, the program is translated into a structured collection of commands that a particular kind of computer has been built to be responsive to. Just as it is important to understand general principles of hardware (architecture in general, as well as the design of individual machines) and general principles of software (software engineering, as well as particular applications), so too it is important to understand not just individual languages, but ideas of language in general. For this purpose, we study models of language.

Why do programming languages take the forms they do and how does a computer process the programs you write? To gain insight into questions like these, we model not only language, but also some mechanisms for processing it. The language-processing models that one uses are simple, imaginary machines called **automata**, and the field of study that seeks understanding of both language structure and processing is often called "Formal Languages and Automata." This field occupies most of Part II.

The study of language models begins with the observation that the two key aspects of language are structure and meaning. As noted in the Preface, a good model strips away the details of a topic, to simplify it, as an aid to understanding. In the case of formal models of language, which is the study of language structure, we make a gross oversimplification: We begin by throwing out language meaning. Of course, meanings have to be addressed, but not right now—that is, not while we are in the midst of looking at structure. Expressing meaning can be done in various ways, many of them related to predicate logic, a topic introduced in Part I: Logic for Computer Science.

Practical treatment of the questions and issues raised in the study of Formal Languages and Automata takes place in courses on Comparative Programming Languages and on Principles of Compiler Design. The modeling approach used here is good preparation for these practical topics. In fact, books on compilers typically begin with one or more chapters on formal languages, and compiler tools are based directly on them. You see one of these tools in Chapter 11.

8.2 Ambiguity and Language Design

Language is a means of communication. This is true of both human languages and programming languages. Comparing and contrasting these two kinds of language reveal useful ideas about the design and implementation of programming languages. Human languages have existed and evolved for thousands of years. Their development appears to be guided by a combination of our communication needs and mental capacities. More recently, computer programming languages have been created. While they too have evolved, there has been more tightly organized control over their design.

The relatively loose design of natural language can be seen in a number of ways. First, there is vagueness, as you can see by imagining a chair becoming wider and wider. At some point it becomes a bench or a couch, but the boundary of the meaning of "chair" is not exact. In contrast, there is no vagueness about the dividing line between integers and reals in a programming language.

Ambiguity differs from vagueness. An ambiguous word is one with multiple unrelated meanings. For example, the word "bank" can refer to a financial institution or to the land that lies beside a river. In either case, "bank" belongs to the same category—that of noun. Consequently, the whole sentence containing it can also be ambiguous, as in "I'm going to the bank." It is up to the listener or reader to figure out from context which meaning is intended.

The word "trip" presents a slightly different form of ambiguity by belonging to two different categories: It can be either a noun (as in "take a trip") or a verb (as in "trip over a shoelace"). This is like allowing a keyword in a programming language, such as "`if`" or "`while`", to also serve as the name of a variable. Many programming language designers have simply ruled out such a practice. The programmer must understand that these items are *reserved* for their predefined use.

An even more interesting, complex, and troublesome kind of ambiguity can arise at the level of phrases and sentences. An understanding of **ambiguity** is crucial for designers of programming languages, and the phenomenon has also been of great interest to psycholinguists studying how humans use our human languages. To begin with an example in English, take the sentence "I used a robot with one hand," which can mean that I used a one-handed robot or that I only needed one of my hands. Notice that these two different sentence meanings do not result just from an ambiguity of a single word in the sentence. Rather the difference has principally to do with how meanings combine.

As another example of structural ambiguity in human language, if one speaks of "old men and women," most people understand it to mean that the women as well as the men are to be old. However, "old people and children" would probably not be taken to mean that the children are old. These two phrases share a pattern, "old X and Y," that can in general be understood in two different ways and is thus structurally ambiguous.

A human listener can, of course, go beyond the pattern to make a distinction based on the meanings of the particular words and the relationships of those meanings. Humans are so good at this kind of reasoning that they are often unaware of having done it. Computers can be made to do this kind of reasoning too, at least to some extent, but the process is complex and time-consuming, both for a human to create and for a computer to execute. It is much easier to design programming languages to avoid presenting structurally ambiguous choices, and we see later on how to go about doing so.

Returning to our phrase "old X and Y," we now explain its two different meanings by saying that it has two different possible grouping structures. We indicate these grouping structures by means of trees. In the tree structure on the left, the words "X and Y" are first grouped together into a subtree and then "old" is associated with that entire phrase. In this case, the interpretation is that both X and Y are old. In the second tree, "old" is initially grouped only with X to mean that X is old.

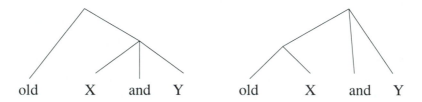

old   X   and   Y   old   X   and   Y

    The same kind of situation arises for programming languages—for example, when they make use of mathematical expressions. Suppose we replace "old" by the function "log" and replace "and" by the operator "+" to get "$\log X + Y$". In this case, mathematicians have invented special rules—called the rules of precedence—about how grouping should be done. They have also introduced the idea of parentheses for overriding the precedence rules. They have thereby paved the way for programming language designers and implementers who have accepted these ideas and proceeded to make compilers that operate accordingly.

    Let us put aside for a moment both the precedence rules and the fact that we can use parentheses. The next two trees highlight two different groupings that underlie two reasonable meanings for "$\log X + Y$". To dramatize the significance of the difference, suppose that $X = Y = 32 = 2^5$ and base 2 is being used for logarithms. Then the structure on the left has the value 6 and the one on the right evaluates to 37. Without precedence and with no parentheses, there would really be no compelling reason to select either one or the other of the two trees as the one intended by the person who wrote the expression. Avoiding such structural ambiguity is important in the design of programming languages and their processors.

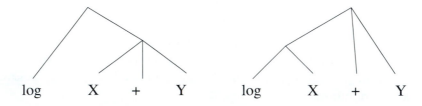

log   X   +   Y   log   X   +   Y

    Another key issue, besides ambiguity, is efficiency. Human beings manage to process each others' sentences in the time it takes to utter them, so that processing time is proportional to sentence length. It is certainly desirable to achieve this same kind of efficiency for the processing of programming languages. The study of language models provides a great deal of insight about both ambiguity and efficiency.

8.3 Formal Languages

Models ignore details to allow a clear focus on particular aspects of interest. The field of formal language models makes a startling choice: It focuses on the statements— the sequencing of their basic symbols—while it ignores the meaning except in the most simplistic way. There is no attempt to specify or characterize the meaning of a sentence or programming statement. The closest one comes to the idea of meaning is to say—as in the discussion of structural ambiguity—that multiple meanings are present because of multiple possible groupings. (The study of formal languages can been extended, in several ways, to incorporate the meaning or *semantics* of sentences; discussions of formal semantics are beyond the scope of this book.)

As just noted, the field of formal models of language focuses on sequences of symbols. These are called *strings*—a term that is neutral between the statements of programming languages and the sentences of human languages and that may also serve to remind us that meaning has been stripped away. The specification of any particular language begins with a finite set of symbols, Σ, which by definition is an **alphabet**. A **string** is defined to be a finite sequence of symbols from an alphabet. (See Sections 1.2 and 1.3 for related definitions.) Then a formal language—called just a **language** hereafter—is defined simply as a set of strings. One can also say that a language is a subset of all the possible strings that can be formed using its alphabet. A key question is, for any particular language or class of languages that interests us, how can we specify precisely the correct strings and no others?

According to these definitions, everything is built up from symbols in some alphabet Σ. For composing the strings (sentences) of English, Σ would be the words of English—a huge set. For a programming language, Σ would be smaller, but still too big to write down easily. Therefore, for convenience in these examples, we use much smaller symbol sets.

Example 8.1 Let $\Sigma = \{a, b, c\}$ be the set of symbols. Some strings composed from the symbols of Σ are *ab*, *bbc*, and *abcba*. We say that these are "strings over Σ."

The strings of Example 8.1, although simple, could find use as the names of variables, constants, and functions in a programming language. In other examples, we take these things (variables, etc.) themselves as the symbols in Σ and build strings that are whole statements. Example 8.2, shown next, is suggestive of aspects of binary arithmetic.

Example 8.2 Let $\Sigma = \{0, 1, +\}$ be the set of symbols. Some strings over Σ are 0, 1+1 and 10+11+10101.

The **length** of a string is the number of symbols in it. In Example 8.1, the length of *abcba* is 5. Vertical bars, which in arithmetic denote the absolute value of a number, are used with strings to denote length, so we can write $|abcba| = 5$. A string can have length one: $|b| = 1$. Notice that *b* can mean either the symbol *b* or the string of length one consisting of the one symbol, *b*. Just as it is useful in arithmetic to have a symbol for zero, so here it is useful to have a symbol for a string with no symbols, the **empty string**, Λ, where $|\Lambda| = 0$. Note that Λ is a string and *not* a symbol. As you can see from the examples, it is not listed in Σ.

Example 8.3 The set of strings over $\Sigma = \{a, b\}$ of length ≤ 2 is $\{\Lambda, a, b, aa, ab, ba, bb\}$.

Example 8.4 The set of strings over $\Sigma = \{0, 1, +\}$ that represent sums of 0s and 1s is $\{$ 0+0, 0+1, 1+0, 1+1, 0+0+0, 0+0+1, $\ldots\}$.

Examples 8.3 and 8.4, by specifying sets of strings, provide our first languages, and they have the beginnings of some relationships to programming language ideas. In Example 8.3, the strings are of limited length—something that is also true of variable names in some languages. The length limit of 2 in the example is of course unrealistic, but Fortran once had 6 as the limit, and early versions of Pascal allowed only eight letters and digits in its variable names. Example 8.4 is also related to programming languages, which almost always include the numerical expressions.

An important difference between these two examples concerns size: The language in Example 8.3 has a finite number of strings—7 to be precise. In contrast, the language described in Example 8.4 has infinitely many strings, so we had to resort to the use of ellipsis ("$\ldots$") when attempting to list the strings. Many useful languages are infinite, such as the set of sentences of English, the set of expressions of arithmetic, and the set of permissible statements of C++. Although a language may be infinite, each of its (infinitely many) strings is finite in length. Also the set of symbols is always finite.

There is one infinite language that we use repeatedly. For a given Σ, there is an infinite language, Σ^*, associated with it:

Σ^* is the language consisting of all possible strings over the symbol set Σ.

For example, $\{a, b\}^*$ represents all strings over the specific symbol set $\Sigma = \{a, b\}$. Here is a list of the first 12 of them in order of increasing length:

$$\{a, b\}^* = \{\Lambda, a, b, aa, ab, ba, bb, aaa, aab, aba, abb, baa, \ldots\}.$$

Any language over $\{a, b\}$ is a subset of $\{a, b\}^*$. One often uses letters near the end of the alphabet, like x and y, to stand for strings. For example, we might have $x = abba$, in which case $x \in \{a, b\}^*$. It is now possible to restate the contents of Example 8.3 using set notation as follows.

Example 8.5 $\{x \mid x \in \{a, b\}^* \wedge |x| \le 2\} = \{\Lambda, a, b, aa, ab, ba, bb\}.$

Since a language is a set of strings, we can, like any set, represent it using extensional or intensional formats. Consider the language in Example 8.5; call it L. At this point, we have seen three different ways to represent L, written next as (i)–(iii). The first is simply an explicit list of elements, the *extensional* format. This format can only be used for small finite sets; otherwise we must use an ellipsis and sacrifice a rigorous definition. By contrast, (ii) and (iii) are *intensional* specifications of the same language. The first, (ii), is a loose description in English, whereas the other, (iii), uses standard terminology of formal languages, sets, logic, and arithmetic. Increasingly, we use this last kind of specification because it is compact, precise, and versatile.

(i) $L = \{\Lambda, a, b, aa, ab, ba, bb\}.$
(ii) $L =$ the set of strings over $\{a, b\}$, of length no more than two.
(iii) $L = \{x \mid x \in \{a, b\}^* \wedge |x| \le 2\}$

8.4   Operations on Languages

As just noted, languages can be specified extensionally, intensionally, and by description. It is also possible, and indeed useful, to be able to build up new languages in terms of existing ones by making use of various *operations on languages*. First, because languages are sets (of strings), they can undergo all of the usual set operations. Given two languages, L_1 and L_2, one can form their *intersection* ($L_1 \cap L_2$), *union* ($L_1 \cup L_2$), *set difference* ($L_1 \setminus L_2$), and *symmetric difference*. Each language L has a *complement* $\Sigma^* \setminus L$ with respect to all possible strings over its alphabet. Speaking of sets, note that just as there is an empty set, there is also an *empty language*, which in fact is the same thing as the empty set, written $\emptyset$, as usual. It is important to distinguish between the empty language, $\emptyset$, and the empty string, Λ.

Example 8.6 $\emptyset$ is the empty language. It has no strings. The language $\{\Lambda\}$ has one string, although that string is the empty string, having length 0. The language $\{\Lambda, a, aa\}$ has three strings of lengths 0, 1, and 2.

Another operation on languages, besides the set operations, is *concatenation of languages*, which is based on concatenation of *strings* introduced in Section 1.3. Remember that, for example, the concatenation of a and b is ab; the concatenation of ab and edc is $abedc$. If x stands for one string and y for another, then xy stands for their concatenation. Notice that no operator symbol is used. This practice is analogous to the way multiplication is usually expressed in algebra, where the product of x and y, each of them standing for a number, is also written xy. The order in which strings are concatenated can be (and usually is) significant, so concatenation is not commutative.

Definition 8.1 Concatenation of strings.
If x and y are strings, xy is the concatenation of x and y. For any string x, we have $x\Lambda = x = \Lambda x$; thus, the empty string is the identity element for concatenation. A string can be concatenated with itself. The concatenation of x with x is xx, sometimes abbreviated to x^2. Concatenating x with x^k gives x^{k+1}. Also, $x^0 = \Lambda$.

Definition 8.2 Concatenation of languages
The concatenation of two languages L_1 and L_2 is written $L_1 L_2$. It contains every string that is the concatenation of a member of L_1 with a member of L_2. That is,

$$L_1 L_2 = \{xy \mid x \in L_1 \wedge y \in L_2\}$$

Since the concatenation of individual strings is not commutative, neither is the concatenation of languages. That is, $L_1 L_2$ can—and usually does—differ from $L_2 L_1$.

Example 8.7 Let $L_1 = \{a, aa\}$ and $L_2 = \{b, bb, bbb\}$. Then the concatenations $L_1 L_2$ and $L_2 L_1$ are as follows:

$$L_1 L_2 = \{ab, abb, abbb, aab, aabb, aabbb\}$$
$$L_2 L_1 = \{ba, bba, bbba, baa, bbaa, bbbaa\}.$$

Notice that there are 6 (the product of 2 and 3) possible ways to select strings to concatenate for $L_1 L_2$ in Example 8.7, and all 6 results differ from each other. However, although the language $L_2 L_2$ has 9 (3×3) ways to select strings, the resulting overlap leads to $L_2 L_2$ having only 5 members: $L_2 L_2 = \{bb, bbb, bbbb, bbbbb, bbbbbb\}$.

Definition 8.3 Superscripts for languages

Superscripts for languages behave analogously to those for strings. That is, for any language L, $L^0 = \{\Lambda\}$ and, for any integer k, $L^{k+1} = LL^k$. It then follows that $L^1 = L$, $L^2 = LL$, $L^3 = LLL$, and so on.

Definition 8.4 Closure for languages

The *closure* of L is L^*, where $L^* = L^0 \cup L^1 \cup L^2 \cup L^3 \cup \cdots$; that is,

$$L^* = \bigcup_{i=0}^{\infty} L^i$$

It may help to think of the "$*$" operator as specifying a kind of loop for building a string of the language of L^*. At each iteration, you decide whether to continue. If you do, you decide which element of L gets added to the string. In Example 8.8, the first string listed for $L^* = \{a, bb\}^*$ is Λ, which is the result of exiting the loop right at the outset. The next two strings result from a single iteration. The four after that are from going around the loop twice, picking either a or bb each time.

Example 8.8 Let $L = \{a, bb\}$. Then $L^0 = \{\Lambda\}$, which is true for any language. Also,

$$
\begin{aligned}
L^1 &= L = \{a, bb\}, \\
L^2 &= LL = \{aa, abb, bba, bbbb\} \\
L^3 &= LL^2 = \{aaa, aabb, abba, abbbb, bbaa, bbabb, bbbba, bbbbbb\} \\
L^* &= \{\Lambda, a, bb, aa, abb, bba, bbbb, aaa, aabb, abba, abbbb, bbaa, ...\}
\end{aligned}
$$

The "$*$" or closure operator in Definition 8.4 is also sometimes called the *(Kleene) star operator*. The use of this symbol is consistent with the definition of Σ^* earlier. In each case, the operator produces a set of strings formed by concatenating any number (zero or more) of instances of its operand. That operand may be the alphabet Σ, a set of symbols, or L, a set of strings. If we regard a and b as strings of length 1 (as opposed to just symbols), then $\{a, b\}$ is a language since it is a set of 2 strings, each of length 1. In that case, the two definitions are in agreement that $\{a, b\}^*$ is the set of all strings over $\{a, b\}$. Definition 8.4 here implies that "$*$" is a unary operator on languages; that is, it operates on one language to produce another. For practically any language L (any except $\emptyset$ or $\{\Lambda\}$, to be precise), the language L^* has infinitely many strings.

8.5   Two Levels and Two Language Classes

For both human languages and programming languages, matters are complicated by the fact that we use symbols to represent two different kinds of things. For a human language, we usually take the symbols to be the individual words. In that case, we often call the symbol set (Σ) a *vocabulary* (rather than "alphabet"), and the strings of the language are its sentences, regarded as sequences of words. However, at a finer-grained level of detail, it is also true that each word can be regarded as a string composed of letters. (At least this is true in many human languages, although by no means all of them.) When we work at this lower level of analysis, the letters become the members of the symbol set (Σ), which is now more appropriately called an *alphabet*.

The situation is similar for programming languages, where symbols standing for two different kinds of things also prove useful for different purposes. Strings of (ASCII) characters make up what are called the **tokens** of a programming language. Tokens correspond to words of human languages and can serve as the symbols in Σ. Some examples of multicharacter tokens in C++ are `for`, `<=`, and `cout`. The tokens in turn combine to form statements. Example 8.9 starts at a low level of detail, using the alphabet of decimal digits to define the positive integer tokens.

Example 8.9 $\Sigma = \{0, 1, 2, 3, 4, 5, 6, 7, 8, 9\}$ $L = \{x \mid x \in \Sigma^* \wedge |x| \geq 1\}$

By contrast, Example 8.10 starts at the word level; it provides a partial vocabulary for English and includes strings of members of that vocabulary to form some sentences of the language. (Note that the inter-word spaces in L are for readability and are not part of the strings.) Here L, which contains some strings over Σ, is meant to illustrate such a language, but of course is not fully defined.

Example 8.10 $\Sigma = \{$a, I, am, an, as, at, be, do, $\ldots\}$
$\qquad L = \{$I am, I do, $\ldots\}$

It is important to be aware of these different uses of symbols. Nevertheless, at any particular time, one is interested in just one particular symbol set. Even if that symbol set has multicharacter symbols (like English words or C++ tokens), we may still get useful insight by using simple symbols like a, b, and c in our language models. It is also typical to use small symbol sets like $\{a, b\}$ and $\{0, 1\}$. This makes it easier to express the key ideas, which then apply to large symbol sets as well. It should not be too surprising that small symbol sets are conceptually adequate since ultimately all computation is done by (huge numbers of) electronic components with just two physical states, corresponding to two symbols.

Consider the case of a typical programming language like C++. The combining of tokens to form statements turns out to be more complex than the way characters combine to make tokens. Therefore, we use two different classes of language. There is no inherent reason why tokens are formed in simpler ways than statements beyond the fact that programming languages were invented by analogy with human languages, where a similar situation exists.

The first and simpler class of languages, used in understanding tokens, is the class of *regular languages*. Despite their simplicity, these languages provide a good conceptual basis for *lexical scanning*, the first phase of a compiler. In fact, their simplicity is beneficial because it leads to ease of programming and efficiency of execution. It turns out, however, that regular languages are inherently limited in ways that make it impossible to use them for analyzing how programming statements are constructed from tokens. Thus, it becomes necessary to introduce another language class, known as the *context-free languages*.

The difference between these two classes of formal language lies in the notion of **recursive structure**: Context-free languages have it and regular languages do not. A sentence or program statement has *structure* in the sense that it can be broken into meaningful parts, which often can be broken into smaller parts and ultimately into words or tokens. In the case of sentences, the smaller parts are various kinds of phrases, like "full of sound and fury" or "four score and seven years ago," which may in turn contain smaller phrases like "four score." In the case of programming languages, many of the parts of statements are marked off explicitly by parentheses, brackets, and braces, as in the C++ statement that follows:

```
for (i=0; i<n; i++) {total += x[i]; count++;}.
```

This C++ statement has another important property: There are statements within it. For example, `total += x[i];` is a statement within a statement. The inner statement bears no restrictions; it can be as complex as any other statement. The statement category in C++ is thus recursive, and this is true of statements in programming languages in general. A construct is *recursive* if it can contain within itself a structure of the same type. (Strictly speaking, we should make a further distinction here as follows. If the inner statement were allowed to occur only at the very beginning or end of its containing statement, then we have a case of the weaker concept of *nonessential* recursion, and such structure can be handled by the mechanisms for regular languages. However, recursion in general does require the more powerful mechanisms used with context-free languages.)

8.6   The Questions of Formal Language Theory

It is easy to define a language to be a set of strings, but that seems to be too general to be useful. How does a computer scientist use this theory? What sort of questions are we going to ask? Answering this helps us understand how we are going to proceed in the next few chapters and motivate the choice of topics.

How is a language specified? The discussion of Example 8.5 emphasizes that languages are sets and can therefore be presented in extensional or intensional formats. The extensional form, which explicitly enumerates the elements, can only be used for small finite languages (although one may sometimes successfully communicate a simple infinite language to another person informally using a few sample strings and '...'). The intensional format uses a specification of the properties of the strings it contains. That statement may be informal or formal; here is an example of each:

$$L = \{x \mid x \in \{a, b\}^* \text{ and } x \text{ contains an equal number of } as \text{ and } bs\}$$

$$L = \{x \mid x \in \{a, b\}^* \wedge N_a(x) = N_b(x)\}.$$

With $N_a(x)$ denoting the number of occurrences of the symbol a in the string x, the informal and formal versions specify the same language here. Thus, for each of them, $abababba \in L$ and $aabaab \notin L$. Formal intensional specifications enable us to prove things about a language, and in that way can be more helpful than informal descriptions and partial listings of strings. However, none of these kinds of representation is suitable for answering the computational questions about language. In subsequent chapters, we therefore introduce a variety of formal representations specifically devised for language that do enable us to deal with such questions.

What are the key computational questions about language? Arguably the central questions are how to generate the sentences and how to recognize them. Let us see what these mean and then go on to other important questions.

Generation: How can we generate the sentences of a language? The interesting and useful languages are in principle of unlimited size—in other words, infinite. Therefore, it is impossible to define them extensionally simply by listing their strings. Rather, we need a finite—indeed compact—way to represent infinite languages. Once we have such a representation, the generation question arises: How can we use that representation to *generate* or display an unlimited number of strings of the infinite language in such a way that any particular string would ultimately occur? This is a computational question. To answer it, we need to specify our languages in a way that lets us produce, step by step, the strings of the language.

The formal rules for the production steps needed to produce strings of a language are the key part of something called a *grammar* for that language.

Recognition: How can we recognize the sentences of a language? The recognition problem is as follows: Given a language L and any string x over the alphabet for L, can we always correctly determine whether $x \in L$? This is a *decision problem*, where the output is "yes" or "no". For a particular language L, it may seem reasonable to think in terms of a computer program that can take any string as input and tell whether it is in L. Such a program is said to *recognize* the language L. There is, however, a downside to expressing the recognition idea in terms of a computer program—namely, that the program would be in some particular programming language and the specific characteristics of that programming language could then unduly influence us. Therefore, we do not describe recognition in terms of a programmed computer, but rather in terms of a simple *computing machine* or *automaton* which is built specifically for L.

What is the best way to specify a language? There is no best approach. We can define and represent a language L by giving an automaton that recognizes it, we can give a grammar that generates it, or we can give an intensional formal definition. The choice among these styles of representation depends on what we are trying to accomplish. We also want to show correspondences among them. We often translate one definition of a language to another dissimilar definition of it. For example, we want to take a grammar that generates a language L and use it to produce an automaton that recognizes L. Another example would be the translation of an automaton into yet another form of representation, the regular expression, introduced later. These translations are done mechanically and are discussed in the coming chapters. The details depend on the language class being discussed.

What is a language class? If Σ contains even a single symbol, then Σ^* contains an infinite number of strings, and so there are an infinite number of different languages over Σ. Some of these are more complex than others. Consider, for example,

$$L_1 = \{x \mid x \in \{a\}^* \text{ and } x \text{ contains an even number of symbols}\}$$

$$L_2 = \{x \mid x \in \{a\}^* \text{ and } x \text{ contains a prime number of symbols}\}$$

so that $aaaaa \in L_2$ but $aaaaa \notin L_1$. Although these look equally complex as specified here, they are quite different computationally. An automaton for L_2 is more challenging than one for L_1, and a grammar for L_2 is trickier to produce than for L_1.

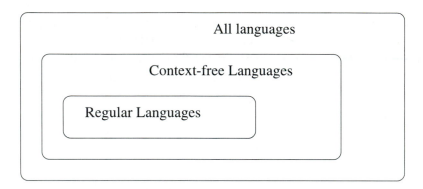

Figure 8.1: Containment of some language classes.

One of the great achievements in the theory of formal languages was the discovery that we can clearly state how and why some languages are more complex than others and that leads to the definition of a language class. We impose some strong restrictions on how an automaton can be built—if we were still speaking in terms of computer programs, those restrictions would be on the number and types of variables allowed. Some languages can be recognized by these restricted machines, and other languages are so complex that no such restricted automaton exists that can recognize them. Therefore, a *language class* is a set of languages, each of which can be recognized by some automaton that abides by the restrictions. In other words, a language class corresponds to a type of restriction on how an automaton can be built.

In parallel to this, we put restrictions on how grammars can be specified. We can define a language class in terms of the type of restriction on the form of the grammar—a language is in the class if there is a grammar for it of the restricted type. What is surprising is that we find that exactly the same language classes can be defined in terms of automata and in terms of grammars.

We have introduced two major language classes: regular and context-free. Figure 8.1 shows what is known about these classes. (Recall that a "class" is just a set, so we can talk about one language class being contained in another language class.) It indicates that every regular language is also a context-free language, but not vice versa. There are also languages that are not context-free; these languages are more complex, in some sense, than context-free languages. We demonstrate these relationships in the following chapters.

These observations lead directly to an outline of what we study herein. First, we study the class of automata that recognize tokens like numbers and the names of variables; then we study the regular expressions, an algebraic notation used to describe how to generate the same languages. Later we come to context-free grammars for the formation of statements from tokens; for these we also study a corresponding class of automata. Finally, we discuss the most powerful model of automata, Turing machines, and their relationship to grammars.

We also pay attention to significant practical issues. For one thing, we extend the conventions of regular expressions to arrive at Lex, a compiler tool for analysis of tokens as character strings. We will also observe how the automata for context-free grammars reflect various strategies for analyzing the structure of programming statements.

Exercises

8.1 State a distinction between the fields of Comparative Programming Languages and Formal Languages and Automata.

8.2 Changes in human languages come from a variety of sources. List some words recently added to English. If you can, state whether they describe new things in our changing world (like "fax"), come from distinct speech communities (like "dis") or come from other languages (like "guru").

8.3 The pattern "a X with Y and Z" has two possible word grouping structures, leading to two distinct meanings.

(a) Use trees as in the examples with "old" and "log" in Section 8.2 to reflect the likely difference in intended structure for "a dog with fleas and cats" and "a dog with fleas and ticks."

(b) Explain your choice of structures in part (a).

8.4 Consult a textbook on compilers or programming languages to find out what it means to *overload* an operator.

(a) In what sense is this a form of ambiguity?

(b) How do compilers figure out which meaning of the operator to use in a particular context?

8.5 Some languages have been called string-processing, list-processing, object-oriented, business-oriented, graphics-oriented, and so on. For one of these categories:

(a) Name a language in the category.

(b) Give an example of a specific operator or kind of structure in the language that is relevant to the category.

(c) State what the operator does or how the structure is used.

8.6 Express each of the following as briefly as possible using correct notation: an alphabet, the set of all strings over that alphabet, the empty string, the empty language, the length of string x, and the closure of language L.

8.7 Give the length of each of the following strings:

(a) $b^3 c^4$

(b) $(a \Lambda a \Lambda b \Lambda b)^2$

(c) Λ^5

8.8 Write the extension of each of the following sets:

(a) $\{x \mid x \in \{a, b\}^* \wedge |x| = 3\}$.

(b) $\{x \mid x \in \{a, b\}^* \wedge |x| = 4 \wedge \exists y : (x = aya)\}$.

8.9 Express the following sets intensionally using formal language terminology:

(a) $\{aa, ab, ac, ba, bb, bc, ca, cb, cc\}$

(b) $\{aa\}^*$

8.10 How many strings are there in the set $\{x \mid x \in \{a, b\}^* \wedge |x| \leq k\}$? Notice that your answer should be a function of k, but not of x.

8.11 How many of the strings over the symbol set $\Sigma = \{a, b, c\}$ are of length exactly 5?

8.12 Use the notation of formal languages, sets, logic, and arithmetic to express in intensional form each of the following sets, using no English.

(a) The set of strings of length 5 over $\{0, 1\}$.

(b) The set of strings over $\{0, 1\}$ that begin with 1 and that represent, as binary numbers, the values from 1 to 31 (in decimal notation).

8.13 Let b and c signify the names of variables and let $+$ have its usual meaning of addition.

(a) Write an intensional definition, using your choice of either English or formal language terminology, of the set of all strings over $\{b, c, +\}$ that legally represent sums.

(b) Is it correct to call the symbols b, c, and $+$ in this example "tokens"? Explain.

8.14 For each of the following operators, state whether it is commutative; and if it is not, give an example showing this: (a) multiplication, (b) logical "and" ($\wedge$), (c) concatenation, (d) union.

8.15 The multiplication operator "$\times$" is associative since for any numbers a, b, and c it is always true that $(a \times b) \times c = a \times (b \times c)$. Is concatenation of strings associative? Explain.

8.16 Let L be the language $\{a, bb\}$ and consider its closure, L^*.

(a) How many strings in L^* are of length 4?

(b) How many strings in L^* are of length 5?

8.17 In each case, write the set of strings of length 5 in the language of the RE:

(a) $a^*(b + cc)$

(b) $a + bb^*$

(c) a^*b^*

8.18 If L is the language of Example 8.5 and L_1 and L_2 are as specified in Example 8.7, give the extensional form of (a) $(L_1 L_2) \cap L$ and (b) $L_1(L_2 \cap L)$.

8.19 Let L be any language. Is it true that $(L^*)^* = L^*$? That is, can applying the closure operator a second time ever yield anything not already obtained by applying it once?

8.20 Show by means of a counter-example that the following statement is false. For any language L, the languages $(LL)^*$ and L^*L^* are the same.

8.21 You have seen the recursive structure of programming statements. Are algebraic expressions (as used in mathematics and programming languages) recursive? Explain your answer both in general and in terms of a specific example.

Chapter 9

Finite Automata and Their Languages

In Chapter 8, we stated that a fundamental computational problem for formal languages was *recognition*. The goal is to design machines that can answer questions of the form: For a given language L and string x, is it true or false that $x \in L$? We approach the problem by designing special-purpose hardware for each language, with no operating systems and no software. Each language L is to have its own machine whose only task is to take arbitrary input strings over the alphabet of L and for each such string decide whether it is a member of L. We call such a machine design an *automaton* (plural: automata). In summary, each language has an automaton that is a complete computational model of a recognition process for that language, handling all of what is normally done by a combination of hardware *and* software.

In this chapter, we introduce a simple way to specify a category of automata, and we determine what class of languages such automata can recognize. In later chapters, these automata are enhanced by extra mechanisms to get more complex categories of automata that recognize broader—and, it turns out, equally important—classes of languages. One interesting and important aspect of this machine-design approach is that it allows us to compare the complexity (or simplicity) of language classes by comparing the complexity of the corresponding classes of automata.

Although we speak only in terms of *design* and not about actual machines, these designs could readily be implemented as real circuitry. Electrical engineers routinely begin the design of hardware with the specification of an automaton. A computer scientist, in contrast, is more likely to translate an automaton into a computer program, which simulates its behavior. In fact, some theories of software engineering specify a program's actions with an automaton. In any event, this formal theory is crucial in understanding the computational aspects of languages.

9.1   Automata: The General Idea

An **automaton** is a specification for a *symbol processing machine*. It differs from the machines that manufacture material goods (e.g., cars) in at least three important ways. First, it is only a *specification*—something we imagine or describe. Second, it operates on *symbols*, not metal, plastic, and other substances. Finally, it has a relatively simple internal structure to study.

Informally, we can think of an automaton for any language L as a "black box" (a box with unknown contents). As its input, such a box can be given any string x over the alphabet of its language. For output purposes, it has a green light that is on when—but only when—the portion of the string processed so far is in L. Consequently, the light may go on and off at various times as the string is processed. If the light is on when the end of x is reached, $x \in L$. To an observer, the automaton's use of its green light shows that it recognizes (the strings of) L. The mechanism of a black box can be quite complicated, but for finite automata the internal mechanism is remarkably simple.

As an automaton executes, various changes occur in its internal condition. Each possible internal condition is called a **state**. We do not ask about the details of the internal machinery that make one state different from another, but rather simply give names (like A, B, ... or q_0, q_1, ...) to the different states. The states are a kind of internal memory for an automaton. A **finite automaton** (**FA**) has a finite number of states and has no other form of memory; this is why it is called "finite." This finiteness places some limits on what it can do. In later chapters, we look at two other kinds of automata—pushdown automata and Turing machines—that have this same form of internal memory and in addition have simple forms of external memory.

We begin by showing the operation of a finite automaton with a simple diagram of it called a *state transition diagram*. Then the formal notation of finite automata is introduced to provide a streamlined way of talking precisely about the diagrams. With this notation in hand, it is easy to write a short, straightforward algorithm for how FAs work. Ultimately, it is this algorithm that provides the solution to the recognition problem.

Many of these diagrams correspond to *non*deterministic finite automata. These automata have the unsettling property that we—and *they*—cannot always be sure what state they are in. Yet, for some languages, nondeterministic automata seem to provide a more natural means of expression than deterministic ones. Moreover, they turn out to play a crucial role in solving the recognition problem. Our strategy for putting them to actual use involves converting them to deterministic finite automata that recognize the same languages.

9.2 Diagrams and Recognition

We approach the study of FAs by introducing the idea of a simple processing diagram called a **state transition diagram**. When FAs are defined formally in the next section, it becomes clear that every FA can be expressed as one of these diagrams. Moreover, the diagram has all the information needed to get back to a complete formal specification of its FA. Therefore, the two representations—one visual, the other symbolic—are completely equivalent.

A state transition diagram receives a string as its input and either **accepts** it or not. The set of strings that a diagram accepts is considered to be its language. Consider the state transition diagram used as the figure for Example 9.1. This diagram accepts precisely the two strings a and bc, as we prove later, but for now just have a look at its general appearance. The name *state transition diagram* comes from the little circles in the diagram called **states** and the labeled arrows called **transitions**.

The rules for using these diagrams for recognition are similar to the King's reading instructions to the White Rabbit: "Begin at the beginning, and go on till you come to the end: then stop." (Quoted from *Alice's Adventures in Wonderland,* by Lewis Carroll.) The beginning point in a state transition diagram is the **start state**. There is always just one of these, indicated by a short arrow pointing to it, not coming from any other state. Corresponding to the start state is the beginning point in the input string. The first symbol of input is initially made the current symbol.

At each step of the process, follow a transition that leads out of the current state and whose labels include the current input symbol. The new current state is the one to which the arrow points, possibly the same as before if the arrow curves back to the state it comes from. Carrying out this step uses up the current symbol of input, making the next one current. The process then repeats. A double circle signifies an **accepting state**. A string that leads from the start state to such a state is **accepted** by the diagram. That is, if the end of input and an accepting state are reached simultaneously, the string is in the language of the state transition diagram. Unless this occurs, the string is not in the language.

These processing instructions, like the King's, go to the end of input and stop there. Where in the *diagram* one stops, however, is less easy to say. A state transition diagram can have more than one accepting state (see the diagram for Example 9.3). Also, accepting states are not necessarily "the end," in the sense that if there is more input, the process is not *required* to stop. Thus, in Example 9.1, with input *aa*, after going from state A to state C processing continues with a transition to state D, so the string is *not* accepted, even though we pass through an accepting state.

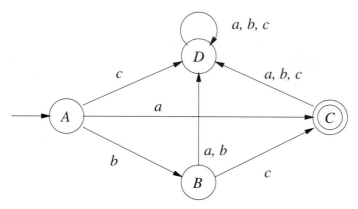

Example 9.1 Let L be the language accepted by the four-state diagram in the accompanying figure. Input strings must be over the alphabet $\Sigma = \{a, b, c\}$. Prove that $L = \{a, bc\}$.

The set equality rule in Section 5.3 guides our proof plan. To prove equality of the sets L and $\{a, bc\}$, we need to show that each is a subset of the other. Invoking the subset rule, also from Section 5.3, we first need to show that $a \in L$ and that $bc \in L$.

The initial state is A. If the first input symbol is a, there is a transition to the accepting state C, so $a \in L$. When the first input symbol is b, the machine makes a transition to the state B. Then if the second input symbol is c, there is a transition from B to the accepting state C, so $bc \in L$.

Next we need to show that $x \in L \to x \in \{a, bc\}$, or, using the contrapositive rule from Section 3.2, $x \notin \{a, bc\} \to x \notin L$. In other words, we need to show that all strings *other than a and bc* are *not* accepted. So let us consider those other strings. Since there are infinitely many of them, we better not try them one at a time, but rather divide them into broad (indeed infinite) categories on the basis of some properties, like what member of the alphabet is the first symbol.

If the first input symbol is c, then we go to state D. The state D has only a transition to itself, so all future transitions stay at D, which is nonaccepting. It follows that all input strings beginning with c – like c, cab, $cccbac$, and so on—end up stuck at D. Strings that begin with a and continue (i.e., excepting a itself as the whole string) go to state C and continue to D, where they stay. The remaining possible first symbol is b, which goes to the nonaccepting state B. From there, if the second symbol anything except c (making bc altogether), you would end up stuck at D. Finally, if you reached state C before the end of the input, the next symbol would take you to D and any additional symbols would leave you there.

The state D in Example 9.1 is an example of a **sink**—a state that once entered cannot be left. A nonaccepting sink, like D, is called a **trap state**. Whenever a trap state is reached, it means that the input seen so far is enough to disqualify the entire string from being accepted. A single trap state in a diagram is enough for this purpose. There are accepting sinks as well (see Examples 9.6 and 9.7). Unfortunately, a trap state, and especially all the transitions to it, clutter up our diagrams. We therefore use *trap-free* diagrams, like the one in Example 9.2, where the trap state is not shown and any missing transitions are assumed to be to the trap state.

Example 9.2 Redraw the diagram of Example 9.1 without the trap state.

We omit not only the trap state, but also all transitions to it. The resulting diagram accepts the same language, $\{a, bc\}$. Note, for example, that the transition for symbol b from state B is implicitly to a trap state that is not drawn.

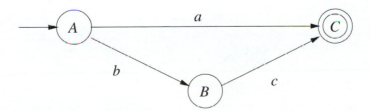

For each state in Example 9.1, we provided exactly one transition out of that state for each symbol in Σ. This important property can be restated as follows: For each state-and-symbol pair, there is exactly one transition. The property also holds for Example 9.2, provided that we regard the removed trap state and the missing transitions as being implicitly present. In fact, it holds for all the diagrams in this section.

Example 9.3 Draw a transition diagram without a trap state for an FA that recognizes the language L, where

$$L = \{x \mid x \in \{a, b\}^* \text{and every } a \text{ precedes every } b\}.$$

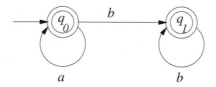

In the set specification of Example 9.3, "every" is used twice to express universal quantification. As stated at the end of Section 4.4, the universal quantifier is always true over an empty set, so L includes all strings that contain no as and/or no bs. We could have given many other equivalent intensional descriptions of the language recognized by this machine—for example,

$$L = \{x \mid x = yz \text{ and } y \in \{a\}^* \text{ and } z \in \{b\}^*\}.$$

$$L = \{x \mid x \in \{a, b\}^* \text{ and there is no occurrence of } ba \text{ in } x\}.$$

Example 9.4 Draw a transition diagram for an automaton that recognizes the language

$$L = \{x \mid x \in \{a, b\}^* \text{ and there is no odd block of } bs \text{ in } x\}$$

where an "odd block of bs" means an odd number of consecutive bs (not contained in a longer block of bs). In other words, for x to be accepted by the machine, consecutive bs must be paired up or else it ends up at a nonaccepting state (possibly the trap state).

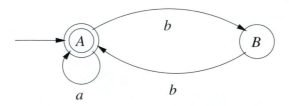

The opposite of acceptance is **rejection**. Now that we are omitting trap states, there are two different ways for a diagram to reject strings. One results from a transition to an implicit trap state. This occurs for the string *abab* in Example 9.4 when trying to process its third symbol. The other is not new: If the end of the string is reached in a state that is not an accepting state, the string is not accepted. This occurs for the string *abbab* with the diagram of Example 9.4.

As a practical example that occurs in C and in C++, consider the problem of trying to recognize strings that look like comments—strings of the form "/* ... */". In other words, comments in these languages begin with a slash-star combination, end with star-slash, and the intervening material is arbitrary except that it does not contain star-slash since that would terminate the comment at an earlier point. In the next example, the situation is simplified, for clarity, by taking a small symbol set, $\{a, b, c, d\}$, and using the ordinary characters "*c*" and "*d*" in place of star and slash. Nevertheless, the pattern we use preserves the essential features of the comment structure.

Example 9.5 Give a transition diagram for the language L over $\Sigma = \{a, b, c, d\}$ that contains all and only the strings x such that (i) x begins with *dc*, (ii) x ends in a substring *cd* (where the *c*s in (i), and (ii) are not the same one); and (iii) between these substrings there is no other occurrence of *cd*.

In the first of the two diagrams shown here, the straight arrows make it clear that all accepted strings must satisfy conditions (i) and (ii). After an opening, *dc* takes us to the middle state, the self-loop keeps us there for any number of input symbols in $\{a, b, d\}$. This enforces rule (iii) so that the language of this diagram has *only* strings of L. However, the diagram does not accept *all* the strings of L since it does not include such strings as *dcaaacbbbcd*, *dcccd*, and many other strings that meet the requirements.

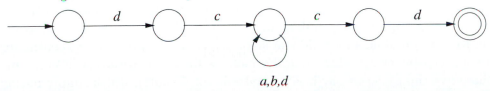

The trouble with the first diagram is that it assumes that from the middle state the occurrence of *c* takes us to a state that *must be* one symbol from the end of the string. That is fine if the next symbol is *d*, but if the next symbol is *a*, *b*, or *c*, it is still possible to end up with an accepted string. The second diagram takes these additional possibilities into consideration (see Exercise 9.5).

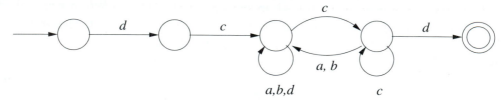

This section has introduced the idea of a state transition diagram. This construct does a nice job of defining languages in terms of a recognition process. This is a pretty clever way to proceed since, for practical purposes, we do need recognition. So let us take a moment to reflect on how someone might have come up with this cleverness. Back in the introduction to Chapter 1, we mentioned the broad applicability of a graph. As noted in Section 1.6, a graph is just a set of vertices and a set of edges, where the edges connect pairs of vertices. You could have taken the idea of vertices and used it here for what we have called states. Similarly, the arrows that represent state transitions are also familiar to anyone who has studied graphs: They are just directed edges. In fact, they are labeled directed edges, with labels coming from the alphabet Σ. So from a graph viewpoint, these diagrams can be called *labeled, connected, directed graphs* in which each path corresponds to a string. We do need something more: start and accepting states, which confine us to the right strings for some particular language.

9.3   Formal Notation for Finite Automata

The diagrams that we have been using up to this point have the advantage of being easy to understand at a glance, but expressing precise ideas about them in ordinary English can lead to clumsy discussions. Moreover, they are not fit for consumption by a computer. To remedy these shortcomings, we turn to formal notation. We observe that a state-transition diagram is composed of (i) states and (ii) symbols, along with information about (iii) starting the recognition process, (iv) continuing it, and (v) accepting or not when done. Formally, a **finite automaton** (FA) is a model of these five things, so we say it is a quintuple (or 5-tuple), which simply means an ordered set of five things that we name. We also name the whole automaton; it is usually called M, for "machine."

Definition 9.1 Finite automata
    A finite automaton, M, is a quintuple, $(Q, \Sigma, q_0, \delta, A)$, where

Q is a finite set of states,

Σ is a finite set of symbols,

$q_0 \in Q$, where q_0 is the start state,

$A \subseteq Q$, where A is the set of accepting states, and

$\delta : Q \times \Sigma \to Q$.

The last line states that δ is a function from $Q \times \Sigma$ to Q. We use q for an arbitrary element of Q and σ for an arbitrary element of Σ. (The latter pair are the Greek lowercase and capital sigma, respectively.) Thus, $Q \times \Sigma$ is the set of all ordered pairs (q, σ) such that $q \in Q$ and $\sigma \in \Sigma$. One writes $\delta(q, \sigma)$ to express the result of applying δ to these arguments. The function δ is understood to be the **transition function** of the finite automaton, specifying the transitions in the corresponding state transition diagram. That is, if the current state of the FA is q and the current input is σ, then the FA's next state is the value of $\delta(q, \sigma)$.

In the automata of this section, the choice of next state is uniquely determined at each step; there is never more than one possibility. This is consistent with the property specified right after Example 9.2—that there is precisely one transition arrow for each state-and-symbol pair. Moreover, there is never less than one possibility; that is, δ is a *total function*, with $\delta(q, \sigma)$ defined for all q and σ. If a trap state is needed to make this true, it is included in Q and used in δ.

Example 9.6 Specify a machine $M = (Q, \Sigma, q_0, \delta, A)$ for the language $\{a\}^*$ by giving the values of Q, Σ, A, and δ, and also by drawing the corresponding diagram.

$Q = \{q_0\}$,

$\Sigma = \{a\}$,

$A = \{q_0\}$ and

$\delta(q_0, a) = q_0$.

a

The next example is motivated by the format of names like X1, TEMP, X3A, and so on that are used for variables, arrays, and functions in programming languages. Typically such names are required to begin with a letter and continue with letters and digits, as well as possibly some other characters, which we ignore for simplicity. As a further simplification, let $\Sigma = \{a, d\}$; think of a as standing for any letter of the alphabet and d for any digit. Then the accepted strings are those that begin with a. This readily leads to this diagram:

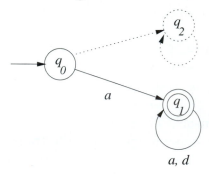

Notice that state q_2 in this FA, shown with a dotted circle, is a trap state. The transitions to and from it are also shown in dotted form. These transitions are needed in the transition function, δ, of Example 9.7, to make it a total function. In Definition 9.1, the function specification is $\delta : Q \times \Sigma \to Q$, so the value of δ is always a member of Q, which means that it is exactly *one* state, not zero states, as would be the case for $\delta(q_0, d)$ if the trap state were omitted. You can see that there is exactly one state in each cell of the table in the next example.

Example 9.7 Let $M = (\{q_0, q_1, q_2\}, \{a, d\}, q_0, \delta, \{q_1\})$, where δ is specified by the following table. Justify the claim that M accepts all strings over $\{a, d\}$ beginning with a and no others.

$$
\delta = \quad
\begin{array}{c|cc}
 & a & d \\
\hline
q_0 & q_1 & q_2 \\
q_1 & q_1 & q_1 \\
q_2 & q_2 & q_2 \\
\end{array}
$$

By Definition 9.1, the start state is found in the third position in the quintuple; as usual, it is denoted q_0. The fifth (last) element of M is always the set of accepting states; it is $\{q_1\}$ in this case. From the middle row of the table for the transition function, δ, you can see that q_1 is a sink since both of its transitions are to itself. The same can be seen for q_2 in the bottom row. In addition to being a sink, q_2 (but not q_1) is a trap state because it is also nonaccepting. Clearly the first symbol of the input is crucial here. If it is d, the automaton M goes into the trap state and the string is rejected. If the first symbol is a, M goes to the accepting sink, so it accepts the string, no matter what else follows. Thus, the language accepted by M consists of all and only the strings beginning with a, as intended.

One way to view the transition function, δ, of an FA is that it tells us the state-to-state movement for each input symbol. Thus, in Example 9.7, the input a can move automaton M from q_0 to q_1, from q_1 to q_1, or from q_2 to q_2. For the extended state-to-state movement resulting from *strings* of symbols, we introduce a new function, δ^*, that works by using as many applications of δ as needed—one for each symbol in the string. It may help to notice the analogy between the star ("*") in δ^*—which indicates multiple applications—and the star in Σ^* for multiple symbols to form strings. In Example 9.7, the string ad can make M go from q_0 (via q_1) to q_1, so we write $\delta^*(q_0, ad) = q_1$. Sometimes called the **closure** (of δ) or the generalized transition function, δ^* has the following formal definition.

Definition 9.2 δ^*, **the closure of the transition function**

Let $M = (Q, \Sigma, q_0, \delta, A)$ be an FA. Then δ^* is a function that takes a state and a string as input and produces a resulting state. That is, $\delta^* : Q \times \Sigma^* \to Q$. (Recall that Σ^* is the set of strings over Σ.) The specific values of δ^* are:

(i) For any $q \in Q$, $\delta^*(q, \Lambda) = q$ and

(ii) For any $q \in Q$, any $\sigma \in \Sigma$ and any $x \in \Sigma^*$, $\delta^*(q, x\sigma) = \delta(\delta^*(q, x), \sigma)$.

Part (i) of Definition 9.2 states that the empty string, Λ, has no effect on the FA, simply leaving it at its current state, q. Part (ii) is for nonempty strings. First notice that x and σ are both variables, but they differ in that σ is a member of Σ and so stands for a single symbol, whereas x has a value in Σ^*, making it a string. Also worth noting is that part (ii) is recursive; it defines δ^* in terms of itself. To avoid circularity, it defines the behavior of δ^* for each string, $x\sigma$, in terms of what happens with a slightly shorter string, x. Part (ii) says that to know what δ^* does with input $x\sigma$, first figure out what it does with x and then apply δ (whose behavior is known from the specification of M) to the resulting state and the one remaining symbol, σ. Next comes a simple but useful result, following directly from Definition 9.2, for applying δ to strings of length 1.

Theorem 9.1 For any state, q, and any string, σ, of length 1, δ^* gives the same values that δ gives when applied to q and σ. That is, $\delta^*(q, \sigma) = \delta(q, \sigma)$.

Proof

$$\begin{aligned}
\delta^*(q, \sigma) &= \delta^*(q, \Lambda\sigma) && \text{Substitution: } \sigma = \Lambda\sigma \\
&= \delta(\delta^*(q, \Lambda), \sigma) && \text{Part (ii) of Definition 9.2, with } x = \Lambda \\
&= \delta(q, \sigma) && \text{Part (i) of Definition 9.2}
\end{aligned}$$

□

Example 9.8 It was noted earlier that from the start state q_0 in Example 9.7, the input string ad should take the automaton M to state q_1. Show how Definition 9.2 formally confirms this result.

$$\begin{aligned}
\delta^*(q_0, ad) &= \delta(\delta^*(q_0, a), d) && \text{Definition 9.2 with } x = a \\
& && \text{and } \sigma = d, \text{ so } x\sigma = ad \\
&= \delta(\delta(q_0, a), d) && \text{Theorem 9.1} \\
&= \delta(q_1, d) && \text{Evaluating the inner } \delta \\
&= q_1 && \text{Evaluating } \delta
\end{aligned}$$

The foregoing definitions—of an automaton, the transition function, δ, and its closure, δ^*—now make it easy to define the language recognized by an FA as the set of strings that take the FA from its start state to an accepting state using δ^*. This idea is made precise by the next definition.

Definition 9.3 The language recognized by a finite automaton
The language $\mathcal{L}(M)$ **recognized** by a finite automaton $M = (Q, \Sigma, q_0, \delta, A)$ is the set of all strings $x \in \Sigma^*$ such that $\delta^*(q_0, x) \in A$. One says that M **accepts** the strings of $\mathcal{L}(M)$ and **rejects** those of its complement, $\Sigma^* \setminus \mathcal{L}(M)$.

Writing a recognition algorithm is now remarkably simple if we allow ourselves to use the generalized transition function δ^*. Following Definition 9.3, to determine whether the input string x is accepted, one would just compute $\delta^*(q_0, x)$ and check whether it is a member of A. This approach assumes that we can implement δ^*. Although Definition 9.2 tells us exactly how to write a recursive function for δ^*, we instead use a simple iterative algorithm.

Algorithm 9.1 Recognizing the language of a finite automaton
Let M be an FA as in Definition 9.1 and let q denote its current state. Let x be the input string and σ the current input symbol. We use "$\Leftarrow$" as the assignment operator. In general, the function *dequeue* removes an element from the front of a queue and returns it. Here it returns the current first symbol of the input string and resets x

to the rest of the string. The following recognition algorithm for M returns TRUE for acceptance (when the value of $q \in A$ is true) and FALSE for rejection.

$$q \Leftarrow q_0$$
$$\textbf{while } x \neq \Lambda \textbf{ do}$$
$$\sigma \Leftarrow dequeue(x)$$
$$q \Leftarrow \delta(q, \sigma)$$
$$\textbf{return } (q \in A)$$

9.4 Finite Automata in Prolog

Implementing FAs in Prolog brings together key techniques from both halves of this book and is surprisingly easy to do. The idea is to get Prolog to carry out the acceptance of exactly the strings that are in a particular FA's language. We do this in two ways. The first method straightforwardly converts the specification for a particular machine directly to a Prolog predicate. The second approach is a more general one involving a rule that is useful for any FA. In this method, Prolog *facts* express the structure of a particular machine—an organization that we argue makes better sense.

To write a Prolog program for machine M by the first method, we create just one predicate, which we call `accept`, to suggest that it accepts strings. We want it to succeed (i.e., be true and give a **yes** answer) when given a string that M accepts; it should fail on all other strings. We assume that input strings are converted to lists; for example, the string *abc* becomes `[a,b,c]`. Conversion facilities from strings to lists and vice versa are often available in implementations of Prolog.

The predicate `accept` has two arguments that together express the current situation: the current state and what remains of the input string. We want to be able to see if a string is accepted by entering a query with that string's list form as the second argument to `accept` and with the start state, q_0, as first argument.

Example 9.9 Consider the FA,

$$M = (\{q_0, q_1, q_2\}, \{a, b, c, d\}, q_0, \delta, \{q_2\})$$

where $\delta(q_0, a) = q_1$, $\delta(q_1, b) = q_1$, $\delta(q_1, c) = q_2$ and $\delta(q_2, d) = q_0$

To test a string such as, say, *abbcdac*, one would enter the query, `accept(q0,[a,b,b,c,d,a,c])`. In this case, the answer should be **yes** since the string is in the language of the automaton. Here is a multiclause rule for `accept`:

```
accept(q₀,[a|Tail])  :- accept(q₁,Tail).
accept(q₁,[b|Tail])  :- accept(q₁,Tail).
accept(q₁,[c|Tail])  :- accept(q₂,Tail).
accept(q₂,[d|Tail])  :- accept(q₀,Tail).
accept(q₂,[ ]).
```

Look at the program in Example 9.9 and begin by noticing that the first argument to the predicate accept is always a state of the FA and the second is always a list. In each clause, the list on the right side is shorter by one input symbol—exactly the one that causes the transition from the state on the right to the state on the left. In addition, the predicate accept succeeds when its first argument is q_2 and its second argument is the empty list. You can see this from the last line. This implements the fact that q_2 is an accepting state. It follows that with q_0 as first argument the program succeeds for any string in $\mathcal{L}(M)$, the language of the FA, and fails for any other string.

Now consider a more general approach to FAs in prolog. Although the Prolog rule in Example 9.9 correctly implements the machine for which it was created, it does not give us any help with other FAs. Therefore, we now put the accept predicate into a form that is more abstract and is therefore also of more general use. In Example 9.10, accept expresses the workings of FAs in general, so its rule can be used, unchanged, in any FA program.

The strategy is to express as Prolog *facts* the information about the transition function of a particular FA, whereas the *rule* is reserved for what is true of all FAs. It is appropriate to use delta as the name of the new predicate for facts about δ. The first and second arguments of delta are therefore the current state and input, whereas the third argument is the resulting new state, which is the value (output) of δ. (The technique of converting a function to a predicate with an extra argument for the result is a common one. You have seen it with append, a three-argument predicate that corresponds to the two-argument function of list concatenation.)

Example 9.10 Transition information for the FA in Example 9.9 now appears as facts about the predicate delta.

```
accept(Q,[S|Tail])  :- delta(Q,S,R), accept(R,Tail).
accept(Q,[ ])       :- acc(Q).
delta(q₀,a,q₁).
delta(q₁,b,q₁).
delta(q₁,c,q₂).
delta(q₂,d,q₀).
acc(q₂).
```

Notice that in Example 9.10 there are only two clauses for the `accept` rule. They reflect Prolog's declarative style in that each of the two clauses makes a statement about the nature of FAs, one dealing with transitions and the other with final states. Moreover, the facts about a particular FA are expressed as Prolog facts, using only `delta`, so there is a clean break between rules and facts, with rules used for general matters and facts used for the specifics of one machine.

The first clause for `accept` specifies how transitions work. Look at its right side. The first conjunct, `delta(Q,S,R)`, means that this clause is useful only if there is a transition (an arrow, in terms of FA diagrams) that goes from state `Q` to state `R` and has `S` as the current input. Since `Q`, `S`, and `R` are all variables, they can refer to any transition in any FA.

Now look at the whole first clause. It says that from state `Q`, with current input `S`, acceptance (success of `accept`) occurs provided that `delta(Q,S,R)` succeeds, where `R` is the new state, and also provided that acceptance occurs from `R` with a slightly shorter input list, diminished by the removal of `S` from the front of it.

The second clause of accept handles the idea of accepting states. It says that if you are in state `Q` and there is no more input, `accept` succeeds provided that `Q` is an accepting state of the FA. The idea of an accepting state is represented by the predicate `acc`. The last line of this Prolog program states that q_2 is an accepting state.

As already mentioned, the `delta` predicate corresponds directly to the δ function of the particular FA. Compare the four lines of the `delta` predicate with the four lines of the δ function. Notice that in each case the third argument of `delta` is the value (output) when δ is applied to the first two arguments.

9.5 Nondeterminism: The General Idea

Before introducing the particulars of nondeterministic finite automata in the next section, it may help to discuss the general idea of nondeterminism. The good news about nondeterminism is that it is a powerful concept that enables us to simplify the way we represent some computations. The not-so-good news is that the idea can be a bit puzzling since—unlike the deterministic automata we have dealt with up to now—the nondeterministic automaton does not directly model real-life circuitry. In this section, we introduce the notion of nondeterminism with a simple example and go on to interpret this unusual concept in practical terms.

Consider the task of writing a three-letter word in Swahili (which is the language of Tanzania and an important commercial language in a broader region of east-central Africa). You have available an electronic device with a data structure that holds Swahili words and allows a lookup operation in which you give the device a string and it says whether that string is a word. Here is your nondeterministic solution to the problem:

1. Choose the first letter.

2. Choose the second letter.

3. Choose the third letter.

4. Look up the resulting string to see if it is a word.

But how do you choose each letter? What if you choose wrong letters? To understand the answers to these questions, imagine that you are a nondeterministic robot with superhuman intelligence. Specifically, you have the somewhat mystical ability to make choices that will turn out, in combination, to give a correct answer if it is at all possible to do so. That is, if any correct answers exist, you—in the role of nondeterministic robot—will make choices that specify one of them. This is the idea of nondeterminism. Well, this is very nice, but since it seems completely unrealistic, what, you may ask, is the value of even discussing it?

A nondeterministic approach should be regarded as a bare-bones description of *what* is being accomplished, but not *how* it is being carried out. In fact, the non-deterministic approach can actually be implemented in some totally realistic ways, but—since they lack the magic described before—they take either more equipment or more time. We describe two such implementations in the context of our word problem: **parallel computation** and **backtracking**.

The parallel computation approach assumes that we have as many parallel processors (multiple CPUs) as we need. One processor is responsible for exploring each possible first letter in a word, 26 processors in all. Each of these processors uses 26 additional processors to explore the various second letters. Each of these uses 26 more processors to try out different third letters, for $26 + 26^2 + 26^3$ processors. If any of the third-tier processors completes a three-letter word found in the Swahili dictionary, then the entire computational effort stops successfully (even if other words could also be found—it does not matter who wins such ties); if no word is found by any processor, the entire collective computational effort fails.

A backtracking algorithm is used when you have a single processor—that is, a traditional sequential computer. For this problem, the algorithm would tentatively choose a first letter, say "a." Then in association with that choice it picks a letter for the second position, say "a," so that now it is looking for words starting with "aa." Then it tries different third letters; it turns out there is no three-letter Swahili word beginning with "aa,", so all 26 attempts fail. The algorithm now backtracks: It gives up on its most recent choice and makes a new choice at that point. If all choices at that point are used up, it backtracks further. In the current context, this means that it gives up on the "a" in second position (but at least for now keeps the "a" in first position) and tries a different second letter, say "b." Now it once again tries different third letters—getting "aba," "abb," and so on. These first two are not Swahili words and neither is "abc," but when "abd" is looked up it is found to be a Swahili word (imported from Arabic actually) and the procedure succeeds. If there were no three-letter words in Swahili, then the procedure would eventually fail after an exhaustive search—that is, after trying all possibilities.

Both the parallel and backtracking approaches succeed when it possible to do so and fail otherwise. They differ greatly in details, but they share the same nondeterministic characterization. The nondeterministic specification is thus a *model* of a solution in that it provides a relatively simple and succinct description of what is to be done while ignoring those aspects of the implementation that do not currently interest us.

9.6   Nondeterministic Finite Automata

Nondeterministic finite automata (NFAs) share several aspects and properties of the FAs formally defined in Section 9.3, which we now call *deterministic* FAs or **DFAs** to make the distinction. Despite substantial similarity in the definitions, NFAs do differ from DFAs in one crucial way: They can have more than one transition for a single symbol out of a state. By contrast, as we saw earlier, in a **deterministic** finite automaton (DFA), the transitions leaving a state must all be labeled with different symbols. Thus, the diagram in Example 9.11 must belong to an NFA since it has *two* transitions labeled a both leaving the start state. You may now wonder what state this automaton goes to when the input begins with a. We come back to that question, but for the moment just remember (from Section 9.5) that nondeterministic automata do not *directly* model real-life circuitry.

Example 9.11 For the finite language $L = \{ab, ac\}$, draw an NFA state transition diagram, giving each string of L its own states and transitions, sharing only the start state.

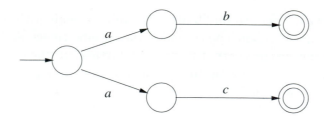

The NFA in Example 9.11 is a natural, straightforward representation of the language $L = \{ab, ac\}$, in the sense that the strings of the language are directly expressed in the diagram, each with its own path, in a way that can easily be extended to *any* finite language (any language consisting of a finite set of strings). However, as already mentioned, this automaton presents a dilemma by having two transitions with the same label departing from some state. For strings that begin with a, one might think that the diagram is in conflict with itself about where to go from the start state. The corresponding dilemma from an automaton viewpoint is: What is the value of $\delta(q_0, a)$? To have a chance of acceptance by this machine, of course, a string must begin with a. After the processing of the a, there are, momentarily, two possible current states. The next symbol then forces a selection between them, assuming that it is b or c. Of course, the string aa is rejected. The crucial idea here is that we have introduced a *choice* of transitions. Informally, as described in the previous section, a nondeterministic machine makes a series of choices that leads to the acceptance of the input whenever that is possible. We need to use formal definitions to state clearly how an NFA works.

The only difference between the two kinds of automata involves the transition function, δ. For DFAs, the (output) value of δ was an element of the set Q—that is, it had to be exactly one state. For NFAs, however, a value of δ can be any subset of the states. For a particular state and input symbol, the number of possible next states may be zero, one, or more than one. You can see that this would create some difficulty for Algorithm 9.1. Specifically, the assignment to q in the next-to-last line of that algorithm should be a single state.

To be more precise about the one difference between DFAs and NFAs, we can say that the difference concerns the *codomain* of δ. The codomain of any function is the set from which its outputs are chosen. Thus, for DFAs the codomain of δ is Q. Since δ for NFAs has values that are *subsets* of the states, its codomain must be all the subsets of states—that is, the power set, 2^Q (see Section 1.2).

Definition 9.4 Nondeterministic finite automata

A nondeterministic finite automaton, M, is a quintuple, $(Q, \Sigma, q_0, \delta, A)$, where Q, Σ, q_0, and A are just as for DFAs—that is, Q is the set of states, Σ is the set of symbols, q_0 is the start state, and A is the set of accepting states, but where

$$\delta : Q \times \Sigma \to 2^Q.$$

For various values of $q \in Q$ and $\sigma \in \Sigma$, the value of $\delta(q, \sigma)$ may be a set of zero, one, or more states. Cases of $\delta(q, \sigma)$ containing more than one state present a choice of what the next state will be. There will be at least one such case in each of the NFAs we present to make the machine genuinely nondeterministic. Contrastingly, a machine for which each of the $\delta(q, \sigma)$ contains zero or one state never has any real choices to make. Although such a machine can formally satisfy the definition of an NFA, it has a decidedly deterministic flavor and is readily rewritten as a deterministic automaton (see Exercise 9.12).

What strings are accepted by an NFA? Informally, a string x is accepted if there exists some choice of transitions, while reading the symbols of x left to right, that will take us from the start state to an accepting state. To make this formal, we need to adapt the definition of δ^* to the case of an NFA.

Definition 9.5 δ^*, **the nondeterministic generalized transition function**

Let $M = (Q, \Sigma, q_0, \delta, A)$ be an NFA. Then δ^* is a function that takes a state and a string as input and produces a resulting set of states. That is, $\delta^* : Q \times \Sigma^* \to 2^Q$. The specific values of δ^* are:

(i) For any $q \in Q$, $\delta^*(q, \Lambda) = \{q\}$ and

(ii) For any $q \in Q$, any $\sigma \in \Sigma$ and any $x \in \Sigma^*$,

$$\delta^*(q, x\sigma) = \bigcup_{p \in \delta^*(q,x)} \delta(p, \sigma).$$

Part (i) of Definition 9.5 is straightforward. In part (ii), the left side, $\delta^*(q, x\sigma)$, *means* the set of all states you can reach from state q by processing $x\sigma$, whereas the right side spells out how to *find* all these states: First find what states x can take you to (subscript on the union operator) and then, continuing from each of those, find the union of the states that you can get to in one more step with σ. For the case in which q is the initial state and $\delta^*(q, x)$ includes some accepting state, the machine accepts the string x. This leads to the definition of the language recognized by an NFA.

Definition 9.6 The language recognized by an NFA

The language $\mathcal{L}(M)$ **recognized** by an NFA $M = (Q, \Sigma, q_0, \delta, A)$ is the set of all strings $x \in \Sigma^*$ such that $\delta^*(q_0, x) \cap A \neq \emptyset$. One says that M **accepts** the strings of $\mathcal{L}(M)$ and **rejects** those of its complement, $\Sigma^* \setminus \mathcal{L}(M)$.

Example 9.12 Consider the language $L = \{x \mid x \in \{a, b\}^*$ and x ends with $ab\}$. This language contains, for example, the string $bbab$, but not $abba$. Draw a state transition diagram for both a DFA and an NFA to recognize L. Make each as simple as possible.

First, here is a DFA for L. Although the machine is small—just three states—it is not straightforward to see how one might have thought of it. Even after it has been presented, it is something of a challenge to characterize the job of each state in ensuring that exactly the right strings are accepted.

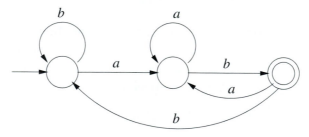

Compare the DFA to the following NFA that also recognizes L. Again we have three states, but now the diagram looks simpler and it is easier to see how it works.

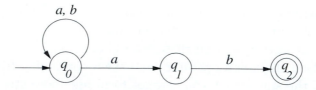

This machine simply loops until, nondeterministically, it verifies that the final two input symbols are ab. The formal notation for this machine is

$$M = (\{q_0, q_1, q_2\}, \{a, b\}, q_0, \delta, \{q_2\}),$$

where δ is specified by the following table.

$\delta =$		a	b
	q_0	$\{q_0, q_1\}$	$\{q_0\}$
	q_1	$\emptyset$	$\{q_2\}$
	q_2	$\emptyset$	$\emptyset$

9.7 Removing Nondeterminism

We have seen what nondeterminism is and how it allows for more readily understood finite automata, and yet important questions remain. First, how can we convert NFAs into real computational devices? We saw in Section 9.5 that this can be done for nondeterminism in general by parallel machines or by backtracking, but in this section we use an implementation method quite specific to finite automata.

A second important question is: Are NFAs more *powerful* than DFAs? In other words, is there some language that an NFA recognizes that is not recognized by any DFA? NFAs certainly *seem* to hold out the promise of additional possibilities, but that promise is *not* fulfilled since it turns out that the DFAs and NFAs represent *the same class of languages*. We prove this by the widely used proof technique of *simulation*, in which any machine of one category has its results achieved by a machine in the other category.

Notice that our two questions get answered simultaneously. "How do we make NFAs real?" is answered by converting them to DFAs, which provides the answer "No" to "Are they more powerful?" This negative answer is actually a good thing as a practical matter since it frees us to design in terms of NFAs, knowing that they can be automatically converted to (real) DFAs.

The recognition problem for an NFA language is *not* simply a matter of using the NFA in Algorithm 9.1—the algorithm for DFA language recognition. That algorithm does not work for NFAs because for NFAs the result of applying δ in the fourth line of the algorithm is a *set* of states. Now if that set has exactly one element, we can proceed as for DFAs; if that set is empty, the string can just be rejected. It is when the set of next states has two or more elements that the difficulty arises. In that case, when we come to δ again, in the next iteration of the `while` loop, its first argument has multiple values. For example, in state q_0 of the NFA in Example 9.12, if a is encountered in input, we have no way to know whether the NFA is in state q_0 or q_1.

Our solution is simply to tolerate this uncertainty. In this particular case, we say that our **state of knowledge** about the current state is expressed by the set $\{q_0, q_1\}$, indicating that the current NFA state must be one or the other of these. We are deliberately using the word "state" in two different ways here—for the states of the NFA and for states of knowledge. The states of knowledge become the states of a new *deterministic* automaton, using the *subset construction*, so named because the states of knowledge that it uses are *subsets* of Q—the set of states of the given NFA. After a detailed explanation in terms of a long example, we sum up the ideas in more general form with a definition and an algorithm.

Example 9.13 Given the NFA, M, in Example 9.12, find an equivalent DFA, M', that accepts the same set of strings, so that

$$\mathcal{L}(M') = \mathcal{L}(M).$$

The given NFA is $M = (\{q_0, q_1, q_2\}, \{a, b\}, q_0, \delta, \{q_2\})$, where δ is specified in the table of Example 9.12. Our strategy for finding the transition function, δ', for an equivalent DFA M' centers on our state of knowledge about what state M is in. Although this knowledge is not always enough to single out just one state, it does determine a *subset* of states that are currently possible. These states of knowledge are the states of the new machine, M'. We examine how one goes to another and record the transitions in a new table.

At the outset, M is known to be in state q_0, so the set of possible states is $\{q_0\}$. With no uncertainty, we simply copy the entries in the top row of the table for δ into a new table that we are now building for δ'. Having done this, we notice in column a that $\{q_0, q_1\}$ is a possible state of knowledge, so we treat it as a state of the new automaton we are building, which means giving it its own row in the table for δ'—specifically, the second row. The partially built table for δ' at this point is shown here.

	a	b
$\{q_0\}$	$\{q_0, q_1\}$	$\{q_0\}$
$\{q_0, q_1\}$		

$$\delta' =$$

To start filling in the second row, suppose that the state of knowledge is $\{q_0, q_1\}$ and the input symbol is a. This tells us that M must not have been in state q_1 after all—if there is to be any chance of acceptance—since $\delta(q_1, a) = \emptyset$. So M must have been in q_0 and must now be in q_0 or q_1—the state of knowledge denoted $\{q_0, q_1\}$. Next, suppose that the state of knowledge is $\{q_0, q_1\}$ and the input symbol is b. Then either M is in q_0 and stays at q_0 (since $\delta(q_0, b) = \{q_0\}$) or else M is in q_1 and goes to q_2 (since $\delta(q_1, b) = \{q_2\}$). Therefore, the new state of knowledge is $\{q_0, q_2\}$, which now gets its own row in δ'.

This third row is processed in the same way. We find that if we are in one of the states in $\{q_0, q_2\}$, then after processing an a our state of knowledge is $\{q_0, q_1\}$. Finally, if we are in either q_0 or q_2 and confront the input b, we must be in state q_0 if we are to continue. In that case, we stay in q_0 and our resulting state of knowledge is $\{q_0\}$. No new states of knowledge have arisen in this row (and none remains from earlier rows), so the table for δ' is now complete.

$$
\delta' = \quad
\begin{array}{c|c|c}
 & a & b \\
\hline
\{q_0\} & \{q_0, q_1\} & \{q_0\} \\
\{q_0, q_1\} & \{q_0, q_1\} & \{q_0, q_2\} \\
\{q_0, q_2\} & \{q_0, q_1\} & \{q_0\} \\
\end{array}
$$

A complete specification of a deterministic FA that accepts the same set of strings as the nondeterministic FA M in Example 9.12 is:

$$M' = (\{\{q_0\}, \{q_0, q_1\}, \{q_0, q_2\}\}, \{a, b\}, \{q_0\}, \delta', \{\{q_0, q_2\}\}),$$

where δ' is as shown in the preceding table. To determine the accepting states of M', we look for any state of knowledge that allows the *possibility* of being in an accepting state of M; specifically, this means sets containing q_2. There is just one such state in M'—namely, $\{q_0, q_2\}$. Consequently, A', the set of *all* such states, is the set $\{\{q_0, q_2\}\}$. Note that A' is a *one*-element set whose sole element is a two-element set of states.

A few comments about the preceding table for δ' are worth making. First, note that there is no row stating where to go from the state of knowledge $\{q_1\}$. This is reasonable since one is never sure of being in state q_1. The same can be said of $\{q_2\}$. The table really is complete since it does have a row for every state of knowledge that can be reached directly or indirectly from $\{q_0\}$. Finally, you may have observed that the table does not look like other DFA tables we have seen. That could be fixed by introducing simpler names.

The next table δ'' shows the result of the substitutions $q_0' = \{q_0\}$, $q_{01}' = \{q_0, q_1\}$ and $q_{02}' = \{q_0, q_2\}$. This new, neater table, clearly displays determinism yet retains—in the subscripts—information on the linkage back to the states of the original NFA.

$$
\delta' = \quad
\begin{array}{c|c|c|}
 & a & b \\
\hline
q_0' & q_{01}' & q_0' \\
\hline
q_{01}' & q_{01}' & q_{02}' \\
\hline
q_{02}' & q_{01}' & q_0' \\
\hline
\end{array}
$$

The start state is q_0' and the set of accepting states is $\{q_{02}'\}$. Note that this is exactly the DFA in Example 9.12, provided we label that machine's states q_0', q_{01}', and q_{02}' from left to right.

The preceding example shows what the subset construction does in a particular case and provides an idea of how it works. It is also important to understand the method in general terms. The construction takes an NFA and produces a DFA, so it actually is an implementation of a function from $\mathcal{N}$, the set of all NFAs, to $\mathcal{D}$, the DFAs. If we call that function $\mathcal{S}$, we can write $\mathcal{S} : \mathcal{N} \to \mathcal{D}$ as the mapping it achieves.

Definition 9.7 The subset construction

The subset construction, $\mathcal{S}$, is a function, $\mathcal{S} : \mathcal{N} \to \mathcal{D}$, that applies to any NFA, $M = (Q, \Sigma, q_0, \delta, A)$, to yield a DFA, $M' = \mathcal{S}(M) = (Q', \Sigma', q_0', \delta', A')$, where the following relationships hold between the parts of M and M' :

$$\Sigma' = \Sigma$$
$$q_0' = \{q_0\}$$
$$Q' \subseteq 2^Q$$
$$\delta' : Q' \times \Sigma \to Q' \quad \text{where } \forall q' \in Q' : \forall \sigma \in \Sigma : \delta'(q', \sigma) = \bigcup_{q \in q'} \delta(q, \sigma),$$
$$A' = \{q' \in Q' \mid q' \cap A \neq \emptyset\}$$

Notice several things here. First, the new alphabet, Σ', is not really new, but is just the same one, Σ that is also part of M. This makes sense since the two automata are to recognize the same language, which means the same strings of the same symbols. Second, $q_0' = \{q_0\}$ because the NFA must start at q_0. Next, consider Q'. Until the algorithm for the subset construction has actually been carried out for a particular automaton, M, we do not know just how big Q' will turn out to be, but we do know that each of its members is a subset of the states of Q. A set with n elements has 2^n subsets, so for an NFA with n states the construction may produce a DFA with up to 2^n states (including the possibility of a trap state, $\emptyset$). In the preceding example, the NFA had 3 states, which could have led to 8 ($= 2^3$) DFA states, although in this case we found only 3.

The fourth line in Definition 9.7 is the heart of the matter, showing the relationship between the new transition function, δ', and the given one, δ. Notice the quantifiers and union. The quantifiers say that this formula applies at each state q' with any input symbol, σ. In each case, the result of applying δ' is the union of all the states that can be reached via a σ-arrow from any state in q' (which is a set of states). Finally, A' is the set of members of Q' containing a member of A.

Algorithm 9.2 The subset construction: NFA to DFA

This algorithm builds the transition function, δ', of the new machine, the required DFA, as specified in Definition 9.7. The implementation of δ' is a table that we construct using a table operation, *record*. This table is like an array except that when you actually try to implement it, you have to deal with the fact that on one of its dimensions each index is a set. The first argument to *record* is a set of states that is to be put at some location in the table. The second argument is that location.

We also assume some operations of queue management. *Enqueue* adds an item at the end and *dequeue* returns an item that it removes from the front. Again, we use "$\Leftarrow$" as the assignment operator.

To-do is a queue in which each member is a *subset* of Q (the states of the original NFA) that needs to become a *member* of Q' (the states of the new DFA). Each of these queue items is waiting to have a row in the δ' table constructed for it. In contrast, the list *Done* contains the subsets for which table entries have already been constructed. Notice that when adding entries to *To-do*, the algorithm does not bother to check on whether they are already present in *To-do* or in *Done*. When an entry is dequeued later on, however, it is checked for membership in *Done* and is ignored at that point if it has already been processed.

$Done \Leftarrow empty\text{-}queue$
$To\text{-}do \Leftarrow empty\text{-}queue$
$\delta' \Leftarrow empty\text{-}table$
$enqueue(\{q_0\}, To\text{-}do)$
while $To\text{-}do \neq empty\text{-}queue$ **do**   // Subsets remain to be processed.
    $q' \Leftarrow dequeue(To\text{-}do)$
    if $q' \notin Done$ **then**   // Avoid repeats.
        $enqueue(q', Done)$
        for each $\sigma \in \Sigma$ **do**   // Create and store cell entry.
          $r' \Leftarrow \emptyset$
          for each $q \in q'$ **do**
            $r' \Leftarrow r' \cup \delta(q, \sigma)$
          $record(r', \delta'(q', \sigma))$
          $enqueue(r', To\text{-}do)$

9.8 Λ-Transitions

Preceding sections have shown how nondeterminism can, for some problems, allow a simple solution that can then be automatically converted to a deterministic form by simulation. This problem-solving strategy can be extended to additional situations by means of a handy new form of nondeterminism, Λ-transitions. In this section, we introduce them, motivate and use them in an example, formalize them, and finally eliminate them without losing their benefits.

In terms of state-transition diagrams, this new extension is just a matter of allowing Λ as a label on transitions, wherever it is convenient. The presence of a Λ-transition from state q_i of an automaton to state q_j means that whenever the automaton is in q_i, it may change its state to q_j without using up any input or even looking at the current input symbol. The notation of the Λ label is consistent with that of ordinary transitions in that—in either case—the label specifies what input is used up, in this case none, signified by the empty string, Λ. The automata that can be formed by adding this capability to those of ordinary NFAs are called Λ-**NFAs**. In Example 9.14, Λ-transitions provide a straightforward solution to a problem for which simplicity is otherwise elusive.

Example 9.14 Design an automaton for the union of L_1 and L_2, where L_1 is all strings of exactly one b *preceded* by zero or more as and L_2 is all strings of exactly one a *followed* by zero or more bs. That is,

$$L = L_1 \cup L_2$$
$$L_1 = \{x \mid yb \wedge y \in \{a\}^*\}$$
$$L_2 = \{x \mid ay \wedge y \in \{b\}^*\}$$

Let us start by trying to design an automaton for L without pre-judging whether it needs to be deterministic. To get L_1's unlimited sequence of as, we need an a-loop—that is, a transition labeled a that goes from some state to itself. Moreover, this state would apparently have to be the start state. In contrast, for the single a that must start each of the strings of L_2, we need an a-transition that does *not* go to itself. Since both of these possibilities are for the beginnings of strings, it seems we need the start state to have both an a-loop and an a-transition to some other state that in turn has a b-loop. Our design so far, with two a-transitions out of the start state, rules out a simple DFA. Even for an NFA, we have a problem since we are already permitting strings to have multiple as followed by multiple bs.

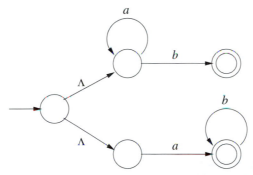

To escape these difficulties, we turn to a Λ-NFA, specifically the one shown here. This automaton begins by choosing to move to one of two states along a Λ-transition. From one of these states, we in effect enter a subautomaton for recognizing L_1. From the other, L_2 can be recognized. For example, the machine accepts $x = aab$ since it *can* initially move up to the first of the two upper states along a Λ-transition. After arriving at this state, it can now process the three symbols of x, leading to an accepting state.

The formal definition of a Λ-NFA includes all the familiar parts of an NFA and in addition a Λ-transition function, denoted λ (lowercase Λ). For each state q, this function tells us which other states are reachable from q via a single Λ-transition.

Thus, a Λ-NFA is a 6-tuple, $(Q, \Sigma, q_0, \delta, \lambda, A)$, where $\lambda : Q \to 2^Q$, and the other five items are as they were for NFAs.

For any state q and current input σ, a λ-NFA chooses its next state nondeterministically among the members of $\delta(q, \sigma) \cup \lambda(q)$, using up σ if the choice is based on δ, but *not* using up σ if the choice is based on λ. In the event of overlap—that is, if the next state is some r such that $r \in \delta(q, \sigma) \cap \lambda(q)$—the input σ may *or* may not be used. In Example 9.14, beginning at the start state, there are two possible Λ-transitions and no ordinary symbol transitions, so one of the Λ-transitions must be chosen, but in general the choice may be broader than that.

Formal definitions of δ^* and $\mathcal{L}(M)$ for Λ-NFAs are analogous to those given for NFAs and are omitted here. However, there is something new that merits attention. In the spirit of δ having a closure, δ^*, we define a λ-closure, denoted λ^*, that yields the set of states reachable by zero, one, or more Λ-transitions (but no ordinary transitions). The λ-closure plays an important role in specifying the languages of Λ-NFAs and their recognition.

Although the general idea of closure is the same for λ and δ, the formulas look a bit different. For one thing, $\lambda(q)$ and hence $\lambda^*(q)$ are functions of only one argument, not two arguments like $\delta(q, \sigma)$ and $\delta^*(q, x)$. Moreover, the closure of δ had to allow for applying δ an unlimited number of times since there is no limit on the length of an input string that serves as the second argument. Here, however, finite successions of Λ-transitions suffice to cover all possibilities since if there are n states, no path from one to another need be longer than $n - 1$. Formally, we first define λ^0 and then $\lambda^1, \ldots, \lambda^{n-1}$, where n is the number of states, $n = |Q|$. Finally, we take the union of all the $\lambda^k(q)$.

Definition 9.8 Λ-Closure

$$\forall q \in Q : \lambda^0(q) = \{q\}$$

$$\forall q \in Q : \lambda^{k+1}(q) = \bigcup_{p \in \lambda^k(q)} \lambda(p)$$

$$\forall q \in Q : \lambda^*(q) = \bigcup_{k=0}^{n-1} \lambda^k(q)$$

The purpose of introducing Λ-NFAs is the same as for NFAs: They permit short proofs of what can be done deterministically while omitting the details of a deterministic scheme. Yet as with NFAs, we need to show how an arbitrary Λ-NFA can be simulated by a DFA. Actually we only need to show how a Λ-NFA can be simulated by an NFA (since we know that an NFA can, in turn, be simulated by a DFA). This simulation technique is called Λ-*elimination*.

Our Λ-elimination method begins with the observation that for any string $x = a_1a_2 \ldots a_n$ to be accepted by a diagram that includes Λ-transitions, there must be a path (actually, there may be more than one) from the start state in that diagram to an accepting state, consisting of the following sequence of transitions: zero or more Λ-transitions, followed by an a_1-transition, then possibly some Λ-transitions, then an a_2-transition, and so on. Finally, after an a_n-transition, there can be zero or more Λ-transitions. For brevity, we use the notation Λ^* to mean zero or more Λs. The sequence of labels on the path from start to accepting state can thus be characterized as $\Lambda^*a_1\Lambda^*a_2\cdots\Lambda^*a_n\Lambda^*$. We can break up this sequence as follows: $(\Lambda^*a_1)(\Lambda^*a_2)\cdots(\Lambda^*a_n)\Lambda^*$.

Viewing the sequence in this way suggests the following steps for getting a new diagram that has no Λ-transitions but accepts the same language. First, for any of the symbols a_i in the sequence, consider the portion of the above path corresponding just to Λ^*a_i, consisting of Λ-transitions followed an a_i-transition. This path starts from some state, q_j, and ends at some state, q_k. (These could conceivably be the same state.) The effect of this path can be achieved by adding an a_i-transition connecting q_j directly to q_k. Formally, we write δ', the transition function for the new machine—a new λ-free NFA—as the following formula, which is to be used in step (ii) of Algorithm 9.3.

$$\delta'(q,\sigma) = \bigcup_{p \in \lambda^*(q)} \delta(p,\sigma)$$

The Λ^* at the end of $\Lambda^*a_1\Lambda^*a_2\cdots\Lambda^*a_n\Lambda^*$ suggests that any state connected by a sequence of Λs to an accepting state should also be accepting. When these two kinds of things have been done in all possible cases, the Λ-transitions are no longer needed and can all be deleted. This process is summarized in Algorithm 9.3.

Algorithm 9.3 Λ-elimination: Λ-NFA to NFA

The new machine, $M' = (Q', \Sigma, q_0, \delta', A')$, is an NFA with the same input alphabet (Σ) and start state (q_0) as the given Λ-NFA, M. Its set of states Q' is also like that of the original machine, the only difference being that some states may end up being unreachable (from q_0) and so can be eliminated. To compute δ' and A', do the following steps. Remember that $\lambda^*(q)$ always includes q. Also note that because Λ-transitions are not present in the new machine M', it does not have a λ-function.

(i) For each $q \in Q$, compute and record $\lambda^*(q)$, which is needed for the next two steps.

(ii) For each $q \in Q$ and $\sigma \in \Sigma$, compute δ' according to the formula in the text above.

(iii) For each $q \in Q$, if $\lambda^*(q)$ overlaps A (i.e., if $\lambda^*(q) \cap A \neq \emptyset$), then make q a member of A'.

(iv) Compute Q' as the set of states reachable from q_0.

The first three steps have been applied to the Λ-NFA in Example 9.14 to get the figure shown here. Note that this result includes an unreachable state. The final step of the algorithm would, in effect, remove that state by failing to include it in the new machine. In general, further simplifications in the resulting NFA might be possible; our intent is only to show that such an NFA exists.

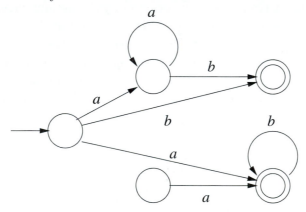

9.9   Pattern Matching

Pattern matching is an important application. Web searching is just one example of the need for techniques for finding occurrences of patterns in text. Pattern-matching algorithms are a well-studied topic. What is interesting here is that some of the best known algorithms are based on finite automata. The whole story is beyond the scope of this book, but we introduce the connection. This also gives us some practice designing FAs.

The standard pattern-matching problem begins with two strings: the *pattern* $P = p_1 p_2 \ldots p_m$ and the *text* $T = t_1 t_2 \ldots t_n$. The simplest goal is to find an occurrence of P in T, typically the first occurrence. For example, if $P = aaba$ and $T = baabbaabab$, then the first (and only) occurrence of P in T begins at the sixth character of T, $p_1 p_2 p_3 p_4 = t_6 t_7 t_8 t_9$.

What is the connection with FAs? Suppose we designed an FA M to accept the language

$$L(P) = \{x \mid x \text{ contains the string } P\}.$$

When processing the input, we know that M must enter an accepting state when it has just finished seeing the first occurrence of P and that thereafter it must remain in some accepting state or other. In other words, M essentially solves the pattern-matching problem when given T as input. Further, M provides an efficient way to search for P; it processes the characters of T very quickly. The main problem is, how do we get the FA M?

One way to design an FA is to start with a trivial NFA. Suppose $P = ababb$ and the alphabet is $\Sigma = \{a, b\}$. This NFA clearly accepts $L(P)$:

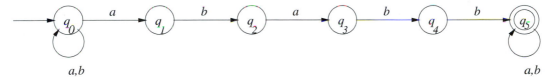

It waits nondeterministically for P to begin, verifies that P has occurred, and then stays in an accepting sink state. Clearly this example generalizes to any P. Now we can use the techniques in this chapter to convert the NFA into an FA. However, that could be time-consuming and yield an FA with a large number of states. Instead, we show how to quickly build an FA that has no more states than the NFA.

We continue to use the example of $P = ababb$ as we motivate the deterministic approach. An FA looking for P does not know, when it sees an a in the input, whether that a is the beginning of an occurrence of P. So when it (first) encounters an a, it must go to a state that corresponds to the fact that has seen the first character of P. Now if we are in this new state and encounter a b, we can go to another state that corresponds to the fact we have just encountered the first two characters of P. Continuing in this fashion, we can motivate the set of states $\{q_1, q_1, \ldots, q_m\}$, where reaching q_i corresponds to the fact that we have just encountered the first i characters of P. We introduce the state q_0 to correspond to the fact that no progress toward forming P has been made up to this point.

We have to be careful. Suppose that we have just processed these six input characters: $ababab$. Should we be in state q_2 (because the last two characters were ab) or state q_4 (because the last four characters were $abab$)? Clearly we need to be in state q_4, otherwise if the next input character were a b and we were in state q_2, we would not realize we had just encountered the fifth character of P. In general, you would never be in state q_i if you could be in state q_j, where $j > i$.

What if you were in state q_4 and encountered an a in the input? It follows that the last five characters of the input were *ababa*. We appear to have a choice between q_1 and q_3, but using the preceding observations we see that we must make a transition to state q_3. This sort of example can be generalized into a single rule: If we are state q_i and the input is σ, then we make a transition to state q_j where

$$ j = \max\{k \mid 0 \leq k \leq m \text{ and } p_1 p_2 \ldots p_k = p_{i-k+2} \ldots p_i \sigma \}. $$

We know that we have just encountered all the characters leading up to the ith character of P, and we try to use as many of those as possible in choosing j. It is important when interpreting this rule to realize there are two degeneracies, when $j = 1$ and $j = 0$. When $j = 1$, none of the prior characters matches up, but we keep track of the fact that the new input σ does match up with the first character of P. When $j = 0$ (recall that $p_1 p_2 \ldots p_k$ is the empty string iff $k = 0$), it is because we go to the state q_0, which means that we have currently made no progress at all toward finding P.

We are now ready to build an FA using only the states $Q = \{q_0, q_1, \ldots, q_m\}$. We make q_m an accepting sink for the same reason we did in the earlier NFA. Using the rule for j above we can generate all the other transitions we need. For our example, $P = ababb$, we get this machine:

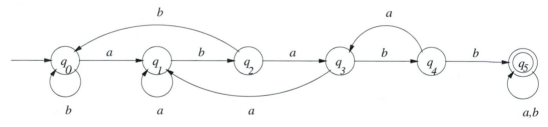

This gives a general technique for building FAs to solve the pattern-matching problem. It is rare that we are able to find such a general technique; most FAs are found less systematically.

9.10   Regular Languages

We are now in a position to define a language class in terms of a type of automaton. More specifically, Definition 9.9 defines a regular language to be one that some FA recognizes. You can think of the FA here as a DFA, but it can equally well be an NFA or a Λ-NFA, because as we have seen, they all have the same capabilities when it comes to what languages can be recognized.

Definition 9.9 Regular Languages

A language L is a regular language if (and only if) there exists an FA M such that $L = \mathcal{L}(M)$.

The class of regular languages has both practical and theoretical significance. In this section, our objective is to give an indication of how far-reaching this language class is. It might seem reasonable to expect that by taking two regular languages and combining them—by various language operations—we could get some new *non*regular languages. However, this turns out to be impossible for several operations, including many of the common set operations like union and intersection, as well as for concatenation and closure, which were developed specifically for languages in Chapter 8. We therefore say that these operations are **closed** with respect to the regular languages. It is as if the language class occupies a room and the door is closed for the operations in question, in the sense that they do not produce new languages outside the room. Thus, the room is quite large.

The fact that an operation is closed over some domain is generally called a *closure property*. Although this makes sense in terms of how English forms suffixes, it may seem confusing since the word "closure" has already been used (in Section 8.4) as an alternative name for the Kleene star operator and earlier in this chapter to talk about λ^* and δ^*. The ideas are actually all related; in particular, the star operator is what lets concatenation be closed.

As indicated before, an operation on languages is said to be closed for a language class if applying it to languages in that class produces other languages in the same class. We show that the class of regular languages is closed for the following operations: concatenation, (Kleene) closure, union, intersection, set difference, symmetric difference, and complementation. For example, if we take any regular languages L_1 and L_2, then their intersection $L_1 \cap L_2$ is also a regular language; that is, there exists an FA that recognizes $L_1 \cap L_2$. In fact, we prove each closure property by showing how to construct the FA for the result. Example 9.15 indicates the potential applicability of the closure properties by reworking an earlier example.

Example 9.15 Design an FA for the following language over $\Sigma = \{a, b\}$:

$$L \;=\; \{x \mid x \text{ is an } a \text{ followed by zero or more } b\text{s}$$
$$\vee\; x \text{ is a } b \text{ preceded by zero or more } a\text{s}\}.$$

It is easy to see that $L = L_1 \cup L_2$ where

$$L_1 = \{x \mid x \text{ is an } a \text{ followed by zero or more } b\text{s}\}.$$
$$L_2 = \{x \mid x \text{ is a } b \text{ preceded by zero or more } a\text{s}\}.$$

It is straightforward to design an FA for L_1 and an FA for L_2. We soon see that this is all we need since the proof of Theorem 9.4 shows how to build the FA for the union L automatically from the FAs for L_1 and L_2.

Theorem 9.2 If L_1 and L_2 are regular languages, then their concatenation $L = L_1 L_2$ (Definition 8.1) is a regular language.

Proof: Since L_1 and L_2 are regular languages, there must be two corresponding FAs M_1 and M_2:

$$L_1 = \mathcal{L}(M_1) \text{ where } M_1 = (Q_1, \Sigma_1, q_{0,1}, \delta_1, A_1)$$

$$L_2 = \mathcal{L}(M_2) \text{ where } M_2 = (Q_2, \Sigma_2, q_{0,2}, \delta_2, A_2)$$

According to Definition 9.9, L is regular if there is an FA, M, such that $L = \mathcal{L}(M)$. (Any kind of FA will do.) We use M_1 and M_2 to build a new Λ-NFA. Writing the new machine M as the 5-tuple

$$(Q_1 \cup Q_2, \Sigma_1 \cup \Sigma_2, q_{0,1}, \delta, A_2)$$

asserts that M contains all the states and symbols of the two original machines, the start state of M is the start state of M_1, and the accepting states of M are the accepting states of M_2. What remains to be described is δ. The new δ contains all of the transitions of δ_1 and δ_2 (which are *within* the two original machines) plus new transitions *between* the elements of Q_1 and Q_2. The new transitions are Λ-transitions from each (accepting) state in A_1 to $q_{0,2}$ the start state of M_2.

To show that $L = \mathcal{L}(M) = L_1 L_2$, we must show that $x \in L$ if and only if $x \in L_1 L_2$. Suppose $x \in L$. For x to be accepted by M, we must have first traversed a path in M_1 from its start state to one of its final states, then made a Λ-transition to the start state of M_2, and then followed a path in M_2 to one of its accepting states. In other words, $x = x_1 x_2$ where x_1 corresponds to the first path and x_2 to the second path. Therefore, $x_1 \in L_1$ and $x_2 \in L_2$ and $x \in L_1 L_2$. Similarly, if we begin by supposing that $x \in L_1 L_2$—so that $x = x_1 x_2$ where $x_1 \in L_1$ and $x_2 \in L_2$—then we can show that x will be accepted by M; so $x \in L$. $\square$

Theorem 9.3 If L_1 is a regular language, then $L = L_1^*$ is a regular language.

Proof: As in the previous proof, we begin with the same definition of M_1, from which we construct a new M, such that $L = L_1^* = \mathcal{L}(M)$. Formally, $M = (Q_1 \cup \{q_0\}, \Sigma, q_0, \delta, \{q_0\})$, where q_0, the only new state, is both the start state of M and the only accepting state of M. The transitions of δ include all those of δ_1 plus additional transitions to and from q_0. In particular, there is a Λ-transition from q_0 to $q_{0,1}$ the start state of M_1, and Λ-transitions from each state in A_1 back to q_0.

To show that $L = \mathcal{L}(M) = L_1^*$, we must show that $x \in L$ if and only if $x \in L_1^*$. Since this is true for $x = \Lambda$, we continue by assuming that x is not empty. Suppose $x \in L$. For x to be accepted by M, we must have made a Λ-transition to the start of M_1, traversed a path in M_1 to one of its accepting states, made a Λ-transition back to the start state of M, and then followed such a loop zero or more times. In other words, $x = x_1 x_2 \cdots x_k$, where x_1 corresponds to the first loop, and so on. Therefore, each $x_i \in L_1$, $1 \leq i \leq k$, and $x \in L_1^*$. Similarly, if we begin by supposing that $x \in L_1^*$—so that $x = x_1 x_2 \cdots x_k$, for some k, where each $x_i \in L_1$—then we can show that x will be accepted by M; so $x \in L$. $\square$

Like the preceding two proofs, the next one is also constructive; that is, to show the existence of a certain machine, we begin by constructing it. This time, the new machine has a set of states that is the cross-product of the state sets of the original machines. This stratagem allows the new machine to keep track of how both of the original machines would process each input.

Theorem 9.4 If L_1 and L_2 are regular languages, then $L = L_1 \cup L_2$ is a regular language.

Proof: As before, L_1 and L_2 must have two corresponding FAs M_1 and M_2:

$$L_1 = \mathcal{L}(M_1) \text{ where } M_1 = (Q_1, \Sigma, q_{0,1}, \delta_1, A_1)$$

$$L_2 = \mathcal{L}(M_2) \text{ where } M_2 = (Q_2, \Sigma, q_{0,2}, \delta_2, A_2)$$

From these two machines we build a new FA, M, such that $L = L_1 \cup L_2 = \mathcal{L}(M)$. Formally, $M = (Q_1 \times Q_2, \Sigma, (q_{0,1}, q_{0,2}), \delta, A)$. Since the new set of states is the cross-product $Q_1 \times Q_2$, the states of M are ordered pairs, in which the first element of the ordered pair is a state of M_1 and the second element is a state of M_2. The new start state combines the two original start states. The new δ is defined as follows:

$$\delta((q_1, q_2), \sigma) = (\delta_1(q_1, \sigma), \delta_2(q_2, \sigma)),$$

for every $q_1 \in Q_1$, $q_2 \in Q_2$, and $\sigma \in \Sigma$. Note that M is deterministic. Before discussing A, consider the behavior of this new machine.

We assert that M simulates the behaviors of M_1 and M_2 simultaneously. In particular, for any string x, if processing x takes you from $q_{0,1}$ to some $q_{i,1}$ in M_1 and processing x takes you from $q_{0,2}$ to some $q_{j,2}$ in M_2, then processing x in M takes you from $(q_{0,1}, q_{0,2})$ to $(q_{i,1}, q_{2,j})$. This can be proved inductively on the length of x.

What should A be? Since M should accept x iff $x \in L_1$ or $x \in L_2$, we define

$$A = \{(q_1, q_2) \mid q_1 \in A_1 \text{ or } q_2 \in A_2\}.$$

In other words, because of the simulation, we accept x iff we reach A_1 while running M_1 or we reach A_2 while running M_2. □

Corollary 9.1 If L_1 and L_2 are regular languages, then $L = L_1 \cap L_2$ is a regular language.

Proof: The construction for this proof is nearly identical to the one in the theorem. The new machine M again uses a cross-product of state sets. Indeed it is the same as the one for Theorem 9.4 with respect to all of its parts except for A, the set of accepting states, which is now as follows:

$$A = \{(q_1, q_2) \mid q_1 \in A_1 \text{ and } q_2 \in A_2\}.$$

Note that with this definition of A a string x is accepted by M iff $x \in L_1$ *and* $x \in L_2$—that is $x \in L_1 \cap L_2$. □

Similar techniques can be used to prove related corollaries. In particular, we leave the proofs for set difference and symmetric difference as exercises. Example 9.16 shows the practical applicability of the cross-product construction from the preceding theorem and corollary.

Example 9.16 Find an FA for the language L, over $\Sigma = \{a, b\}$, of strings that have both an odd number of as and an odd number of bs. Now clearly $L = L_1 \cap L_2$ where

$$L_1 = \{x \mid x \in \{a, b\}^* \wedge x \text{ contains an odd number of } a\text{s}\}, \text{ and}$$

$$L_2 = \{x \mid x \in \{a, b\}^* \wedge x \text{ contains an odd number of } b\text{s}\}.$$

We begin by designing the comparatively simpler FAs corresponding to L_1 and L_2.

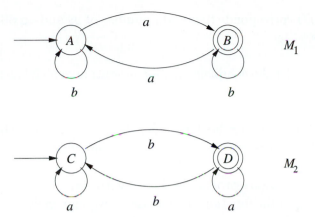

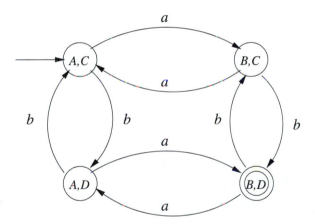

For example, state A represents the fact that the number of as so far is even; state B corresponds to an odd number of as. We now construct M as described in the corollary.

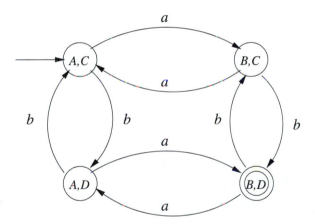

Notice how this simple technique turns a difficult task into a routine exercise. Also note that the interpretations of the new states follow directly combined interpretations of the original states.

- (A, C) corresponds to an even number of as and an even number of bs so far.

- (B, C) corresponds to an odd number of as and an even number of bs so far.

- (A, D) corresponds to an even number of as and an odd number of bs so far.

- (B, D) corresponds to an odd number of as and an odd number of bs so far.

Finally, we consider the complementation operation, which has the simplest proof of all.

Theorem 9.5 If L_1 is regular language, then $L = \Sigma^* \setminus L_1$, the complement of L_1 with respect to Σ, is a regular language.

Proof: As in the previous proofs, we begin with $M_1 = (Q_1, \Sigma, q_{0,1}, \delta_1, A_1)$. We assume that δ_1 is a total function; if necessary, we can make this so by adding a trap state. From M_1, we construct a new M, such that $L = \Sigma^* \setminus L_1 = \mathcal{L}(M)$. In particular, $M = (Q_1, \Sigma, q_{0,1}, \delta_1, Q_1 \setminus A_1)$. In other words, M differs from M_1 in that set of accepting states is complemented. Therefore, x is accepted by M iff x is not accepted by M_1. $\square$

Exercises

9.1 Redraw the diagram of Example 9.3 including its trap state and all the transitions associated with that state.

9.2 Draw a state transition diagram for each of the languages specified. Omit trap states. Be sure that each diagram, besides accepting all the strings described, also excludes all others. The languages are the sets of all strings over $\{a,b,c\}$ that:

    (a) start with c.

    (b) end in c.

    (c) contain exactly one c.

    (d) contain at least one c.

    (e) contain at least one c and are of length exactly 2.

    (f) are of length at most 2.

    (g) are of length at most n for some integer n.

9.3 Express the language L of Example 9.3 as $L = L_1 L_2$ by specifying L_1 and L_2 formally.

9.4 Draw a state transition diagram for comments in C or C++. These are the strings that (i) begin with /*, (ii) end in */ without overlap (so /*/ is excluded), and (iii) have no other occurrence of */. Hint: Look at Example 9.5.

9.5 Example 9.5 defines a language L in terms of three conditions that its strings must satisfy. Let M be the *second* (correct) state transition diagram given there. *Prove* that $L = \mathcal{L}(M)$.

Hints: (1) You are being asked to prove the equality of two languages. You can do this by showing that each string must be in both or neither. Alternatively, you can show that each language is a subset of the other. (2) It helps to break the problem into cases on the basis of whether a string is or is not of the form $dcycd$ for some y. (3) For a string of this latter form to be in $L = \mathcal{L}(M)$, y must correspond to a path in M from the middle state to either that state or the one immediately to its right.

9.6 Formally specify a machine $M = (Q, \Sigma, q_0, \delta, A)$ by giving the values of Q, Σ, q_0, A, and δ corresponding to

(a) the state transition diagram in Example 9.4, as shown, with δ being a partial function.

(b) the same diagram except that you first add the trap state and the transitions associated with it. Note that δ is now a total function.

9.7 Let $M = (\{q_0, q_1, q_2, q_3\}, \{a\}, q_0, \delta, \{q_1, q_3\})$, where δ is specified by the following table.

$$\delta = \quad \begin{array}{c|c} & a \\ \hline q_0 & q_1 \\ q_1 & q_2 \\ q_2 & q_3 \\ q_3 & q_0 \end{array}$$

(a) Draw the state transition diagram for this finite automaton.

(b) Very briefly describe the language $\mathcal{L}(M)$ in English.

(c) Using a quintuple, give a complete specification of a two-state automaton that accepts $\mathcal{L}(M)$.

9.8 Specify just the transition function of a finite automaton for the second state transition diagram in Example 9.5. Omit the trap state. Label the states q_0, q_1, q_2, q_3, and q_4.

9.9 For your automaton in Exercise 9.8, give the values of δ^* for the arguments shown here.

(a) $\delta^*(q_0, dcba)$

(b) $\delta^*(q_1, \lambda)$

(c) $\delta^*(q_1, dcba)$

(d) $\delta^*(q_2, dcba)$

(e) $\delta^*(q_0, dcd)$

(f) $\delta^*(q_0, dccccd)$

9.10 Following the technique in Example 9.8 in its use of Definition 9.2, *prove* that for the finite automaton of Example 9.7, $\delta^*(q_0, dad) = q_2$.

9.11 In the discussion leading up to Algorithm 9.1 for recognizing the language of a finite automaton, an alternative algorithm is suggested that consists of (i) defining a recursive subroutine for δ^* and (ii) calling it from a main program. Write this two-part algorithm either in the pseudocode of this text or in a high-level programming language.

9.12 Let $M = (Q, \Sigma, q_0, \delta, A)$ be an NFA with no genuine choice. In other words, for every q in Q and σ in Σ, the value of $\delta(q, \sigma)$ either has one element or is empty. Formally specify a new *deterministic* automaton, M' that accepts the same language as M. That is, formally specify the five parts of the quintuple for M' so that $\mathcal{L}(M') = \mathcal{L}(M)$.

Hint: Introduce a trap state—call it q_t'—and then specify δ by formally specifying what must happen (i) when $\delta(q, \sigma) = \emptyset$ and (ii) when $\delta(q, \sigma) = \{p\}$; that is, when δ yields the one-element set containing only state p.

9.13 For both the DFA and NFA in Example 9.13, evaluate $\delta^*(q_0, x)$ for each of the following strings, x.

(a) a

(b) b

(c) ab

(d) *ba*

(e) *abab*

(f) a^k, where $k \geq 1$

9.14 Create an NFA for the set of all strings over $\{a, b\}$ ending in *abab* and use the subset construction to convert it to a DFA. (Your NFA should have a self-loop on the start state labeled with both *a* and *b*. Transitions labeled *a* and then *b*, *a*, and *b* should take the NFA from q_0 to q_1 and then to q_2, q_3, and q_4, which is accepting.)

9.15 This problem concerns automata for the language L consisting of all strings over $\{a, b\}$ that end in *either abab or baa*.

(a) Draw the transition diagram of an NFA for L by starting with the same states and transitions as in Exercise 9.14 and adding some states by a similar technique so that transitions labeled *b* and then *a* and *a* take the NFA from q_0 to a new accepting state. Label the new states q_5, ...

(b) Use the subset construction to convert your NFA to a DFA expressed as a quintuple.

9.16 Algorithm 9.2 for the subset construction maintains a queue of states, *To-do*, that are among those to be used in the new DFA, but that have not yet been processed to find how they must behave in the new transition function. Hand simulate the algorithm to the extent necessary to enable you to write down a trace of the values of *To-do* over the entire course of the execution of the algorithm when it operates on

(a) the NFA in Example 9.14

(b) the NFA in Example 9.15

9.17 In the seventh line of Algorithm 9.2, to avoid repeated processing of a state, the algorithm checks whether q' is a member of the queue, *Done*.

(a) Explain what this entails, taking into account that *Done* is a sequence of sets.

(b) Discuss the efficiency of alternative ways to maintain the sets and accomplish this test.

9.18 Build an FA for $L(P) = \{x \mid x$ contains the string $P\}$ for these patterns:

   (a) $P = aaab$

   (b) $P = abba$

9.19 Give both a nondeterministic and a deterministic finite automaton for the language L in which each string contains the substring aa and at some later point the substring bb. Thus, for example, $baaababba \in L$, but $bbaa \notin L$.

9.20 Carry out the following steps to get a simple, correct state-transition diagram for a^*b^*. Begin with the simple diagram for a^* in Example 9.6 and a similar one for b^*. Use these two diagrams together with the correct diagram construction operation for concatenation (introducing a Λ-transition) to get a diagram for a^*b^*. Draw this diagram. Then demonstrate the process of Λ-elimination by showing the successive results of applying steps (i)–(iii) of Algorithm 9.3.

9.21 In a manner similar to that specified in Exercise 9.20, draw a state transition diagram for $a^* + b^*$. You again need a Λ-transition. Draw this diagram. Then demonstrate the process of Λ-elimination by showing the successive results of applying steps (i)–(iii) of Algorithm 9.3.

9.22 Drawing on the ideas of Exercises 9.20 and 9.21, give an automaton with Λ and another without Λ for the language L in which each string consists of an even number of as followed by an even number of bs. Recall that 0 is even.

9.23 Show that the regular languages are closed under set difference. In particular, show that if L_1 and L_2 are regular then $L_1 \setminus L_2$ is also regular.

9.24 Consider Definition 9.8, which defines repeated application of the function λ for Λ-NFAs.

   (a) Why does it make sense to stipulate that for any q, $\lambda^0(q) = \{q\}$?

   (b) Prove that for any q the following holds: $\lambda^1(q) = \lambda(q)$.

   (c) In defining λ^*, we stated that "no path from one [state] to another need be longer than $n - 1$." Prove, in graph-theoretic terms why this is so, by arguing that in this context any path of length n or more can be replaced by a shorter path. Hint: You may find a use for the pigeon-hole principle here.

9.25 Use the cross-product technique to build an FA for this language over $\Sigma = \{a, b\}$:

$$L = \{x \mid \text{there is no } b \text{ before an } a \text{ in } x \ \wedge \ |x| \text{ is even}\}.$$

9.26 Use the cross-product technique to build an FA for this language over $\Sigma = \{a, b\}$:

$$L = \{x \mid \text{there is at most one } a \text{ in } x \ \wedge \ \text{ there is at least one } b \text{ in } x\}.$$

9.27 Prove by mathematical induction that if L is a regular language (an FA language), then $\forall k \in \mathcal{N} : L^k$ is a regular language (an FA language).

9.28 The two Prolog implementations of FAs were presented for deterministic FAs. Would they work for NFAs?

Chapter 10

Regular Expressions

In Chapter 9, we explored finite automata motivated by the computational task of *language recognition*. In particular, we studied FAs and the class of languages that FAs recognize. Remarkably, the range of languages belonging to this class turned out to be the same whether FA was taken to mean DFA, NFA, or Λ-NFA. In this chapter, we turn to the other main computational task for languages: *language generation*. The focus is on describing languages so that we can readily produce their strings.

One approach to generation issues is to use *grammars*. A grammar is basically a set of rules—called *grammatical rules*—that specify how to build up longer and longer strings in the language while avoiding the production of strings that are not in the language. These rules for specifying what is and is not in a language are more precise than the statements in traditional grammars of English and other human languages. Important as this technique is, however, we postpone treatment of it to Chapter 12, where we discuss grammars not only for the languages that FAs recognize, but for other language classes as well.

An alternative approach to the study of language generation is *regular expressions* (REs), the principal topic of this chapter. These turn out to be especially appropriate for the languages of FAs, which is why we take them up at this particular point.

REs represent languages with just three of the several language operations introduced in Chapters 8 and 9, yet turn out to have all the generative power of FAs. That is, any FA language is also an RE language; the converse is true too. REs and their variants are widely used to represent sets of strings in programming contexts. For example, REs provide the foundation for the compiler tool known as Lex, which is the topic of Chapter 11.

10.1   Regular Sets

Before taking up our main topic, let us try to prevent a possible confusion involving names. The FA languages were called the *regular* languages in the preceding chapter and that is in fact a correct way to refer to them since historically researchers have called them that. However, the name "regular languages" seems to prejudge the question of whether these FA languages are related to the REs. One might assume that *of course* regular languages and REs are related; after all, they are both regular. So here the languages recognized by FAs are called "FA languages." When we ultimately find that these are identical to the languages generated by REs, which look very different from FAs, we will be suitably amazed. With that said, let us proceed.

An important approach to language generation uses language operations and takes advantage of their *closure properties* with respect to FA languages (see Section 9.10). Recall that this use of the word closure refers to the question of whether a set is closed with respect to an operation—in particular, the class of FA languages is closed with respect to union, intersection, concatenation, and some other language operations including the operation called *closure* in the other sense of that word, where it refers to the operation also known as "Kleene star."

Language operations provide a way to generate languages. For example, if you have two FA languages, you can generate a new FA language by taking the union (concatenation, etc.) of the two that you already had. This *suggests* that if we start with some small collection of FA languages as a basis, we might be able to build up exactly the class of all and only the FA languages by applying operations that are closed with respect to FAs. We do know—from closure properties—that several operations are safe: They give us *only* FA languages. But this does not ensure getting *all* the FA languages.

Not only do we get them all, but it turns out that we do not need all of the closed operations. It is sufficient—and simpler—to use just three of them: concatenation, union, and closure. We first define the sets of strings that can be generated with these operations and then prove that these sets are indeed exactly the entire class of FA languages. These sets, which we call *regular sets*, are sets of strings so they are also languages. Yet we call them regular *sets* because the phrase "regular languages" is, as noted before, already associated with FAs, and we do not want our use of names to prejudge the outcome. The following definition has three parts: the first specifies the simplest imaginable sets, which serve as the building blocks; the second states the rules for combining, by the three operations, both the building blocks and results of previous combining; and the last part rules out everything else.

Definition 10.1 Regular sets

The regular sets of strings over the alphabet Σ meets these conditions.

1. $\emptyset$ and $\{\Lambda\}$ are regular sets. $\forall \sigma \in \Sigma : \{\sigma\}$ is a regular set.

2. If S is a regular set, S^* is regular.
   If S_1 and S_2 are regular sets, $S_1 S_2$ and $S_1 \cup S_2$ are regular.

3. No other sets over Σ are regular.

Condition 1 states that the very simplest sets of strings are regular. That is, $\emptyset$ and the set consisting of only the empty string, $\{\Lambda\}$, are regular, as are the sets of strings consisting of a single string of length 1. For example, with $\Sigma = \{a, b\}$, the sets $\{a\}$ and $\{b\}$ are regular. The second condition says that the operations of concatenation, union, and closure applied to regular sets produce regular sets. The last condition in the definition adds nothing but limits the languages to those specified in the earlier conditions.

Theorem 10.1 A set of strings is a regular set if and only if it is an FA language.

After we prove this theorem, we will be justified in using the terms *regular set* and *FA language* interchangeably. We will also be able to resume using the phrase *regular language* without confusion since it is defined to be the same as FA language, and we will have shown that everything we have called "regular" really is related in the ways suggested by the shared phrasing. The *if* part of Theorem 10.1 is Theorem 10.2 in Section 10.3, and the *only if* part is Theorem 10.3 in Section 10.4.

Note that the recursive definition of *regular sets* naturally leads to more complicated expressions. Whenever one has several operators that can be used to build up complex expressions, it is important to know the order in which they are meant to be applied. Parentheses can always be used for this purpose, but it is also helpful to establish a *precedence ranking* as well. For example, in the algebraic expression $x + 3y^2$, the exponentiation comes first, then multiplication, and finally addition. For regular sets, closure and exponents have higher precedence than concatenation, which in turn has precedence over union. (Recall that exponents in such an expression are just shorthand for repeated concatenation.)

Example 10.1 To form the set corresponding to $S_1 \cup S_2 S_3^*$ from string sets S_1, S_2 and S_3, first form S_3^*, the closure of S_3. Then concatenate S_2 and S_3^* to form $S_2 S_3^*$. Finally, take the union of S_1 and

$S_2 S_3^*$ to form the desired language, $S_1 \cup S_2 S_3^*$. In other words, these parentheses are implicit: $(S_1 \cup (S_2(S_3^*)))$. Of course we must use parentheses if precedence would give something other than what we intended. For example, $(S_1 \cup S_2)S_3^*$ indicates that we first take the union and the closure before the final concatenation.

Example 10.2 In the preceding example, let us replace S_1, which is a name for a set, by some particular set—specifically the set $\{a\}$. Similarly, let $S_2 = \{b\}$ and $S_3 = \{c\}$. With these changes, the example becomes $\{a\} \cup \{b\}\{c\}^*$. The shortest few strings in this regular set can be written as follows: $\{a, b, bc, bcc, bccc, \ldots\}$.

10.2   Regular Expressions and What They Represent

When working with regular sets, it is tedious to write them out as expressions corresponding to the recursive definition. Consider this regular set over the alphabet $\{a, b, c\}$:

$$(\{a\}\{b\}\{b\} \cup \{c\})^* \cup \{a\}(\{b\}\{c\})^*.$$

This is an unwieldy way to express this set especially since it is pretty clear that the braces, "{" and "}", are unnecessary. **Regular expressions** (REs) represent regular sets by omitting the braces and using a plus sign in place of the union sign. For example, the preceding regular set corresponds to this RE:

$$(abb + c)^* + a(bc)^*.$$

REs are thus more succinct and in fact look like abbreviations for the regular sets they represent. Moreover, their resemblance to ordinary algebraic expressions suggests the correct precedence, making them easy to read and understand. Variations on this improved representation occur in many computer science contexts, most notably in the Lex language-recognition software, coming up soon (Chapter 11).

It is worth noticing that "b" now has three related but distinct meanings. Within the symbol set "$\{a, b, c\}$," it is a symbol. In the phrase "the language $\{b\}$," it must be a string since a language is a set of strings. The length of this particular string is one. Finally, to say "b is an RE" is to claim (correctly) that b is an RE, specifically the RE representing the language $\{b\}$. The symbol Λ is the regular expression that represents the language $\{\Lambda\}$, while the expression $\emptyset$ represents itself, so to speak. Taken together, Λ and the symbols are the primitives or building blocks of REs. In addition to them, we need operators to build up more complex ones.

REs have three operators: concatenation, alternation, and closure. The concatenation of two REs represents the concatenation of their sets. Similarly, the closure of an RE, formed by applying "$*$", represents the closure of its regular set. The **alternation** operator gets its name from the fact that it provides for alternatives. Its symbol is "$+$" and it corresponds directly to the union of sets. For example, $a + b$ is the RE for $\{a\} \cup \{b\}$, that is, the language $\{a, b\}$. Unlike concatenation, alternation is commutative (e.g., $a + b = b + a$). This certainly makes sense in terms of sets since the order of the elements does not matter.

Example 10.3 The following table gives some REs and their languages. The expressions that use closure have infinite languages, so one cannot list all their strings. In these cases, we may settle for listing several of the shorter strings followed by "$\ldots$" or we may specify an infinite set intensionally, as in the last row of the table.

RE	Corresponding Regular Set
$a + bc$	$\{a, bc\}$
$a(b + c)$	$\{ab, ac\}$
$(a + b)(a + c)(\Lambda + a)$	$\{aa, ac, ba, bc, aaa, aca, baa, bca\}$
$a^*(b + cc)$	$\{b, cc, ab, acc, aab, aacc, aaab, aaacc, \ldots\}$
$a + bb^*$	$\{a, b, bb, bbb, bbbb, bbbbb, \ldots\}$
$(a + bb)^*$	$\{\Lambda, a, bb, aa, abb, bba, bbbb, aaa, \ldots\}$
a^*b^*	$\{\Lambda, a, b, aa, ab, bb, aaa, aab, abb, bbb, \ldots\}$
$((a + b)(a + b))^*$	$\{x \mid x \in \{a, b\}^* \wedge \lvert x \rvert \text{ is even.}\}$

Examples can be helpful, but to be clear about *all* the possibilities, we now define the REs formally. Each one expresses a particular corresponding language, and Definition 10.2 specifies that correspondence. The strict parallels between this definition and Definition 10.1 make it clear that REs represent regular sets and nothing else.

Definition 10.2 Regular expressions (REs) and their languages
The following conditions specify the set of REs, R, over the symbol set Σ and also their languages.

1. $\emptyset \in R$ and it represents the set $\emptyset$.
   $\Lambda \in R$ and it represents the set $\{\Lambda\}$.
   $\forall \sigma \in \Sigma : \sigma \in R$ and it represents the set $\{\sigma\}$.

2. If $r \in R$, then $(r^*) \in R$, representing the closure of r's set.
   If $r_1 \in R$ and $r_2 \in R$, then $(r_1 r_2) \in R$ and $(r_1 + r_2) \in R$, representing the concatenation and union of the sets that r_1 and r_2 represent.

3. There are no other REs over Σ.

Definition 10.3 The language function $\mathcal{L}$
  If r is an RE, $\mathcal{L}(r)$ is the set it represents.

Example 10.4 What strings are in $L = \mathcal{L}((a + bb)^*)$?

  L is the set that the RE $(a + bb)^*$ represents. This language contains all strings over $\{a, b\}$, in which the all-b substrings must be of even length.

Notice that in part 2 of Definition 10.2, each new RE introduces a new set of parentheses. Therefore, all the REs formed according to this definition are fully parenthesized. The outermost parentheses are always unnecessary. Additional pairs of parentheses are unnecessary in some REs because of precedence. The precedence rules correspond to those for regular sets: closure is highest, followed by concatenation, and finally alternation, with lowest precedence.

A good way to improve understanding of REs is to try to translate back and forth between them and either English or set notation. In one direction, you would start with either a description in ordinary English for some set of strings or else an intensional set specification for such a set. In either case, you would try to write a corresponding RE—one that represents the given set. Alternatively, you could try to do the opposite. In the next few examples, we start from English.

Example 10.5 Find an RE for the set of all strings over $\Sigma = \{a, b\}$.

  To translate this English specification to an RE, we can clearly use $(a + b)^*$. In fact, since "+" is commutative, as noted earlier, we can just as well give $(b+a)^*$ as the answer. In fact, $(a+b)$ can be replaced by $(b + a)$ anywhere, specifically in several of the examples below, with no effect on the set expressed.

Example 10.6 Find an RE that is simpler than $(a^* b^*)^*$ but represents the same set.

  Example 10.3 shows that $\mathcal{L}(a^* b^*)$ is a superset of $\mathcal{L}(a + b)$. Taking the closure of each, it follows that $\mathcal{L}((a^* b^*)^*)$ must surely contain everything in $\mathcal{L}((a+b)^*)$. It cannot contain more since $\mathcal{L}((a+b)^*)$ contains everything. So $\mathcal{L}((a^*b^*)^*) = \mathcal{L}((a+b)^*)$, which is the set of all strings over $\Sigma = \{a, b\}$. Getting back to the original question: To simplify $(a^*b^*)^*$, write $(a+b)^*$.

Example 10.7 Find an RE for all strings of bs with at least two bs.

Since a string here can have any length except 0 or 1, the set is infinite, which suggests the use of closure. To get lengths of "at least 2," we start with lengths of "at least 0," for which we can use b^*, and then increase all lengths by 2 by adding bb. That is, b^*bb is an RE for the strings of at least two bs. The extra bs could have been added anywhere: $bbb^* = bb^*b = b^*bb$ are all correct answers. In these last expressions, note that each "*" applies only to the b right before it according to the precedence rules.

Definition 10.4 An extension of REs
Let r be any RE. Then $r^0 = \Lambda$ and for all $k \geq 0$, $r^{k+1} = rr^k$.

For example, an RE for all strings of length exactly 4 is $(a+b)^4 = (a+b)(a+b)(a+b)(a+b)$. Strictly speaking, these superscripts are not part of RE notation, but sometimes, as in the next example, we use them to simplify the REs.

Example 10.8 Use the notation of Definition 10.4 to write an RE for (i) all strings of length k over $\Sigma = \{a, b\}$, and (ii) all strings of length $\leq k$ over $\Sigma = \{a, b\}$.

(i) $(a+b)^k$ represents all strings of length k over $\{a, b\}$.

(ii) $(a+b+\Lambda)^k$ represents all strings of length $\leq k$ over $\{a, b\}$.

Definition 10.5 Another extension of REs
Let r be any RE. Then r^+ represents all strings in r^* except Λ.

It follows immediately that $r^* = \Lambda + r^+$. Another way to describe r^+ is to say that it stands for one or more rs concatenated. It is also true that $r^+ = rr^*$.

Example 10.9 Write an RE for real numbers in binary notation as follows: one or more binary digits followed by a period (".") followed by one or more binary digits.

$$(0+1)^+.(0+1)^+$$

Example 10.10 Find an RE for all strings over $\Sigma = \{a, b\}$ in which the number of bs is: (i) exactly 2, (ii) at least 2, (iii) even, or (iv) odd.

(i) For exactly two bs, write them down and then allow for arbitrarily many as anywhere: $a^*ba^*ba^*$.

(ii) The case of at least two bs can be handled similarly by replacing each a in the preceding expression by $(a+b)$ to get $(a+b)^*b(a+b)^*b(a+b)^*$. However, some simpler expressions work too, such as $a^*ba^*b(a+b)^*$.

(iii) Since the even numbers are the multiples of 2, we might think of applying closure to the expression for two bs to get $(a^*ba^*ba^*)^*$. However, this expression leaves out all strings with zero bs except Λ. It turns out that a slightly simpler expression works: $a^*(ba^*ba^*)^*$.

(iv) By adding one more b (and any number of as), we get $a^*ba^*(ba^*ba^*)^*$ for strings with an odd number of bs.

Example 10.11 Describe the regular set represented by the RE $\Lambda + b + bb + bbbb^*$.

Here we go in the direction opposite to that of the preceding examples: from an RE to English. By analogy with Example 10.7, $bbbb^*$ represents the strings of 3 or more bs. The rest of the expression takes care of lengths 0, 1, and 2, giving the set of all strings of bs. Thus, the given RE simplifies to b^*. A description of the language is "all strings of zero or more bs."

Example 10.12 Describe the regular set represented by the following RE:

$$0+(1+2+3+4+5+6+7+8+9)(0+1+2+3+4+5+6+7+8+9)^*$$

Ignoring the "$0+$" out front, we have an expression that represents one or more decimal digits in which the first of them is not zero. Thus, we have all the positive decimal numbers without leading zeroes. The "$0+$" at the beginning allows the digit zero to appear alone. Our description of the set is "the set of nonnegative integers."

Figure 10.1: Diagrams for all the REs—$\emptyset$, Λ, a, and b—over $\{a, b\}$ without operators.

10.3 All Regular Sets Are FA Languages

In this section, we prove the first part of Theorem 10.1: Every regular set is in fact an FA language. In other words, the set of strings represented by an RE is an FA language. More briefly, RE languages are FA languages. The proof can draw on the relationship of the definition of regular sets to the closure properties. Alternatively, we could have a more direct proof, where we explicitly build an FA that accepts the language represented by an RE. This latter approach is also discussed.

We prove the result by induction. Recall that induction is used for theorems about integers, so how can we apply it here? We use the number of operations in the RE. For example, a involves zero operations and $(abb + c)^* + a(bc)^*$ is the result of 8 operations: 4 concatenations, 2 alternations, and 2 closures. Further, because of the recursive nature of the definition, there can be no doubt about which operation was the last to apply; in the preceding example, it was the alternation of $(abb + c)^*$ and $a(bc)^*$.

Theorem 10.2 The set of strings represented by an RE is an FA language.

Proof: We prove this by induction on the number of operators in the RE. In particular, we show:

> If r is an RE containing k operations,
>
> then $\mathcal{L}(r)$ is an FA (regular) language, for $0 \le k$.

The basis of the proof is $k = 0$. Figure 10.1 shows state transition diagrams for these simplest REs, the ones with no operators. These are $\emptyset$, Λ, a, and b, assuming that $\Sigma = \{a, b\}$. Notice that the string Λ is accepted by the second diagram because no input is needed for getting from the start to the accepting state as they are the same state. The $\emptyset$-diagram is included for completeness, but plays no further role and is not discussed again.

Now assume that the RE r has $k > 0$ operations. By the (strong) inductive hypothesis any RE with fewer than k operations represents an FA language. By definition, r is either r_1r_2, $r_1 + r_2$, or r_1^*, where r_1 and r_2 contain fewer than k operations. By the inductive hypothesis, $\mathcal{L}(r_1)$ and $\mathcal{L}(r_2)$ are regular languages. By Theorems 9.2, 9.3, and 9.4, it follows that $\mathcal{L}(r_1)\mathcal{L}(r_2)$, $\mathcal{L}(r_1)^*$, and $\mathcal{L}(r_1) \cup \mathcal{L}(r_2)$, respectively, are all regular languages. Therefore, $\mathcal{L}(r)$ is an FA language. $\square$

Although this proof is quite short and mathematical, it is based on the closure results for regular languages. If you look at the proofs of those results, you see *very* clear instructions for building finite automata (Λ-NFAs) to accept the more complex regular languages resulting from REs. We can use these constructive proofs to explicitly build a Λ-NFA that recognizes $\mathcal{L}(r)$ for any RE r.

1. Decompose r, using the recursive definition, down to zero-operation REs.

2. Use FAs in Figure 10.1 for each zero-operation RE.

3. Recompose r, building Λ-NFAs at each stage, using the constructive proofs.

This process is illustrated in Figure 10.2, where the last two examples involve more operations, and so several hidden steps.

It is clear from these examples that the Λ-NFAs are somewhat complex. Further, to build a DFA for a given RE, we first need to remove the Λ-transitions and then remove the nondeterminism. Both of these processes were detailed in Chapter 9. Unfortunately, they result in (exponentially) larger and even more complex DFAs.

Although our primary concern is in the *existence* of FAs, it is certainly appealing to build as simple a DFA as possible. Moreover, for some computer applications, there are economic benefits from doing so. The problem of transforming a DFA into another equivalent DFA (one that recognizes the same language) with as few states as possible has been studied. The algorithms for doing this are not discussed in this book, but do exist and are not difficult to implement. These are called *state minimization algorithms*.

It is tempting to do an informal sort of minimization because it seems easy and often works. We call it *careless merger* to emphasize that sometimes it give wrong results; beware! The idea is simply to take any Λ-transition and shrink that edge, so to speak, until it disappears, at which point the two states that were its endpoints become merged into one state and the Λ-transition is gone. We can see in Figure 10.3 the effect of doing careless merger to the diagrams in Figure 10.2. In the simplest cases it works, but in general it does not create an automaton that is language-equivalent to what we started with.

The diagrams in the top half of Figure 10.3 are successful careless mergers of the first three diagrams in Figure 10.2. Alternatively, they can be seen as constructed directly from the basis diagrams in Figure 10.1. On this latter view, the diagram for

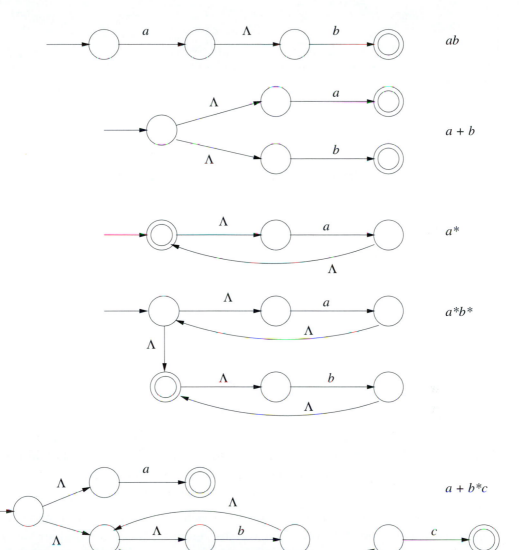

Figure 10.2: Diagrams built according to the constructive proofs.

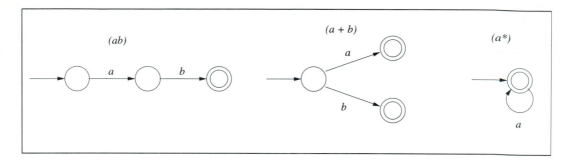

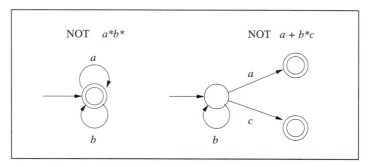

Figure 10.3: Correct and incorrect transition diagrams formed by the careless merger method.

the concatenation ab is achieved by taking the diagrams of a and b from Figure 10.1 and merging the accepting state for a with the start state for b. The alternation $a + b$ is the result of merging the start states of the a and b diagrams. The diagram for the closure a^* merges the start and accepting state of the a diagram.

The damage of the careless merger approach shows up in the bottom half of Figure 10.3, where we try to extend careless merging to more complex diagrams. First consider the diagram on the left in the bottom half of Figure 10.3, which is an attempt at converting a^*b^* to a diagram. We have taken the diagram for a^* from the top half of the figure and a similar one for b^* and then carried out careless merger for concatenation: The accepting state for a^* (actually its only state) has been merged with the start state of b^*. As you can see, the resulting diagram allows all strings over $\{a, b\}$, which is clearly an unsatisfactory result since a must never follow b in the language of a^*b^*. The corresponding analysis for $a + b^*c$ is left as an exercise.

Consider what went wrong. The careless merger method breaks down the boundary between what two different nodes are supposed to do. This becomes important when repeatable nodes are involved in the merger. A node is repeatable in a diagram if there is a sequence of transitions that leads from that node back to itself. In graph theory terms, any sequence of directed edges (arrows, transitions) is a path; a *cycle* is a path that begins and ends at the same vertex (node). What we are calling a *repeatable node* is one that is on a cycle. For example, the single node in the diagram for a^* is repeatable and so is the one for b^*. Merging these into a single node to form the diagram for a^*b^* allows the as and bs to intermingle, contrary to what the RE allows.

How does one produce a DFA for a given RE? Previously we outlined a general multistep procedure that is easily automated but tedious to do by hand. For simple REs, when doing them by hand, we use as much art as science. We use a blend of insight, analogies with previous problems, and the parts of the multistep procedure to build our FA. Insight and automation each have their own virtues.

10.4   All FA Languages Are Represented by REs

In this section, we prove the second half of Theorem 10.1. We have seen that any RE can be converted to an FA by a series of constructions. It is also possible to make the opposite conversion in all cases. That is, for any FA, there is an RE that expresses exactly the language that the FA accepts.

We explicitly show how to construct the RE that represents the language recognized by a given FA. There are various methods for doing this, and some are quite difficult to comprehend. Our method constructs the RE in step-by-step fashion while in some sense dismantling the given FA. To allow for this dismantling we need to generalize the concept of an FA as follows. (The generalization is used solely in this section.)

A **generalized finite automaton** (GFA) is an NFA with generalized transitions. In an NFA, a transition from state p to state q is labeled with a single symbol σ, which means that when in state p and with the next input symbol being σ we can (nondeterministically) process that input symbol and make a transition to state q. In some cases, we have found it convenient to indicate a set of symbols, like "a, b, c," on an arc to show that it can be used with any of those symbols as input. Doing so can save clutter in diagrams but adds no capability since we could use a separate transition for each symbol. Now we further extend the class of arc labels by allowing strings as well.

Thus, suppose we allow a transition from p to q to have as its label a string x of k symbols. Then if at some point the machine is in state p and the next k input symbols are the string x, we can process those k symbols and make a transition to state q. A *generalized transition* is a transition that has been labeled with a set of strings. We make a transition from p to q if the current input matches, in the foregoing sense, any of the strings labeling that transition. Since this is nondeterministic, if several strings could be used, at some point in time, the one used is chosen nondeterministically.

Rather than labeling a transition explicitly with a set of strings, in this section we label a transition with an RE. Of course, using the RE label r on a transition is the same as labeling it with the set of strings $\mathcal{L}(r)$. A transition may be labeled with an infinite set of strings. Note that Λ could be $\mathcal{L}(r)$ and would be treated exactly like a Λ-transition; in this sense, Λ-NFAs are a special case of GFAs.

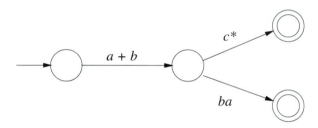

Example 10.13 This transition diagram corresponds to a GFA that recognizes the language represented by $r = (a+b)(c^*+ba)$. Suppose the input was $bccc \in \mathcal{L}(r)$. The edge from the start state is labeled with the set of strings $\{a, b\} = \mathcal{L}(a + b)$. Since one of those two strings matches the initial b of the input, we process that input letter and make a transition to the middle state. Now we have two possible transitions with labels $\{\Lambda, c, cc, ccc, \ldots\} = \mathcal{L}(c^*)$ and $\{ba\} = \mathcal{L}(ba)$. Since the next three input characters match a label of the first of these, we *can* make a transition to a final state while processing all of the input. Therefore, $bccc$ is accepted by this GFA. You should also show that these strings are accepted: b, aba, and ac.

To simplify our technique, we wish to restrict how the start state and accepting states are used.

Lemma 10.1 For any regular language L, there exists a Λ-NFA that recognizes L and that has the following properties:

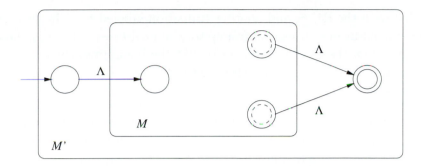

Figure 10.4: The construction in the proof for Lemma 10.1.

- no transition to the start state
- a single accepting state
- no transition from that accepting state
- transitions into and out of every other state

Proof: Suppose that a given regular language L is recognized by FA M, where M has k accepting states. We build a new machine M' from M that also recognizes L. M' contains all the states and transitions of M. In addition, there is a new start for M' that is connected to the old start state of M with a Λ-transition. Further there is just one accepting state in M', a new state, and there is a Λ-transition to it from each of the k old accepting states of M. These old accepting states are carried along as *non*-accepting states in the new machine. All of this is illustrated in Figure 10.4. Clearly M' satisfies each of the first three properties in the lemma.

For the fourth property, suppose there were other states in M' that did not have transitions both entering and leaving them. Clearly such a state cannot appear on any path from the new start state to the new accepting state. Therefore, such states can be removed without any effect on what is accepted by M' $\square$

The procedure for producing an RE for given FA is based on two operations for modifying a GFA. The first, *transition merging*, removes parallel edges in the diagram. The second, *state removal* reduces the number of states. By repeatedly applying these two operations, we slowly dismantle the GFA while building the corresponding RE. Recall that each transition is labeled with an RE.

- **Transition merging**—This operation applies whenever there are two parallel transitions. In other words, from state p to state q, there is one transition labeled with the RE r_1 and another transition labeled r_2. The two transitions are replaced by one transition from p to q labeled $r_1 + r_2$. Clearly the language recognized by the GFA is unchanged. (At the beginning, this also means that a transition labeled "a, b", which is just shorthand for two parallel transitions, becomes "$a + b$".)

- **State removal**—This operation removes a state that has transitions both entering and leaving it. Let q be the state we wish to remove. Suppose there is a transition from p to q labeled r_1, and another transition from q to s labeled r_3. Further, suppose that r_2 is the label on the transition from q to itself (if there is no such transition, then we take $r_2 = \Lambda$). For every such p and s, we add a transition from p to s labeled $r_1 r_2^* r_3$. Do this even if p and s are the same state—that is, if there is a transition from p to q and from q back to p (which results in a transition from p to itself).

Why does the state-removal operation work? The removal makes some other changes necessary since we want the resulting GFA to recognize the same language. Consider an accepting path through the GFA before the state removal. Each time the path passes through q, it must come from a state p and continue on to a state s after looping back from q to itself zero or more times. Each of these two or more transitions that together lead from p over to s corresponds to a language of one or more strings. The new transition from p to s is labeled with an RE representing exactly the same set of strings that could have been formed by concatenating these two or more languages. It follows that the language recognized by the GFA before the state removal is the same as that recognized by the GFA after the removal.

Algorithm 10.1 Constructing an RE from an FA
    Let M be a deterministic FA.

> $M' \Leftarrow$ the result of applying Lemma 10.1 to M
> Perform any possible transition-merging operations.
> **while** M' has more than two states **do**
>> Select any state q of M' except the start state or accepting state.
>> Perform a state-removal operation on q.
>> Perform any possible transition merging operations.
> **return** (the RE label on the single remaining transition)

We are now in a position to prove Theorem 10.3. It then follows that Theorem 10.1 is established.

Theorem 10.3 Any FA (regular) language is the set of strings represented by an RE.

Proof: Algorithm 10.1 gives a constructive approach, so we need to establish the correctness of the algorithm. That is, we need to argue that after each iteration the new GFA recognizes the same language. We outline an inductive proof, where the induction is on the number of states removed. The basis is trivial; that is, when no states have been removed, nothing can possibly have changed. Earlier we discussed why each operation leaves the language unchanged, so we essentially have shown the inductive step.

Since the algorithm inevitably terminates with a single transition from the new start state of M' to the only accepting state of M', the RE labeling that ultimate transition must be equivalent to the language recognized by the original GFA (and all the intermediate GFAs). □

Example 10.14 Find an RE for the language recognized by the diagram shown at the top of Figure 10.5.

First apply Lemma 10.1 to the top diagram to get the Λ-NFA in the second diagram, with a new start state and a new accepting state. The states that were originally accepting are shown with solid outer circles but dashed inner ones. To get each of the next three diagrams, we remove the original states one by one. As an example, in the first of these diagram changes (from the second diagram to the third), removing a state interrupts two paths. One of those paths has a label sequence a, b, giving the RE ab, which merges with an existing c-transition to change the latter's label to $ab + c$. The other interrupted path has the label $a\Lambda$, giving a new a transition. The final diagram is a GFA with a single transition bearing as its label the RE that solves the problem. Notice that the correctness of the algorithm does not depend on the order in which the states are removed. In fact, if the states are removed in a different order, you can obtain a distinct but equivalent RE.

As a footnote, we observe that our definition of GFA allows any set of strings to label an edge. As we soon see, there are languages that are not regular, so it would seem that we could label an edge with a set of strings constituting a nonregular language; in that case, the GFA could accept a nonregular language. However, that presents no difficulty. GFAs are not necessarily equivalent to FAs. We *only* use them to prove that we can transform an FA into an RE.

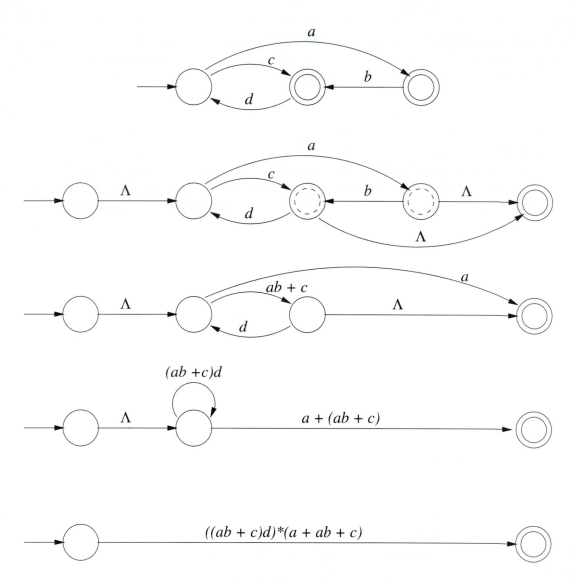

Figure 10.5: Building an RE while dismantling a GFA.

Exercises

10.1 Write down all strings of length 3 in each of the following regular sets, where $S_1 = \{a\}$, $S_2 = \{b\}$, and $S_3 = \{c\}$.

(a) $S_1 \cup S_2 S_3^*$

(b) $(S_1 \cup S_2) S_3^*$

(c) $(S_1 \cup S_2 S_3)^*$

10.2 For each of the following REs, r, give the set $\{x | x \in \mathcal{L}(r) \wedge |x| = 3\}$.

(a) $a + bc*$

(b) $(a + b)c*$

(c) $(a + bc)*$

10.3 Simplify each of these REs by writing another RE with fewer operators that represents the same language.

(a) $a + a^*$

(b) $a + aa^*$

(c) $a^* a^*$

(d) $(a^* b^* c^*)^*$

10.4 Let $L = \mathcal{L}((aaa + aaaa)^*)$.

(a) List all the strings over $\{a\}$ that are *not* in L.

(b) Prove informally that there are no others.

10.5 What is the shortest string over $\{a, b\}$ that is *not* in the language corresponding to $(a + ba)^* b^*$?

10.6 Write REs for the following sets of strings over $\{a, b\}$. In each case, the language your RE represents should contain all and only the strings described.

(a) The strings that do not end in *bb*.

(b) The strings in which there is no *b* followed immediately by *b*.

(c) The strings containing exactly one occurrence of *bb*.

10.7 Write an RE for the real numbers using a minus sign for negatives and an optional plus sign for positives.

(a) Start by allowing any such string of digits with at most one decimal point, such as 1.2, -00.5, +.0, and 10.

(b) Continue part (a), but disallow extra leading zeroes, while allowing trailing zeroes to the right of the decimal point; a single leading zero before a decimal point is allowed. The language of your RE should include these examples: +3.77, 200.0, -3.000, -33.0007, -.666, and 0.01; it should exclude 000.1.

(c) Continue part (b) by restricting the representations of zero to: 0, 0., 0.0, 0.00, etc.. Note that zero should not have a sign.

(d) Now include scientific notation so that each number allowed in part (a) can be immediately followed by an E, an optional plus or minus, and an integer.

10.8 The text describes and rejects the method of "careless merging" for diagram construction corresponding to the RE operators. This method can lead to incorrect results, as it does in the case of the state transition diagrams in the lower half of Figure 10.3.

(a) Explain how the method leads to those diagrams.

(b) What REs do those diagrams represent?

10.9 Convert this state transition diagram into an RE by applying Algorithm 10.1 as follows:

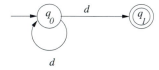

(a) Draw the state transition diagram that includes the new start and accepting states, along with the required Λ-transitions.

(b) Show the result of removing one of the original states.

(c) Show the final result with both original states removed.

10.10 The first FA in Example 9.16, shown in the form of a state transition diagram, recognizes the set of those strings over $\{a, b\}$ with an odd number of as. Apply the construction in Algorithm 10.1 to this FA to get an RE.

10.11 The resulting FA in Example 9.16, shown in the form of a state transition diagram, recognizes the set of those strings over $\{a, b\}$ in which both the number of as and the number of bs are odd. After adding new start and accepting states and making the associated adjustments, choose the state that was originally the start state as the first one to be removed.

   (a) Show the result of removing that state. Notice that $5 \, (= 3 + 2)$ transitions need to be removed and that $6 \, (= 3 * 2)$ need to be inserted.

   (b) State whether it must always be true that, for some m and n, the number of transitions removed is $m + n$ and the number inserted is mn (for the same m and n).

10.12 In Example 10.5, the FA is converted to an RE by removing states from right to left.

   (a) Show what happens when you remove states from left to right, starting with removal of the state that was originally the start state.

   (b) The resulting RE is *not* the same as the result in the example. Yet the two REs are supposed to represent the same language. Give several reasonably long strings that are in the language of each. Give others that are in neither's language. Can you find any strings that violate the claim that these REs and the FA all represent the same language?

10.13 Give an RE for these languages over the alphabet $\Sigma = \{0, 1\}$:

   (a) $L_1 = \{x \mid x \text{ contains } 010\}$.
   (b) $L_2 = \{x \mid x \text{ does not contain } 010\}$.
   (c) $L_3 = \{x \mid x \text{ contains exactly one } 010\}$.

10.14 Draw the transition diagram for a deterministic FA that recognizes the language represented by:

   (a) $(aa + ab)^*$.
   (b) $(aaa + abb)^* b$.
   (c) $(a + aab)^* b$.

Chapter 11

Lex: A Tool for Building Lexical Scanners

Having learned something about regular expressions (REs), you are ready for Lex. Lex is a powerful software tool that has been created by extending the RE approach to pattern representation and implementing the recognition of the resulting patterns. Moreover, the Lex programmer can specify—in C or C++—what to do when a string is found that matches a pattern. Given these capabilities, Lex can help you to create more readable and maintainable code and to do it faster, when building a wide variety of software applications that involve looking for patterns in strings. It is best known for its widespread use in creating the lexical scanning component of compilers.

The first section gives the basic idea of how Lex works. We then look at several Lex operators and see how they allow certain ideas to be expressed more compactly than in REs. Next comes a specification of the structure of Lex programs and how they are processed. Then come some more examples, this time taking more advantage of special Lex notation and also providing a few remarks on C. The following section specifies the sequence of things you must do to use Lex successfully on a real computer. Finally, we introduce Flex (fast Lex), a newer variant that allows you to use C++ in place of C.

11.1 Overview

The Lex notation for symbol patterns extends REs by permitting some useful operations that are not part of the core definition of REs. (Recall that REs only have the operations of alternation, concatenation, and closure.) Yet this notation is only an extension and not a whole new kind of representational system in that practically any Lex expression (LE) can be rewritten as an RE. Still in many cases of interest, the use of Lex's extra operators allows the LE to be more compact than the corresponding RE. Summarizing the relationship between the two:

- LEs and REs represent the same class of languages.

- LEs modify (slightly) and extend the RE notation.

- The extra operators in Lex can make LEs simpler than REs.

Example 11.1 Write an RE and LE corresponding to all strings over the first six letters of the alphabet in lowercase.

The RE is $(a + b + c + d + e + f)^*$. The LE can be briefer. In Lex, brackets indicate a choice among characters, so it is possible to write `[abcdef]*`. Moreover, within brackets, the hyphen ("-") can be used for a range of characters having successive ASCII code numbers, so `[a-f]*` represents the set of same strings.

Notice that we use `Courier` type face for actual Lex patterns and other code, both in this example and throughout the chapter.

Example 11.2 Write an LE for unsigned integers.

Lex uses the plus sign to mean "one or more consecutive occurrences," so the simple pattern `[0-9]+` does the job. We have more to say about plus signs later. This pattern allows leading zeroes (zeroes at the beginning of the integers that match) so it matches strings like 0073. The pattern `[1-9][0-9]*` disallows this possibility, but also disallows zero.

Each statement in the body of a Lex program consists of an LE pattern and optionally a C statement. The input to Lex is a (usually long) string in which we expect to find substrings that match certain ones among your patterns. Often the input string is the entire contents of one file; this may be a program or document, but it is regarded as a sequence of characters, including newline (end-of-line) characters. At any point in the processing of the input text, there is a contest among the various LEs to see which one can match the longest substring starting at the current position in the input string. If some patterns are tied, the winner is the one among them that occurs earliest in the Lex program. If the winning LE is accompanied by a C statement, the C statement is executed. On some systems and with some variants of Lex, it is possible to use C++ instead of C. Briefly, Lex works likes this:

- Lex searches for the longest string that fits any of your LEs.

- The search is in some input text, like a program or document.

- You specify, in C or C++, what happens when an input string fits a pattern.

Example 11.3 Suppose you want to remove from a file each occurrence of a number sign (#) along with anything that comes after it on the same line. Doing this actually removes all comments from some Unix files—for example, the shell-initialization (.cshrc) file—since the "#" in that type of file means that the rest of the line is a comment. The following two lines constitute a complete Lex program will does the job:

```
%%
#.* ;
```

The first line in Example 11.3 (%%) separates the program's **declarations** from its **body**. In this case, there are no declarations, as you can see, but the %% is needed anyway, to show that. The body in this example consists of only one line—the second line. The second line has three parts: a Lex expression (#.*) followed by whitespace (in this case, just one blank) and an empty C statement consisting of only a semicolon, which does nothing. This three-part sequence—Lex expression, whitespace, and a C statement—is the normal structure for a line of the body.

Now we look at the second line one symbol at a time. The #-symbol has no special role in Lex so it matches any occurrence of itself in the input. The period matches any character at all except for newline (end of line). This use of the period to mean *any symbol* is a useful Lex convention that is not part of ordinary RE terminology. The asterisk (*), or star, is the LE closure operator. Just like the RE closure operator, it allows unlimited repetition of whatever it applies to—in this case, the period. The period–star pattern (.*) matches any input sequence of any length up to the end of a line. This is just what we need since comments can contain anything. Therefore, this pattern does what we set out to do: It matches a single-line comment starting with # and continuing with anything.

Whenever a Lex pattern succeeds in matching some input, the matched material is removed and the associated C statement is executed. In this case, the C statement does nothing, so we accomplish our objective of removing a comment and doing nothing else. The Lex program then moves on to the next character, which in this case is at the beginning of the next line of input, and it continues in this fashion through the rest of the input.

* Star in Lex stands for zero or more occurrences of its operand, just as it does in REs.

| The vertical bar separates alternatives in Lex, instead of the plus sign used in ordinary REs.

Concatenation is the same in Lex as in REs.

() Parentheses are used in the ordinary way for grouping. They do not add any meaning.

Figure 11.1: Lex notation corresponding directly to REs.

11.2 Lex Operators and What They Do

Lex has quite a few operators beyond the standard notation for REs. One of them, the period, was already seen in Example 11.3. Before we get to the extensions, however, take a quick look at Figure 11.1, which shows how Lex expresses the standard RE operations. The only difference is that alternation, which is expressed by the plus sign in RE notation, is expressed by the vertical bar, "|", in Lex.

This deviation allows Lex to use + for something else—specifically, to mean one or more occurrences of something. For example, a+ matches any string in the set $\{a, aa, aaa, \ldots\}$. The only difference between this set and the one for "*" is that Λ is left out. Both of these operators are unary (taking just one operand), and both yield an infinite number of results. It also follows that for any regular expression r, the Lex expressions r+ and rr* represent the same language. Thus, the new operator is a convenience, but does not add to what can already be expressed by REs. The same can be said for the other operators in Figure 11.2, but the convenience is considerable. For example, the LE (0|1){8} corresponds to the RE $(0+1)(0+1)(0+1)(0+1)(0+1)(0+1)(0+1)(0+1)$. Yet another unary operator is the question mark, signifying zero or one occurrences of its operand, thereby making it optional. These number-of-occurrence operators are gathered for easy reference in Figure 11.2.

It is easy to be fooled by the plus sign since it is a unary operator in Lex. This contrasts with its usual role as a binary operator in REs, mathematical notation and the programming languages to which Lex is applied. (Further, although the plus sign is unary in its role for signed integers, it is a prefix operator there, whereas

* See Figure 11.1. Star in Lex belongs to a family of notations for matching different numbers of occurrences.

+ Plus means one or more occurrences of whatever it is applied to. It is *not* used to separate alternatives. That role is taken by the vertical bar.

? A question mark after something makes it optional, so `b?` stands for the RE, $(b + \Lambda)$. This operator has the same high precedence as star and plus. For example, the expression `ab?cd+e` can match with *acde*, *abcde*, *acdde*, *abcdde*, *acddde*, *abcddde*, ... Another example is `-?(0|1)+`, which matches nonempty sequences of binary integers with or without a unary minus out front.

{} Braces around a number indicate that something should be repeated that number of times, so `x{12}` matches *xxxxxxxxxxxx*. Braces around a comma-separated pair of numbers indicate a range of possible numbers of repetitions; for example, `[A-Z]{1,8}` matches 1 to 8 capital letters. (Another use of braces appears in Figure 11.4.)

Figure 11.2: Lex notation for number of occurrences.

in Lex it is postfix.) Moreover, when you type it at the keyboard, the plus sign will of course *not* be raised like an exponent, although we wrote it that way in extended REs to express the meaning it has in Lex. Thus, the plus sign here has quite an unexpected look. As a simple example, `a+b` matches one or more as followed by `b`.

Additional related groups of Lex operators are gathered in Figures 11.3, 11.4, and 11.5. Although the RE symbols do not have to be precisely the set of ASCII characters, from a practical standpoint it is often handy to use that set along with its ordering conventions. Lex does just that by means of the notational items gathered in Figure 11.3. Thus, for example, when we say that Lex provides a wild-card symbol, the period, which can stand for anything except the newline character, what we really mean is any *ASCII character* except newline. Similarly, when the caret symbol is used in brackets to create the complement of a set of characters, that complement is meant to be taken with respect to the set of ASCII characters.

Most characters simply denote themselves in Lex, although, as we have already seen, some have special roles as operators. Then in any particular program, some characters may have been defined to stand for something else. Figure 11.4 describes how to *use* a definition to let one thing stand for another. It also describes the use

[] Brackets denote a choice among characters, so [aeiou] means any vowel just like (a|e|i|o|u). Brackets retain their usual capacity to indicate grouping. Inside brackets, most of the special symbols lose their special properties; for example, [*/] represents a choice between star and slash, and [.?!] denotes a choice among sentence-ending punctuation marks. Blanks behave normally inside brackets, just denoting themselves. Thus, [,] denotes a choice of comma or blank. However, note that the hyphen does have special properties in this context; see the next entry.

- Characters with consecutive ASCII codes can be expressed with a hyphen in brackets; for example, [a-z] is a pattern for any lowercase letter. Using both this and the bracket notation just introduced, Lex takes [a-zA-Z] to be any letter. However, a hyphen at the beginning or end of a bracketed choice behaves normally, so [-+] denotes a choice of sign and [-+]? stands for an optional sign.

^ When caret ^ appears at the start of a bracketed pattern, it negates the remaining characters. Thus, [^aeiou]+ means a sequence of one or more consonants.

. A period matches any single character except newline. The pattern ".*" matches an arbitrary sequence within a line.

Figure 11.3: Lex notation for alternative characters.

of backslash and double quotes to *avoid* the special meanings of the Lex operators. Finally, Figure 11.5 shows how to establish context in Lex. A pattern can specify that—in addition to satisfying some pattern properties—any string that is to match it must occur at the beginning of a line, at the end of one, or immediately followed by certain things specified in another LE pattern. Taken together, Figures 11.1 to 11.5—although not a complete description of all the features of Lex—illustrate how REs can be extended for practical use and should be plenty to allow you to experiment with Lex.

Example 11.4 Convert some simple Lex expressions to regular expressions using the symbol set $\Sigma = \{a, b, c, d, e, f, g, h, +, -\}$. Note that because the lowercase letters occur consecutively within the ASCII

{} Braces can surround a defined term to invoke its definition. The definition itself should appear in the section for definitions and declarations, before the first "%%". If D has been defined as [0-9], then {D} can be used to match any digit. The pattern \${D}+\.{D}{2} would then match an amount of dollars and cents.

\ Backslash before an operator makes it behave like an ordinary character. For example, \+ matches an input plus sign and \. matches a period or decimal point. However, just as in the C language, \t stands for the tab and \n means newline. Thus, [\t]+ matches whitespace within a line and [\t\n]+ can match whitespace across line boundaries. Bringing the caret notation from Figure 11.3 into play here, we can also write [^\n\t]+ as a pattern that matches one or more *non*-whitespace characters.

As noted earlier and demonstrated by these examples, blank behaves normally inside brackets. Outside brackets, however, blank must be preceded by backslash; otherwise the blank signals the end of the lex pattern and the beginning of the C or C++ code.

" " Double quotes are used in pairs to make the included characters lose their special status. Because double quotes have this special role, they need backslash protection to be used as themselves, so a suitable pattern for quoted material up to the end of a line is \"[^"\n]*["\n].

Figure 11.4: Lex notation for changing or retaining interpretations.

character sequence, we can use, for example, [a-d] to represent a choice among *a*, *b*, *c*, and *d*. Also notice the ambiguity of the plus sign in REs.

Finally, [+-]? is okay for denoting an optional sign—plus, minus, or nothing—even though the minus sign is the same character as the hyphen, which can have a special role inside brackets. Here the minus (hyphen) is the last symbol inside brackets, and in this position (or when it is first) it *can't* link the characters before and after it to form a range of characters.

^ Caret used outside of brackets at the start of a pattern requires the material potentially matching that pattern to appear only at the start of the input line.

$ Dollar sign at the end of a pattern requires the material potentially matching that pattern to appear only at the end of the input line.

/ Slash allows a pattern to stipulate a right-hand context. For example, the pattern ab/cd matches the string ab if and only if the next two letters are cd. Only the ab is used up.

Figure 11.5: Lex notation for establishing context.

Lex	RE
.	$a + b + c + d + e + f + g + h + + + -$
a*	a^*
a+	aa^*
a|b	$a + b$
a?	$a + \Lambda$
[ace]	$a + c + e$
[a-d]	$a + b + c + d$
[a-cf-h]	$a + b + c + f + g + h$
(ab){5}	$ababababab$
a\-b	$a - b$
[+-]?	$+ + - + \Lambda$
[^c+-]{1,2}	$(a + b + d + e + f + g + h)(a + b + d + e + f + g + h + \Lambda)$

11.3   The Structure and Processing of Lex Programs

Somewhere in a Lex program there must be a line that begins with two percent signs (%%) and contains nothing else. On lines before that, there can be definitions and declarations, as in Example 11.7 later in this chapter, or nothing, as in Example 11.3. After the %% comes the body of the program, consisting of Lex patterns, each of which can be accompanied by a C statement. Later in the program there may also be a second %% line followed by subroutines in C, but this is not required and is not used in the elementary Lex examples here.

A crucial role is played by **whitespace**. Within a line, whitespace consists of at least one blank or tab or any mixture of both. Whitespace separates a Lex pattern from its associated C statement. Therefore, the Lex pattern must be placed at the beginning of the line with *no spaces or tabs before it or within it* (except inside brackets, etc.). Then can come whitespace and a C statement, telling what to do when the Lex pattern is matched. The C statement can continue onto more than one line, but the continuation lines must begin with whitespace.

One way to think about the processing of input by your Lex program is to imagine each of your patterns competing with the others by examining the input and trying to match itself with as long a sequence of input as it can, starting with the current symbol (which is initially the first symbol of input). The winning pattern is the one that finds the longest string to match. The matched string becomes accessible by a local variable with the special name `yytext`; the characters in that string have no further role as input since the current symbol becomes the next one after the matched string. The C statement associated with the winning pattern is then executed. If you want the matched material to appear in your output, you must have this statement do the job using `yytext`. In other words, unless you do something about it, your output contains only *un*matched input.

If no match is found starting at the current character, that character passes right through to the output and a new contest for longest match is started at the next input symbol. If two or more patterns are tied for longest string matched, the one occurring earliest in your program wins, and processing continues in the manner described earlier, as if this winner of tiebreaking had been the longest or only successful pattern.

11.4 Lex Examples with C

Since Lex came along at a time when C was widely used for system programming and when C++ did not exist—nor Java either for that matter—many classic instructional examples of Lex programming are laced with C code. Therefore, we have written a few examples here with C, but we also provide information on using Flex with C++ in Section 11.7. For the following examples, the only new thing a C++ programmer needs to know is the `printf` function, which is provided in the standard C library.

The first argument to `printf` must be a string enclosed in a pair of double quotes, possibly including such things as "%s", showing where to insert a **string** and "%d", showing where to insert a **decimal** integer. Subsequent arguments provide the material to insert in the corresponding order. Thus, if the current value of k is 3 and x is the string "abc", invoking `printf("The length of %s is %d\n", x, k)` causes output "`The length of abc is 3`" (without quotes), followed by a newline, which is expressed inside the first argument as "\n".

As you study the following examples, note that strings are arrays of characters and that array indexing in C starts at zero, so the first character in the string `yytext` is `yytext[0]`. Its length always becomes the value of the special variable `yyleng`. Although we say that each Lex pattern has *an* associated C statement, this is not really a limitation since that C statement can be a compound statement using braces, "{...}", as in Example 11.7.

Example 11.5 Look for a string of (zero or more) Ps followed by a `Q`, print it out with some decoration, and keep on doing this. For example, if "PPPQ" is found, print out the string ">>> PPPQ <<<". Discard everything else.

In the Lex program shown, the Lex pattern `P*Q` matches the specified strings. The C `printf` statement prints out its first argument, which should be a string, except for the `%s`, which shows where to insert some material from another argument. Here that other argument is `yytext`, which always contains the matched piece of input. Other characters are captured, one at a time, by the period in the last line and discarded.

```
%%
P*Q printf(">>> %s <<<",yytext);
 .      ;
```

Example 11.6 Find capital letters in the input and replace them by their lowercase counterparts. Make no other changes.

The Lex pattern `[A-Z]` matches any capital letter. The C `putchar` statement puts one character into the output stream. We take the first and only character of `yytext`, that is `yytext[0]`, and treat it as an integer—a technique not permitted in modern, more strongly typed languages. Notice that the last line of the code in Example 11.5 does not appear here. Therefore, this code lets characters other than capital letters pass through to output unchanged.

```
%%
[A-Z]   putchar(yytext[0]+'a'-'A');
```

Example 11.7 Find hexadecimal numbers (base 16), flagged by an "x"
(either x or X), and print them out with their length and base-ten
value.

The first line in the following Lex program begins with a blank (and
then a few more blanks). This initial whitespace shows that the material on this line is C code and not a Lex pattern. This line of C
declares i, x, and y to be integers. Then come two Lex *definitions*.
The second of them defines H as matching any of the first six letters of the alphabet, capitalized or not. After %% comes the body.
The principal pattern begins with x or X, used as specified, to help
identify the occurrence of a hexadecimal number. Notice how to use
definitions. After D has been defined in the definition section, its
defined meaning can be specified as part of a pattern by using {D}
in the body. The braces are essential for this purpose. D without
braces would just match the letter "D" despite the definition. Most
of the C code is straightforward, but the first argument to printf
may look a bit daunting. It uses %s, %d, and %d again to insert a
string and two decimal numbers from the next three arguments; we
use \t for tab and \n for newline to format the output.

```
     int i,x,y;
D [0-9]
H [a-fA-F]
%%
[xX]({H}|{D})+ {y = 0;
      for( i=1 ; i < yyleng ; i++)
          {x=yytext[i];
          if (x >= '0' && x <= '9') x = x - '0';
          if (x >= 'A' && x <= 'F') x = x - 'A' + 10;
          if (x >= 'a' && x <= 'f') x = x - 'a' + 10;
          y = y * 16 + x;}
      printf("%s\t%d\t%d\n", yytext, yyleng - 1, y);}
   . ;
```

11.5 States

Suppose you wish to write a Lex expression for comments in C or C++. These
must begin with "/*" and end in "*/". Remembering that both "/" and "*"

are special characters in Lex, you might think of using the pattern \/*.**\/. Unfortunately, there is a bug in this Lex pattern. Consider the input "<code1> /*comment1*/ <code2> /*comment2*/". Since Lex looks for a match involving the longest possible string, it matches our pattern with the string that includes *both* comments and everything in between.

There is another shortcoming in the preceding pattern. Since the period does not match a newline character, the pattern is confined to matching within a line. To match multiline comments, you might think of replacing the ".*" by (.|\n)*. Unfortunately, this has the unacceptably inefficient behavior of always searching all the way to the end of the program for the last occurrence of "*/". If there are at least two comments in a program, then our new pattern—adjusted as just described for multiline comments—matches all comments *and* code all the way from the beginning of the first comment to the end of the last one.

To cope with this problem, we can use a capability of (most versions of) Lex that involves the concept of a *state*. States are used in a manner directly motivated by finite state automata. In particular, we begin in an initial state (which is by default called INITIAL) and make transitions from state to state. The transitions are not automatic, but are in response to the special action BEGIN in the C code. We can require a pattern to be applied only when we are in a particular state. The action(s) carried out when Lex finds a particular pattern can include changing the state. If a pattern is preceded by the name of a state enclosed in angle brackets (e.g., "<SOMESTATE>") then that state must be the current one for the pattern to be available for use. To put it the other way around, when SOMESTATE is the current state, the only active patterns are those that have no state specified *or* begin with <SOMESTATE>. Before showing how states can help us deal with C/C++ comments, we present a simpler example—a Lex program that makes use of states to recognize an old friend, the language {$a^n b^n$}. Following the program is a sample of input, with the resulting output.

Example 11.8 Write a Lex program using states as needed that will find occurrences of $a^n b^n$ within each line of the input. Such an occurrence is not preceded by any *a*s or followed by any *b*s. In particular, it would find *aaabbb* and *ab*, but would not find *aaaabbb* (although it contains *aaabbb*). Any such occurrences are replaced in the output by "<n a's and b's>", where *n* is the appropriate actual number. All other input (including such occurrences as *aaabbbb*) goes to the output unchanged.

```
%s   LOOKING_FOR_B
     int acount;
     char *astring;


%%
<INITIAL>a+          {astring = strdup(yytext);
                     acount = yyleng;
                     BEGIN LOOKING_FOR_B;}
<LOOKING_FOR_B>b+ {if (yyleng == acount)
                         printf("<%d a's and b's>", yyleng);
                     else printf("%s%s",astring, yytext);
                     BEGIN INITIAL;}
.|\n                 {printf("%s",yytext);
                     BEGIN INITIAL;}
```

There is no single LE to match the sort of pattern we are looking
for. The program finds the *a*s with the Lex pattern a+, saves them,
and then goes into a state reflecting that it is ready for *b*s. The
state is appropriately called LOOKING_FOR_B. To ensure that processing must be in this state at the beginning of the pattern b+, we write
<LOOKING_FOR_B>b+, rather than simply b+. This state is declared
in the declaration section by writing %s LOOKING_FOR_B. The default
state is INITIAL and need not be declared.

We begin in the INITIAL state and are looking for a block of *a*s in the
input. If we find them, we change to the LOOKING_FOR_B state after
recording what we just found in program variables. Now when we
are "looking for b," if we in fact see a block of *b*s, we check whether it
is the same length as the block of *a*s. If it is, we process it. If it is not
of the same length, we need to send to the output not only these *b*s,
but also the block of *a*s that we have been tentatively holding back.
However, in either event, we go back to the INITIAL state because
we need to start looking for *a*s again.

The final pattern, ".|\n", is enabled if we are in either state. Because
it can match only a single character and appears last among the
patterns, it can have effect only when the others both fail (whether on
the basis of state or pattern). The code accompanying this pattern
merely echoes the input to the output. It has the important side

effect of taking us immediately back to the INITIAL state if we are looking for a *b* and see any other character. (Actually, the first pattern a+ does not need to be preceded by <INITIAL>, but it is easier to understand as shown.) For these lines of input:

```
aabb
aabaaabbbabb
aaabb
```

the compiled lex program produces these lines of output:

```
<2 a's and b's>
aab<3 a's and b's>abb
aaabb
```

Notice that there are three aspects to the use of states: *declaring* a state, *constraining* a pattern to apply only in a particular state, and *changing* from one state to another.

- Declaring states: To declare an ordinary state called "STATENAME," put "%s STATENAME" in the declaration section of your Lex program before the first "%%". You can also use "%x STATENAME" (using x instead of s) to declare an *exclusive* state. When you are in an exclusive state during processing, only patterns explicitly specifying that state can be used for matching.

- Constraining a pattern: Use "<STATENAME>pattern", where "pattern" is any Lex pattern to confine the pattern's use to the state called "STATENAME". Be sure to have *no* whitespace before the pattern since whitespace still signals the transition from the Lex portion to the C portion.

- Changing the state: When processing begins, the state is assumed to be a state called INITIAL that you do not have to declare. After that, execution of C statements like BEGIN STATENAME; change the state to STATENAME.

Example 11.9 Write a Lex program that recognizes C/C++ comments. In particular, in the output, replace the entire comment by the string "comment begun - comment ended"; the rest of the input is unchanged.

```
%x      COMMENT   /* processing inside a comment */
%x      HALF_OUT  /* lacking "/" to leave a comment */


%%

.|\n                    printf("%s", yytext);
                                    /* other material printed */
\/\*                    {BEGIN COMMENT; printf("comment begun - \n");}
<COMMENT>\*             BEGIN HALF_OUT;
<COMMENT>[^*]           ;               /* includes newline */
<HALF_OUT>\*            ;
<HALF_OUT>\/            {printf("comment ended\n"); BEGIN INITIAL;}
<HALF_OUT>[^*/]         BEGIN COMMENT;
```

This Lex program makes use of states called COMMENT, HALF_OUT, and INITIAL. After seeing "/*" in the input, the state goes to COMMENT, indicating that the processing is taking place inside a comment. This state continues so long as the input consists of characters—including occurrences of the newline character—other than a star ("*"). A star alters the state to HALF_OUT, so named since only a slash ("/") is needed to complete the comment. In state HALF_OUT, additional stars leave the state unchanged whereas a slash completes the comment, moving the state to INITIAL. All other symbols—other than slash and star—send the state back to COMMENT. (This could have been written without using the additional state HALF_OUT, but it is included to illustrate the features more fully.)

Note that the two defined states are exclusive states. This is important since the first pattern ".|\n" is disabled when we are in either of the defined states; this prevents characters from inside the comment being echoed to the output.

11.6   Using Lex in Unix

What do you have to do to actually use Lex? First, of course, you have to gain access to it, but that is easy because it is widely available. In particular, Lex is on nearly all computers that run some version of the Unix operating system. Since Lex is a Unix command, there is an entry for it in the online manual. You can get that documentation by typing "man lex" at the operating system prompt. Note that the correct spelling is with all lowercase letters, "`lex`", just like other Unix commands. To learn more about Lex and its uses, consult various books on Lex, Unix or compilers; some are mentioned in the bibliography. Here is the sequence of steps you need to carry out. If you wish to use C++ instead of C for the actions in your Lex program, see the next section.

1. Create a file containing a Lex program. The file can have any name; we call it `LF`. Use a simple program to get started, such as the one in Example 11.3. Be sure not to put any blanks ahead of the Lex expression on its line, but do put a blank before the C code.

2. Convert your Lex program file to a C program with the following command. Like other Unix commands, "lex" must be entirely in lowercase letters.

   ```
   lex LF
   ```

3. Your resulting C program is put into the file `lex.yy.c` in the current directory. Compile this program with the `cc` command and the needed library material by typing the command shown here (ending in two lowercase Ls).

   ```
   cc lex.yy.c -ll
   ```

4. Your executable program is now in a file called `a.out` (unless you used the `-o` option in Step 3 to give the file a different name). You can use this executable file interactively with this Unix command:

   ```
   a.out
   ```

   Then you type in a string, followed by ⌐return⌐ (or ⌐enter⌐), and the system responds. Repeat, using various strings, to test your Lex patterns. For example, for the Lex program in Example 11.3, use strings with and without the number symbol (#). To stop, type (two keys at once): <control-d>.

5. Create a file containing data for your Lex program. This gives you an orderly way to plan what strings to use and to have a record of that. We call this file `DF`.

6. To use your program with your data file, you can type

```
a.out < DF
```

The less-than sign introduces an input file. After some trial runs like this, you should redirect your output to a file (say, OF) by using a greater-than sign as shown next:

```
a.out < DF > OF
```

11.7   Flex and C++

If you are a C++ user who is not familiar with C, you may wish to use C++ for your commands instead of C. Since Lex is translated to C and your code is carried over intact, this yields a mixture of C and C++. Now if you have heard that there is supposed to be upward compatibility from C up to C++, you may think you are done. Unfortunately, not every version of Lex makes this work, but read on.

Flex, a version of Lex, does generate C code that is C++ compatible. However, since the resulting file is named `lex.yy.c`, a compiler may assume that the ".c" extension of the file name means that the code is to be compiled as C, not C++. For example, the g++ compiler will do this and it expects a ".cpp" extension for a C++ file. A simplistic way to deal with this is to rename the file by hand to `lex.yy.cpp`. A better solution is to leave the file name unchanged and instead use the "-x c++" option on the command line, before the file name, to inform g++ that this is a C++ file. If the file that holds your program is called LF, as in Section 11.6, you can use the three commands below to

(i) create a C++ program in the file lex.yy.c,

(ii) compile that file, and

(iii) run the executable on input from a file named DF, saving the result to file OF.

```
prompt>> flex LF
prompt>> g++ -x c++ lex.yy.c -ll
prompt>> a.out < DF > OF
```

Example 11.10 Here is a complete Flex program that simply copies its input to the display (i.e., copies stdin to stdout) double-spaced:

```
#include <iostream.h>    // permits the use of I/O in C++

%%

.* cout << yytext; // match anything on a line; pass it to output
\n cout << endl << endl; // match newline; send two to output

%%

main(){yylex();}
```

Exercises

11.1 Give some idea of the differing roles of the plus sign in REs versus Lex expression, by doing the following:

(a) Write the set of all strings of length 4 in the language of the Lex expression a+bcc*.

(b) Write the set of all strings of length 4 in the language of the RE $a+bcc*$.

(c) Write the Lex expression a+bcc* as an RE.

11.2 To show how Lex can unfold into lengthy REs, translate the following Lex expressions into REs, assuming that the symbol set is just the digits 0 through 9.

(a) [0-5]?

(b) [^01]

(c) .{2}

(d) 01[01]{2,4}

11.3 Translate the following REs into Lex expressions. To emphasize the compactness of Lex, make the expressions as short as possible.

(a) $(a + b + c + d + e + f)(a + b + c + d + e + f)(a + b + c + d + e + f)$

(b) $(a + b + \Lambda)(a + b + \Lambda)(a + b + \Lambda)$

(c) $9.99

11.4 Write Lex expressions for these familiar concepts.

(a) Word: one or more letters, all lowercase except that the first one may possibly be a capital.

(b) Symbol name: a letter, which may be capital or lowercase, followed by zero or more characters, each of which must be a digit, an underscore, a hyphen (same as a minus sign), or a capital or lowercase letter.

(c) Whitespace: a string of blanks, tabs, and newline characters that has at least one occurrence of at least one of them.

(d) Money: a dollar sign, at least one digit (although that may be the digit "0"), then a decimal point, and finally two more digits. Leading zeroes are acceptable.

11.5 Describe in English the sets of strings accepted by each of the following Lex expressions, stating which ones are proper subsets of which other ones.

(a) `[^\n\t ]+`

(b) `.*`

(c) `(.|\n)*`

11.6 Write patterns that look for

(a) a semicolon occurring anywhere, along with everything after it on the same line;

(b) a semicolon, which must be at the start of its line, along with whatever uninterrupted whitespace follows it on that line;

(c) same as part (b), but also including uninterrupted whitespace from the start of the line up to the semicolon.

For each of the following problems:

- Write the Lex program as specified, add print statements that keeps a user informed about all kinds of good and bad input, and explain how your program achieves its goals.

- Create a data set that fully tests the program, state the key variations in your data set that make it a complete test of good and bad input and provide the results of testing.

11.7 Write a single Lex program that recognizes both the integers—with an optional plus or minus sign—and also the reals. For the reals, use the specification in Exercise 10.7, including part (b) of that exercise for the possibility of scientific notation. Remember that the decimal point or period is a special symbol in Lex, and so are the plus and minus signs. In contrast, the letter *E* here is just an ordinary letter, not a definition. Begin your program with definitions, including

- one or two symbols to stand for choice among digits, and

- a symbol that stands for an optional sign: plus, minus, or nothing (not blank).

11.8 Example 11.7 evaluates hexadecimal numbers. Enhance that code so that it works properly not only for hexadecimal, but also for binary and octal numbers. Where the given code uses "x" as the signal for hexadecimal, you should allow either "x" or "hex". Make this signal case-insensitive (i.e., allow any combination of capital and lowercase letters, like "hEX"). Make "b" and "bin" the signals for binary, and make "o" and "oct" indicate octal, all case-insensitive.

11.9 Word counting is a popular utility. Write a Lex pattern that matches any single word, where a word is a string of non-whitespace characters followed by *some* whitespace (blanks, tabs, and/or newlines), but with the whitespace not part of what goes to yytext. Use the "/" Lex pattern operator. Replace each string of non-whitespace by a single "X" so that "ab cd ef" becomes "X X X". Declare a variable, initialize it to 0, increment it for each word, and print out its final value when input has been completed. To simplify matters, assume the input ends with the string "EOF". You will find that input from the keyboard looks peculiar because of the dual role of the newline character, so create at least one file of test data right away and take input from there when executing your compiled program.

11.10 Comments in the Lisp programming language can consist of a semicolon and everything after it to the end of the line. Some programmers use two or more semicolons for comments at different levels of organization. Write a Lex program that changes the indentation of those one-line Lisp comments that are preceded only by whitespace according to the following scheme:

- 1 semicolon: Start the line with that one semicolon followed by three spaces.

- 2 semicolons: Start the line with those two semicolons followed by five spaces.

This can be done with three Lex patterns—one to remove whitespace that appears between the start of the line and semicolon and two more that recognize one or two semicolons followed by an arbitrary string to the end of the line. For the first of these, consult Figure 11.5, "Lex notation for establishing context." With respect to the second, pay attention to the order in which you place the two rules.

11.11 Write a Lex program for evaluating the password proposed by a user on a single line of input. To qualify as acceptable, the proposed password must contain at least one letter (capital or lowercase), at least one digit, and at least one character that is something other than a letter, digit, blank, or tab. Trailing whitespace (blanks and tabs between the last whitespace character and the end of the line) is allowed but discarded. Other whitespace disqualifies the password. (Hint: Put patterns for bad strings first.)

Chapter 12

Context-Free Grammars

Context-free grammars (CFGs) can express important languages including many that are *non-regular*, and they can assign a useful *structure* to individual strings. These two important capacities combine to give CFGs a central role in both formal models of language and the design and implementation of practical compilers.

As a motivation for introducing a new class of language models, the first section presents some simple, important languages for which the models we have seen so far are *inadequate*. We show that for these languages there can be no finite automaton that succeeds in accepting exactly the strings of the language; they are nonregular. Nor can these languages be represented by regular expressions.

Section 12.2 then introduces CFGs and shows how they *can* represent these and many other non-regular languages. Moreover, we do not seem to lose anything because CFGs can also express all the regular languages as shown in Section 12.3. The only price to pay is that we lose some simplicity and efficiency of the recognition process. Recognition of CFGs is discussed in Chapter 13.

Besides specifying the strings for a wide range of languages, CFGs also provide an account of the *phrase structure* of each string in their languages. These structures, which were briefly introduced in Section 8.5, are the focus of Section 12.4, where we show how they can play a role in extracting the *meanings* of programming statements. Some CFGs provide more than one structure for some strings. This somewhat awkward result is known as *structural ambiguity*. Although it turns up frequently in human languages, it is usually regarded as something that can and should be avoided when designing programming languages.

The languages represented by CFGs are known as the context-free languages (CFLs). After our study of regular languages, it should perhaps come as no surprise that CFLs also have *other* representations—most notably, Backus Normal Form and syntax diagrams. Both of these formalisms have been widely used for specifying the permissible statements in a particular programming language. These alternative formalisms are presented in Section 12.5. The final section is devoted to proofs, including one of some practical significance.

12.1   Limitations of Regular Languages

You have seen that regular languages (RLs) can be expressed in several equivalent formalisms, including regular expressions (REs), deterministic finite automata (DFAs), and nondeterministic finite automata (NFAs), possibly allowing Λ-transitions. Despite their simplicity, RLs are adequate to express all the required character patterns needed to specify integers, real numbers, variable names, operators, and other kinds of tokens used in programming languages. Moreover, the simplicity of the formalisms for expressing regular languages makes it possible to create simple and efficient algorithms for using them. Lex is a tool for creating lexical scanners for compilers using a slightly altered notation for regular expressions. In addition, operating systems and editors use REs to specify search patterns for selecting files and finding material within files.

Not all potential language applications can get by with such a simple kind of language model, however. We must also understand the limitations of RLs to avoid trying to use them where they cannot possibly work. A simple example of an aspect of languages that is beyond the representational capacity of RLs is the balancing of parentheses, as used in algebra, logical expressions, and programming languages. We get a simple *model* of the balancing idea by taking the language formed by ignoring everything else in these expressions. Thus, for the expression $\log(a(b + c)(d + e))$, we are left with the string "(( ) ( ))". The symbol set for this language is $\{(,)\}$. Another string of balanced parentheses is "(( ) (( ) ( )))".

Parentheses are only one example of what are called *delimiters*. Other delimiters include brackets (sometimes called *square brackets*) and braces (sometimes called *curly brackets*), which are used in mathematics and in many programming languages, including C and C++. Another delimiter pair is made up of BEGIN and END in Pascal. The hypertext markup language HTML uses "<" and ">" as well as multicharacter delimiters like "<H2>" and "</H2>". Each of these delimiter pairs must be balanced. Some languages permit more than one kind of delimiter pair and allow nesting but not arbitrary intermingling, so that "{ ( ) ( ) }" would be allowed, for example, but not "{ ( ) (})".

Example 12.1 To make things a bit more precise, we provide definitions
of some balanced, one-delimiter languages. Two of the languages

here are each specified in three ways: in English, in an incomplete extensional form using ellipsis ("..."), and in intensional form.

L_1 = the strings of n occurrences of a followed by n occurrences of b
L_2 = the strings of n occurrences of "(" followed by n occurrences of ")"
$L_1 = \{\Lambda, ab, aabb, aaabbb, aaaabbbb, \ldots\}$
$L_2 = \{\Lambda, (\,), (\,(\,)\,), (\,(\,(\,)\,)\,), \ldots\}$
$L_1 = \{a^n b^n\} = \{x \mid x = a^n b^n \wedge n \geq 0\}$
$L_2 = \{(^n\ )^n\}$
L_3 = the balanced strings over $\{(,)\}$
$L_2 \subset L_3$

Although L_2 is only a subset of the balanced strings, it does capture the important idea of nesting: You can form a new balanced string by placing an existing one inside a new delimiter pair. Moreover, even the relatively simple subset L_2 is too complex to be expressed as a regular expression. We explore this claim by looking at L_1, which is just the same as L_2 except that, to avoid confusion, it uses different symbols. Anything that can be said about L_1 can also be said about L_2 simply by substituting "(" for a and ")" for b.

We show that L_1 is not regular by showing that there can be no finite automaton for it. The argument makes crucial use of the concept of **distinguishability**, which is a relationship among three things: two strings and a language.

Definition 12.1 Distinguishability

Let L be a language over Σ and $x, y \in \Sigma^*$. Then x and y are distinguishable with respect to L if for some $z \in \Sigma^*$ one of the strings xz and yz is in L but the other is not in L. Otherwise they are *in*distinguishable.

Two strings x and y are distinguishable with respect to a language L if they differ in either of two ways: acceptance now or acceptance in the future as they are examined from left to right. Differing with respect to "acceptance now" means that one is in L and the other is not. This idea is implied by Definition 12.1 because we can choose Λ as the value of the string z. Differing on future acceptance means that the string z in the definition is not Λ. When a string z is concatenated at the end of x (or y) to form xz (or yz), we call it a *continuation*.

Example 12.2 Are the strings aa and $aaaaaaa$ distinguishable with respect to the language L represented by the RE, $a^*bb(a+b)^*$?

First, the two strings are the same with respect to acceptance now since neither of them is in L. Second, they are also the same with respect to acceptance in the future since both aa and $aaaaaaa$ can (and would have to) be part of the a^* portion of the RE. So for any continuation, z, both aaz and $aaaaaaaz$ belong to L if and only if $z \in L$. Since they do not differ in either way, the two strings are indistinguishable.

Example 12.3 Are the strings aaa and $aaaaa$ distinguishable with respect to the language $L_1 = \{a^n b^n\}$ introduced in Example 12.1?

The two strings are the same with respect to acceptance now since neither of them is in L_1, but they differ with respect to future. Using the continuation string $z = bbb$, we have $xz \in L_1$, but $yz \notin L_1$. Therefore, the two strings are distinguishable with respect to L_1.

This result extends to any two sequences of as that are of different lengths. That is, for any two unequal non-negative integers i and j, the strings a^i and a^j are distinguishable with respect to L_1, using either $z = b^i$ or $z = b^j$ as the continuation.

This last result in Example 12.3 means that we have found an *infinite number* of strings (all of the strings in the language of a^* to be precise) that are pairwise distinguishable strings with respect to L_1. Now suppose you are trying to design a DFA for L_1. Take any two different non-negative integers, i and j. Since a_i and a_j are distinguishable, the state reached from the start state, q_0, with a_i as input must be different from the state reached with a_j. Why? Suppose that these two strings bring the DFA to the same state, q. Then suppose the next symbols are b^i. Should the resulting state, $\delta^*(q, b^i)$, be an accepting state?

There is no satisfactory answer to this last question. The state $\delta^*(q, b^i)$ must be accepting to accept $a^i b^i$, but it must be nonaccepting to reject $a^j b^i$. Our assumption that q could exist has led to an absurdity and so it is false. In other words, $\delta^*(q_0, a^i)$ and $\delta^*(q_0, a^j)$ must be two different states and so every non-negative integer—that is, each of the *infinitely many* non-negative integers—must have its own state. It follows that no *finite* state automaton can handle this language; it is not regular. We now summarize a key idea here in more general terms for future use in showing languages to be nonregular.

Theorem 12.1 Let Σ be a symbol set and let L be a language over Σ. If there is an infinite set $\{x_i \mid i \geq 0\}$ of strings over Σ that are pairwise distinguishable with respect to L, then L is not regular.

Proof: Suppose, to the contrary, that L is regular so that some DFA, M, accepts exactly the strings of L. Being a finite automaton, M has a finite number of states; let n be that number.

We invoke the pigeonhole principle: To fit $n+1$ pigeons into n pigeonholes, some pair must share a pigeonhole. As pigeonholes, we take the n states of M. As pigeons, for each of the first $n+1$ strings $\{x_i \mid 0 \le i \le n\}$, we take the state, $\delta^*(q_0, x_i)$, to which x_i leads from the start state. By the pigeonhole principle, two of the latter states must share the same state; that is, for two of the strings, say x_j and x_k,

$$\delta^*(q_0, x_j) = \delta^*(q_0, x_k).$$

It follows that x_j and x_k are not distinguishable since for any string $z \in \Sigma^*$,

$$\delta^*(q_0, x_j z) = \delta^*(\delta^*(q_0, x_j), z) = \delta^*(\delta^*(q_0, x_k), z) = \delta^*(q_0, x_k z).$$

But we know that x_j and x_k *are* distinguishable since that is part of the conditions of the theorem. So the assumption that L is regular has led to a contradiction and we conclude the opposite—that L is not regular. $\square$

To summarize, when building a DFA for a language, we need *distinct states* for strings that are (pairwise) distinguishable with respect to the language. If the language has an infinite number of distinguishable strings, there would have to be an infinite number of states, contrary to the definition of a DFA ("F" is for "finite") as a machine with a *finite* number of states.

We also know that if a language cannot be expressed in terms of a DFA, it is also true that there is no NFA or RE for it. Returning to the languages of Example 12.1, L_1 is not a regular language. It follows, simply by changing symbols, that L_2 is not regular either. For L_3, the same infinite set of distinguishable strings as for L_2 can be used, together with Theorem 12.1, to show that it too is nonregular. Distinguishability can also help us prove that many other important languages are beyond the expressive power of regular languages. We therefore turn to different and more powerful kinds of representation.

12.2   Introduction to Context-Free Grammars

Context-free grammars (CFGs) are an important formalism for representing both programming languages and human languages. They can express all of the regular languages, as demonstrated in the next section, and their capacity goes well beyond that. In this section, we content ourselves with defining them and showing that they can express the languages L_1, L_2, and L_3 of Example 12.1, which were discussed at some length in the preceding section.

12.2.1   The Four Parts of a CFG

A context-free grammar G has four parts, of which the crucial one is the set of **rules**. The grammar G_1 in Example 12.4 has rules $S \to a \, S \, b$ and $S \to \Lambda$. The **terminal symbols** of a grammar—in this case, a and b—can appear in the strings of its language. S is an example of a **nonterminal symbol**. Nonterminals help determine what the strings of the language $\mathcal{L}(G)$ are, but do not appear in those strings. One of the nonterminals is designated as the *start symbol*. In the case of G_1, the only nonterminal is S, which also serves as the start symbol.

> **Definition 12.2 Context-free grammars**
> A context-free grammar G is a quadruple, (V, Σ, S, P), where
>
> V is the set of nonterminal symbols (also called variables);
> Σ is the set of terminal symbols, the symbol set for the strings of $\mathcal{L}(G)$;
> S is the start symbol, which must be a member of V; and
> P is a set of rules, each of the form $\alpha \to \omega$, where $\alpha \in V$ and $\omega \in (V \cup \Sigma)^*$.
> That is, the left side of a rule is a nonterminal and the right side is any sequence of terminals and/or nonterminals.

> **Example 12.4** $G_1 = (\{S\}, \{a, b\}, S, \{S \to a \, S \, b, \; S \to \Lambda\})$. We soon see that $\mathcal{L}(G_1)$, the language of G_1, is the language $L_1 = \{a^n b^n\}$ studied in Section 12.1.

12.2.2   Deriving the Strings

> **Example 12.5** To show that a particular string of terminals is in the language of some grammar, we **derive** that string from the start symbol. Here is a derivation (see Definition 12.4) of *aaabbb* from S, the start symbol of G_1:
>
> $$S$$
> $$a \, S \, b$$
> $$a \, a \, S \, b \, b$$
> $$a \, a \, a \, S \, b \, b \, b$$
> $$a \, a \, a \, \Lambda \, b \, b \, b \; = \; a \, a \, a \, b \, b \, b$$

After the start symbol in the first line of this derivation come three lines each based on replacements using the rule $S \to a\, S\, b$. The last line is obtained by using $S \to \Lambda$. It is useful to have an operator symbol, " $\Rightarrow$ ", for the idea of making a replacement (see Definition 12.3). The derivation can be rewritten as shown here:

$$S \Rightarrow a\, S\, b \Rightarrow a\, a\, S\, b\, b \Rightarrow a\, a\, a\, S\, b\, b\, b \Rightarrow a\, a\, a\, b\, b\, b.$$

Be sure to use this double-bar arrow in derivations and the single-bar arrow (" $\to$ ") in the grammar rules.

A few comments about CFG notation are in order. First, it is common practice to specify a CFG solely in terms of its rules, allowing the other three parts to be inferred from them. Suppose, for example, that only the rule set $S \to a\, S\, b$, $S \to \Lambda$ of G_1 were given. To determine the other parts of G_1, we could first notice that S occurs on the left side of at least one rule, so it must be a nonterminal, whereas a and b, which are not on any left sides, must be terminals. As the only nonterminal, S must be the start symbol. An additional clue is that it is typical, although not required, to use S as the start symbol; note that "s" is the initial letter of "start," "statement" and "sentence." It is also common for the start symbol to be the left side of the first rule.

It is conventional, at least in simple examples, to use capital letters for the nonterminals and lowercase letters as terminal symbols. Another convention is to use a symbol near the start of the Greek alphabet, like α or β, to stand for some unspecified nonterminal. The last few letters of that alphabet, especially ϕ, ψ, and ω, often represent strings in $(V \cup \Sigma)^*$ containing terminals and/or nonterminals.

We saw in Example 12.5 that finding a string in the language of a grammar is accomplished by derivation—a process of successive replacements. A rule of the form $\alpha \to \omega$ allows an occurrence of α to be replaced by ω. The next two definitions put matters in more general terms.

Definition 12.3 The replacement operator, $\Rightarrow$, and its closure

The replacement of α by ω in the string $\phi\alpha\psi$, using the rule $\alpha \to \omega$, is written $\phi\alpha\psi \Rightarrow \phi\omega\psi$.

The closure of this replacement operator, written " $\overset{*}{\Rightarrow}$ ", expresses the result of 0 or more replacements. Thus, if $\psi_0 \Rightarrow \psi_1 \Rightarrow \psi_2 \Rightarrow \cdots \Rightarrow \psi_n$, we can write $\psi_0 \overset{*}{\Rightarrow} \psi_i$ for any i from 0 to n.

Definition 12.4 Derivations in a grammar

A derivation in some grammar G is a sequence of strings in which each one after the first is derived from the one before it by replacement using a rule in G.

Definition 12.5 Terminal strings

A terminal string of G is a string containing only terminal symbols of G. (Λ is considered to be a terminal string.)

Definition 12.6 The language generated by a grammar

A string x belongs to $\mathcal{L}(G)$, the language of G—also called the language that G *generates*—if and only if there exists a derivation $\psi_0 \Rightarrow \cdots \Rightarrow \psi_n$, such that

- ψ_0 consists of (one occurrence of) the start symbol of G,

- each step uses a rule of G, and

- ψ_n contains only terminal symbols of G.

Example 12.6 The language generated by G_1, specified in Example 12.4, was shown in Example 12.5 to contain *aaabbb*. It is not hard to prove that $\mathcal{L}(G_1)$ is the language $L_1 = \{a^n b^n\}$, introduced in Example 12.1.

Example 12.7 What language is generated by the following grammar?

$$G_2 = (\{S\},\ \{(,)\},\ S,\ \{S \to (\,S\,),\ S \to \Lambda\})$$

It is important to remember that "(" and ")" are just ordinary terminal symbols. Since this grammar is just like G_1, except for replacing a and b by left and right parentheses, the same is true of the resulting language: $\mathcal{L}(G_2)$ is the language $L_2 = \{(^n\,)^n\}$ introduced in Example 12.1.

12.2.3   Balanced Parentheses

Now that you have developed some skill at using CFGs, it is time to look for a CFG for *all* strings of balanced parentheses, not just those of L_2. However, except for giving some examples, we have never really said what strings of balanced parentheses *are*. Since there are infinitely many of them, a recursive definition is appropriate.

Definition 12.7 Strings of balanced parentheses

Let B denote the language of strings of balanced parentheses. Then,

1. $\Lambda \in B$.
2. If $s_1 \in B$ and $s_2 \in B$, then $s_1 s_2 \in B$.
3. If $s \in B$, then $(\,s\,) \in B$.
4. Nothing else is in B.

The third line captures the main idea of parentheses: that to use them you surround a legal expression by putting "(" in front of it and ")" after it. Line 2 says that two legal expressions can go side by side. Line 1 just lets us get started, and line 4 is the usual final disclaimer in this kind of definition.

Of course, when parentheses appear in ordinary mathematical expressions, there are other things mixed in with the parentheses, both within and between balanced pairs, as well as before and after, but here we are ignoring everything else. We are now in a position to write a grammar for the language of balanced parentheses simply by mimicking lines 1 to 3 of Definition 12.7.

Example 12.8 All strings of balanced parentheses—and no other strings— belong to the language of the grammar G_3, with the following rules:

$$S \to \Lambda \qquad S \to S\,S \qquad S \to (\,S\,)$$

In other words, we claim that $L_3 = \mathcal{L}(G_3)$ is the language of balanced parentheses. The following derivation shows that the string $(\,(\,)\,(\,)\,)$ is in $\mathcal{L}(G_3)$. The symbol that is replaced next is underlined.

$$\underline{S} \Rightarrow (\,\underline{S}\,) \Rightarrow (\,\underline{S}\,S\,) \Rightarrow (\,(\,S\,)\,\underline{S}\,) \Rightarrow (\,(\,\underline{S}\,)\,(\,S\,)\,) \Rightarrow (\,(\,)\,(\,\underline{S}\,)\,) \Rightarrow (\,(\,)\,(\,)\,)$$

The proof of the claim that $\mathcal{L}(G_3)$ is the language of balanced parentheses is straightforward, using mathematical induction and drawing on the similarity of the three rules of G_3 to, respectively, lines 1, 2, and 3 of Definition 12.7. Line 4 of that definition corresponds to the words "and only if" in Definition 12.6 for the language of any CFG.

The two key reasons for our interest in the language L_3 involve modeling and nonregularity. First, the language serves as a model of how parentheses, and delimiters in general, behave. Recall that models simplify yet retain essential features.

In this case, the simplification is to remove all other material, whereas the essential feature retained is described in line 3 of Definition 12.7 and echoed in the third rule of G_3 in Example 12.8: Parentheses *surround* expressions.

We turn now to the other motivation for introducing L_3—the fact that it is a nonregular language. The nonregularity of L_2 has already been demonstrated, and it may seem predictable that L_3, with its additional strings that require a more complex description, must therefore also be nonregular. Although that is essentially correct, do not get the mistaken idea that extra strings necessarily make a language more complex. After all, the set of *all* strings over an alphabet is regular and recognizable by a one-state DFA.

The next example proves that, although the simple CFG G_3 is sufficient to generate it, L_3 cannot be the language of any finite automaton and so is not regular.

Example 12.9 Prove that L_3 is not regular.

By Theorem 12.1, a language is nonregular if it has an infinite set of pairwise distinguishable strings. For L_3, we claim that such a set is provided by the language corresponding to the RE (*—that is, the set of sequences of any number of left parentheses. Simply note that $(^i$ and $(^j$ for $i \neq j$ are distinguishable by $)^i$.

12.3 RE Operators in CFGs

The CFGs as a class are more powerful than regular expressions since the CFGs can represent all of the regular languages and also some nonregular languages. We have proved the second part of this two-part claim, although we have not yet gotten around to the first. Specifically, we have seen three CFGs—G_1, G_2, and G_3—each of which expresses a language that has been proved nonregular by means of distinguishability arguments invoking Theorem 12.1. There are many more CFGs that generate nonregular languages of great usefulness, including the language consisting of algebraic expressions and widely used programming languages.

So CFGs represent important languages beyond the regular languages. But what about the regular languages themselves? Is there a CFG to generate each and every one of them? The answer is "yes" as Theorem 12.2 shows. Since every regular language can be represented by a DFA, we just find a CFG for each DFA.

Theorem 12.2 Every regular language can be generated by a context-free grammar.

Proof (using DFAs): Let $M = (Q, \Sigma, q_0, \delta, A)$ be a DFA. Then $G = (V, \Sigma, S, P)$ is a CFG that generates the language accepted by M provided that $V = Q$, $S = q_0$

and

$$P = \{q \rightarrow \sigma q' \mid q' = \delta(q, \sigma)\} \cup \{q \rightarrow \Lambda \mid q \in A\}$$

As nonterminals of the CFG, we use the DFA states. The key idea—expressed in the left-hand operand of "∪"—is that for each DFA transition in δ there is a grammar rule. Then for any input string accepted by M, the steps of the derivation corresponds exactly to the state transitions for that input. In particular, the derivation *simulates* the path through the transition diagram; at each step of the derivation, the nonterminal is the state we would have arrived at after each corresponding transition. Formally, $\delta^*(q_0, x) = p \leftrightarrow S \overset{*}{\Rightarrow} xp$, which can be established by induction on the number of steps in the derivation.

Finally, if the state p thus reached is an accepting state—that is, a member of A—the right-hand operand of "∪" lets Λ replace the state name, p. Making these replacements, we can conclude that for any terminal string x,

$$\delta^*(q_0, x) \in A \leftrightarrow S \overset{*}{\Rightarrow} x$$

We now invoke the definitions of the language of an FA and the language of a CFG to get, for any terminal string x,

$$x \in \mathcal{L}(M) \leftrightarrow \delta^*(q_0, x) \in A \leftrightarrow S \overset{*}{\Rightarrow} x \leftrightarrow x \in \mathcal{L}(G)$$

□

Example 12.10 The following DFA transition diagram is a copy of an example from Chapter 9, except that here we label the states C, D, E, and F. C is the start state and F is the only accepting state. Like the earlier diagram, this one accepts the language of strings with an odd number of as and of bs. Convert the DFA to a CFG that accepts the language.

Following the specifications in the proof of Theorem 12.2 yields the grammar

$$G_4 = (\{C, D, E, F\}, \{a, b\}, C, P),$$

which generates the required language, where P consists of the rules in the first three columns here. The rules in the first two columns have been constructed according to the left-hand operand of "∪" in the theorem. The rule in the third column comes from the right-hand operand of "∪" and could be replaced by the parenthesized rules in the fourth column to eliminate unnecessary use of Λ in the grammar. This change would involve replacing the right-hand argument of "∪"

by $\{q \to \sigma \mid \delta(q, \sigma) \in A\}$. The resulting trees would be simpler, but the proof would become more complicated.

$$
\begin{array}{llll}
C \to a\,D & C \to b\,E & & \\
D \to a\,C & D \to b\,F & F \to \Lambda & (D \to b) \\
E \to a\,F & E \to b\,C & & (E \to a) \\
F \to a\,E & F \to b\,D & &
\end{array}
$$

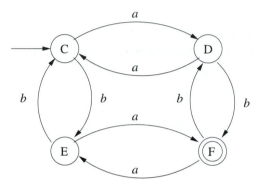

You should verify the idea in the proof of Theorem 12.2 for various x; for example, $\delta^*(C, aab) = E$ and $C \overset{*}{\Rightarrow} aabE$.

It should be noted that the grammars the above proof creates have a special structure. Is it significant that we only need simple rules to generate regular languages? The answer is "yes," and the following definition specifies how to constrain CFGs.

Definition 12.8 Regular grammars

A *right-regular* grammar is one in which the right-hand side of each rule has one terminal symbol possibly followed by one nonterminal.

A *left-regular* grammar is one in which the right-hand side of each rule has one terminal symbol possibly preceded by one nonterminal.

A *regular* grammar is a grammar that is either right-regular or left-regular.

It makes sense to call this special subset of the CFGs regular because a language is generated by a regular grammar iff it is a regular language. We have just seen that any regular language is generated by a right-regular grammar—that is how the proof works. It turns out that it is easy to reverse the construction in the proof so that we can create a corresponding FA from any right-regular grammar. Hence, any language generated by a right-regular grammar is regular. (Similar, but more complex, arguments hold for left-regular grammars.)

Note that a grammar is *not* regular if the right-hand sides of its rules include terminal and nonterminal symbols in both orders. Consider, for example, the grammar with rules $S \rightarrow aT$, $S \rightarrow \Lambda$, and $T \rightarrow Sb$. Although the rule $S \rightarrow aT$ could belong to a right-regular grammar and the rule $T \rightarrow Sb$ could belong to a left-regular grammar, the two of them cannot both belong to the same regular grammar. Moreover, it is not hard to see that the language of this grammar is our old friend L_1 from Example 12.1—our first example of a *non*regular language.

The proof of Theorem 12.2 showed that there is a CFG for every regular language since there is one for every DFA. Since every regular language can also be represented by an RE (as well as by a DFA), an alternative approach to proving the theorem is to show how to create a CFG for every RE. This in turn can be accomplished informally by checking that each of the three RE operations—concatenation, alternation, and closure—is included among the tools of CFG production rules.

- **Concatenation:** Notice that a rule like $A \rightarrow B\,C$ expresses concatenation since whatever B generates is followed by whatever C generates. Thus, the concatenation operation is implicit in the definition of CFGs.

- **Alternation:** Alternation is choice among alternatives. A CFG allows for choice by letting a nonterminal have two or more right-hand sides. For example, using both $A \rightarrow B$ and $A \rightarrow C$ lets A be replaced in a derivation by either B or C. In fact, these two rules can be collapsed, by convention, to the abbreviated form, $A \rightarrow B \mid C$. The vertical bar ("|") here expresses a choice among alternatives (just as it does in Lex).

- **Closure:** The effect of unlimited repetition can be achieved by writing a recursive rule like $A \rightarrow B\,A \mid \Lambda$, which gives the same strings as if one were permitted to write $A \rightarrow B^*$. Here B is a nonterminal symbol, so B can expand to the equivalent of a complex RE.

We now reprove Theorem 12.2, this time by converting REs to CFGs. Although this approach is more complex than converting DFAs to CFGs, it does give more practice in manipulating the CFG formalism. Let Σ be the symbol set for the REs and the set of terminal symbols for each grammar. From Definition 10.2, the REs are: $\emptyset$; Λ; each symbol of Σ; and whatever can be constructed from REs by concatenation, alternation, and closure. We show how CFGs are systematically constructed for the languages of all these REs. The result then follows directly by mathematical induction on the number of operators in an RE.

Proof of Theorem 12.2 (using REs):

A grammar for the RE $\emptyset$ is $(\{S\}, \emptyset, S, \emptyset)$.

A grammar for the RE Λ is $(\{S\}, \emptyset, S, \{S \to \Lambda\})$.

For each $\sigma \in \Sigma$, a grammar is $(\{S\}, \{\sigma\}, S, \{S \to \sigma\})$.

Suppose that we already have CFGs G_1 and G_2 for the REs r_1 and r_2; that is
$$G_1 = (V_1, \Sigma, S_1, P_1) \text{ and } \mathcal{L}(G_1) = \mathcal{L}(r_1) \text{ , and}$$
$$G_2 = (V_2, \Sigma, S_2, P_2) \text{ and } \mathcal{L}(G_2) = \mathcal{L}(r_2).$$
Then
$$G_3 = (V_3, \Sigma, S_3, P_3)) \text{ is a CFG that generates } \mathcal{L}(r_1 + r_2), \text{ where}$$
$$S_3 \notin V_1 \cup V_2$$
$$V_3 = \{S_3\} \cup V_1 \cup V_2$$
$$P_3 = \{S_3 \to S_1, \quad S_3 \to S_2\} \cup P_1 \cup P_2$$

$$G_4 = (V_4, \Sigma, S_4, P_4) \text{ is a CFG that generates } \mathcal{L}(r_1 r_2), \text{ where}$$
$$S_4 \notin V_1 \cup V_2$$
$$V_4 = \{S_4\} \cup V_1 \cup V_2$$
$$P_4 = \{S_4 \to S_1 S_2\} \cup P_1 \cup P_2$$

$$G_5 = (V_5, \Sigma, S_5, P_5) \text{ is a CFG that generates } \mathcal{L}(r_1^*), \text{ where}$$
$$S_5 \notin V_1$$
$$V_5 = \{S_5\} \cup V_1$$
$$P_5 = \{S_5 \to S_1 S_5, \quad S_5 \to \Lambda\} \cup P_1$$

Consider G_3 for simulating alternation of REs. In addition to all the existing symbols and rules, we add—using set union—a new start symbol and include it in the new set of variables. Then we add new rules that generate S_1 and S_2 to get the component grammars (G_1 and G_2) started. Similar strategies go into the construction of grammar G_4 for simulating concatenation and G_5 for closure. □

Note: The grammar names G_1 to G_5 here apply only within this proof. They are not particular grammars, but rather are generic—in that they can stand for any grammar of a certain kind, in this case, any regular grammar. Thus, they are not the grammars called G_1 to G_5 elsewhere in this chapter and should not be confused with them.

Example 12.11 Write a CFG that generates the language of the regular expression, $a + b^*c$.

For this example, we faithfully follow the method prescribed in this second proof of Theorem 12.2, based on REs. As the names of new start symbols, we use A, B, C, ... Thus, a grammar generating the one string a has the rule set $A \rightarrow a$. Similarly, use $B \rightarrow b$ and $C \rightarrow c$. For a grammar generating b^*, we can now use $D \rightarrow B D \mid \Lambda$. Next for b^*c, we have $E \rightarrow D C$, and finally, using S as the overall start symbol, we get

$$G_5 = (\{S, A, B, C, D, E\}, \{a, b, c\}, S, P),$$

where $\mathcal{L}(G_5) = \mathcal{L}(a + b^*c)$, and P consists of these rules:

$$
\begin{array}{ll}
S \rightarrow A \mid E & A \rightarrow a \\
E \rightarrow D C & B \rightarrow b \\
D \rightarrow B D \mid \Lambda & C \rightarrow c
\end{array}
$$

Example 12.12 Write a CFG with the same language as the RE, $(a + b)^*b(a + b)^*$.

Grammar G_6 does the job, although it departs in a couple of ways from the method in the proof of Theorem 12.2, to simplify the resulting grammar. Notice the rule with three symbols on the right-hand side. By definition only two REs can be concatenated at a time, so this rule actually reflects repeated concatenation. Also notice the two occurrences of $(a + b)^*$ in the regular expression. According to the method in the proof, these would be handled independently, but G_6 does not bother with two separate sets of equivalent rules:

$$G_6 = (\{S, A, D\}, \{a, b\}, S, P),$$

where P consists of these rules:

$$
\begin{array}{l}
S \rightarrow A b A \\
A \rightarrow D A \mid \Lambda \\
D \rightarrow a \mid b
\end{array}
$$

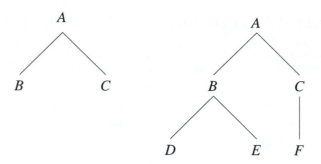

Figure 12.1: Derivation trees using: $A \to B\,C$ then $B \to D\,E$, and $C \to F$.

12.4   Structure, Meaning, and Ambiguity

We model the structure of the derivation of a string and show how that structure can have an effect on the meaning of the string. Then we use these ideas to design a grammar of algebraic expressions.

12.4.1   Modeling Structure for Meaning

A **derivation tree** is a diagram of a derivation. For example, the left side of Figure 12.1 shows the derivation tree for a one-step derivation using the rule $A \to B\,C$. In such a case, we say that we have *expanded* the node A. The derivation tree in the right side of the figure starts the same way and then expands B and C using the two additional rules $B \to D\,E$ and $C \to F$. In general, a parent in the tree must be labeled by the left side of some rule and its children must be labeled by, in order, the symbols on the right side of the same rule.

The second tree in Figure 12.1 can be regarded as a **model** of the derivation

$$A \Rightarrow B\,C \;\Rightarrow D\,E\,C \;\Rightarrow D\,E\,F,$$

in the sense that it ignores some parts of the derivation to focus on other aspects of it. In particular, the tree does not specify in what order B and C are expanded, and often we do not care.

The derivation tree is a model of structure in the sense that it emphasizes certain structural relationships. For example, the lines in the derivation tree that descend from B to its children D and E show that B is composed of D and E. This information is not explicit in the derivation; it is there, but one has to infer it by looking at what has changed from before the arrow to after it in the derivation step $B\,C \Rightarrow D\,E\,C$.

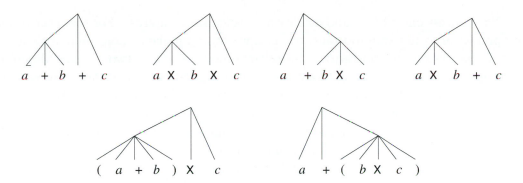

Figure 12.2: Tree structures for the correct application order of operators.

The kind of structural information that is present in derivation trees plays a crucial role in figuring out the **semantics** (roughly speaking, the meanings) of strings in useful CFGs. To understand an expression like $a + b \times c$—to know its semantics— one must at least know that "+" calls for adding, that "×" calls for multiplying, and that the multiplication is to be done first. This last point, the issue of which operator to apply first, is what concerns us here. More generally, we want the derivation trees in our grammar for algebraic expressions—which we design later—to provide an answer to this question: When an expression has two or more operators, in what order should they be executed? *You* know the answer, but the question has to be answered by software—by an interpreter that executes the expression or by a compiler that translates it to machine code for future execution.

So we seek a grammar whose derivation trees always provide the correct order for applying operators. We do this for a simplified language of algebraic expressions using just the two operators "+" and "×", parentheses, and a few variables. However, the ideas are broadly applicable to algebraic expressions for programming languages with numbers, variables, parentheses, functions, arrays, and a wide range of other operators. Consider the expressions and tree structures in Figure 12.2. These trees are *not* derivation trees since they lack nonterminal symbols as labels on some nodes, but they do express the correct order for applying the operators.

Each branching in these trees associates an operator with its two operands. In the case of $a + b \times c$, for example, the lower three-way branching groups "×" with b and c to form $b \times c$. Then the upper branching groups the "+" with this result and a. The tree as a whole correctly reflects the fact that "×" takes **precedence** over "+" and should be performed first. We also want to be able to overrule precedence by using *parentheses*, as shown in the diagram for $(a + b) \times c$, where the lower branching does the grouping for addition first.

The expressions $a+b+c$ and $a\times b\times c$ are also of some interest. For them the order of application is not so important, but still we should make a choice and stick to it, rather than using an **ambiguous** grammar—one that allows two or more different structures for the same string. An ambiguous grammar can allow the software that has to find these structures to go into excessive searching for possibilities, which is inefficient. The branching structures for these two expressions also suggest the repeatable nature of these operators—the fact that a single expression can use these operators as many times as a programmer needs. We achieve this repetition by **recursion** in CFGs here and by iteration in other formalisms in Section 12.5.

Definition 12.9 Recursive Rules, Grammars, and Symbols
A *recursive rule* in a CFG has the form $A \to \phi A\psi$, so that the symbol on the left side also appears on the right. (By convention, ϕ and ψ are arbitrary sequences, possibly empty, of terminal and/or nonterminal symbols.) A *recursive grammar* has some nonterminal for which there is a derivation $A \overset{*}{\Rightarrow} \phi A\psi$ with at least one step. The symbol involved in either case (here A) is a *recursive symbol*—directly recursive for a rule and indirectly recursive in the case of a multistep derivation.

12.4.2   A Grammar of Algebraic Expressions

The foregoing ideas about structure and meaning are now applied to the practical task of designing a grammar of algebraic expressions. Our goal is a grammar for which the derivation trees always imply the correct order of application for the operators, taking into account the four concepts mentioned earlier: recursion, ambiguity, precedence, and parentheses.

Example 12.13 Write a grammar for the algebraic expressions using only "+" and "×" as the operators, confining the variables to just a, b, and c and not including numbers at all.

The grammar G_7 does the job. E, standing for "expression," is the start symbol of the grammar and its only nonterminal. The terminal symbols are a, b, c, $+$, and $\times$. Each of the first two rules is recursive and therefore leads to unlimited repetition of the operators, which is what we want. However, this grammar has the undesirable property of being ambiguous, according to the next definition, as we will see in the next example.

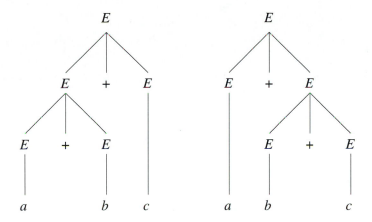

Figure 12.3: Trees for Example 12.14.

Rules for G_7:
$$E \to E + E$$
$$E \to E \times E$$
$$E \to a \mid b \mid c.$$

Definition 12.10 Ambiguity

An *ambiguous string* with respect to a CFG is one that the grammar can generate with at least two different derivation trees. An *ambiguous grammar* is one that generates at least one ambiguous string.

Example 12.14 Draw derivation trees that show repetition and that prove the ambiguity of G_7.

Either one of the recursive rules is sufficient to show these things. The repetition effects of $E \to E + E$ are clear from either one of the derivation trees in Figure 12.3. Repeated use of the rule occurs in each, and further repetition would yield larger trees and longer strings, as needed, without limit. Since there are two trees for the string $a + b + c$, that string is ambiguous and so is the grammar, G_7, that generated them.

Example 12.15 Can we produce another grammar that is not ambiguous and still generates the same language?

The ambiguity of G_7 arises from having two Es on the right side of the recursive rules. One of those Es allows left branching and the

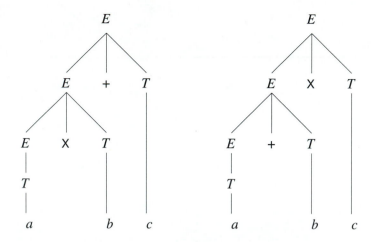

Figure 12.4: Trees for Example 12.16.

other one allows right branching. So let us use rules with no more than one E on the right. The rule set for G_8, shown next, results from a technique like the one used to get regular grammars and does indeed give us an unambiguous grammar.

Rules for G_8:
$$E \rightarrow E + T$$
$$E \rightarrow E \times T$$
$$E \rightarrow T$$
$$T \rightarrow a \mid b \mid c.$$

Example 12.16 How does G_8 avoid ambiguity?

All the branching in the derivation trees of G_8 is to the left, as shown in each of the trees in Figure 12.4. For strings of a given length, there is only one tree shape or branching pattern. In fact, the Es and Ts must always be in the same places in all trees of a particular size, just as in these two trees. All this uniformity makes ambiguity impossible.

Despite being unambiguous, G_8 has a flaw. Unfortunately, some derivation trees generated by G_8 violate precedence. In particular, the derivation tree for the string $a + b \times c$ on the right side of Figure 12.4 incorrectly suggests applying "+" before "×". (The grammar G_7 has a similar shortcoming.)

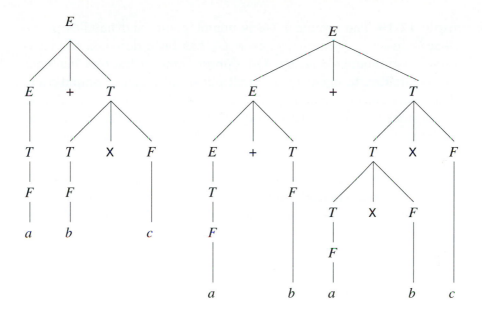

Figure 12.5: Trees for Example 12.18.

Example 12.17 Find a new grammar whose trees respect precedence.

The trees in Example 12.16 reveal a flaw in the rules of G_8: That grammar makes no distinction in the way it handles the two operators, but instead treats them identically, so it can generate them in any order. The grammar G_9 fixes this by generating "+" first and "×" later, so all occurrences of "×" are lower in the derivation trees. Therefore, the trees correctly suggest an interpretation in which all occurrences of "×" are applied before any of the pluses in accord with its higher precedence.

$$\text{Rules for } G_9: \qquad E \to E + T \mid T$$
$$T \to T \times F \mid F$$
$$F \to a \mid b \mid c.$$

Example 12.18 The effect of introducing "×" in its own rule in G_9 can be seen in the derivation trees shown in Figure 12.5. For example, in the tree for $a + b + a \times b \times c$ on the right, both multiplications are performed before the result, $a \times b \times c$, is added to $a + b$ at the top level.

Example 12.19 The grammar G_9 is unambiguous and handles precedence correctly. However, suppose G_9 has been designed to generate a programming language and a programmer using that language
needs addition to occur before multiplication in some computation.
The programmer might like to write $(a + b) \times c$, but is unable to
do so since G_9 has no parentheses. How can we modify G_9 to allow
derivation trees that respect precedence but let parentheses override
it?

We can correctly allow for this possibility by extending our approach
to handling precedence. Note that parentheses have the effect of
a very high precedence, so we make them occur even later in the
grammar than "$\times$". We now have a grammar G_{10} that meets all
four of the criteria established at the outset. Notice that in choosing
nonterminal symbols, we have picked "T" for terms in a sum and
"F" for factors in a product.

$$\text{Rules for } G_{10}: \qquad
\begin{aligned}
E &\to E + T \mid T \\
T &\to T \times F \mid F \\
F &\to (E) \\
F &\to a \mid b \mid c
\end{aligned}$$

Example 12.20 The rule for introducing parentheses appears in a derivation tree for $a \times (b + c)$ using G_{10} in Figure 12.6.

12.5   Backus Normal Form and Syntax Diagrams

There are other language formalisms, in addition to context-free grammars, with
expressive power that goes beyond regular languages. Each of them is capable of
expressing any regular language and other useful languages. Some of these additional formalisms can be shown to be equivalent to each other, in that any language
expressible by one is expressible by the other and vice versa. This section is a brief
introduction to two other formalisms that are equivalent to CFGs: **Backus Normal
Form** (BNF) and **syntax diagrams**.

12.5.1   Backus Normal Form

Where linguists often use CFGs, computer scientists tend to use Backus Normal
Form (sometimes called Backus-Naur Form) or BNF for short. BNF rules expressing

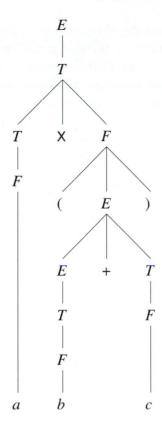

Figure 12.6: Tree for Example 12.20.

concatenation and choice among alternatives look very much like CFG rules, as shown in the two equivalent rules in Example 12.21. A superficial difference between them is the use of "::=" in the BNF rule in place of the CFG arrow. This choice originates simply from the absence of the arrow symbol on a standard keyboard. Also, strictly speaking, the vertical bar, "|", is an operator in BNF, whereas in CFGs it is a notational convenience.

Example 12.21 The following rules are equivalent:

$$\text{CFG: } A \to B\,C \mid D\,E$$
$$\text{BNF: } A ::= B\,C \mid D\,E$$

Unlike the CFG formalism, BNF also permits explicit use of closure—that is, unlimited repetition. However, rather than using "*" as the closure operator, as REs do, the BNF notation expresses the closure of an expression by surrounding it with braces. For example, one writes $\{a\}$ rather than a^* while $\{a|b\}$ corresponds to the regular expression $(a + b)^*$. Notice that in the notation $\{a|b\}$, both "+" and "$*$" have been relieved of the special grammatical significance given to them in REs, thus freeing us to use them with their ordinary meanings of addition and multiplication. Example 12.22 takes advantage of this possibility, using "$*$" to mean multiplication (instead of "$\times$"). Notice that the BNF rule here achieves unlimited repetitions by iteration, whereas the CFG uses a recursive rule for that purpose.

Example 12.22 The following rules are equivalent:

$$\text{CFG: } T \to T * F \mid F$$
$$\text{BNF: } T ::= F \{ * F \}$$

12.5.2   Syntax Diagrams

Syntax diagrams are another way to express the same set of languages as CFGs and BNF. To specify a language, one typically uses a collection of several diagrams, each of which is labeled by a nonterminal symbol. Example 12.23 is a syntax diagram version of the CFG and BNF rules in the preceding example. The nonterminal symbol out at the left—in this case T—is the label of the whole diagram. It corresponds to the symbol on the left side of a CFG or BNF rule. To use the diagram to process input, simply follow the arrows. A terminal symbol like "$*$" in the diagram should match the current input symbol. A nonterminal like F indicates a detour to the diagram with that label. When the end of that diagram is reached, processing returns and continues where it left off just as if a subroutine had concluded.

Example 12.23 The following syntax diagram is equivalent to the rules in Example 12.22. Unlike them, it achieves repeated multiplication, as in "$F * F * F * F$", by iterating its loop rather than via recursion.

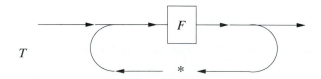

Syntax diagrams look and act quite a bit like the state transition diagrams of FAs, in that both kinds of diagrams have arrows and they follow those arrows when processing input. In fact, *some* syntax diagrams can be converted into FAs, as we see for Example 12.23. However, keep in mind that this conversion is *not* a general process. The following state transition diagram expresses the same strings as the syntax diagram of Example 12.23:

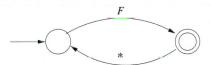

To convert from the syntax diagram (SD) to the state transition diagram (TD), we begin by noticing that the SD has no states, so we put some in. Specifically, put a state wherever arrows come together or split apart. Also, although this is not relevant to Example 12.23, if there is a directed edge from a to b, then insert a new state into that edge between a and b. Next, to determine the start state of the TD, look at where the SD has an arrow entering from the left. Accepting states in the TD are determined by where arrows exit to the right in the SD.

The two kinds of diagrams also differ in where they put symbols: Where a TD has a symbol next to an arrow as a label for it, the syntax diagram inserts that symbol into the arrow, breaking it in two. Therefore, we need to replace every " $\rightarrow a \rightarrow$ " in the SD by an arrow in the TD labeled "a".

The third and most important difference between a syntax diagram and an FA is one that cannot be fixed because it is not just cosmetic, but involves the significant difference between them. Notice that in the syntax diagram, *nonterminal* symbols of the grammar are allowed to appear wherever terminal symbols can (surrounded by a box for emphasis). It is this last difference that gives syntax diagrams the same representational capacity as CFGs and BNF. Example 12.24 shows that a single syntax diagram can, by using recursion, represent a nonregular language. In fact, the language of this diagram is our old friend L_2.

Example 12.24 The language of the following syntax diagram is $L_2 = \{(^n)^n \mid n \geq 0\}$.

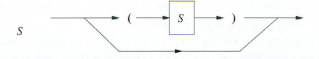

One way to show that the language of the diagram in Example 12.24 really is L_2, as claimed, is to show that the diagram essentially consists of the rules of G_2, which we already know generates L_2. To establish this in the diagram, first note that there are only two paths from start to finish. The lower path uses arrows that do not run into any symbols, so this path for S is equivalent to the rule $S \to \Lambda$. Next, following the upper path, we see "(", then S, and finally ")", providing the rule $S \to (\,S\,)$.

Let us also look directly at the input processing that the diagram specifies. First, given the empty string as input, the diagram succeeds via the lower path, so Λ is in the language. Now suppose that the input is "( )". Following the upper path, the first symbol, "(", is processed successfully. Then S can process Λ, as already shown, and processing can resume with ")" in the diagram, which matches the second symbol, thus accepting the whole input "( )".

With this result in hand, we see that the sequence "(", "( )", ")" is accepted. This is the string (( )) . In this way, it can be seen that longer and longer strings of L_2 are in the language of this syntax diagram.

Functions are crucial in both mathematics and programming. Example 12.25 shows how a syntax diagram can be used to represent a language of function calls. It does not allow for type specification or other information sometimes found in function declarations.

> **Example 12.25** Draw a syntax diagram for functions calls. Use *Fcall* for function calls, *Fname* for function names, and E for expressions. Function arguments are expressions separated by commas, all surrounded by parentheses.

Fcall

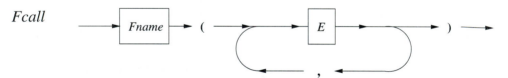

12.6   Theory Matters

In Section 12.4, we saw a progression of grammars for algebraic expressions that gradually added several important properties. The last of those grammars, G_{10}, definitely seemed like the best one to use. However, because it is somewhat more complex than the simple grammar G_7 that we began with, it is reasonable to ask whether G_{10} really generates all the strings we want it to and no others. To establish that it does, one can actually prove that it generates the same language as a simpler grammar (one similar to G_7) whose language is more obvious. We give some hints here about how that proof can be done. First, we practice using some of the ideas that are needed by taking up a much simpler example—one that is amusing but has no particular practical significance.

12.6.1 Practicing Proving with Palindromes

A palindrome as noted in Chapter 7 is a string that reads the same forward and backward; it is the reverse of itself. The empty string and all strings of length one are palindromes. A string of length two is a palindrome if and only if its two symbols are the same. Among the words of English, some palindromes are "a", "gag", "eke", "deed", "noon", "level", "tenet", "redder", and "reviver". Here is a more precise statement about palindromes:

Definition 12.11 Palindromes over Σ

Λ is a palindrome.

For any $\sigma \in \Sigma$, σ is a palindrome.

If x is a palindrome and $\sigma \in \Sigma$, $\sigma x \sigma$ is a palindrome.

The last line defines longer palindromes in terms of shorter ones, using a recursive approach that is by now familiar. Notice that a new palindrome $\sigma x \sigma$ is longer by 2 than x, so Λ in the first line of the definition gets us started only on the even-length palindromes. We also need all the $\sigma \in \Sigma$ (all the strings of length 1) in the second line to get started on the odd-length palindromes. For simplicity, we confine attention to the even-length palindromes.

Example 12.26 Create rules for a grammar for the even-length palindromes over $\Sigma = \{a, b\}$ and write the derivation of $a\,b\,b\,b\,b\,a$.

$$\text{Rules for } G_{11}: \qquad S \to a\,S\,a$$
$$S \to b\,S\,b$$
$$S \to \Lambda.$$

A derivation in G_{11}:

$$S \Rightarrow a\,S\,a \Rightarrow a\,b\,S\,b\,a \Rightarrow a\,b\,b\,S\,b\,b\,a \Rightarrow a\,b\,b\,b\,b\,a$$

Example 12.27 Prove that G_{11} can generate only even-length strings.

Proof. It is sufficient to consider just a single derivation provided that it is arbitrarily chosen. That is, we must make no assumptions about its properties that are not shared by all derivations. For an arbitrary derivation, we prove by mathematical induction that at each step the number of terminal symbols is even.

Basis: A derivation begins with just the start symbol, hence *no* terminal symbols. Zero is an even number.

Inductive step: As each rule applies in a derivation, it either increases the number of terminal symbols either by 2 (for $S \to a\,S\,a$ or $S \to b\,S\,b$) or zero (for $S \to \Lambda$). An even number plus 2 or 0 gives an even result.

We introduced palindromes here with the informal statement that each one is the reverse of itself. Presumably this means that in a string $x = x_1 x_2 \ldots x_n$, we have $x_1 = x_n$, $x_2 = x_{n-1}$ and, more generally, $x_i = x_{n+1-i}$ for every i such that $1 \le i \le n$. (Note that each x_i is a symbol, not a substring.) However, Definition 12.11 and grammar G_{11} do not mention reverses. The next example relates reverses to G_{11}.

Example 12.28 Prove that every string $x_1 x_2 \ldots x_n \in \mathcal{L}(G_{11})$ is the reverse of itself; in other words, $x_i = x_{n+1-i}$ for every i such that $1 \le i \le n$. We also regard Λ as its own reverse.

Proof. This time (instead of considering a single arbitrary derivation as in the proof of Example 12.27), we take on all *terminal* derivations (those that lead to terminal strings) at once. The induction is on the number of steps, p, in the derivations.

Basis: All derivations begin with just the start symbol, which is not a terminal, so there are no 0-step terminal derivations. To get a 1-step terminal derivation requires using a rule that gets rid of S—that is, using $S \to \Lambda$ with result Λ. Thus, Λ is the only terminal string that results from a 1-step derivation.

Inductive step: The inductive hypothesis is that each terminal derivation of p steps produces a string of length $n = 2(p-1)$ that is its own reverse. Consider a terminal derivation of $p+1$ steps and look at its first derivation step. There are three possibilities:

Case 1: The first derivation step is $S \to \Lambda$. In this case, we get Λ.

Case 2: The first derivation step is $S \to a\,S\,a$. From the resulting S, by the inductive hypothesis, the remaining steps derive $x_1 x_2 \ldots x_n$, which is its own reverse. In all, the resulting string is $y = a x_1 x_2 \ldots x_n a$. Using the same convention for y as for x, we write $y = y_1 y_2 \ldots y_m$, where $m = n + 2$. To show that y is its own reverse, first we note that $y_1 = a = y_m$. For $2 \le i \le m - 1$, we have

$$y_i = x_{i-1} = x_{n+1-(i-1)} = x_{n+2-i} = x_{m-i} = y_{m+1-i}.$$

Case 3: The first derivation step is $S \to b\,S\,b$. This is just like case 2.

12.6.2 Proving that G_{10} Does the Right Thing

The grammar G_{10} from Section 12.4 appears to be unambiguous, handle precedence and parentheses correctly, and generate exactly the language we wanted for algebraic expressions with the operators $+$ and $\times$. It is possible to prove that all these things are true, but we settle for a partial proof that G_{10} generates the right language. The following definition summarizes what we mean by the "right" language for algebraic expressions with $+$, $\times$, parentheses, and the symbols a, b, and c.

Definition 12.12 Expressions (simplified algebraic expressions)
a, b, and c are expressions.
If x_1 and x_2 are expressions, then $x_1 + x_2$ and $x_1 \times x_2$ are expressions.
If x is an expression, so is (x).
Nothing else is an expression.

Recursive definitions like this are used widely in formal work, and this one should remind you of the ones for regular expressions and their languages in Section 10.2 and the one for propositions in Section 2.1. Since the grammar G_{12} has a rule for each kind of expression in Definition 12.12 and no other rules, the language $\mathcal{L}(G_{12})$ is the one specified in the definition. G_{12} is $(\{E\}, \{+, \times, a, b, c, (,)\}, E, P)$, with the rule set P shown next.

$$\text{Rules for } G_{12}: \qquad \begin{aligned} E &\to E + E \\ E &\to E \times E \\ E &\to (\, E\,) \\ E &\to a \mid b \mid c. \end{aligned}$$

To show that G_{10} generates the language we want, it is now sufficient to show that its language is the same as that of G_{12}. We let $G = G_{12}$ and $G' = G_{10}$ and also replace E by E' in G'. The two grammars are now as follows, where $\Sigma = \{a, b, c, +, \times, (,)\}$ is the shared set of terminal symbols, with $+$ and $\times$ in a different font to distinguish them from other uses of these symbols.

$$G = (\{E\}, \Sigma, E, P) \qquad\qquad G' = (\{E', T, F\}, \Sigma, E', P')$$

$$\begin{array}{ll} P: & \begin{aligned} E &\to E + E \\ E &\to E \times E \\ E &\to (\,E\,) \\ E &\to a \mid b \mid c. \end{aligned} \qquad\qquad P': & \begin{aligned} E' &\to E' + T \mid T \\ T &\to T \times F \mid F \\ F &\to (\,E'\,) \\ F &\to a \mid b \mid c \end{aligned} \end{array}$$

To simplify the discussion of derivation trees, we just call them just **trees**. A **sum node** means a node with a child labeled $+$; others may be called a **non-sum** nodes. A **unary** node has one child, a **binary** node has two and a **ternary** node three.

Theorem 12.3 G' generates the same language as G.

Proof: Languages are sets (of strings); to prove two of them equal, we prove that each is a (improper) subset of the other. Thus, the proof has two major parts. Recall, to prove a subset relationship, $A \subseteq B$, we prove that $x \in A \to x \in B$.

Part 1. $\mathcal{L}(G') \subseteq \mathcal{L}(G)$ (by showing that $x \in \mathcal{L}(G') \to x \in \mathcal{L}(G)$).

Proof (of Part 1). The proof is by mathematical induction on string lengths.

Basis. Since G' does not generate Λ, its shortest strings are a, b, and c (e.g., $E' \Rightarrow T \Rightarrow F \Rightarrow b$). G also generates these strings (e.g., $E \Rightarrow b$).

Inductive step. The inductive hypothesis is that all strings in $\mathcal{L}(G')$ of length $\leq k$ are also in $\mathcal{L}(G)$. We need to prove the same thing for $k + 1$. Consider $x \in \mathcal{L}(G')$, where $|x| = k + 1$ and take some tree for x. We divide this part of the proof into cases based on where the first ternary node occurs in the tree, starting at the root.

Case 1: at the root. A ternary root arises from the rule $E' \to E' + T$, so the derivation must be of the form $E' \Rightarrow E' + T \overset{*}{\Rightarrow} x$, with $x = y + z$, where y and z are strings derived from E' and T, respectively. Also, $|y| + |+| + |z| = |x| = k + 1$, so $|y| \leq k$ and $|z| \leq k$ (since $|+| = 1$). Since y is derived from E', it is in $\mathcal{L}(G')$ and therefore in $\mathcal{L}(G)$ by the inductive hypothesis. Next, although z has actually been derived from T, that means it can be derived from E' by a derivation $E' \Rightarrow T \overset{*}{\Rightarrow} z$, so it too is in $\mathcal{L}(G')$, hence in $\mathcal{L}(G)$. We have now shown that y and z are each in $\mathcal{L}(G)$, hence derivable from E. It follows that the overall original string x is in $\mathcal{L}(G)$ by the derivation $E \Rightarrow E + E \overset{*}{\Rightarrow} y + z = x$.

Case 2: right below the root. If the root is unary, but its child is ternary, $E' \Rightarrow T \Rightarrow T \times F \overset{*}{\Rightarrow} x$ and $x = y \times z$, where y and z are strings derived from T and F. Thus, as before, they can be derived from E' (by the derivations $E' \Rightarrow T \Rightarrow F \overset{*}{\Rightarrow} z$ and $E' \Rightarrow T \Rightarrow y$). The rest is similar to case 1.

Case 3: at the grandchild of the root. Two unary nodes and then a ternary one yields, $E' \Rightarrow T \Rightarrow F \Rightarrow (E') \overset{*}{\Rightarrow} x$ with $x = (y)$, where $E' \Rightarrow y$ and $|y| = k - 1$. The rest is similar to case 1. There is no "Case 4" since three unary nodes would mean a derivation like the one in the basis.

Part 2. Any member of $\mathcal{L}(G)$ is also a member of $\mathcal{L}(G')$.

Proof. As for Part 1, the proof uses mathematical induction on string lengths.

Basis. Neither grammar generates Λ and both generate a, b, and c.

Inductive step. The inductive hypothesis is that all strings in $\mathcal{L}(G)$ of length $\leq k$ are also in $\mathcal{L}(G')$. Consider $x \in \mathcal{L}(G)$, where $|x| = k + 1 > 1$. The derivation of x in G

1. can begin with $E \rightarrow (\,E\,)$ or

2. can begin with $E \rightarrow E + E$ or

3. (failing to qualify for 1 or 2) *must* begin with $E \rightarrow E \times E$.

Case 1: $E \Rightarrow (\,E\,) \overset{*}{\Rightarrow} x$. This one is easy since it implies that $x = (\,y\,)$ for some y, where y is a string of length k-1 (shorter by 2 than x) derived from E and hence also, by the inductive hypothesis, derivable from E'. It follows that $E' \Rightarrow T \Rightarrow F \Rightarrow (\,E'\,) \overset{*}{\Rightarrow} (\,y\,) = x$.

Case 2: $E \Rightarrow E + E \overset{*}{\Rightarrow} y + z = x$. Since y is derived from E and has length $\leq k$, it must be in $\mathcal{L}(G)$ and, by the inductive hypothesis, in $\mathcal{L}(G')$. This is true of z as well. Unfortunately, this does not establish that x is in $\mathcal{L}(G')$ since, to get a $+$ in a G' derivation, we must use the rule $E' \Rightarrow E' + T$. Although the inductive hypothesis ensures that E' can generate y, we cannot establish that T will generate z. However, T can generate any string w in the language having a tree with a non-sum node as its root since then $E' \Rightarrow T \Rightarrow w$. Therefore, we recursively try to break up y and z, just as x is broken up in the statement of Case 2, ultimately breaking x into as long a sum, of the form $x_1 + x_2 + \cdots + x_n$, of non-sums as possible, where $n \geq 2$, by the conditions of this case.

Each x_i is derived from E and so is in $\mathcal{L}(G)$; it has length $\leq k$, hence also belongs to $\mathcal{L}(G')$; and being a non-sum, it is derivable from T. It follows that there is a derivation of x in G' as follows:

$$E' \Rightarrow E' + T \Rightarrow E' + T + T \overset{*}{\Rightarrow} T + T + \cdots + T \overset{*}{\Rightarrow} x_1 + x_2 + \cdots + x_n = x$$

Case 3: Left as an exercise. $\square$

Exercises

12.1 Use a distinguishability argument to show that L_3 in Section 12.1, the language of balanced parentheses, is not regular. To do this, you need to specify an infinite set of pairwise distinguishable strings in the language, give correct notation for a typical pair, x and y, and specify a string z that extends exactly one of them to a string in the language.

12.2 Using G_3, write derivations for the following strings:

(a) $(\,)\,(\,(\,)\,)$
(b) $(\,(\,(\,)\,(\,)\,)\,)$

12.3 Write a CFG for the language of balanced braces and balanced angle brackets. Your grammar should permit nesting and concatenation, but not arbitrary permutations. For example, "{ < > { } } < { } >" is in this language, but not "{ < } >".

12.4 Let L be the set of strings of equal numbers of left and right parentheses in arbitrary order.

(a) Specify the subset relationships among the languages L, L_2, L_3, and Σ^*, where L_2 and L_3 are as specified in Section 12.1 and $\Sigma = \{), (\}$. Use $\subset$ and/or $\subseteq$ as appropriate. Wherever you specify $\subset$, give an example of a string in the relevant set difference.

(b) Use a distinguishability argument to show that L is not regular.

12.5 Let L_e be the set of strings of equal numbers of *a*s and *b*s in arbitrary order.

(a) Devise a grammar, G_e, for this language, such that $\mathcal{L}(G_e) = L_e$.

(b) *Prove* that for your grammar G_e in part (a), every string of $\mathcal{L}(G_e)$ is in L_e. Hint: Depending on your G_e, you may be able to use mathematical induction on the lengths of derivations to show that there is an equal number of *a* and *b*s *at each step* of every derivation.

(c) Prove that, for your G_e, every string of L_e is in $\mathcal{L}(G_e)$.

12.6 Give examples of languages that satisfy the following conditions:

(a) L_r is regular and infinite, L_n is nonregular, and $L_r \subset L_n$.

(b) L_r is regular, L_n is nonregular, and $L_n \subset L_r$.

(c) L_1 and L_2 are nonregular, but $L_r = L_1 \cap L_2$ is regular.

12.7 Write a regular grammar for the language corresponding to the regular expression $((a + b^*c)d)^*$.

12.8 In light of the discussion in and around Example 9.5, write a regular grammar for C++ comments.

12.9 We can extend the definition of regular grammars by permitting a string of terminals where the definition allows a single terminal. Even with this extended definition, any regular grammar can still be converted to a DFA. Consider the grammar:

$$G = (\{S,T\}, \{a,b,c\}, S, \{S \rightarrow a\,b\,S \mid a\,b\,c\,T, \; T \rightarrow b\,c\,T \mid a\}).$$

(a) What aspect(s) of the grammar make it regular according to this extended definition?

(b) Write a (possibly nondeterministic) state transition diagram that has $\mathcal{L}(G)$ as its language.

(c) Give a normal right-regular grammar for $\mathcal{L}(G)$. Indicate how this might be done in general.

12.10 Write a syntax diagram for the language corresponding to the regular expression:

$$((a + b^*c)d)^*.$$

12.11 Express the grammar G_{10} in BNF taking advantage of the BNF capacity to express iteration within a rule as demonstrated in Example 12.23.

12.12 Draw a syntax diagram that corresponds directly to the BNF rule in Example 12.23 and draw additional syntax diagrams in the same iterative style so that all of them taken together express the language of G_{10}.

12.13 For the grammar G_{11},

(a) Prove by mathematical induction that it is possible to derive from S any string of the form $x \, S \, x^R$, where x is any string over $\{a, b\}$ and x^R is its reverse. You may assume a recursive definition of reverse: (i) $\Lambda^R = \Lambda$, and (ii) $(x \, a)^R = a \, x^R$

(b) Use the result of part (a) to prove that $\mathcal{L}(G_{11})$ is the set of even-length palindromes.

12.14 What rules can be added to the grammar G_{11} for even-length palindromes to yield a grammar for all palindromes (including odd lengths)?

12.15 Complete the final case of the proof of Theorem 12.3.

12.16 The set of balanced parentheses, B, was specified by Definition 12.7. There is another way to characterize B. First, for any string x, let $m(x)$ be the number of left parentheses and $n(x)$ the number of right parentheses. Also, recall that y is a *prefix* of x iff there is a string w (possibly empty) such that $yw = x$. Let

$$B = \{x \mid x \in \{(,)\}^* \wedge m(x) = n(x) \wedge \forall y : y \text{ a prefix of } x \rightarrow m(y) \geq n(y).\}$$

To put it another way, as we process a string from left to right, suppose we keep track of the difference between the number of left and right parentheses. That difference ends up at zero and never goes negative along the way. Show that the two definitions of B are equivalent.

12.17 Give a CFG for the expressions of propositional logic, including all three operators. Recall that, although the formal definition of proposition did not rely on precedence, expressions are rarely fully parenthesized and rely on precedence rules to be interpreted. Negation has the highest precedence and conjunction has the lowest. Make use of the techniques introduced for the grammar of algebraic expressions to create a grammar that deals with all the issues raised there. In particular, your grammar should be unambiguous and should create structures that reflect the way that precedence and parentheses group the propositions during correct evaluation.

12.18 Give a CFG for these languages:

(a) $\{x \mid x = a^i b^{2i}, i > 0\}$.

(b) $\{x \mid x = a^i b^j, i \neq j\}$.

(c) $\{x \mid x = a^i b^j c^k, j = i + k\}$.

(d) $\{x \mid x = a^i b^j c^k, \text{ and } i = j \lor j = k\}$.

12.19 What is the language generated by: $S \to SSS \mid a$?

Chapter 13

Pushdown Automata and Parsing

In earlier chapters, you learned about an important class of languages—the regular languages—and about a class of automata, the finite automata, that can recognize all of those languages and no others. You might therefore wonder whether there is some category of automata that is precisely suited to recognize the broader class of languages introduced in Chapter 12—those that can be generated by context-free grammars (CFGs). There is indeed a type of automaton for this task, the **nondeterministic pushdown automaton** (NPDA). NPDAs, along with their cousins the deterministic PDAs (DPDAs), are the topic of this chapter. We simply write PDA when determinism or its absence is not the focus of discussion.

NPDAs are of interest for computer science mainly because of their relationship to CFGs: For every CFG, G, there is an NPDA that recognizes G's language, $\mathcal{L}(G)$; that is, it accepts all and only the strings of $\mathcal{L}(G)$. In the course of demonstrating a simple way to find such an NPDA, we see where the nondeterminacy comes from. Later we prove that nondeterminism is not only convenient, but necessary. That is, for some CFGs and their languages, there is no DPDA that recognizes them. It follows that the class of NPDAs is larger than the class of DPDAs. This situation is different from what we found with NFAs and DFAs, which are equivalent with respect to the class of languages they accept.

We already know—from several suggestive examples in Chapter 12—that CFGs play a key role in specifying programming languages. If G is a CFG specifying the grammar of some programming language, then $\mathcal{L}(G)$ *is* that programming language from the formal language viewpoint. In other words, each correct computer program in that language is a string in $\mathcal{L}(G)$, typically a very long one. Now that is not the whole story since the strings of a programming language have meanings. However, it also turns out—as you will see in detail if you take a compiler course—that grammars can also provide a structural basis for meanings in programming languages.

When compiling a program expressed as a string s, the compiler must analyze whether and how G could have generated s. This key phase in compiling—of inferring how the string was derived—is called **parsing**. In Sections 13.3 to 13.5, we construct PDAs that mimic some crucial aspects of parsing and thus qualify as *models* of parsing. Despite the absence of some details of true parsers, we see how different PDA construction techniques correspond to different parsing strategies.

13.1   Visualizing PDAs

It is now time to see just what a PDA actually is. PDAs have states, like FAs. However, a PDA is different in that it maintains a memory device called a (pushdown) stack. Symbols can be **PUSH**ed onto the stack and later removed by an action called **POP**ping. **POP**ping the stack removes the most recently added (**PUSH**ed) symbol. Because there is no limit on the **PUSH**ing, the stack provides unlimited—infinite, one might say—memory.

Recall the state transition diagrams (STDs) used to introduce finite automata. Augmenting STDs by adding stack information yields **stack-augmented STD**s, which can express all the information of PDAs in a way that is easy to understand. In a stack-augmented STD, the labeling of each transition is more extensive than in the STDs used earlier. There each transition in an ordinary STD was just labeled by an input symbol. Here, in addition to an input symbol, the label also includes a stack symbol and a stack action. The stack symbol specifies what must be at the top of the stack for the transition to be used. An example of a stack action is to **PUSH** one or more symbols onto the stack; another possibility is to **POP** the top symbol. It is also possible to **POP** and then **PUSH** or simply to leave the stack unchanged.

> **Example 13.1** A stack-augmented STD appears in Figure 13.1. This particular one recognizes the language $\{a^n b^n\}$ as explained next.

What do the labels on the transition arrows mean in a diagram like Figure 13.1? Within each label, the information before the slash ("/") gives conditions under which the transition may be used, whereas the material after slash tells what to do when in fact the transition is used. As with STDs for FAs, we sometimes use multiple labels on a transition to avoid clutter. For example, the self-loop at q_0 here has two (multipart) labels.

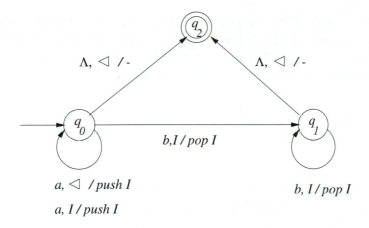

Figure 13.1: A stack-augmented state transition diagram.

To see how such diagrams work, consider the transition from q_0 to itself that has the label "$a, I/$**PUSH** I". The a and I specify that the transition can only be used when the current input is a and the symbol at the top of the stack is I. "**PUSH** I" means just what it says: Using this transition results in **PUSH**ing an I onto the stack. The arrow has the same role as in the STDs in Chapter 9—in this case, requiring that the state be q_0 immediately before and after using this transition.

The other transition from q_0 to itself—the one labeled "$a, \lhd/$**PUSH** I"—is similar except that it requires the symbol at the top of the stack to be $\lhd$. This is a special symbol placed on the stack at the beginning of the process. The $\lhd$ is never removed and is there to indicate the bottom of the stack. A stack containing only $\lhd$ is regarded as an *empty stack* since there is nothing above the "bottom of the stack." Both transitions considered so far respond to an a in input by **PUSH**ing an I onto the stack, the difference being that one—the one with the $\lhd$—is used to get started and the other is used thereafter. The Is serve as markers for counting how many as have been processed so far in the input. In fact, for small numbers, the stack looks like it is counting the as with Roman numerals: $I, II, III, \ldots$, as you can see in the "Stack" column of the table for Example 13.2.

When bs start to appear after some as in an input string, the first b causes a transition to state q_1 and causes one I-marker to be **POP**ped. Additional bs cause processing to continue in q_1, **POP**ping Is until the stack is empty, which occurs when the number of bs equals the number of as that preceded them. This means that the string so far processed is a member of $\{a^n b^n\}$. Since that is the language we claim to be recognizing here, such a string should be accepted. In fact it is, since at this point $\lhd$ is the top symbol on the stack, so the transition to the accepting state, q_2, can be used. This transition is labeled $\Lambda, \triangleleft/—$. Using Λ like this means that the input symbol, if any, is ignored in determining whether the transition can apply and is not processed. The symbol "—" is used here to mean that there is no change in the stack.

Example 13.2 What happens when *aaabbb* is the input string to the STD in Figure 13.1?

The sequence of events is shown in the following table. The first three columns of each row constitute a **configuration**, telling all there is to know about the status of the computation at one particular moment in time. For example, the starting configuration is $(q_0, aaabbb, \triangleleft)$. We can indicate a transition from this configuration to the next one, using the symbol $\vdash$, so that $(q_0, aaabbb, \triangleleft) \vdash (q_0, aabbb, I\triangleleft)$. The last column tells us only part of what is done at each step. The other part is a move to the next state (possibly the same as the current state), which is found at the start of the next row. Underlining shows which symbols in the input and stack are the current ones. These along with the state determine the choice of a transition arrow in the figure and so justify the changes made in going to the next row of the table.

State	Input	Stack	Stack Action
q_0	$\underline{a}aabbb$	$\underline{\triangleleft}$	**PUSH** I
q_0	$\underline{a}abbb$	$\underline{I}\triangleleft$	**PUSH** I
q_0	$\underline{a}bbb$	$\underline{I}I\triangleleft$	**PUSH** I
q_0	$\underline{b}bb$	$\underline{I}II\triangleleft$	**POP**
q_1	$\underline{b}b$	$\underline{I}I\triangleleft$	**POP**
q_1	$\underline{b}$	$\underline{I}\triangleleft$	**POP**
q_1	Λ	$\underline{\triangleleft}$	—
q_2	Λ	$\underline{\triangleleft}$	(Accept)

One might think that the language of balanced parentheses—L_3, presented in Example 12.1—would be a more challenging example than $\{a^n b^n\}$ or $\{(^n\ )^n\}$ since it involves interesting complicated patterns like "((( )) ((( ) ( ))))" that are not part of the language $\{(^n\ )^n\}$. Surprisingly, however, the stack-augmented STD for it—shown in Figure 13.2—is quite simple.

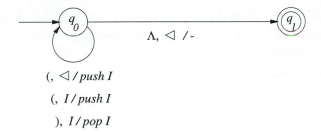

Figure 13.2: A stack-augmented STD for balanced parentheses.

Example 13.3 The stack-augmented STD in Figure 13.2 recognizes the
language of balanced parentheses. (This diagram can be obtained
by merging two states in Figure 13.1 and relabeling.) Describe the
changes that the stack and state undergo as the string "( ) ( )" is
processed.

In state q_0, an I is **PUSH**ed and then **POP**ped. Then I is again
PUSHed and **POP**ped. Finally, state q_1 is entered and the string is
accepted.

Although the language L_3 is generated by the grammar G_3 of Example 12.8, that
grammar bears no obvious or direct relationship to the structure of Figure 13.2.
Given this, and in view of the diagram's surprising simplicity, how can we be so sure
that this stack-augmented STD really does recognize L_3? To demonstrate that it
does so, we first need a precise statement about B, the set of balanced parentheses.
One such statement is provided by Definition 12.7. However, for the purposes of
Example 13.3, we prefer to use the definition of B given in Exercise 12.16, as well
as some notation used there:

$$B = \{x \mid (x \in \{(,)\}^*) \;\wedge\; m(x) = n(x) \;\wedge\; (\forall y : y \text{ is a prefix of } x \to m(y) \geq n(y))\}.$$

One of the exercises is to prove that the STD of Figure 13.2 recognizes B as currently
defined. The key idea is verifying that $m(y) - n(y)$ remains non-negative.

13.2   Standard Notation for PDAs

This section is about converting stack-augmented STDs to the standard notation for
PDAs. This entails two changes. First, observe that there are three kinds of stack
action specifications in Figure 13.1: **PUSH**, **POP**, and the dash ("–"), which specifies

not changing the stack. It simplifies matters to express all of these possibilities within a single notation. To do that, we adopt the convention that the stack is **POP**ped as an automatic first stage in the stack action of each rule. Then to specify any possible stack action, it is only necessary to provide a string (containing zero or more symbols) to **PUSH**.

The second change is to introduce a transition function, δ, somewhat like the one in FAs. Here, δ has three arguments: a state and an input symbol as in FAs, and a stack symbol. This makes it possible for the top symbol of the stack to influence what happens. The output of δ is ordered pairs, where a pair consists of a next state as in FAs and also a string (possibly Λ) of stack symbols to **PUSH**. These symbols enter the stack in reverse order so that, for example, **PUSH**ing abc leaves a at the top of the stack.

The most noticeable change is that we do not use the straightforward **PUSH** and **POP** operations that appear in the foregoing STD examples. Why not use normal **PUSH**es and **POP**s? The reason that we are studying PDAs is specifically to explore their connection with CFGs. It turns out that the PDAs directly associated with CFGs always do a **POP** followed by **PUSH**ing a string. Our PDA definition takes advantage of this fact by *assuming* a **POP** (rather than mentioning it explicitly). This design decision makes the automata built for CFGs look simpler and more natural.

The general definition of NPDAs involves seven items. Five of these are the ones in the quintuples (5-tuples) used in Chapter 9 to represent FAs. Not surprisingly, NPDAs require additional items involving the stack—specifically, a set of stack symbols and the special stack symbol, $\lhd$.

Definition 13.1 Nondeterministic Pushdown Automata

A pushdown automaton is a septuple (7-tuple), $M = (Q, \Sigma, \Gamma, q_0, \lhd, A, \delta)$, where

> Q is a finite set of states;
> Σ is a finite set of input symbols;
> Γ is a finite set of stack symbols;
> $q_0 \in Q$, where q_0 is the start state,
> $\lhd \in \Gamma$, where $\lhd$ is the starting symbol for the stack;
> $A \subseteq Q$, where A is the set of accepting states, and
> δ is a transition function,

$$\delta : Q \times (\Sigma \cup \{\Lambda\}) \times \Gamma \to 2^{Q \times \Gamma^*}.$$

Note that the codomain of this δ function shares an important characteristic with the δ used for NFAs: The value of δ is a set of transitions. The key difference is that here any transition is an ordered pair, specifying the new state and the string to be written to the stack.

Example 13.4 Express the transitions in Figure 13.1 in terms of the PDA transition function, δ.

- The transition from q_0 to q_1 in Figure 13.1 requires input b and stack symbol I, so it concerns $\delta(q_0, b, I)$. This transition is called a **POP** in the figure, so (q_1, Λ) is the result since the stack symbol I is automatically **POP**ped first and then nothing (Λ) is put back. To allow for nondeterminism in general, we could describe this transition by saying that $(q_1, \Lambda) \in \delta(q_0, b, I)$. However, in this case, there is only one transition so we can put it into a one-element set and make the stronger statement that $\delta(q_0, b, I) = \{(q_1, \Lambda)\}$.

- The transitions from q_0 to q_0 in Figure 13.1 are called **PUSH**es there. The one requiring a as input corresponds to $(q_0, II) \in \delta(q_0, a, I)$. Note the string II. **PUSH**ing one of these two Is has the effect of undoing the automatic **POP**; then **PUSH**ing the other accomplishes a net gain of one I on the stack.

- The transition from q_1 to q_2 has no effect on the stack, as indicated in the figure by the dash. This transition corresponds to $(q_2, \lhd) \in \delta(q_1, \Lambda, \lhd)$. The $\lhd$ that appears here as δ's third argument calls for a $\lhd$ at the top of the stack. That $\lhd$ is automatically **POP**ped, but then a $\lhd$ replaces it, yielding no net change. Also note that when Λ is the input symbol, no input is used up. Thus, the only real effect of this rule is the state change to the accepting state, q_2. The idea of this transition is to provide for acceptance when the stack is empty.

PDAs have four distinct kinds of stack actions. Each is listed next in terms of the transition function, δ, and is then described. The form of δ is the same in all cases except for the output string, which plays the key distinguishing role.

POP $(r, \Lambda) \in \delta(q, a, g)$ **PUSH**ing nothing (the string Λ) leaves the automatic **POP** as the only change.

no change $(r, g) \in \delta(q, a, g)$ **PUSH**ing the symbol that was on top of the stack, g, undoes the automatic **POP**, leaving the stack unchanged.

PUSH $(r, xg) \in \delta(q, a, g),$ **PUSH**ing a string that ends in g means that
with $x \neq \Lambda.$ g goes onto the stack first, undoing the effect of the automatic **POP**, so that the result is purely a **PUSH** of the string x.

POP; **PUSH** $(r, x) \in \delta(q, a, g),$ This is a **POP** of g followed by a **PUSH** of x.
with $x \neq \Lambda$ and
x not ending in g.

Example 13.5 The diagram in Figure 13.1 can be written as the 7-tuple

$$(\{q_0, q_1, q_2\}, \{a, b\}, \{I, \triangleleft\}, q_0, \triangleleft, \{q_2\}, \delta),$$

where δ still needs to be specified. In the following table, we present three of the transitions needed for δ and thereby demonstrate the ideas of Example 13.4, by showing a transition for each of three kinds of stack change: a **POP**, a **PUSH**, and a "no-change." Also in Figure 13.1 are three more transitions, one of each kind. These are handled similarly. One of the exercises is to provide the rest of this table specifying δ.

from state Q	input symbol $(\Sigma \cup \{\Lambda\})$	stack symbol Γ	$\rightarrow$	to state Q	push symbol(s) Γ^*
q_0	a	I		q_0	II
q_0	b	I		q_1	Λ
q_1	Λ	$\triangleleft$		q_2	$\triangleleft$

The language recognized by an NPDA is the set of strings that (nondeterministically) lead to an accepting state. The notion of nondeterminism used here is identical to the one discussed at length for NFAs. In particular, a string is accepted iff there *exists* a sequence of choices of transitions that lead to an accepting state.

13.3   NPDAs for CFG Parsing Strategies

We now explore an important computing application of the pushdown stack: algorithms that perform CFG parsing, which is a key stage of any compiler. The **parsing problem** is to take an input string and a grammar and produce the derivation tree(s) for that string. If the string is not in the language generated by the grammar, then the parsing process is expected to fail. For compilers, we strongly prefer unambiguous grammars, so that for any input there is only one tree.

The pushdown stack is handy for CFG parsing, and this convenience hints at an even stronger relationship between CFGs and NPDAs. Just as NFAs and regular grammars specify the same class of languages, so too do CFGs and NPDAs as stated in the following theorem.

> **Theorem 13.1** A language is recognized by an NPDA if and only if the language is generated by a CFG.

Rather than prove this theorem, we present and analyze a construction technique that converts a CFG to an NPDA for accepting the language of the CFG. The description of the method makes it clear that the construction works for any CFG. We omit discussion of going in the opposite direction, from NPDAs to CFGs, since it is more difficult and less useful.

Parsing methods can be named for where in the tree they begin and in what direction the process moves. We look first at **top–down** parsing, since it proceeds in a familiar way, similar to the creation of a derivation tree. An alternative starting point characterizes **bottom–up** parsing, the topic of Section 13.5. Whatever the strategy, the goal is a **parse tree**, which is the same as a derivation tree but gets a new name in this context.

Starting at the top of the tree means establishing its root, which by convention appears at the top of the diagram. The root is labeled by the start symbol of the grammar. From the root, one expands the tree downward using rules of the grammar. Besides moving downward from the top, it is also convenient to go **left to right**, always expanding the leftmost nonterminal symbol—call it α—that is already in the (partial) tree, but has not yet been expanded. Doing this can involve any rule $\alpha \rightarrow \omega$ for that nonterminal. The α node is connected downward to new nodes labeled by the symbols in the string ω. But suppose there are two or more right-hand sides available for the same α. How do we choose which one to use? Keep this question in mind as you read Example 13.6.

> **Example 13.6** Let G be the CFG $(\{S\}, \{a, b\}, S, \{S \rightarrow a\,S\,b, S \rightarrow \Lambda\})$, which generates the language $\{a^n b^n\}$. How can top–down parsing succeed on the input string $aabb$?

Beginning at the top, we initially have the *partial* parse tree consisting of just S. To expand this node, we must use a rule with S on the left side. For this, the current grammar provides a choice between $S \to a\, S\, b$ and $S \to \Lambda$. For choosing between right-hand sides (here $a\, S\, b$ and Λ), we use the longer rule, $S \to a\, S\, b$, until the tree is big enough and then use $S \to \Lambda$ once. Here are the successive results:

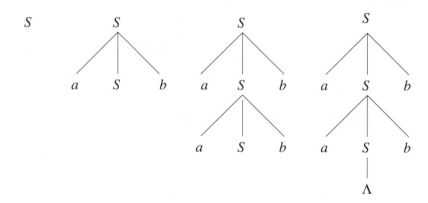

In Example 13.6, the strategy used for selecting a right-hand side each time an S had to be expanded was successful, but that strategy was left vague. Note that we chose to expand S in two different ways, at different times. How to make such choices is the core issue in parsing. For now we explore making the choice nondeterministically, presenting only the choice that makes the result come out nicely, thereby showing that the nice outcome is *possible*. In the next section, we explore how the choices might be made deterministically.

The next example specifies an NPDA that accepts the language $\mathcal{L}(G) = \{a^n b^n\}$ from Example 13.6. Moreover, it does so in a way that reflects the grammar G used there. Ideally this machine would not only accept each string of $\mathcal{L}(G)$, but would also produce its derivation tree. Typically acceptance of strings is a "yes/no" computation, but we at least want the *steps* the machine takes—in arriving at its yes/no answer—to provide a clear indication of the derivation tree so that it *could* be recorded and produced as output by a straightforward extension of the NPDA. We see in Example 13.8 that the NPDA's steps do indeed precisely mirror the derivation, thereby implying the correct tree.

Example 13.7 This is an example of a nondeterministic PDA for top–down parsing. As in Example 13.6, let G be the CFG ($\{S\}, \{a, b\}, S$, $\{S \to a\, S\, b,\ S \to \Lambda\}$), which generates the language $\{a^n b^n\}$. The

#	type	from	input	stack	changes
1	Start	q_0	Λ	$\lhd$	$\{(q_1, S\lhd)\}$
2	Expand	q_1	Λ	S	$\{(q_1, aSb), (q_1, \Lambda)\}$
3	Match	q_1	a	a	$\{(q_1, \Lambda)\}$
4	Match	q_1	b	b	$\{(q_1, \Lambda)\}$
5	Stop	q_1	Λ	$\lhd$	$\{(q_2, \lhd)\}$

Figure 13.3: Transitions for Example 13.7.

NPDA M accepts all the strings of $\mathcal{L}(G)$ and no others, where

$$M = (\{q_0, q_1, q_2\}, \{a, b\}, \{a, b, S, \lhd\}, q_0, \lhd, \{q_2\}, \delta),$$

and δ is specified by the table in Figure 13.3. Specifically, the columns labeled *from*, *input*, and *stack* tell what the state, input symbol, and stack-top symbol must be for the rule to apply. The *changes* column gives the possible choices for the resulting change, each consisting of a new state and a stack action. By convention, when a rule is applied, it uses up a symbol of input equal to the one specified in its *input* column. If that symbol is Λ, no input is used up. Notice that the grammatical symbols a, b, and S are also used as stack symbols.

In the δ-table of Example 13.7, the first two columns are not part of the formal specification. The first simply numbers the rules for easy reference. The words in the second column suggest the roles of the various rules as follows:

- **Start:** At the start of processing, **PUSH** S.

- **Expand:** If the symbol currently at the top of the stack is a nonterminal, nondeterministically replace that symbol by each of its possible right-hand sides. Each of these replacement actions may be regarded as a prediction that each symbol put into the stack will ultimately be justified, in the proper order, by some subsequence of input.

- **Match:** If the same terminal symbol appears as both the current symbol of input and the top of the stack, it means that the prediction embodied in the stack symbol—that it would be justified by input—has indeed come true. In recognition of this, **POP** it from the stack and advance past this input symbol to the next position in the input string. Now that the stack and input symbols have been matched, they have no further role.

- **Stop:** If the input is done and the stack is empty, stop.

The nondeterminacy of Example 13.7 can be seen in Rule 2 of its δ table, which has a set of two changes (each consisting of a state-string pair) in the *changes* column. These two possible changes for the NPDA correspond to the two rules in the CFG that have the symbol S on the left side. The automaton makes a nondeterministic choice of one transition or the other. Also notice the similarity of Rules 3 and 4 in that table. Together they say that, for any input symbol, if it matches the stack then advance the input and **POP** the stack. Each handles the fulfillment of a prediction as described under *match*. The table in Example 13.8 shows how this NPDA accepts *aabb*, step by step, with the nondeterministic choice of a rule being the correct one at each step. Other possible steps would lead to failure, so what the table shows is the *existence* of an accepting scenario, which is all we require.

> **Example 13.8** Here is the sequence of steps by which the NPDA of Example 13.7, based on grammar G of Example 13.6, recognizes the language $\mathcal{L}(G)$ in a way that corresponds to the derivation and its trees in Example 13.6. In particular, Rule 2—for the nondeterministic expansion of S—is used with the right side aSb twice and then with Λ. These are *possible* choices.

State	Input	Stack	Rule #
q_0	$\underline{a}abb$	$\triangleleft$	1
q_1	$\underline{a}abb$	$\underline{S}\triangleleft$	2 (with $a\,S\,b$)
q_1	$\underline{a}abb$	$\underline{a}Sb\triangleleft$	3
q_1	$\underline{a}bb$	$\underline{S}b\triangleleft$	2 (with $a\,S\,b$)
q_1	$\underline{a}bb$	$\underline{a}Sbb\triangleleft$	3
q_1	$\underline{b}b$	$\underline{S}bb\triangleleft$	2 (with Λ)
q_1	$\underline{b}b$	$\underline{b}b\triangleleft$	4
q_1	$\underline{b}$	$\underline{b}\triangleleft$	4
q_1	Λ	$\underline{\triangleleft}$	5
q_2	Λ	$\underline{\triangleleft}$	(Accept)

The sequence of steps detailed in the table of Example 13.8 not only shows that the input *aabb* is accepted, but *why*. It does this by *simulating* the derivation of the string *aabb* in such a direct way that we can state exactly what rules were used in the derivation. The next table emphasizes this point by presenting the same sequence of events, with the same stack sequence, but with an "Input Seen" column, showing the input already processed, rather than what *remains* to be processed as in the foregoing table.

In each row of this new table, let us place in the final column the concatenation of the entries in the first two columns (with the $\triangleleft$ omitted) so that the third column is an overall record of what has occurred so far. Examining the strings in this third column, we can see that each one is a step (sometimes repeated) in the *derivation* of the terminal string. The *expand* parsing steps correspond to replacement steps in the derivation, and the *match* parsing steps correspond to the computation catching up with and confirming the previous expansion.

$$S \Rightarrow aSb \Rightarrow aaSbb \Rightarrow aabb$$

Input Seen	Stack	Derivation
Λ	$\triangleleft$	—
Λ	$S\triangleleft$	S
Λ	$aSb\triangleleft$	aSb
a	$Sb\triangleleft$	aSb
a	$aSbb\triangleleft$	$aaSbb$
aa	$Sbb\triangleleft$	$aaSbb$
aa	$bb\triangleleft$	$aabb$
aab	$b\triangleleft$	$aabb$
$aabb$	$\triangleleft$	$aabb$

13.4   Deterministic Pushdown Automata and Parsing

With FAs, we began by discussing deterministic machines because they were simple and realistic. Moreover, it turned out that NFAs were no more powerful than DFAs in terms of the class of languages recognized. In contrast, for PDAs, we began with the *non*deterministic ones principally because they *are* more powerful, and we need that power to recognize all context-free languages. We show that there are context-free languages that cannot be recognized by any deterministic PDA. The proof is deferred until the next chapter, because it depends on results from that chapter. Despite that limitation, however, determinism is still highly desirable for those grammars that *can* be parsed by DPDAs since it corresponds to simpler, more efficient algorithms. Before delving into deterministic parsing—first things first—let us define these things.

Definition 13.2 Deterministic Pushdown Automata (DPDA)
    A DPDA is a septuple (7-tuple), $M = (Q, \Sigma, \Gamma, q_0, \triangleleft, A, \delta)$, where the parts are the same as in Definition 13.1 except that the δ function does not provide any choices. In particular,

$$\delta : Q \times (\Sigma \cup \{\Lambda\}) \times \Gamma \to Q \times \Gamma^*,$$

so that the codomain of δ is ordered pairs, not sets of ordered pairs. This implies that if a Λ-transition is defined for some $q \in Q$ and $g \in \Gamma$—for example, $\delta(q, \Lambda, g) = (p, x)$—then there can be no other transitions defined for that q and g. This restriction keeps the DPDA from having a choice of whether to use the Λ-transition.

The challenge now is to parse deterministically. The approach for parsing with NPDAs was to simulate a derivation for the grammar. When there was a choice between competing right-hand sides, the NPDA sidestepped the issue by nondeterministically trying all (both) possibilities. DPDAs confront such choices deterministically and they have to get the right answer every time.

To get the choices deterministically correct—yet retain a top–down orientation—we design DPDAs to use input symbols as a guide. The resulting **lookahead** methods pay attention to the next symbol in the current input—or in some methods the next two or more symbols—and let it influence the choice of which right-hand side to use when more than one is available. Implementing this strategy makes the lookahead decision table more complex. On the benefit side it is simpler to write a simulation algorithm for DPDAs than one for NPDAs, and it is also more efficient. The next example is a DPDA that illustrates top–down, lookahead parsing for a particular grammar.

Example 13.9 This is an example of top–down parsing with lookahead by a deterministic PDA. As in Examples 13.6 and 13.7, let G be $(\{S\}, \{a, b\}, S, \{S \to a\,S\,b, S \to \Lambda\})$. The NPDA M accepts all the strings of $\mathcal{L}(G)$ and no others, where

$$M = (\{q_0, q_1, q_2\}, \{a, b\}, \{a, b, S, \vartriangleleft\}, q_0, \vartriangleleft, \{q_2\}, \delta),$$

and δ is specified by the following table.

#	type	from	input	stack	change
1	Start	q_0	Λ	$\vartriangleleft$	$\{(q_1, S\vartriangleleft)\}$
2	Careful-Expand	q_1	a	S	$\{(q_a, aSb)\}$
3	Careful-Expand	q_1	b	S	$\{(q_b, \Lambda)\}$
4	Back-Match	q_a	Λ	a	$\{(q_1, \Lambda)\}$
5	Back-Match	q_b	Λ	b	$\{(q_1, \Lambda)\}$
6	Match	q_1	a	a	$\{(q_1, \Lambda)\}$
7	Match	q_1	b	b	$\{(q_1, \Lambda)\}$
8	Stop	q_1	Λ	$\vartriangleleft$	$\{(q_2, \vartriangleleft)\}$

Notice the two new types of rules, *careful-expand* and *back-match*, in the δ table of Example 13.9. The careful-expand Rules 2 and 3 divide up the nondeterministic Rule 2 in Example 13.7 into two deterministic parts, basing the choice on whether the input is a or b. Applying this DPDA to the string $aabb$ yields the sequence of events in Example 13.10. These results correspond directly to the NPDA results displayed earlier, but here they are the *only* possibility, not just one among many nondeterministic possibilities, most of them wrong.

The careful-expand rules are the heart of the lookahead strategy, but unfortunately they *use up* the input they look at—by definition of how PDAs operate—just as if we had processed it, whereas all we really wanted to do was take a peek (look ahead) at that symbol. To make it possible to deal with this unwanted consequence, M must somehow remember the looked-at input. It does this by going into a special state, either q_a to remember a or q_b to remember b. These states can then match up against the stack according to the back-match rules, 4 and 5, which use up *no* input, thus compensating for the input used up in lookahead by Rules 2 and 3. The *start*, *match*, and *stop* states here are the same as in Example 13.7.

Example 13.10 Here are the deterministic steps in the acceptance of $aabb$.

State	Input	Stack	Rule #
q_0	$\underline{a}abb$	$\triangleleft$	1
q_1	$\underline{a}abb$	$\underline{S}\triangleleft$	2
q_a	$\underline{a}bb$	$a\underline{S}b\triangleleft$	4
q_1	$\underline{a}bb$	$\underline{S}b\triangleleft$	2
q_a	$\underline{b}b$	$a\underline{S}bb\triangleleft$	4
q_1	$\underline{b}b$	$\underline{S}bb\triangleleft$	3
q_b	$\underline{b}$	$\underline{b}b\triangleleft$	5
q_1	$\underline{b}$	$\underline{b}\triangleleft$	7
q_1	Λ	$\triangleleft$	8
q_2	Λ	$\underline{\triangleleft}$	(Accept)

Not all CFGs can be handled so easily by lookahead. To see why, we need to understand the idea of a **recursive** rule—that is, one whose left-side symbol also appears on the right side. Recursive rules come in different varieties. Our immediate concern is with **left-recursive** rules, those in which the left-side symbol appears *first* on the right (e.g., $S \to S\,a$). The next example shows how left-recursion frustrates lookahead.

Example 13.11 The grammar $(\{S\}, \{a, b\}, S, \{S \to S\, a, S \to b\})$ generates the language of the regular expression ba^*. Since every string
begins with b, looking (ahead) at the first symbol never helps decide
between the two right-hand sides for S.

The foregoing example of left recursion is *direct* since it occurs within a single
rule. It is somewhat more difficult to detect the kind of recursive situation exem-
plified by the pair of rules $X \to Y\, a \mid b$ and $Y \to X\, c \mid d$. Here X can left-descend
to Y and then Y can left-descend to X. Thus, X can left-descend to itself through
Y. This means that X is indirectly left-recursive (and so is Y), but that is not clear
from looking at any individual rule. This *indirect left-recursion* is just as damaging
to top–down parsing with lookahead as the direct kind. To seek out all indirect
left-recursion, possibly involving several rules, involves following all possible paths
from left-side symbol in a rule to first-on-the-right symbol in the same rule. This
can be accomplished by the algorithm for finding cycles in graphs.

Fortunately, it is possible to get rid of all forms of left-recursion. The next example does this for one case of direct recursion, but the technique can be generalized
to handle any left recursion, direct or indirect, including multiple cases of it in the
same grammar. To generalize this next example somewhat, notice that a and b
could each have been replaced by any string of terminal and nonterminal symbols
and the same approach to left-recursion removal would still apply.

Example 13.12 Convert a grammar with left-recursive rules to another
grammar that has no such rules but that nevertheless generates the
same language. In particular, do this for the grammar in Example 13.11 with the language $\{ba^n\}$.

Watching a derivation in this grammar unfold, we see the derivation
string grow from right to left as the left-recursive rule applies repeatedly. This growth is duplicated, but in a left-to-right fashion, by
creating a new grammar for the same language using right-recursive
rules but no left-recursive ones. In particular, the new grammar is

$$(\{S\}, \{a, b\}, S, \{S \to b\, T, \quad T \to a\, T, \quad T \to \Lambda\})$$

and you can confirm that its language is $\{ba^n\}$ as required. The rule
$T \to a\, T$ is **right-recursive** since its left-side symbol appears last on
its right side.

Right-recursive rules cause problems of their own for top–down lookahead parsing. Note that we cannot look ahead to decide whether we should choose to use
the $T \to \Lambda$ rule because we need that rule exactly when there are no more symbols

in the input—that is, when lookahead would go off the end of the string, thereby violating its boundary. In short, the difficulty is that a DPDA (unlike an NPDA) that is parsing a right-recursive grammar, needs to know when the end of the input is reached. Our formal machine model does not permit the machine to know this even though it is normal in practice to know when there is no more input.

Detecting the end of input should not be a big deal. Since ordinary programs have things like end-of-file markers, it seems fair enough to allow ourselves the same kind of technique with automata. In particular, we can augment each string in the language L by appending a new symbol that is not in the original alphabet of L. Any symbol will do; we choose $\lhd$.

$$L^\lhd = \{x \mid x = y\lhd \ \wedge \ y \in L\}$$

The new symbol is called a *sentinel* since it should be the final symbol of any valid input, and so it will alert the machine that the input is finished. At least, it will do so if we design the machine appropriately. For the preceding example, the grammar for $L^\lhd$ is

$$(\{S\}, \{a, b\}, S, \{S \to bT\lhd, \ T \to aT, \ T \to \Lambda\})$$

13.5 Bottom–Up Parsing

To motivate the technical material of bottom–up parsing and put it in context, we compare three parsing methods and mention some properties of the particular automaton to be used in this section before proceeding to design and specify it.

13.5.1 Comparison and Properties

Both parsing methods introduced so far begin processing at the top of the tree and try to extend downward from there. In contrast to those top–down strategies, we turn now to a method that begins at the bottom, where the input is, and tries to build upward. On the face of it, this **bottom–up** strategy may seem a lot more sensible since, after all, if you are going to try to parse the input, why not start by *looking at it*. Of course, one could defend the top–down approach by saying if you are going to parse with some particular grammar, you had better pay attention to what *that grammar* can generate, starting with its start symbol.

Lying between the purely top–down method of Section 13.3 and the purely bottom–up method to be introduced in this section is the top–down-with-lookahead approach of Section 13.4. That method works at the top, paying attention to the grammar, but takes the current input into account when making choices among right-hand sides that are possible downward expansions for the current nonterminal. Although for bottom–up parsing we look only at its pure form, it too has a lookahead version. As in the top–down case, the NPDAs have simpler specifications than the DPDAs, whereas from a practical standpoint the implementation is more straightforward and efficient in the deterministic case.

Our presentation here is only for NPDAs. Although we do not present a DPDA example for bottom–up parsing, by now you can perhaps guess that a lookahead strategy would be useful in moving to a deterministic automaton just as in the top–down world. If you did guess that, you would be right. Bottom–up parsing with lookahead is an important topic in the study of compilers.

Bottom–up parsing (assuming it is also left to right) starts at the lower left corner of the parse tree, working on the first symbol of input. From there it builds the tree upward and rightward as it gradually moves rightward through the input. This approach is sometimes called *shift-reduce parsing* after the two kinds of rules it employs.

Shifting brings the next input symbol into active consideration. A nondeterministic PDA does this by pushing it onto the stack. Since reading a symbol removes it from the input, this is a *shift* from the input to the stack. To **reduce** means to find, among the actively considered symbols, all the symbols of the right-hand side of a rule and to upward-connect them in the parse tree to a new parent node labeled by the symbol on the left side of that rule. Thus, *reducing* here is the opposite of *expanding* in a derivation, and these two words consistently reflect the fact that the left side of a rule has just one symbol, whereas the right side typically has one, two or more.

We find that a lot of the nondeterminism in a shift-reduce NPDA comes from the fact that there are two kinds of rules. There is always a possible shift move (except after the input is used up), so there is nondeterminism whenever a reduce move is also applicable.

13.5.2   Design and Construction of the NPDA

It is now time to design the automaton. Like the earlier PDAs, this one does not actually record the tree structure, but it does proceed in a manner that reveals that structure, moving through it in this case from the bottom-left corner. Our nondeterministic PDA implements the reduce operation by popping the right-hand symbols from the stack and replacing them by the symbol on left-hand side of the same rule. This description blithely ignores the fact that only the top symbol on a stack can be looked at, by the definition of a PDA.

There are two ways around this limitation on the PDA's vision. One is to pop the right-hand symbols one by one and use special states to keep track of what popping has been done so far when part-way through the pops needed for a single right-hand side. Recall that special states q_a and q_b proved handy in Section 13.4 for undoing the unwanted consumption of input by lookahead. However, the special-states trick makes for a long specification that obfuscates the simplicity of the method. Instead, we define an extended version of NPDAs with a pop capability that can pop not just the single top symbol on the stack, but a contiguous substring that includes the top symbol. We will call it a string-popping NPDA (**SP-NPDA**). We claim that for any such machine there is an ordinary NPDA that could be constructed by precisely the special-state trick just mentioned.

The SP-NPDA—which is not a standard approach—can be defined as the same 7-tuple as an ordinary NPDA, except for the δ-mapping, which here is as follows:

$$\delta : Q \times (\Sigma \cup \{\Lambda\}) \times \Gamma^* \to Q \times \Gamma^*$$

Example 13.13 Write an SP-NPDA that performs bottom–up parsing on strings of $\mathcal{L}(G)$, where $G = (\{X\}, \{a, b, f, g, (,), ,\}, X, P)$ and P contains the rules

$$X \to f\ (\ X\ )\ |\ g\ (\ X\ ,\ X\ )\ |\ a\ |\ b.$$

Note the use of the comma ("**,**") here as one of the terminal symbols of G. It is printed in boldface to make it look slightly different from the ordinary commas that are being used in their usual role of separating the items of a set. For this grammar, $\mathcal{L}(G)$ includes strings like b, $f(a)$, $g(b,a)$, and $g(f(b),f(b))$.

The SP-NPDA uses the terminal symbols of G as its input symbols. It augments them with the nonterminal set $\{X\}$ and the stack-bottom symbol $\lhd$ to form the set of stack symbols. The only states are the start state, q_0, and an accepting state, q_1. Here is the transition function δ:

#	type	from	input	stack	change	
1-7	Shift	q_0	σ	Λ	$\{(q_0, \sigma)\}$	for each $\sigma \in \Sigma$
8	Reduce	q_0	Λ	a	$\{(q_0, X)\}$	
9	Reduce	q_0	Λ	b	$\{(q_0, X)\}$	
10	Reduce	q_0	Λ	$f(X)$	$\{(q_0, X)\}$	
11	Reduce	q_0	Λ	$g(X,X)$	$\{(q_0, X)\}$	
12	Stop	q_0	Λ	$\lhd X$	$\{(q_1, \lhd)\}$	

Next comes an actual parse using this SP-NPDA. For this example, we reorient the presentation of the stack on the page so that the stack top is at the *right* end. Since we continue to use the same stack-bottom symbol, "$\triangleleft$", the left-pointing triangle, the tip of the triangle now points *away* from rest of the stack throughout the next example; this appearance can already be inferred by looking at Rule 12, the *stop* rule in the preceding example. What we achieve by doing this and by placing the *Stack* column just to the left of the *Input* column in Example 13.14 is that the concatenation of these two columns (row by row) is the derivation of the input string in reverse order and with some repetition. The underlining in the stack shows what string (if any) is about to be popped by this string-popping automaton.

Example 13.14 Here are the steps in the acceptance of $f(f(a))$.

State	Stack	Input	Rule #	Stack+Input
q_0	$\triangleleft$	$f(f(a))$	3	$\triangleleft f(f(a))$
q_0	$\triangleleft f$	$(f(a))$	5	$\triangleleft f(f(a))$
q_0	$\triangleleft f($	$f(a))$	3	$\triangleleft f(f(a))$
q_0	$\triangleleft f(f$	$(a))$	5	$\triangleleft f(f(a))$
q_0	$\triangleleft f(f($	$a))$	1	$\triangleleft f(f(a))$
q_0	$\triangleleft f(f(\underline{a}$	$))$	8	$\triangleleft f(f(a))$
q_0	$\triangleleft f(f(X$	$))$	6	$\triangleleft f(f(X))$
q_0	$\triangleleft f(\underline{f(X)}$	$)$	10	$\triangleleft f(f(X))$
q_0	$\triangleleft f(X$	$)$	6	$\triangleleft f(X)$
q_0	$\triangleleft \underline{f(X)}$	Λ	10	$\triangleleft f(X)$
q_0	$\triangleleft \underline{X}$	Λ	12	$\triangleleft X$
q_1	$\triangleleft$	Λ	(Accept)	$\triangleleft$

13.6   Pushdown Automata in Prolog

Implementing PDAs in Prolog brings together key techniques from both halves of this book. PDAs embody major concepts in programming language analysis, which our Prolog program expresses essentially as logic while also bringing the computation into the real world. Our strategy for PDAs in Prolog builds on the Prolog program for FAs in Section 9.4 just as PDA concepts extend those of FAs. Once again we take advantage of Prolog's declarative nature and its rule–fact distinction to separate the general ideas of an automaton class, expressed as rules, from what is true of particular automata, expressed as facts.

To emphasize practicality, we choose for our Prolog implementation a PDA that is formed systematically from a given grammar to embody a useful parsing technique. This PDA comes from Example 13.9 in Section 13.4; it accepts all and only the strings of the language $\{a^n b^n\}$.

As with FAs, we express the facts of a particular PDA transition function δ with the appropriately named predicate `delta`. As the PDA definition specifies in general—and as diagrams and tables for particular PDAs also show in various ways—each transition has five parts: a source state, an input symbol, a stack symbol, a destination state, and a string of symbols (possibly empty) to push onto the stack. This string becomes a list in the Prolog implementation. In Line 2 of Example 13.9, the five items are, respectively, q_1, a, S, q_a, and aSb. Correspondingly, we get the Prolog fact

$$\text{delta}(q_1, \text{ a, S, } q_a, \text{ [a,S,b]}).$$

All the Prolog facts that arise in this way from the transitions appear in Figure 13.4(a). The other transitions are handled similarly, but the presence of Λs as an input in some of them requires an adjustment, since Λ is not really an input at all. Instead it indicates that the current input is temporarily ignored; we return to this point. Yet when Λ is used to specify a list of symbols to push onto the stack, matters are straightforward because Λ specifies something that *is* a list: the empty list.

We use the predicate `acc` to specify that a state is accepting. In particular, we take note of the fact that q_2 is an accepting state for the current automaton by writing the fact `acc`(q_2) in Figure 13.4(b).

As with FAs, the operation of PDAs is specified just once for an entire automaton class, and again we name the predicate "`accept`." PDAs, however, are a bit more complicated than FAs. The predicate `accept` now needs three arguments instead of two. The first two are the state and the remaining input as for FAs. The third is the stack represented as a list. For example, consider the query

$$\text{accept}(q_0, \text{[a,a,a,b,b,b]}, \text{ [}\triangleleft\text{]}).$$

The purpose of this query is to ask what happens when processing begins at the start state, q_0, with input *aaabbb*, and with the stack holding its initial contents, $[\triangleleft]$. For the PDA that we are going to try to implement, the Prolog program should answer "**yes**" since the language to be recognized is $a^n b^n$.

Let us now build the rule for `accept` so that this works out. We need clauses for transitioning from state to state and for recognizing success in an accepting state. Acceptance is the easier of the two: We write `accept(Q,[ ],_) :- acc(Q).` as

(a) Transition facts:

$$\begin{aligned}
&\texttt{delta}(q_0,\ \Lambda,\ \triangleleft,\ q_1,\ \texttt{[S,}\triangleleft\texttt{]}\ ).\\
&\texttt{delta}(q_1,\ \texttt{a, S, } q_a,\ \texttt{[a,S,b]}\ ).\\
&\texttt{delta}(q_1,\ \texttt{b, S, } q_b,\ \texttt{[ ]}\ ).\\
&\texttt{delta}(q_a,\ \Lambda,\ \texttt{a, } q_1,\ \texttt{[ ]}\ ).\\
&\texttt{delta}(q_b,\ \Lambda,\ \texttt{b, } q_1,\ \texttt{[ ]}\ ).\\
&\texttt{delta}(q_1,\ \texttt{a, a, } q_1,\ \texttt{[ ]}\ ).\\
&\texttt{delta}(q_1,\ \texttt{b, b, } q_1,\ \texttt{[ ]}\ ).\\
&\texttt{delta}(q_1,\ \Lambda,\ \triangleleft,\ q_2,\ \texttt{[}\triangleleft\texttt{]}\ ).
\end{aligned}$$

(b) Accepting state fact:

$$\texttt{acc}(q_2).$$

(c) Acceptance rule:

```
accept(Q,[ ],_) :- acc(Q).
```

(d) Transition rule, using input:

```
accept(Q,[S|T1],[Z|T2])   :- delta(Q,S,Z,R,P),
                             accept(R,T1,Y),
                             append(P,T2,Y).
```

(e) Transition rule, no input (Λ):

```
accept(Q,T1,[Z|T2])       :- delta(Q,Λ,Z,R,P),
                             accept(R,T1,Y),
                             append(P,T2,Y).
```

Figure 13.4: A Prolog program for a PDA.

shown in Figure 13.4(c). This says that acceptance occurs when (i) the input has been used up, indicated by the empty list, [ ], on the left side to permit matching; and (ii) the PDA is in an accepting state, checked by using the predicate `acc` on the right side in "`acc(Q).`"

We turn now to the clause of `accept` whose purpose is to deal with transition rules (with ordinary input, not Λ). In Figure 13.4(d), look at the first conjunct on the right-hand side, `delta(Q,S,Z,R,P)`. All the arguments of `delta` here are variables, so this transition rule can be used for any PDA. In general, such a PDA rule is supposed to permit going from state Q to state R (the first and fourth arguments) with input S and with the stack getting its top symbol Z replaced by the list P. To see that this is exactly what the clause does, compare the arguments of the two uses of `accept` in this clause. As we go from one to the other, state Q in the first argument position is replaced by state R. In the second position, symbol S is popped. Finally, in the third position, Z is popped and replaced by the list P as can be ascertained by noting that the use of `append` requires Y to be the concatenation of P and the stack-tail, T2. (The predicate `append` is built into some versions of Prolog and provided in Section 7.7.)

Finally, as noted before, the use of Λ as input in a PDA rule requires some adjustment in Prolog. Comparing the transition rules with and without input in Figures 13.4(d) and 13.4(e), we see that in the latter there is a Λ in place of S as an argument of `delta`, which is not surprising. Less straightforward is that there is no symbol S that is popped. That is, the input list is the same in the second argument position of the two occurrences of the `accept` predicate.

13.7 Notes on Memory

The stack provides memory, but it is not the only kind of memory we have seen. Recall that an FA has memory too: It "remembers" which of its states it is in. Although many FA examples only use a few states, real devices—even relatively simple ones—have huge numbers of states. A 16-bit register, for example, has $2^{16} = 65,536$ states, whereas for a single 32-bit register, there are over 4 billion states. Strictly speaking, a large modern computer with large but fixed memory could be regarded as an FA with an astronomical number of states. Given that it is easy to have an incredibly large number of states in a real FA, what is the point of introducing the extra memory that the stack provides?

One answer is that PDA memory is not finite, but infinite. In the world of mathematics, the difference between finite and infinite is clear and crucial. We have seen that an unlimited supply of memory is important since we have proved that, without it, FAs cannot recognize important context-free languages. What about in the world of real computers? As a practical matter, computers of modest size by current standards can—despite their finiteness—carry out the recognition of long strings from useful CFGs. Do not let the large size of real machines blind you to the conceptual significance of the distinction between the finite and infinite. Of course, as seen in this chapter, we never use an infinite amount of memory; instead we require an *unbounded* amount of memory. Alternatively, we insist that all requests for memory be filled, which can not be true if we start with some finite amount of memory.

Another way to look at the PDA is to say that each time a symbol is **PUSH**ed, the new symbol is on a newly added position of the stack. There is a second sense in which the PDA has extra memory beyond that of FAs: It has an entirely new *form* of memory—its pushdown stack. The stack provides last-in-first-out storage. Allowing the automaton to consult only the most recently added symbol (but not the ones below it on the stack) is, of course, a constraint on how it can proceed, so we should not be too surprised to find that there are automata even more powerful than PDAs. That turns out to be true, as we see in the next chapter on Turing machines. However, a constraint can be helpful if it directs our attention to the most useful information. That is why pushdown stacks are useful for depth-first tree traversal and for processing function calls—two crucial kinds of algorithms used extensively in real computation.

Exercises

13.1 For each of the following strings, show what happens when it is provided as an input to the diagram of Figure 13.1. In each case, use a table like in Section 13.1.

   (a) *aabb*

   (b) *aab*

   (c) *aabbb*

13.2 In the diagram of Figure 13.2, replace each left parenthesis by *a* and each right parenthesis by *b*. State as explicitly as you can the ways in which the resulting diagram is similar to that of Figure 13.1.

13.3 Using a table like the one for *aaabbb* in Section 13.1, show the steps by which the STD in Figure 13.2

   (a) accepts the string "(( ) ( ))", and

   (b) rejects the string "( ))) (".

13.4 Prove that the diagram in Figure 13.2 recognizes L_3. To do this, you should show that (i) some of the transitions in the diagram keep track of the difference, $m(x) - n(x)$, (ii) the conditions on **POP**ping prevent the difference from becoming negative, and (iii) transition to an accepting state is possible when, and only when, the difference is zero.

13.5 The table in Example 13.5 specifies the transition function δ for three of the six transitions of Figure 13.1. Complete the table by specifying δ for the remaining transitions.

13.6 Specify an NPDA that recognizes L_3 using the proper formalism.

13.7 In Definition 13.1, the mapping specification given for the transition function is

$$\delta : Q \times (\Sigma \cup \{\Lambda\}) \times \Gamma \to 2^{Q \times \Gamma^*}.$$

(a) Explain why $(\Sigma \cup \{\Lambda\})$ is used instead of just Σ, commenting on the need for Λ.

(b) Explain why $2^{Q \times \Gamma^*}$ is used instead of just $Q \times \Gamma^*$.

13.8 Let G be the CFG $(\{S\}, \{a, b\}, S, \{S \to a\, S\, b\, S, S \to \Lambda\})$, which generates what we might call "the language of balanced as and bs" since the strings of $\mathcal{L}(G)$ can be obtained from those of L_3 by substituting a for "(" and b for ")". The following questions concern a deterministic PDA, M, that parses top–down with lookahead and that recognizes the language $\mathcal{L}(G)$.

(a) Since the grammar is right-recursive, modify it to generate $\mathcal{L}(G)^\triangleleft$ (see Example 13.12).

(b) Specify for the new grammar the septuple for M, including …

(c) …a table for the transition function δ.

(d) Create a table that shows the sequence of events for the input $aababb\triangleleft$.

13.9 Let G be the CFG of Example 13.12, $(\{S, T\}, \{a, b\}, S, \{S \to bT,\ T \to aT,\ T \to \Lambda\})$. For a deterministic PDA, M, that parses top–down with lookahead and that recognizes the language $\mathcal{L}(G)$, answer questions (a), (b), and (c) of Exercise 13.8.

13.10 For the language $\{x \mid x = a^i b^j c^k, i < k\}$:

(a) Informally describe a DPDA.

(b) Formally describe a DPDA.

Chapter 14

Turing Machines

Just as we discovered that there are nonregular languages, which led to the discussion of context-free grammars and their languages, so also we find that there are languages beyond the representational power of CFGs. This leads us to consider a more powerful formulation of grammars. On the automaton side of things, we discovered that finite-state automata were not powerful enough for recognizing nonregular languages, which led to pushdown automata, which recognize context-free languages. For noncontext-free languages, we need to formulate a more powerful machine model.

Specifically, we introduce *unrestricted grammars* and the *Turing Machine* (TM) models. These are advanced topics, so we confine our attention to key ideas illustrated by a continuing example, a particular language. We show that this language is not context-free, provide an unrestricted grammar that generates it, and finally exhibit a TM that recognizes it. In the field of formal languages and automata, these and many other types of languages, grammars, and machines have been studied, but we do not pursue these topics in this book. An example is *context-sensitive languages*, which we briefly mention.

Turing Machines are the most versatile category of automata. The most important thing about this category is the following assertion: *For every possible algorithm, no matter how complex, there is a TM that carries it out*. Although this assertion is not provable, no counterexample has been found, as discussed in Section 14.9. For this and other reasons, the assertion is widely believed. In fact, the TM model is used as a definition of computability. The determination of what is computable and what is not is in the realm of theoretical computer science, but the practical value of knowing that something is impossible—that for some problem there is no algorithm that solves it in general—should not be underestimated. It tells us that we must reformulate the problem, perhaps restricting the scope of what we hope to accomplish.

14.1   Beyond Context-Free Languages

Canonical examples of context-free languages, such as the set of strings of balanced parentheses, exhibit two-way balance—a later symbol (or symbols) being paired up with an earlier symbol (or symbols). However, if the notion of structure in the language is more complex than two-way balance, we might find that context-free languages are not powerful enough.

Consider the language L, which has *three-way* balance:

$$L = \{a^n b^n c^n \mid n \geq 0\}.$$

To gain insight into why there is no context-free grammar for L, you should try to devise one. We begin by establishing simple properties of CFGs that lead to the result.

> **Lemma 14.1** For any infinite context-free language L, for any particular CFG G that generates L, there is no bound on the height of the derivation trees required of G by strings of L.

Proof: First note that any context-free grammar G has a finite number of rules and each rule has a finite number of symbols on its right-hand side. Consequently, there must be some maximum length k for right-hand sides of the rules in G. Now suppose, contrary to the statement of the lemma, that there is a bound h on the heights of the derivations trees that L needs in G. Then by the properties of trees, terminal strings could have no more than k^h symbols. But L, being an infinite language, has strings longer than this. □

> **Lemma 14.2** For any infinite context-free language L, for any particular CFG G that generates L, some tree that G generates has a downward path to a leaf with two occurrences of the same nonterminal symbol.

Proof: Since L is an infinite language, by Lemma 14.1, there are derivation trees of unbounded height corresponding to G. In particular, we must have derivation trees for some strings in L that have heights exceeding $n = |V|$, the number of nonterminal symbols in G. Let T be such a tree. T must have—by the definition of height—a path of length greater than n from its root to some leaf, and that path

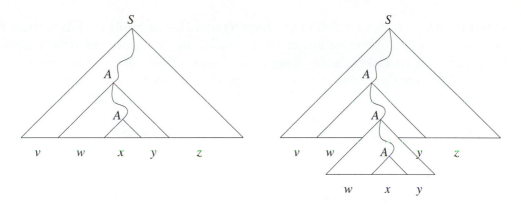

Figure 14.1: In tree T at the left, replace the lower A-rooted subtree by a *copy* of the upper A-rooted subtree to get tree T' at the right.

must have the same nonterminal appearing twice by the pigeon-hole principle. The left side of Figure 14.1 depicts the situation, with a path running down from S through two occurrences of A. □

Theorem 14.1 $L = \{a^n b^n c^n \mid n \geq 0\}$ is not a context-free language.

Proof: Suppose that there is a context-free grammar $G = (V, \Sigma, S, P)$ such that $\mathcal{L}(G) = L$; we find that this assumption leads to a contradiction.

Since L is an infinite language, by Lemma 14.2, G generates some derivation tree with the same nonterminal occurring twice on some path; call it A, as shown in the left-hand diagram of Figure 14.1. Let x be the string that the lower A generates. Then the upper A generates a string that *contains x*, that is, wxy for some w and y. We can assume that either w or y (possibly both of them) is a nonempty string here; otherwise the portion of the derivation between the upper A and the lower A is pointless. (We can prohibit subderivations like $A \overset{*}{\Rightarrow} A$ in general without affecting what G can generate.) The entire string generated by the S at the root is $u = vwxyz$ for some v and z. Since $u \in L$, we know $u = a^m b^m c^m$ for some m.

Now a copy of the whole subtree rooted at the upper A can replace the subtree rooted at the lower A, creating a new valid derivation tree T'. This is shown in the right-hand diagram of Figure 14.1. The string generated by the root of T' is $u' = vwwxyyz$. Clearly T' is a valid derivation tree using G, so $u' \in \mathcal{L}(G)$ or equivalently $u' \in L$. Therefore, $u' = a^l b^l c^l$ for some l.

A string is *homogeneous* if it is composed of only one symbol possibly repeated. We claim that w is homogeneous, for suppose, to the contrary, that w contained two different symbols, say an a and a b. In that case, ww would have a b before an a, and so would u', which is in violation of the requirement that $u' = a^l b^l c^l$. Similarly, y is homogeneous. Now u' must be longer than u so $l > m$. Yet since the only increase in the number of symbols in going from u to u' comes from an extra occurrence of each of the two homogeneous strings w and y, there must be one terminal symbol among the three—an a, b, or c—that is not in w or y and hence still appears only m times in u'. Consequently, the string u'—which is generated by G—cannot be in L. This result contradicts the assumption that there *could* exist a grammar G generating $L = \{a^n b^n c^n \mid n \geq 0\}$. $\square$

14.2 A Limitation on Deterministic Pushdown Automata

Before exploring more powerful grammars, we return to an important point mentioned in the last chapter: Deterministic PDAs are less powerful than nondeterministic PDAs. This might not seem surprising except that there was no such distinction for FAs. We are now in a position to prove this result since we make use of Theorem 14.1. The crux of the proof is a particular CFG language for which there cannot be a DPDA recognizer. The existence of such a language is all we need since for the language of *any* CFG it is straightforward to construct a *non*deterministic PDA with the start, expand, match, and stop rules used in Section 13.3.

> **Theorem 14.2** There exists a context-free language not recognized by any DPDA.

Proof: We exhibit a specific language and show that it cannot be recognized by a DPDA. In particular, consider the following context-free language over the alphabet $\Sigma = \{a, b\}$:

$$L = \{x \mid x = a^i b^i,\ i > 0\} \cup \{x \mid x = a^i b^{2i},\ i > 0\}$$

so that, for example, $a^3 b^3 = aaabbb \in L$ and $a^3 b^6 = aaabbbbbb \in L$. To fix ideas, we argue in terms of these two specific strings, although the arguments are valid in general. Also note that Exercise 14.1 asks you to show that L really is a CFL.

Assume (for the sake of contradiction) that there exists a DPDA M such that $L = \mathcal{L}(M)$, where $M = (Q, \Sigma, \Gamma, q_0, \triangleleft, A, \delta)$. Consider the behavior of M on the nine-symbol string $a^3 b^6$. After the first six symbols, M has seen $a^3 b^3$, which is in L so M must be in one of its accepting states. Moreover, the deterministic nature of M means that there is no choice about which state this will be. From there the remaining symbols (the seventh, eighth, and ninth) take M to a state (possibly the same one) that also is accepting. This sort of observation motivates a subproof that

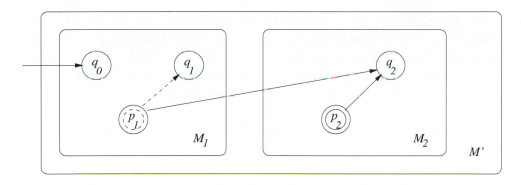

Figure 14.2: The construction of M' that could recognize the language of Theorem 14.1 if M could recognize the language of Theorem 14.2.

from the existence of M as just described one would be able to construct another PDA M' that accepts the language $L = \{a^n b^n c^n \mid n \geq 0\}$. But that is impossible according to Theorem 14.1, so M' cannot exist, and hence neither can M, which leads to it. The construction is described next and depicted in Figure 14.2.

From M we construct M' by first making two equivalent but disjoint copies of M, called M_1 and M_2, by relabeling states so that corresponding states in the two copies can be distinguished. To complete the construction of the single machine M', we then modify and augment the components so that:

- The start state of M' is the start state of M_1.

- The accepting states of M' are those of M_2 (but *not* those of M_1).

- The new transitions to get from M_1 to M_2 are formed from a special set of M_1 transitions: those that go out from an *accepting* state on input b (with any stack symbol). For such a transition, say from p_1 to q_1 (where p_1 must be accepting, but q_1 can be any state, possibly even p_1), M' instead has a transition on input c (instead of b) from p_1 to q_2, where q_2 is the state in M_2 that corresponds to q_1.

- In M_2, change all bs to cs.

Figure 14.2 is a schematic illustration of M'.

Consider what happens when $x = a^3 b^3$ is the input to M'. Of course x takes us to a state of M_1 corresponding to an accepting state of M. Now what about the input $y = a^3 b^3 c^3$? After processing the first six symbols, we make a transition into M_2 on the first c and continue within M_2 on the next two cs. What is the state q_2

where we first reach M_2? It is the state corresponding to the state in M arrived at after processing a^3b^4. Further, the state in M_2 that is reached after processing $a^3b^3c^2$ corresponds to the state we would have reached in M on the input a^3b^5. Finally, y takes us to a state corresponding to the state M reached on a^3b^6; this must be an accepting state of M so it is an accepting state of M'. Therefore, $y \in \mathcal{L}(M')$.

The prior example can be easily generalized. We find that $a^ib^ic^j$ reaches a state in M' (specifically in M_2) that corresponds to the state reached in M on the input a^ib^{i+j}. Further, since M' must reach the states of M_2 to accept a string, any string accepted by M' must begin with a^ib^i, and therefore the behavior outlined before is not only possible, it is forced. It follows that $a^ib^ic^j$ is accepted exactly when $j = i$. So M' is a PDA that accepts the language of Theorem 14.1. However, that language is not context-free and therefore cannot be accepted by any PDA. Hence, we have a contradiction to the assumption that M exists. $\square$

There are, of course, many other context-free languages that could have been used to prove this theorem. A notable example is the set of palindromes (see Definition 12.11). Informally, the language of palindromes is not deterministic because a DPDA cannot know when it has reached the middle of an input string.

14.3   Unrestricted Grammars

The **unrestricted grammar** (UG) class gets its name from the fact that the constraints on rules are relaxed. In particular, we drop the CFG constraint of using a single symbol on the left-hand side of rules, not to mention the stringent requirements on the right-hand sides in regular grammars. This lack of constraints yields a significant gain in representational power. In fact, these grammars are language-equivalent to Turing Machines (taken up next in Section 14.4), which are believed able to compute anything computable. The definition of a UG looks familiar; it is a quadruple $G = (V, \Sigma, S, P)$, where each production in P is of the form:

$$\alpha \to \beta, \quad \alpha, \beta \in (V \cup \Sigma)^*.$$

The four parts here correspond directly to those of CFGs, and derivation steps are defined the same way (with any production $\alpha \to \beta$ permitting the derivation step $\phi\alpha\psi \Rightarrow \phi\beta\psi$). The difference is that where CFGs allowed just a single nonterminal on the left, UGs allow any sequence of terminals and nonterminals.

Theorem 14.1 made clear the need for a formulation of grammars more powerful than CFGs if we are going to generate $L = \{a^nb^nc^n \mid n \geq 0\}$. One view of CFG shortcomings is that the left-hand side of the production $A \to \alpha$ can be applied *any* time A appears during a derivation. To control the use of a replacement—so that it can occur in some contexts but not others—is something that context-*free* productions cannot do. (The so-called context-*sensitive* grammars also overcome this shortcoming of CFGs. They give rise to *context-sensitive languages* and their corresponding class of machines, the *linear-bounded automata*; see Exercise 14.5).

Example 14.1 The UG production $aAb \rightarrow aCb$ permits an A to be replaced by a C, but only when, at some point in a derivation, it has the surrounding context a_b. So a possible derivation step would be $abaAbAc \Rightarrow abaCbAc$, replacing the first A. The string $abaAbCc$ could *not* be derived instead because the second A does not have the required context.

Our demonstration of the limitations of CFGs was based on their inability to cope with the particular language $\{a^n b^n c^n \mid n \geq 0\}$. That language is therefore a suitable challenge for UGs, and Example 14.2 presents a UG for it.

Example 14.2 Show that the unrestricted grammar with productions shown here generates exactly the strings of the language

$$L = \{a^n b^n c^n \mid n \geq 0\}$$

$$
\begin{aligned}
S &\rightarrow WDZ \mid \Lambda \\
D &\rightarrow ABCD \mid ABC \\
CA &\rightarrow AC \\
CB &\rightarrow BC \\
BA &\rightarrow AB \\
WA &\rightarrow aW \\
WB &\rightarrow bX \\
XB &\rightarrow bX \\
XC &\rightarrow cY \\
YC &\rightarrow cY \\
YZ &\rightarrow \Lambda
\end{aligned}
$$

First observe that the second production permits the derivation $D \overset{*}{\Rightarrow} ABCABCABC$ and more generally $D \overset{*}{\Rightarrow} (ABC)^n$ for any $n \geq 1$. So S clearly can derive an intermediate string beginning with a W, ending with a Z, and containing an equal number of As, Bs, and Cs in between. Unfortunately, the As, Bs, and Cs are all mixed up, so if we just made them lowercase, with productions like $A \to a$, we would fail to have all the as before all the bs before all the cs.

The third, fourth, and fifth productions can be used to rearrange the As, Bs, and Cs, putting all the As before all the Bs before all the Cs. Consider this example:

$$S \Rightarrow WDZ \Rightarrow WABCDZ \Rightarrow WABCABCZ$$

$$\Rightarrow WABACBCZ \Rightarrow WABABCCZ \Rightarrow WAABBCCZ$$

These interchanges of adjacent As, Bs, and Cs constitute a *sorting* process—sorting the As, Bs, and Cs. This example clearly generalizes to longer strings.

However, just because a rule *can* be used does not mean it *will* be. Therefore, we must examine what happens if this sorting process is not fully carried out. We see that it becomes impossible to complete a derivation. First note that any nonempty string $x \in \mathcal{L}(G)$ must have a derivation in which the first replacement introduces an instance of Z (as well W and D). Since Z is a nonterminal, it must ultimately be removed. Note that the only production that can remove a Z is the last one, $YZ \to \Lambda$. In other words, for x to be derived, we must find Z in the context of a preceding Y. Looking at G, we see that the appearance of such a Y must have been triggered by the appearance of an X, which was triggered by a W. Consider the following continuation of the previous derivation:

$$WAABBCCZ \Rightarrow aWABBCCZ \Rightarrow aaWBBCCZ \Rightarrow aabXBCCZ$$

$$\Rightarrow aabbXCCZ \Rightarrow aabbcYCZ \Rightarrow aabbccYZ \Rightarrow aabbcc$$

This illustrates how the grammar dictates the behavior of the derivation. In particular, the W symbol sweeps across the As (and only As) leaving as behind. When the W reaches a B it changes to an X, which then sweeps across Bs (and only Bs) leaving bs in its wake. Finally, the X becomes a Y, which changes the Cs it encounters into cs. In other words, for a Y to reach the Z, we must have all the As before all the Bs before all the Cs. In this way, the grammar forces any valid derivation to begin with the sorting process. Hence, any string derived with G is in L.

Example 14.2 illustrates how much more powerful an unrestricted grammar is than a context-free grammar. The grammar in the example has a distinct *algorithmic* flavor. It forces three phases: building, sorting, and checking. There are mechanisms that can force certain productions to be applied before others. Although checking can begin before sorting is completed (or building is completed for that matter), no *part* of a string can be checked until it is sorted.

Given this grammar with its algorithmic flavor, it is perhaps not surprising that we next propose a machine model with mechanisms that allow local changes in a string and the ability to sweep back and forth across a string.

14.4 The Turing Machine Model

In the 1930s, Alan Turing devised a model of computation, now called a **Turing Machine** (**TM**), to explore questions about the limits of computability. Remarkably, his investigations predate the design of the first modern digital computers (which later Turing was to help design). Because it is a model of what must be true of *any* computational device, the TM is far simpler (though less efficient) than our current notion of what a computer is. For proving things, it helps to make the model as simple as possible. Despite its simplicity, however, the TM model has been shown to be every bit as powerful—in terms of what TMs can ultimately compute—as any more realistic model of a computer that has been proposed to date.

A TM shares characteristics of FAs and PDAs. It has a finite control unit with a finite number of internal *states*. The distinction between the models is in the amount of memory and how it can be accessed. For an FA, the input is considered to be in read-only memory that can only be processed left to right; the only other "memory" is the implicit knowledge of what each state encodes about the past. For a PDA, the input is still found in read-only memory, processed left to right, but there is an additional read-write memory of unbounded size that is constrained to behave like a stack. A TM also allows an unbounded amount of read-write memory, but without the stack constraint on its use. Further, to simplify the model, the input is assumed to be found in the same read-write memory that is used for the rest of the computation.

The memory of a TM consists of a set of consecutive cells. At each step, the machine looks at the symbol in a cell. On the basis of what it sees there, along with its internal state, the TM writes a symbol, enters a state, and moves. The movement must be to an adjacent cell. This access mechanism has suggested to some that we call the memory a **tape**; a tape is a read-write storage mechanism accessed by a **tape head** that can move back and forth on the tape. The cells are *not* given addresses, so there is no notion of random access. To get the TM to access a distant cell, you have to arrange for it to move there one cell at a time.

More formally, a TM consists of a finite control with a tape that is unbounded in one direction; that is, it has a first cell, a second, and so on indefinitely. Initially the TM is in a designated initial state and the input string x is found right next to the start of the tape beginning in the second cell. The first cell is blank. The **blank symbol**, denoted Δ, is a distinguished element of the *tape alphabet*. The infinitely many tape cells beyond the input string are also blank (contain Δ) at the outset. The Δ symbol is not part of the *input alphabet*. Because Δs surround the input but cannot be part of it, a TM can detect where the input string begins and ends.

Initially the tape head is at the first cell. The machine makes a sequence of state transitions. If it arrives at the **halt state**, h, the input is accepted by the TM and the machine halts. It follows that, unlike other states, h has no outward transitions. Therefore, we do not include it in the set Q. This aspect of TM operation differs from that of FAs and PDAs, which can continue from an accepting state. TMs have no ordinary accepting states.

Like FAs, TMs have transitions that depend on a state and a symbol. Here the symbol is the one in the tape cell where the tape head is currently positioned. Based on these two values, the TM decides three things:

1. what state to be in next (possibly unchanged, possibly the halt state),

2. what symbol to write in the current tape cell (possibly the same symbol), or

3. where to go: move one cell left or right.

We express TMs with transition diagrams similar to those for FAs and PDAs, but with information corresponding to the foregoing specifications of what happens during a transition. Suppose there is a transition from state p to state q (which may be the same in the case of a self-loop), with the label "$X/Y, \mu$", where X and Y are tape symbols and μ ("mu") is the *move*, which can be $L =$ left or $R =$ right. Then this transition can be used when the machine is in state p and the current tape cell contains the symbol X. As a result, the machine enters state q and, after overwriting the X with Y, makes the move that μ specifies.

Definition 14.1 Turing Machines

Formally we define a Turing Machine M by a quintuple $M = (Q, \Sigma, \Gamma, q_0, \delta)$, where

Q is a finite set of states

Σ is a finite input alphabet, where $\Delta \notin \Sigma$

Γ is a finite tape alphabet, where $\Sigma \subseteq \Gamma$ and $\Delta \in \Gamma$

$q_0 \in Q$ is the initial state, and

δ is the transition function, where

$$\delta : Q \times \Gamma \rightarrow (Q \cup \{h\}) \times \Gamma \times \{L, R\}.$$

As promised, the definition has no set of accepting states. Moreover, the halt state h—which forces acceptance and termination and which is not in Q—shows up only as a possible *result* of δ (as part of $Q \cup \{h\}$) and not as a possible input. This makes sense since h is *not* an ordinary state with outbound transitions. The set $\{L, R\}$ in the definition corresponds to the two possible tape head movements: left or right. The transition described before, from p to q with label "$X/Y, \mu$", is denoted $\delta(p, X) = (q, Y, \mu)$.

If a TM M with x as input enters the halt state h, then M **accepts** x; the set of all strings accepted by M is $\mathcal{L}(M)$. If a string x causes M to reach a situation where no transition is defined and it is not in h, then M halts without accepting x. However, if x causes M to proceed endlessly without ever halting—an infinite loop— then x is also not accepted. This second way of not accepting a string is clearly undesirable; we prefer a TM that always halts whatever its input. Unfortunately, as we show later, there are languages that require both ways of failing to accept strings. A language that is accepted by some TM that always halts is said to be **recursive**; if there is any TM at all that accepts it—even a TM that does not halt on all inputs—it is said to be **recursively enumerable**. (This terminology comes from the mathematics of recursive function theory.)

Example 14.3 Show that $L = \{a^n b^n c^n \mid n \geq 0\}$ is recursive; that is, give a TM M that always halts and for which $\mathcal{L}(M) = L$.

The state transition diagram for such a TM M is given in Figure 14.3. The double circle at the top represents the accepting halt state h. This machine is supposed to verify that the input x is in L. In particular, M enters h in those cases (and no others) when the tape started out with "$\Delta a^n b^n c^n \Delta$" as the symbols in the first $3n + 2$ cells for some $n \geq 0$. M does its work by making repeated passes across the input. Passing left to right, it changes one a, one b, and one c each into the symbol X. Passing right to left, it searches for the Δ at the beginning and then turns around to start the next left-to-right pass. A rightward pass skips over any Xs left from earlier passes. If

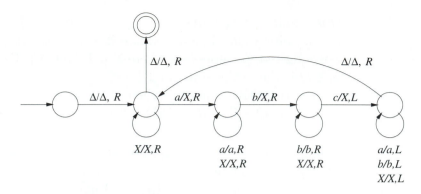

Figure 14.3: A Turing Machine for $L = \{a^n b^n c^n \mid n \geq 0\}$.

a rightward pass encounters only Xs before encountering the trailing Δ, then it accepts the input.

What if this M halts without accepting the input? Suppose we halt in the middle state. In that case, we have already encountered an a on a rightward pass. After possibly skipping some Xs, we expect to find a b to match up with the a. If we halt then, it is because we saw some other symbol; in other words, we have found the input to be ill-formed and, therefore, not in L. Halts in the other nonaccepting states have similar interpretations.

Example 14.3 demonstrates typical behavior for a TM: running up and down the tape looking for symbol patterns to initiate certain activities. As a result, TMs have a reputation for being tediously slow. (Actually, although slow, they are not *too* slow, but that is beyond the scope of this discussion.) What is important to us is this: *Can* a TM recognize some language L?

The preceding TM is *deterministic* inasmuch as M never had a choice of two transitions. We can define *nondeterministic* TMs by augmenting δ to allow choices. However, it can be shown—like FAs and unlike PDAs—that the power of nondeterminism does not permit TMs to solve any more difficult problems.

14.5   Infinite Sets

Turing machines are studied for two complementary reasons. First, they allow us to describe succinctly what any computer *can* do; we return to this topic in Section 14.9. Second, they allow us to explore what a computer can*not* do. The idea of a computational task that no computer can perform may seem counterintuitive, and the work of *proving* that such tasks exist may seem daunting. Indeed it must be admitted that the proofs are indirect and somewhat complicated even when treated informally. To get a handle on them, we need to begin with a better understanding of infinite sets.

Recall that a finite set is a set with a cardinality that is an integer. So $\{a, b, c\}$ is a finite set since its cardinality is 3. Also recall that two sets have the same cardinality if and only if there is a one-to-one correspondence between them. So $\{a, b, c\}$ and $\{1, 2, 3\}$ have the same cardinality because of this mapping:

$$
\begin{array}{ccc}
1 & 2 & 3 \\
\updownarrow & \updownarrow & \updownarrow \\
a & b & c
\end{array}
$$

This use of mappings to determine that two sets have the same cardinality carries over to infinite sets. The most important infinite set is the set of non-negative integers, $\mathcal{N} = \{0, 1, 2, 3, 4, \ldots\}$. We can define $\mathcal{N}$ formally, but that would take us beyond the scope of this book. Informally, $\mathcal{N}$ is defined by starting with 0 and using the rule that if i is in $\mathcal{N}$ then $i + 1$ is also in $\mathcal{N}$; clearly there is no largest element of $\mathcal{N}$. Consider the following one-to-one correspondence between $\mathcal{N}$ and $\mathcal{E}$, where $\mathcal{E}$ is set of even non-negative integers:

$$
\begin{array}{ccccc}
0 & 1 & 2 & 3 & 4 & \cdots \\
\updownarrow & \updownarrow & \updownarrow & \updownarrow & \updownarrow \\
0 & 2 & 4 & 6 & 8 & \cdots
\end{array}
$$

This mapping shows that two infinite sets can have the same cardinality, even though one is a proper subset of the other. This is just one of many counterintuitive properties of $\mathcal{N}$. We must be careful using the word "infinite," as will soon become clear. A set with the same cardinality as $\mathcal{N}$, such as $\mathcal{E}$, is said to be *countably infinite*. This makes sense because the mapping explicitly shows how we count the elements; every element is eventually reached and counted. Are there sets with so many elements that they have more elements than $\mathcal{N}$? The answer is "yes." Moreover—and equally important here—*the set of all languages over an alphabet is uncountable.*

First consider the idea of an infinite string. Recall that, by definition, a string is composed of a finite number of symbols, so let us define a new term ω-**string** for strings with a countably infinite number of symbols. The *occurrences* of symbols of an ω-string can be put in one-to-one correspondence with the elements of $\mathcal{N}$. An example of an ω-string is the decimal representation of a irrational real number, such as $\pi = 3.141592653589\ldots$.

Recall that in an infinite language, although there is no limit on how long a string can be, each string must be finite. So *no* language we have studied so far—although most of them have been infinite—has contained an ω-string. So as not to disturb this terminology, we say "sets of ω-strings" when that is what we mean and we do not call them *languages*. In particular, let $\mathcal{W}$ be the set of all ω-strings over the alphabet $\{0,1\}$. Although the remainder of this section uses only this alphabet, the results can be generalized to any alphabet.

A finite binary string can be regarded as the binary representation of an integer; in this sense, every language we have discussed can be regarded as a set of integers and is therefore a subset of $\mathcal{N}$ (ignoring the empty string for the present argument). As with $\mathcal{E}$, every infinite subset of $\mathcal{N}$ is countable, so it follows that every infinite language is composed of a countably infinite number of (finite) strings.

We want to build an ω-string from a given infinite language L by concatenating all the strings of L together. However, since a language (like any set) is unordered, it is not clear what order should be used in building the ω-string. Therefore, we artificially restrict our attention to infinite languages with exactly one string of each possible length. One example of such a language is $\mathcal{L}(a^*)$ and another is the language of the regular expression $(ab)^*(a + \Lambda)$. One that we return to is $L = \mathcal{L}((11)^*) \cup \mathcal{L}(0(00)^*)$. If the strings of such a language are sorted by length, the result looks like an infinite version of the so-called *rhopalic sentences*. (Rhopalic is an obscure but real adjective describing things that grow in length; for example, "I am not sure you'll notice growing rhopalic sentences" is a rhopalic sentence since the word lengths increase one letter at a time.) For present purposes, a **rhopalic language** contains exactly one string of length i for each $i \in \mathcal{N}$.

If we concatenate the strings of a rhopalic language in order by increasing length, we unambiguously create an ω-string; let $c(L)$ be that ω-string for a rhopalic language L. Take, for example, the language L expressed before as a union of RE languages: $L = \{\Lambda, 0, 11, 000, 1111, 00000, 111111, \ldots\}$. For this language, $c(L) = 011000111100000111111\cdots$. Further, notice that any ω-string can be sliced up into strings of increasing size, resulting in a unique rhopalic language. It follows that there is a one-to-one correspondence between the set of rhopalic languages and $\mathcal{W}$ (defined before to be the set of all binary ω-strings). So $\mathcal{W}$ and the rhopalic languages have the same cardinality.

Next, we show that $\mathcal{W}$ is so large that the elements of $\mathcal{W}$ are uncountable. It follows that the set of rhopalic languages is uncountable. Since the set of rhopalic languages is a subset of the set of all languages, Theorem 14.3 will follow.

Theorem 14.3 If $\Sigma \geq 2$, the set of all languages over Σ is uncountable.

We show that $\mathcal{W}$ is uncountable by contradiction. Assume $\mathcal{W}$ is a countably infinite set, so that its elements can be put in one-to-one correspondence with $\mathcal{N}$. This is equivalent to saying that we can make a list of all the elements of $\mathcal{W}$. Once the correspondence is chosen, we can unambiguously talk about the ith element of $\mathcal{W}$. By hypothesis, this list contains every possible binary ω-string, but we show that there must be an ω-string that cannot be on the list. Define the ω-string x as follows: The ith bit of x is 0 if the ith bit of the ith string in $\mathcal{W}$ is 1, and vice versa. (We are using a 0-based indexing.) An illustration of this construction is

$$x = \quad 1 \quad 1 \quad 0 \quad 1 \quad \cdots$$

0th	0	1	1	0	0	1	$\cdots$
1st	0	0	1	0	1	1	$\cdots$
2nd	1	1	1	1	0	1	$\cdots$
3rd	1	0	1	0	0	1	$\cdots$

The key observation is that x is an ω-string and hence should be on the list of all ω-strings. Yet for any i, the construction prevents x from being the ith string on the list since it differs from that string in the ith bit. Hence a contradiction. $\square$

This proof is an example of the technique called **diagonalization**. We use it again soon. (It is worth remarking that the preceding argument is almost identical to the proof that the number of real numbers between 0 and 1 is uncountably large. To see the relationship, note that any such real can be represented in binary notation as an ω-string preceded by a "binary point." There are some additional technical details since some reals have more than one representation.)

14.6 Universal Turing Machines

We have promised that the TM is a general model of computation (Section 14.4). The prospects for such a claim seem dubious so far, however, since a general-purpose computer can run all kinds of software, but the TM in Example 14.3—the only TM we have seen—can do only one thing: determine whether each input string is in the language L. The goal of this section is to dispel this appearance of TM rigidity by presenting a design strategy for a TM that can accept as input a description of any other TM—much as a real computer accepts software—and then carry out the behavior of that other TM on whatever data is provided as a second input. Such a TM is called a **Universal Turing Machine (UTM)**.

If one TM is to be input to another (the UTM), that first TM is going to have to be expressed in terms of symbols that are allowed to appear on the tape of the second. In particular, if the UTM uses $\Sigma = \{0,1\}$, there has to be an **encoding scheme** that represents any TM M in 0s and 1s. The encoding of a machine M is denoted $\langle M \rangle$. It needs to be emphasized that there is no single correct encoding scheme. Various schemes could be used that agree in spirit but differ in details. To get a clearer understanding of encoding schemes, it is best to look at one.

> **Example 14.4** Give an encoding scheme for converting a given TM $M = (Q, \Sigma, \Gamma, q_0, \delta)$ into a binary string, $\langle M \rangle$.
>
> The encoding of each TM element is a string of 1s (possibly empty), with each string separated from the next by a single 0. First we represent the states $Q = \{q_0, q_1, \ldots, q_n\}$ by the strings $\{\Lambda, 1, 11, 111, \ldots, 1^n\}$, where q_i corresponds to 1^i. The halt state h becomes 1^{n+1}. Similarly, we can represent the symbols in the tape alphabet $\Gamma = \{x_0, x_1, x_2, \ldots, x_m\}$ by the strings $\{\Lambda, 1, 11, 111, \ldots, 1^m\}$, where x_i corresponds to 1^i. This takes care of Σ since $\Sigma \subseteq \Gamma$. The blank symbol is $\Lambda = 1^0$; $\Delta = x_0$. Finally, for the tape head, movements $\{R, L\} = \{\mu_0, \mu_1\}$ represent the move μ_i by the string 1^i.
>
> Consider a generic transition of the TM, $\delta(q_i, x_l) = (q_j, x_k, \mu_m)$. We encode this transition by the string $1^i 0 1^l 0 1^j 0 1^k 0 1^m 0$. We represent all of δ by concatenating together the representations of each and every transition to form one long string, w. In fact, w represents a complete description of M, so we let $\langle M \rangle = w$.

Although there may be wide variations among rule encodings with respect to the number of 1s, the number of 0s for the encoding of each transition is always 5, a fact that helps the UTM keep track of where it is. For example, moving from the beginning of the tape past five 0s brings the tape head to the second transition rule.

Since an encoding scheme makes a string out of each TM, the set of TM encodings is a language. Now consider a TM encoding, followed by a special symbol ("$\diamond$"), followed by an input string that TM accepts. This too is a string, and the set of all *these* strings is a language. We denote this language L_U and call it the *universal language*. It is universal in that it represents all TM computations that succeed in halting. Formally, we write

$$L_U = \{ \langle M \rangle \diamond x \mid \text{TM } M \text{ accepts } x\},$$

where the diamond, $\diamond$, is a new symbol used only as the divider, allowing any string in L_U to be broken down unambiguously into an encoding of M and another string taken to be the input to M. We assume, without loss of generality, that input strings, like encodings, use the alphabet $\{0, 1\}$. Thus, there are three symbols in the symbol set for L_U: $\{0, 1, \diamond\}$.

We now claim that there exists a TM M_U that accepts L_U. Such a TM is a *universal TM* or UTM because it has the behavior discussed earlier. That is, it accepts the encoding of any TM with its data and simulates that TM's behavior. In this way, it is analogous to a general-purpose computer running a program. The strongest way to support this claim would be to give the details of a UTM. Although UTMs exist with as few as five states and a five-symbol alphabet, the task of specifying one requires many TM design techniques. An example of such a technique is the one used in Example 14.3: A self-loop with the label $X/X, R$ lets us "move rightward across Xs." A slight extension of this idea, which we could use here where $\Gamma = \{0, 1, \diamond\}$, would be to "find the diamond, to the right" by moving rightward across 0s and 1s with a self-loop labeled both $0/0, R$ and $1/1, R$. Rather than develop and deploy a bag of TM tricks, we content ourselves with a rough and informal—but we hope reasonably convincing—description of M_U.

Given the input "$\langle M \rangle \diamond x$," a UTM simulates the execution of M on the input x and accepts its input iff the simulation indicates that M accepts x. It works on the portion of the tape to the right of the $\diamond$ as if it were the tape used by M. It also needs to allocate a portion of the tape to hold the encoding of the current state that M would be in as the simulation progresses. Thereafter, the UTM simulates M by scanning down to find what symbol is currently being scanned by the simulated M (assuming that position is marked in some way) and then it scans to find within $\langle M \rangle$ the transition that M must make at this time (it needs to use the current state of M to determine this). It then executes that transition by changing the encoding of M's current state, the currently scanned symbol, and moving the tape head (by moving the "mark") as appropriate. This above discussion of the design strategy provides some confidence that M_U exists. The details of M_U and its operation are messy, but have been worked out in various ways in the literature. The existence of M_U establishes the next theorem.

Theorem 14.4 The language L_U is recursively enumerable.

Note that the proof of this theorem, only sketched here, involves the simulation of M. If M does not halt on the input x, then our M_U does not halt on the input $\langle M \rangle \diamond x$. Hence, we have *not* established whether L_U is recursive.

In the following section, we talk about the "ith TM." To see that such a notion is meaningful, note that for any TM M its encoding, $\langle M \rangle$ is a bit-string (a string over $\{0,1\}$), which in turn can be read as a unique integer i in binary (base 2). In this way, the TMs map into the integers. Now consider the mapping in the other direction—from integers to bit strings to TMs. Disallowing leading 0s—which never occur in our encodings—every integer i has its own unique bit-string; call it $bin(i)$. (For example, if $i = 9$, then $bin(i)$ is the string 1001, not 0001001.) Now this bit-string may be a valid encoding of a TM, but it may not because the encoding process imposes constraints on what strings it can produce. Still for simplicity, we make the "ith TM" the one that maps to i, so $\langle M_i \rangle = bin(i)$. For any i where $bin(i)$ is not a valid encoding, we may think of M_i as being ill formed and accepting no strings so that its language is empty.

14.7   Limits on Turing Machines

The TM model has been presented as the most powerful model of computation, a point to which we return in Section 14.9. Still there are limits to what this class of machines can do. For some languages, there is no TM at all; such a language is not recursively enumerable. Other languages, although they are recursively enumerable, are not recursive; for these there is no TM that reliably halts.

> **Theorem 14.5** There exists a language that is not recursively enumerable.

Proof: Theorem 14.3 states that the number of languages is uncountable. However, we showed in Section 14.6 that each TM can be encoded as an integer, so it immediately follows that the set of all TMs is only countably infinite. Thus, there are more languages than TMs, so after you map TMs to the languages they accept, there must be languages left over that do not correspond to any TM. □

This proof is not very satisfying. It shows that such a language must exist without exhibiting it. We can get a specific language that is not recursively enumerable by applying the diagonalization technique used Section 14.5 directly to TMs. Recall that M_i is the ith TM as defined in Section 14.6:

$$L_D = \{\ bin(i) \mid i \text{ is a positive integer and TM } M_i \text{ does not accept } bin(i)\}.$$

Although this is a peculiar language, since M_i is uniquely defined there is no ambiguity as to whether some string x is in L_D. Since $\langle M_i \rangle = bin(i)$, a string $x \in L_D$ iff the machine whose encoding is x does not accept x. This is the sense in which this is a diagonalization argument.

Theorem 14.6 The language L_D is not recursively enumerable.

Proof: Suppose, for the purpose of contradiction, that L_D is accepted by some TM M so that $L_D = \mathcal{L}(M)$. Since $\langle M \rangle = bin(i)$ for some i, it follows that $M = M_i$. Now consider whether M accepts $x = bin(i)$. If M accepts x, then $x \in \mathcal{L}(M)$ and so $x \in L_D$. However, if M accepts x, then x cannot be in L_D by the definition of L_D. This contradiction implies that M cannot exist. $\square$

There are many properties of recursive and recursively enumerable languages that can be proved. We only need the following one. Recall that the complement of a language L over an alphabet Σ is $\overline{L} = \{x \in \Sigma^* \mid x \notin L\}$.

Lemma 14.3 If a language L is recursive, then $\overline{L}$ is also recursive.

Proof: Let L be the recursive language. Then by definition there is an M that accepts L and halts on all inputs. We can build a new TM $\overline{M}$ for $\overline{L}$ by modifying M. The modification changes the state h into a nonaccepting sink. Further, for each of the undefined transitions (which are what cause M to halt without accepting), add a new transition to a new halt state. For any input x, $\overline{M}$ halts and $\overline{M}$ accepts x iff M does not accept x. $\square$

Define $L_A = \overline{L}_D$.

Corollary 14.1 The language L_A is not recursive.

Proof: If $L_A = \overline{L}_D$ were recursive, then L_D would be recursive, by Lemma 14.3, but we know that it is not even recursively enumerable. $\square$

With these results, we are now prepared to give an example of a language that is recursively enumerable but not recursive. Recall that in Section 14.6 we showed that L_U, the universal language, was recursively enumerable.

Theorem 14.7 The language L_U is not recursive.

Proof: Suppose, for the purpose of contradiction, that there exists a TM M_U that accepts L_U and halts on all inputs. We use this to build a TM M_A that accept L_A and halts on all inputs (which we now know is impossible by Corollary 14.1). First, the TM M_A checks whether the first symbol is a 0 (if it is, it cannot begin a $bin(i)$ for any $i > 0$, or $i = 0$; in either case, it is in L_A and M_A can halt). If the input starts with a 1, then M_A begins, when given $x = bin(i)$ as input, by making a duplicate of x and placing the symbol $\diamond$ between the two copies of x. Since $\langle M_i \rangle = bin(i)$, the tape now contains the string $\langle M_i \rangle \diamond x$. At this point, M_A switches over and starts behaving like M_U. Since, by hypothesis, M_U always halts, it follows that M_A always halts, which gives us a contradiction. $\square$

Why is recognizing L_U so difficult? Recall that we argued that $\langle M \rangle \diamond x$ can be accepted by M_U simulating M on input x. Now if M halts on all inputs, the M_U would halt on all inputs. However, if our TM M_U could determine whether the simulation would halt, it would know when M did not accept x and could halt without accepting its input. Hence, the underlying reason that L_U is not recursive is because it is too difficult, in general, to decide whether a TM will halt. This is pursued in the next section.

14.8   Undecidability

In this chapter we have been concerned with the question of testing whether we can find a machine that recognizes a given language. This is an example of a **decision problem**. Informally, a decision problem is a problem for which we need to compute "yes/no" answers. This decision problem has been discussed at length:

- Is string x in language L?

However, we could add many others to such a list, such as:

- Does a given string contain an even number of symbols?

- Is a given number prime?

- Does TM M halt on input x?

- For a given context-free grammar G, is $\mathcal{L}(G)$ regular?

They seem different in character, but it is important to realize that these last four questions, and all other decision problems, are special cases of the first example: "Is string x in language L?"

We need to recast each decision problem as a language-recognition problem. For each problem, we specify how instances of the problem can be regarded as strings and then define the set of strings that correspond to instances for which the answer is "yes." This set of strings is a language, and testing membership in that language is tantamount to answering the decision problem. For example, the preceding list of four questions can be recast as the following languages:

- $L_1 = \{x \mid x$ is of even length $\}$

- $L_2 = \{bin(i) \mid i$ is prime $\}$

- $L_3 = \{\langle M \rangle \diamond x \mid \langle M \rangle$ is an encoding of a TM M and M halts on x $\}$

- $L_4 = \{\langle G \rangle \mid \langle G \rangle$ is an encoding of a CFG G and $\mathcal{L}(G)$ is regular $\}$

where $\langle G \rangle$ is some encoding of the grammar G into a (binary) string; by analogy with $\langle M \rangle$, we can concatenate together encodings of each of the productions of G.

It is the ability to cast diverse problems as language tasks that gives the study of formal languages its crucial role in computation theory. Many of the languages in this text may seem artificial, but that is only because we need to start with simple examples. In fact, the power of languages is in their ability to capture the essence of natural problems.

Some decision problems are fairly straightforward. The decision problem corresponding to L_1 can be solved by a simple FA; therefore it can be solved by a TM that always halts. It is also possible to give a TM that accepts L_2 that always halts. However, L_3, which corresponds to the decision problem known as the **Halting Problem**, is more difficult. In Section 14.7, after we proved that L_U is not recursive, we gave an argument showing that L_3 is also not recursive. (If it were recursive, then L_U would be recursive.)

A decision problem is said to be **undecidable** if the corresponding language is *not recursive* (even if it is recursively enumerable). We can say the "halting problem is undecidable." (Sometimes we say the "language L is undecidable," but properly we should refer to the corresponding decision problem.) Note that *undecidability* refers to our inability to design a single computer (TM) that correctly solves the problem for all inputs. In other words, you might be able to build a TM that almost always gets the right answer, but if the problem is undecidable then your TM must give the wrong answer for at least one input!

Some undecidable problems are artificial, but many, such as the halting problem, have direct impact on computer scientists. If someone tells you he or she has a program that can do a complete analysis of, say, C++ code, then you should doubt them. After all, their program cannot always decide if some given C++ code even halts, so how can they decide if it works? (This is the reason we stressed the notion of proofs of *partial correctness* in Chapter 6.) Sometimes the most innocent problems turn out to be undecidable. For example, the problem of determining whether a CFG corresponds to a regular language—L_4 above—is undecidable. Unfortunately, the proof is too complicated to give here.

14.9   Church–Turing Thesis

Alonzo Church and Alan Turing simultaneously defined models of computation. Church's model, called the λ-*calculus*, was later found to be equivalent to TMs. Both researchers contended that their models were truly universal models of computation. In other words, they were sure that any other model, including specifications for real computers, would not be any more powerful than theirs with respect to the question of which computations are possible. This was a bold and unprovable thesis since it makes a statement about any model of computation that will ever be devised in the future. The **Church–Turing Thesis** can be paraphrased as: Any computational task can be accomplished by a TM.

To appreciate this claim, we need to expand slightly our notion of what a TM does; so far, a TM can only solve decision problems. A TM can be thought of as computing a function f, where if x is the input, then whatever is on the tape when the machine halts is $f(x)$. The Church–Turing Thesis has been verified to the extent that there is no known function f that can be computed by some other model, but not by a TM. This has remained true since the 1930s despite the fact that many alternate models have been proposed, often with the intent of falsifying the thesis.

Will the thesis continue to hold? Perhaps not, if we are willing to push the limits of the notion of "computation." For example, people have seriously investigated to what extent brain functions are not computable by a TM. Alternatively, researchers of so-called *quantum computers* who make use of the uncertainties of subatomic reactions feel that TMs may not be able to keep up. These ideas are speculative. For all practical purposes we can rely on the thesis.

It is because of the general support for the Church–Turing Thesis that the TM has a central role in theoretical computer science. Another entire textbook could be written to explore what is known about TMs. We mention one such topic in the next section.

14.10   Computational Complexity

In the second part of this book, we have dealt exclusively with questions of what can or cannot be done. For example, $L = \{a^n b^n \mid n > 0\}$ is a language for which we cannot give a regular grammar, but we can give a context-free grammar. In practice, computer scientists wish to go beyond whether they *can* solve a problem to how hard it is to solve the problem. By sorting problems into language classes, we can gauge how hard a problem is. After all, if one problem can be solved with an FA and another requires a TM, there is a sense in which the first problem is easier.

However, if a regular language requires an FA with a number of states exponentially larger than a TM would require to recognize the same language, then the simplicity of the FA is moot.

In computer science, we have traditionally evaluated the difficulty of a problem by the amount of resources consumed by the (optimal) computer program that solves that problem. Typically the resource studied the most is execution time, but memory usage is also important. In an Algorithms course, these issues are studied extensively. However, there are important issues about efficiency that can be studied theoretically with TMs.

We confine our attention to decision problems in this section, which is equivalent to concentrating on language-recognition tasks. In Chapter 8, we discussed sorting languages into language classes as dictated by various models of computation, grammars, and so on. Now, instead, we wish to sort languages into **complexity classes** according to the amount of resources a TM must use to recognize that language. This leads to a whole field of study known as *computational complexity*, which would require a semester to survey. In this section, we indicate some directions that can be pursued in that field.

> **Example 14.5** What resources—that is, how much time and space—are required by the TM in Example 14.3 when it begins with $x = a^n b^n c^n$?
>
> The TM repeatedly scans the tape, back and forth, until it eventually halts. In particular, it scans all $3n$ symbols plus the two bracketing blanks (Δs) n times left-to-right and n times right-to-left, plus a final left-to-right pass. Careful counting shows that it takes the TM $(2n + 1)(3n + 1) + 1$ steps to accept x. Generally we are looser and simply state that it takes a quadratic number, $O(n^2)$, of steps. It can also be seen that it takes a quadratic number of steps to reject an input of n symbols. The TM does not use any additional tape cells beyond the $3n + 2$ already mentioned; we say it uses a linear amount of space, $O(n)$.

We need more formal definitions. Recall that the $O(\cdot)$ notation was defined in Section 1.5. We say a TM M "accepts a language L in time $T(n)$" if for every $x \in L$, of length n, M accepts x in $O(T(n))$ steps. Further, we say a TM M "accepts a language L in space $S(n)$" if for every $x \in L$, of length n, M accepts x using $O(S(n))$ tape cells.

We have noted that nondeterminism does not allow a TM to accept a language that is not accepted by some deterministic TM. However, nondeterminism may allow a TM to accept the strings of a given language using fewer resources than any deterministic TM. Of course, this sort of speedup is only of theoretical interest since only deterministic machines exist. Surprisingly, the theory of nondeterminism turns out to lead to some practical insights. Here are two types of time complexity classes:

$$DTIME(T(n)) = \{L \mid L \text{ is accepted by a deterministic TM in time } T(n) \}$$

and

$$NTIME(T(n)) = \{L \mid L \text{ is accepted by a nondeterministic TM in time } T(n) \}.$$

Note that a complexity class is a set of languages that share the property of being equally difficult to recognize, in some sense. The space complexity classes $DSPACE(S(n))$ and $NSPACE(S(n))$ are defined analogously.

There are literally thousands of theorems known about various complexity classes, with most depending on the growth rates of $T(n)$ and $S(n)$. A simple example of such a theorem is

$$DTIME(f(n)) \subseteq DSPACE(f(n)).$$

To prove this, you need only observe that if a TM uses $f(n)$ steps it uses at most $f(n)$ cells, but a TM using $f(n)$ cells could use far more time. These results ultimately inform us about the relative difficulty of the various decision problems.

The best-known area of complexity theory concerns the two complexity classes $\mathcal{P}$ and $\mathcal{NP}$:

$$\mathcal{P} = \{L \mid L \text{ is accepted by a deterministic TM in polynomial time } \}$$

$$\mathcal{NP} = \{L \mid L \text{ is accepted by a nondeterministic TM in polynomial time } \}$$

which can defined more formally as

$$\mathcal{P} = \bigcup_{k=0}^{\infty} DTIME(n^k)$$

$$\mathcal{NP} = \bigcup_{k=0}^{\infty} NTIME(n^k),$$

Although these are defined in terms of language recognition, we continue to interpret them as pertaining to decision problems. A decision problem is in $\mathcal{P}$ if it can be solved deterministically in $O(n^k)$ time for some integer k.

When k is small, say $k = 2$, then we have a runtime of a reasonably efficient machine, but if $k = 1,000,000$, then such an implementation is incredibly impractical. So why is *polynomial time* central to these definitions? There are three reasons.

First, even if membership in $\mathcal{P}$ does not guarantee a practical implementation, it is certainly true that *not* belonging to $\mathcal{P}$ means that the decision problem has no practical solution for large n. We label a decision problem *intractable* if it is not in $\mathcal{P}$. Second, although a TM seems tediously slow, it is known that a TM can simulate a single step of a normal modern random-access computer in polynomial time. (In fact there is a whole literature on the complexity of various machine simulations.) Third, polynomials have simplifying closure properties; for example, a polynomial number of steps, each taking polynomial time to execute/simulate, takes a cumulative time that is also polynomial. (Experience has shown that for natural problems when a polynomial time algorithm exists the value of k is small. However, we can easily invent problems that require larger values of k.)

Membership in $\mathcal{NP}$ is of no *direct* practical significance. In fact, nondeterminism appears to be helpful in allowing unrealistically fast implementations. A nondeterministic TM can guide the computation by making shrewd guesses whenever it has a choice of transitions and so avoid having to search for evidence that a string should be accepted. It is obvious that

$$\mathcal{P} \subseteq \mathcal{NP}$$

since the power of nondeterminism can only improve the time needed to accept a language. In fact it seems likely that there would be problems solvable in polynomial time nondeterministically, that cannot be solved by any polynomial time TM. Any such problem is, of course, intractable.

In fact, $\mathcal{NP}$ is of great *indirect* practical significance because of the class of $\mathcal{NP}$-complete languages. The definition of $\mathcal{NP}$-**complete** languages is too technical to give here, but the upshot is that these are the languages in $\mathcal{NP}$ that are the hardest to solve. In particular, if *any* language in $\mathcal{NP}$ is intractable, then *every* $\mathcal{NP}$-complete language is intractable.

Despite its abstract definition, the class of $\mathcal{NP}$-complete problems contains tens of thousands of decision problems that people have actually needed to solve in real life. A few examples of $\mathcal{NP}$-complete decision problems are:

- **Partition** – Given a set of integers, can it be partitioned into two disjoint sets such that the sum of the elements in each set is the same?

- **Hamiltonian Cycle** – Given a graph, is there a subset of the edges that forms a cycle that goes through every vertex exactly once? (The related **traveling salesperson** problem uses an edge-weighted graph and asks for the hamiltonian cycle of least total weight.)

- **Scheduling** – Given a set of tasks, with their durations and deadlines, is there a schedule for two (or more) processors that has all the tasks completed by their deadlines?

- **Satisfiability** – Given a boolean formula, is there a truth assignment to the boolean variables such that the formula is true?

This short list begins to illustrate that the class of $\mathcal{NP}$-complete problems is diverse and of practical interest. It is worth pointing out (given the emphasis on logic in this text) that the satisfiability problem is the problem on which all of the rest of the theory is based! Why is satisfiability so important? Briefly, it is because boolean expressions can "express" that certain problems are as hard as some other problems.

The thousands of $\mathcal{NP}$-complete problems have an interesting property in common. Although they have attracted much attention by people trying devise efficient algorithms (because of their real-life importance), no researcher has ever devised a polynomial time implementation that solves any such problem. It can be shown that if any $\mathcal{NP}$-complete problem can be solved in polynomial time, then every $\mathcal{NP}$-complete problem can be solved in polynomial time. These observations provide strong *circumstantial evidence* that none of the $\mathcal{NP}$-complete problems has a polynomial time solution.

In summary:

- If any problem in $\mathcal{NP}$ is intractable (not in $\mathcal{P}$), then every $\mathcal{NP}$-complete problem is intractable. Alternatively, if any problem in $\mathcal{NP}$ is tractable (in $\mathcal{P}$), then every $\mathcal{NP}$-complete problem is tractable.

- Every $\mathcal{NP}$-complete problem appears to be intractable because the combined efforts of thousands of researchers have failed to show even one such problem is in $\mathcal{P}$.

Taken together, these strong observations lead people to *expect* that these problems—like the satisfiability and the partition problem—will have no polynomial time algorithms that solve them. However, there is no known proof of this conclusion.

Exercises

14.1 For the language L in the proof of Theorem 14.2:

(a) Give a CFG that generates L.

(b) Give an NPDA that recognizes L.

14.2 Show that $L = \{a^i b^j c^k \mid i < j < k\}$ is not a CFL using the same proof technique as in Theorem 14.1.

14.3 Given a CFL L_1 and a regular language L_2, show that the intersection $L_3 = L_1 \cap L_2$ is a CFL.

14.4 Consider the language $L' = \{x \in \{a, b, c\}^* \mid x$ contains an equal number of as, bs, and cs $\}$. Using Exercise 14.3, show that L is not context-free.

14.5 A *context-sensitive grammar* (CSG) is a grammar in which each production $\alpha \to \beta$ has the property that $|\alpha| \le |\beta|$; no step in a derivation results in a shorter string of terminals and nonterminals.

(a) Explain why any language generated by a CSG does not contain the empty string.

(b) Give a CSG for $L' = \{a^n b^n c^n \mid n \ge 1\}$.

14.6 Show that each of the following sets is countably infinite by providing a one-to-one mapping between that set and $\mathcal{N}$.

(a) the perfect squares

(b) the set of all integers (including the negatives)

14.7 Design a TM that recognizes $\{ww \mid w \in \{a, b\}^*\}$, the language of repeated strings like *aabaaaba*. Hint: The most difficult part is locating the first symbol of the second half.

14.8 Specify a finite automaton that accepts exactly the strings that are valid encodings of Turing machine transition functions, according to the encoding scheme used in Section 14.6.

Bibliography

1. Alfred V. Aho and Jeffrey D. Ullman, *Foundations of Computer Science*, Computer Science Press, 1995.

   A comprehensive introduction to nearly every theoretical area of Computer Science.

2. Alfred V. Aho, Ravi Sethi, and Jeffery D. Ullman, *Compilers: Principles, Techniques, and Tools*, Addison-Wesley, 1986.

   A classic text that extends and applies formal language concepts in the domain of compiling.

3. M. Ben-Ari, *Mathematical Logic for Computer Science*, Prentice-Hall, 1993.

   A sophisticated, readable account that includes but goes well beyond the logic portion of this text.

4. George Boole, *An Investigation of the Laws of Thought*, Dover, 1958.

   The original work on the mathematical approach to logic, originally published in 1854.

5. Ivan Bratko, *Prolog: Programming for Artificial Intelligence: Second Edition*, Addison-Wesley, 1990.

   A good treatment of Prolog that makes a strong connection to the field of artificial intelligence.

6. Thomas H. Cormen, Charles E. Leiserson, Ronald L. Rivest, and Clifford Stein, *Introduction to Algorithms: Second Edition*, The MIT Press, 2001

   A thorough and excellent algorithms text that emphasizes loop invariants.

7. Peter J. Denning, Jack B. Dennis, and Joseph E. Qualitz, *Machines, Languages, and Computation*, Prentice-Hall, 1978.

   A more complete introduction to the topics in Part II.

8. Michael R. Garey and David S. Johnson, *Computers and Intractability: A Guide to the Theory of NP-Completeness*, Freeman, 1979.

   Still the standard reference work on $\mathcal{NP}$-completeness, although it was published in 1979.

9. Andrew Hodges, *Alan Turing: The Enigma*, Simon & Schuster, 1983.

   A biography that puts Turing's many contributions in perspective.

10. John E. Hopcroft, Jeffery D. Ullman, and Rajeev Motwani, *Introduction to Automata Theory, Languages, and Computation, Second Edition*, Addison-Wesley-Longman, 2000.

    A new edition of an advanced but readable book on languages and automata.

11. Efim Kinber and Carl Smith, *Theory of Computing: A Gentle Introduction*, Prentice-Hall, 2001.

    A new text that gives a "gentle" treatment of the topics in Part II.

12. Robert A. Kowalski, *Logic for Problem Solving*, North Holland, 1979.

    This book unifies important computing concepts as logic and asserts that "Algorithm = Logic + Control."

13. John R. Levine, Tony Mason, and Doug Brown, *lex & yacc*, O'Reilly, 1992.

    A source of some good applications of lex and its big sibling, yacc.

14. Peter Linz, *An Introduction to Formal Languages and Automata*, D. C. Heath & Co., 1990.

    An excellent text that goes beyond this one in Turing Machines and related topics.

15. James Martin, *Introduction to Languages and the Theory of Computation: Second Edition*, McGraw-Hill, 1997.

    An excellent text for those already motivated; goes well beyond the formal language and automata portion of this text.

16. Ernest Nagel and James R. Newman, *Gödel's Proof*, New York University Press, 1958.

    A remarkably simple introduction to the very complex subject.

17. David Poole, Alan Mackworth, and Randy Goebel, *Computational Intelligence: A Logical Approach*, Oxford University Press, 1998.

    An artificial intelligence text showing the remarkably broad range of what a logic-oriented approach can achieve.

18. Rudy Rucker, *Infinity and the Mind*, Birkhaüser, 1982.

    An introduction to the broad mathematical, scientific, and philosophical implications of infinity.

19. Raymond Smullyan, *Forever Undecided: A Puzzle Guide to Gödel*, Knopf, 1987.

    A lively puzzle-oriented approach to undecidability and related concepts.

20. Raymond Smullyan, *Satan, Cantor and Infinity*, Knopf, 1992.

    A recreational look at the relationship between logic and infinity.

21. A. B. Tucker, A. P. Bernat, W. J. Bradley, R. D. Cupper, and G. W. Scragg, *Fundamentals of Computing: I. Logic, Problem Solving, Programs, and Computers*, McGraw-Hill, 1995.

    Provides a good introduction to program verification.

22. Tu Van Le, *Techniques of Prolog Programming*, Wiley, 1993.

    A Prolog text with significant advanced techniques and applications.

Index

Δ, blank symbol, 314
δ function, 165
δ^* function, 167
$\exists$, existential quantifier, 58
$\forall$, universal quantifier, 58
Λ, empty string, 5
Λ-NFA, 182
Λ-closure, 184
Λ-elimination, 185
$\mathcal{L}(G)$, language of a grammar, 252
$\mathcal{L}(M)$, language of a machine, 176
$\mathcal{L}(r)$, language of a regular expression, 206
ω-string, 317

acceptance
    finite automaton, 168
algebraic expression, grammar, 273
alphabet, 143
alternation operator, 205
ambiguity, 141, 263
anonymous variable, 104
assertion, 100
associative operator, 2
assumption, 35
atomic formula, 64
automaton, 158
    finite (FA), 158
    Turing Machine, 313
axiom, 34

backtracking, 172
Backus Normal Form (BNF), 266
balanced parentheses, language, 253
biconditional operator, 26
binary relation, 6
blank symbol (Δ), 314
Boolean, 16
bound variable, 60

case analysis, 21
Church–Turing Thesis, 326
clause in Prolog, 110
closed language operator, 189
closed operator, 1
closure
    δ, 167
    Λ, 184
    of replacement operator, 251
    operator for languages, 147
commutative operator, 1
complete system in logic, 83
complexity classes, 327
concatenation
    language, 146
    string, 146
conclusion, 36
conditional operator, 25
conjunction operator, 18
conjunctive normal form, 27
consistent system in logic, 83
constant, logic, 16